The Limits
of Power

America since World War II

Warren F. Kimball, editor

The Limits
of Power

THE NIXON AND FORD ADMINISTRATIONS

John Robert Greene

*Indiana
University
Press*

BLOOMINGTON AND INDIANAPOLIS

The paper used in this publication meets the minimum
requirements of American National Standard for Information Sciences—
Permanence of Paper for Printed Library Materials, ANSI Z39.48-1984.

MANUFACTURED IN THE UNITED STATES OF AMERICA

Library of Congress Cataloging-in-Publication Data

Greene, John Robert, date
The limits of power : the Nixon and Ford administrations / John
Robert Greene.
p.   cm.—(America since World War II)
Includes bibliographical references and index.
ISBN 0-253-32637-0
1. United States—Politics and government—1969–1974.   2. United
States—Politics and government—1974–1977.   3. Nixon, Richard M.
(Richard Milhous), 1913–   .   4. Ford, Gerald R., 1913–   .
I. Title.   II. Series.
E855.G7   1992
973.924—dc20   91-47014

1 2 3 4 5   96 95 94 93 92

For Patty, T. J., and Christopher

Contents

Foreword

"How come we never get past World War II?" Teachers of United States history must hear that refrain a hundred times a year, and in all too many cases the complaint is valid. Having lived through the 1950s, 1960s, and 1970s, many of us find it hard to think of those years as textbook-type history, and we have often failed to take the time to sit back and make the historical judgments that must precede any attempt to teach about those decades. An even greater problem is posed by the scarcity of solid, fully researched syntheses dealing with the more immediate past. That gap is precisely what the series America since World War II is designed to fill.

Some will quarrel with the decision to construct the series along the traditional lines of presidential administrations. Granted, such an organization does tend to disguise the broader social, political, and economic trends which developed or continued after 1945 without regard for what Winston Churchill called America's "quadrennial madness." Yet, in each volume, the authors have consciously examined such trends and, when read as a whole, the series provides an overview of the entire postwar period. Periodization is not only a useful teaching device but also has a validity all its own. As will quickly become clear to the reader, each of these administrations possessed a personality that, while reflecting the broader ideals and attitudes of the American nation, nonetheless remained unique and identifiable. Nor have the authors merely summarized the political history of the period. Rather, each has carefully examined the cultural, social, and economic history which make an era much more than just dates and names.

Richard Milhous Nixon has engendered more emotion, more fervor, more anger than any other twentieth-century president. And he has had some serious competition from Woodrow Wilson, Franklin Roosevelt, and Lyndon Johnson. A public official for nearly thirty years, vice-president for eight, twice elected president, Nixon was, as pundit William Safire put it, a "presence" in our lives, whether we loved or hated, despised or admired him.

The intensity of emotions has made it virtually impossible for historians of Nixon's own generation to examine his presidency with any semblance of objectivity. Vietnam and Watergate are more than just events in United States history; they have become concepts that evoke conditioned responses. But twenty years have passed since Richard Nixon sat in the Oval Office, and a new array of historians has appeared on the scene. It is time for a new assessment of the Nixon years—the good, the bad, and the ugly.

What might be called the Nixon effect has also warped our view of the administration of Gerald Ford—the only president never elected to the office. Ford is generally dismissed as the man who pardoned Nixon, and as little else. His years in office are seen as nothing more than an unimportant interim between Nixon and Jimmy Carter. That is both untrue and unfair. Ford, like Nixon, has awaited the arrival of historians whose minds were not already made up by their own experiences.

The first two volumes of this series set high benchmarks. Charles Alexander's *Holding the Line: The Eisenhower Era* proved to be the opening salvo in the reassessment of Eisenhower's presidency that has characterized recent studies of that period. With exceptional insight and despite very limited access to archival materials, Alexander outlined all the major themes the Eisenhower "revisionists" have offered since the documents began to become available in the 1980s. Beginning with the question of how the man who so successfully led the Anglo-American-Soviet military coalition in World War II could be the bumbling, indecisive president depicted in most histories to that point, Alexander concluded that whatever the wisdom of Eisenhower's decisions, Ike was most definitely in charge. The book was a model for using the public record to reconstruct both the facts and the context of history.

Jim Heath's *Decade of Disillusionment: The Kennedy-Johnson Years* provided an early and perceptive analysis that went deeper than the forceful personalities who captured the headlines. Subsequent research has expanded our knowledge of that era, but Heath's study has remained one of the best overall summaries of foreign and domestic politics, culture, and society in an era when Americans questioned and tried to reshape their own national self-image.

Bob Greene's study likewise marks a new departure in histories of that era. The intensity of the partisan disputes over Richard Nixon's presidency, along with the congressional investigations that accompanied those debates, set forth a public record of remarkable depth and breadth. Reams of documents that government would normally hide from public view for decades appeared in hearings and then in newspapers. In addition, the players from both administrations are still with us, and most proved willing to talk. Because of this new documentation, Greene departs from the format of his predecessors and includes a number of citations so that students and scholars can benefit from his research.

Greene has taken this documentation and constructed a fascinating picture of a Nixon aware that the government he headed was less able to control and shape events, foreign and domestic, than any other since World War II. But such shrewd assessments were combined with a thin-skinned sensitivity that clouded his judgment. Principle and opportunism often underlay a single policy. Many will be surprised at the perceptiveness of Nixon's domestic policies, particularly his commitment to equal opportunity for African Americans. Yet he alienated black America. His foreign policy successes in China and in Soviet-American relations are offset by failures in Southeast Asia and the Middle East. Gerald Ford emerges from these pages as a real person with real policies that helped shape U.S. history, rather than just a caretaker president. All this is done in a literate, lively narrative that makes real people out of Nixon, Ford, and those around them. At the same time, Greene provides a readable, digestible synthesis for students of the history of the United States during the Nixon-Ford years.

Warren F. Kimball
Rutgers University

Preface

"THAT DEPENDS ON WHO WRITES THE HISTORY"

In researching and writing this book, I asked many of my colleagues around the nation for interviews and advice. It would be fair to say that the vast majority of my academic friends hate Richard Nixon. I was intrigued, in fact, by the substantial number of them who tried to convince me that writing an objective study of the Nixon administration was impossible. For but one example, a noted and respected scholar of the presidency sent me a gracious letter that included this word of warning: "As for Nixon, I hope you're not getting lost in some angle that forgets the big one. To put it most radically: no one wants to write about Hitler's office management."

When asked during an interview with this author how he wanted to be remembered as president, Gerald Ford replied, "I want to be remembered as a nice person, who worked at the job, and who left the White House in better shape than when I took it over. . . . If I can achieve those goals by being a nice guy, that's [a] pretty good recommendation."

Moments after Nixon resigned the presidency on national television, he walked from the Oval Office to the family residence with Henry Kissinger. Struck by the gravity of the moment, Kissinger commented that history would rank Nixon as one of the great American presidents. No doubt with a smile, Nixon replied, "That depends, Henry, on who writes the history."[1]

Richard Nixon and Gerald Ford have become stereotypes. With but one or two notable exceptions in a vast biographical literature, Nixon is evaluated solely in light of the abuses of power committed during his administration, and he is treated as a lifelong, irredeemable crook. In a much smaller literature, Ford is universally seen as a likable but somewhat bumbling steward. Studies of their administrations have built on these themes. Nixon's tenure is treated as corrupt and essentially valueless, Ford's as a caretaker presidency. Nixon's only success is seen to be in foreign policy; Ford gets credit for few successes at all. British historian Herbert Butterfield would have recognized the tone of these works. In his 1931 masterpiece, *The Whig Interpretation of History,* he warned against "the practice of abstracting things from their historical context and judging them apart from their context."

It would be folly of me to argue that my work is free of the biases placed there by years of reading, interviewing, thinking, and writing on the subject. Historians who believe they have been completely unprejudiced in their work know nothing about history; besides, as Butterfield observed, a history without bias is "the dullest of things." Nevertheless, it seems that there is room in the literature for a study that looks at the events of the years 1969–1977—arguably the most seminal of the postwar period in terms of the evolution of the American political system—with some amount of balance. When that is done, it is indeed possible to be more objective regarding these two turbulent tenures and to come to a number of thoughtful conclusions.

One theme threads through both these administrations: the period represents a stage in United States history when the nation discovered its limits in the world, probably for the first time, and had to face the fact that it could no longer do everything it wanted to do. In this same period Americans came to believe that there should also be limits on the actions of the president and proceeded to put such limits into effect. Every moment of the Nixon and Ford presidencies was an effort to deal with these new limits, to come to grips with a new American attitude toward government.

Many people helped this historian write this history.

Most authors choose to thank those closest to them last; I would like to thank them first. The research and writing of this work has spanned seven years and the birth of two children. If it was not for my family's patience with ever-moving deadlines and with a study that seemed to have a perpetually closed door, this work would never have been written. It is to them that this book is dedicated.

Thanks to all my students at Cazenovia College and Syracuse University's University College, especially those in my honors seminars who read many drafts as they progressed. Particular thanks go to those students who helped me either as research assistants or as secretaries. I am particularly grateful for the extra efforts of Christine Caffrey, Heather Clark, Sarah Hundemann, Kim King, Melissa Klish, Frances Vigliotti, Bethany Welch, Stephanie Winters, and Anne White.

Part of this study was funded through a grant from the Harry S. Truman Library Institute and a research grant from the Rockefeller University. I also benefited greatly from a research sabbatical granted me by Cazenovia College. I thank Dr. Stephen M. Schneeweiss and Dr. Carolyn B. Ware for granting me that opportunity.

So many archives and libraries were visited during the course of the research for this book that to thank them all would take a separate chapter. A parenthetical note: only those who toil in the historical vineyard know the true value of an archivist. While it takes persons of special skills to truly know the manuscripts of historical value donated to them, their impact does not stop there. Though ever acute to the needs and time limitations of a writer on the road, their profession demands that they remain in the background. We historians would not have a profession were it not for them.

Two archives are of particular import for this work. My first hint of the extent that historians had both understated and undervalued Ford's administration was the enormous amount of material I found at the Gerald R. Ford Library in Ann Arbor, Michigan. I thank my friend Supervisory Archivist David Horrocks for helping me wade through it all.

Particular thanks must go to a group of archivists working in what some might consider the least desirable archival situation in the country: the caretakers of the Richard Nixon Presidential Project in Alexandria, Virginia, many of whom have moved to different positions since I did the bulk of my research. I was given help beyond the call of duty by Project Director Jim Hastings, Ray Geselbracht, Maarja Krusten, Dick MacNeil, Scott Parham, and Sue Ellen Stanley. Without the counsel and friendship of Joan Howard, Supervisory Archivist during my research tenure, this book would not have been completed.

Also of inestimable help were the Hofstra University Conferences on the Modern Presidency. The Nixon (1987) and Ford (1989) meetings brought together an impressive array of alumni from both administrations, and the conferences were run with such precision and grace that all scholars could not help but benefit. Particular thanks to Natalie Datlof and Professor Bernard Firestone.

I interviewed many of the principals of both the Nixon and Ford administrations for this work. I have listed their names in the bibliographical essay, and I am indebted to all of them for their valuable time. The vast majority of them agreed to be interviewed on the record, and given the general flavor of Nixon literature, I have spared the reader an overuse of unattributed interviewing material (the proverbial "high government source in the Nixon administration").

I am greatly indebted to former President Gerald R. Ford for taking the time to talk to me at his home. His graciousness and his time opened many new doors when my work was at a critical phase. It should be noted for the record that despite many attempts, former President Richard Nixon declined to be interviewed for this work.

Many people read parts of this work; many people shared with me helpful material; many people offered their help and encouragement: Stephen Ambrose, John and Kathy Bell and their family, David Caputo, Jennifer Ferguson, Carol Goehner, J. Justin Gustainis, Robert Hartmann, James Heitzman, Graeme Johnson, Deborah Nygren, Kelly O'Keefe, Margot Papworth, Margery Pinet, Robert Shogan, Maurice

Stans, Donna Gates Thomas, Shirley Anne Warshaw, Dolores Weiss, and Frederic Williams.

No one writes a book alone, but one must draw one's own conclusions. My judgments, while growing out of many kindnesses, are my own.

The Limits
of Power

CHAPTER ONE

To Reform the Sixties

O N January 23, 1968, a North Korean submarine chaser and three patrol boats boarded the USS *Pueblo* off the Korean coast. In the struggle that followed, four of the seventy-five crew members were wounded, one fatally. The crew members were taken hostage and imprisoned, and the ship was taken into the nearby port of Wonsan. The North Koreans charged that the *Pueblo* was a spy ship that had been conducting intelligence activity inside the twelve-mile international boundary. Bent on humiliation as well as revenge, the North Koreans filmed the ship's commander, Lloyd Bucher, while he was giving a forced confession of his activities as a "spy." After negotiations that lasted for over a year, the Koreans finally set the crew free, claiming a gigantic victory over Western imperialism.

When cornered by a press that had long since stopped taking his pronouncements at face value, President Lyndon Johnson admitted only that the *Pueblo* might have "inadvertently drifted" within the twelve-mile limit. In reality, the *Pueblo* was a top-of-the-line spy ship. The Koreans knew all about its activities and were content to let it spy as long as it stayed twelve miles out to sea. It didn't, and the crew paid the price.

The plight of the *Pueblo* gave many Americans their first taste of what *Time* magazine called the "impotence of power." When news of the capture reached American eyes and ears, the reaction was one of amazement. The photograph of Bucher confessing to his North Korean captors was galling, particularly since, as one writer later observed, "this was surrender to Mickey Mouse."[1] The United States Navy was also forced to swallow the fact that to free the crew it had to release an official apology to the North Koreans for spying. The Cold War mentality of the early 1960s, marked as it was by American arrogance, had received quite a jolt. If the United States couldn't control the North Koreans, how could it hope to win a victory in Vietnam? Nothing this mortifying had happened in the war against North Vietnam, a war which, according to most reports, the United States was winning.

The reports, however, were wrong. As if by some grotesque design, one week after the *Pueblo* was captured all hell broke loose in Vietnam. On January 30 some 600,000 Vietcong guerrillas celebrated the Chinese new year, Tet, by staging the most startling offensive of the war. The well-coordinated attack was aimed at seven major urban centers in South Vietnam. U.S. and South Vietnamese forces were caught completely off guard; American planes were burned on the ground in Da Nang. Once again the enemy's strength had been grossly underestimated. While the North Vietnamese were eventually repulsed, the damage was widespread. The ancient city of Hue was destroyed. Most of the Mekong Delta lay in the hands of the enemy. The United States Embassy in Saigon had been infiltrated and took nearly six hours to retake. Following Tet, both the North Vietnamese Army and the Vietcong fought with a newfound vigor. Nevertheless, Johnson told his military advisers that the attack had been a "complete failure." Senator George D. Aiken of Vermont wryly observed that "if this is failure, I hope the Viet Cong never have a major success." [2]

Before Tet most Americans were under the impression that the United States was winning the Vietnam War. This was understandable, since that was the picture presented by the military and generally reported in the media. Tet destroyed this illusion. It was said that when Walter Cronkite heard of the attack, the normally unruffled newscaster snapped, "What the hell is going on? I thought we were winning the war!" [3] If the *Pueblo* represented the feeling of defeat that was creeping into American society in 1968, Tet represented that and more. More and more Americans were coming to the conclusion that the government and the military had deceived them about Vietnam.

Close on the heels of Tet, students at a major American university demonstrated once again that they were more than aware of this deception. Several factors combined to set off a bloody confrontation at Columbia University in New York in April 1968. One issue, Columbia's housing of the Institute of Defense Analysis, a twelve-college think tank used by the U.S. Defense Department, had been a smoldering concern for some time. A second problem had just made its appearance that spring. Columbia owned several buildings in adjacent Harlem, and the school's administration had decided to raze several of them to erect a gymnasium. The two issues fused, with leaders of the campus chapters of Students for a Democratic Society (SDS) and the Afro-American Society banding together on April 23 to march on the administrative offices in Low Library.

The supposedly unified demonstration soon disintegrated into bitter factionalism. The predominantly white members of SDS occupied the library, taking over the office of President Grayson Kirk. Students drank

Kirk's liquor, smoked his cigars, rifled his files, and defecated in his wastebasket. When boredom set in they moved to Mathematics Hall. There they were joined by such luminaries as Tom Hayden, an intellectual icon representing what the student movement had meant at its inception. By this point the African-American students, who had been pushed out by SDS, moved across campus to Hamilton Hall, the center of the undergraduate college, where they occupied "their own" building. The protesters were by no means unchallenged by their fellow students. A sizable group of athletes, calling themselves "Students Opposing SDS," dubbed the protesters the "Pukes" and organized an effort to cut off the food supply to the occupied buildings.

The protest ended with violence of a kind that had come to be expected in the course of campus confrontations in the late sixties. On the morning of April 25, early enough so that Harlem would still be asleep, President Kirk called in the police. About one thousand answered the call. The black students in Hamilton Hall surrendered peacefully, but the SDS enclaves had to be stormed. The police arrested 700 students and, flailing their nightsticks, injured 148.

Actually, since 1963 the nation had been slowly bleeding to death. The first wound had come in Dallas on November 22 of that year. The nation had never recovered from that shock, and it reeled dazedly through the sixties as violence became the norm. The litany of bloodshed had become all too familiar. Birmingham, Selma, and Oxford had all been bloody testing grounds in the drive for civil rights for African Americans. Watts had been burned to the ground, with thirty-four people dead. Riots had defamed Newark, Rochester, Harlem, Cincinnati, and Detroit. Not only John Kennedy but also Martin Luther King, Jr., had been assassinated, and Robert Kennedy's killing would soon follow. Some observers thought it was a nation trying to commit suicide.

The fury of the late sixties seemed particularly apocalyptic to those Americans who had lived through the Great Depression and World War II. In their eyes the deprivations of the thirties had been far worse than the problems of the sixties. Yet they believed that the national character had been strengthened, not weakened, by those earlier crises. They had brought their land back from the ashes of economic collapse and had been victorious in their struggle to make the world safe from murderous dictators. As their children blithely wore buttons warning that "You Can't Trust Anyone over Thirty," many Americans of the older generation feared that their values were in danger of being permanently displaced.

For some of these Americans, the problem seemed to be that their country had gotten "soft." Protesters should be jailed or drafted, they felt; violence in the streets should be met with an equivalent amount of counterviolence, and the Vietnam War should be ended with a grand, brutal military stroke. Yet these hardliners, called "hawks" by the press, were as much a minority as were the "doves" who hoped for a societal revolution and instant withdrawal from Vietnam. The vast majority of voters occupied the ideological territory between the hawkish far Right and the dovish far Left. They were in the Middle, unable to tolerate the solutions proposed by either extreme. Predominantly white, members of all economic classes, and politically active, by 1968 Middle Americans had had enough. They longed to replace the climate of welfare, violence, defeat, and deception with a leadership that championed the old-fashioned American values of peace, honor, and honesty. As they geared up for the 1968 presidential election, they searched for a candidate who would reform America and end the political experimentation of the sixties.

Richard Nixon would be that candidate. He had ridden the center to victory throughout his career. His political defeats had come after campaigns in which voters of the Middle had abandoned him; his many political victories, both local and national, had come after campaigns designed to court them. No politician on the national scene in 1968 better understood exactly what the Middle wanted than did Nixon. Indeed, by virtue of both his background and the niche that he had cut out for himself in politics since 1952, he was one of them.

Born in 1913 and reared in southern California, young Nixon was exposed to an excess of religion and discipline but not of money or status. Those who remember him emphasize his scholarly nature, his thoughtfulness, and his love of music and reading. The death of Nixon's youngest brother from tuberculosis in 1925 traumatized his father, who threw himself into revivalist religion as a cure; Nixon, however, reacted with the quiet stoicism of his Quaker mother. No one was surprised when this serious young man signed up for prelaw in high school, telling a classmate that he would someday be a politician. A strong pupil who excelled at rhetoric and debate, Nixon was acclaimed the "best all-around student" at graduation. Yet an expensive college was out of the question. Nixon's eldest brother had now contracted tuberculosis, and his care had drained the family's savings. Nixon later admitted that he "had dreamed of going to college in the East," but he was forced to settle for tiny Whittier College, a local liberal arts school with ties to the Quaker church.[4]

Nixon's career at Whittier was not easy. He commuted to college while still maintaining a rigorous work schedule at the family grocery store. In his junior year his eldest brother died. Despite these difficulties, Nixon is again remembered by his classmates for his hard work. He stayed on the honor list all four years, was elected class president in his senior year, and continued to excel at debate. He did, however, develop one form of noncerebral recreation. Despite his limited physique, Nixon threw himself into football. Only a third stringer, he nevertheless was remembered by his teammates for the passion that he brought to the game. As an adult he would be an astute armchair quarterback, and watching the game became one of his true forms of relaxation.

The Whittier experience also began Nixon's move away from Quakerism. Nixon's most astute biographer, Stephen Ambrose, notes that at Whittier Nixon developed a skepticism for the literal word of the Bible. Nixon himself recalled that after taking a course entitled "The Philosophy of Christian Reconstruction," he approached the Bible from a predominantly symbolic point of view. For example, he still felt "that Jesus was the son of God, but not necessarily in the physical sense of the term."[5] Ambrose notes that this conviction made religion "from that point on . . . no longer important to him."[6] Nevertheless, several of his teachers viewed Nixon's critical mind as first-rate, and he won a full-tuition scholarship (of $250) to Duke University Law School in Durham, North Carolina, in 1934.

Duke was the beginning of a new phase in Nixon's life in many ways. There were new sacrifices as the Depression took its toll. To save money Nixon lived for a time in a toolshed with no stove. Nixon also found the work of law school surprisingly difficult. He was forced to admit that although he had long excelled at memorizing facts, he had a difficult time analyzing information and synthesizing it in a legal brief. Unnerved but not intimidated by the requirement that all scholarship students keep a B grade average, Nixon bore down so hard that his fellow classmates gave him the nickname "Gloomy Gus." As usual his hard work paid off. Once again a superior student, he graduated third in his class and made the law review.

Even more important than the formal education that he received was the fact that Duke was in the South. In California Nixon had for the most part been insulated from racial prejudices. Now both of his roommates were southerners, and he lived and studied in a racially segregated city. His attitude toward African Americans did not change; he was appalled at the way they were treated in Durham. Yet despite this introduction to racism, he found much in the quiet southern way of life of the mid-1930s that appealed to him. Indeed, he developed an affection for southerners that few northern or western politicians of the 1960s would share.

After his graduation in 1937 and a brief job search in New York, Nixon returned to Whittier and joined the law firm of Wingert and Brewley. Business was slow. Nixon did some trial work, but the balance of his time was spent doing routine clerking chores. To fill up his time he quickly found his way into local politics. Nixon became a sought-after speaker on the civic club circuit, had two short-lived candidacies for city attorney and the State Assembly, and campaigned for Wendell

Willkie in the presidential election of 1940. Nixon also met Thelma "Pat" Ryan, a business education teacher who had recently graduated from the University of Southern California. After two years of an intense courtship, they were married in June 1940.

As a Quaker, Nixon could have applied for an exemption from wartime service as a conscientious objector. Yet he could ill afford to do nothing to help the war effort and still entertain thoughts of a political career. In 1942 he moved to Washington and took a job at the Office of Price Administration (OPA), the agency in charge of wartime price controls and rationing. Nixon was an assistant attorney in the Rationing Coordination Section. This experience was as seminal in Nixon's development as Duke had been. It was here that Nixon had his first taste of close work with eastern liberal lawyers, for whom he developed an active distaste. He also became quickly convinced that the tinkering with the economy that was being done by New Dealers was wrong. This was also Nixon's first look at government bureaucracy, and the OPA was a red-tape nightmare. In short, he hated it. In August 1942 Nixon volunteered for service in the U.S. Navy.

Biographers have often mocked Nixon's wartime service, which he performed primarily in the South Pacific, with several stateside stops as well. They have sneered at "Nick's Snack Shack," a stand set up by Nixon on Green Island to serve free food to pilots. They have made fun of the stories of his playing poker to while away the boredom. Yet World War II changed Nixon, as it did other young men from small towns who were suddenly seeing the world. He saw active duty, served with distinction, and received a letter of commendation for his efforts. Like John Kennedy, he was a lieutenant (J.G.), commissioned after only two weeks' training. Unlike Kennedy, Nixon did not face any life-or-death decisions for his men (a fact that Kennedy handlers exploited, with much success, in 1960), whom he supervised as they loaded and unloaded cargo planes. Nixon did, however, endure constant shelling, did see death (an airplane crash, from which he helped carry away the bodies),[7] and—most important—did grow up. It is of no small import that Nixon made the final break with his Quaker pacifist beliefs in order to go on active duty. For Nixon this decision opened a world that would have been denied him had he not compromised his religious beliefs. The man who returned from the South Pacific was better dressed for the bruises of political battle than he had been before he enlisted.

Nixon wasted no time in parlaying his status as a decorated veteran into political capital. The election of 1946 in California's Twelfth Congressional District has a certain legendary quality about it. There is no question but that Nixon's campaign against Democratic incumbent Jerry Voorhis was dirty. Nixon falsified the voting record of his opponent, understated the number of bills that Voorhis had introduced, and linked him to a labor political action committee that had disowned Voorhis two years earlier. Yet it was the anti-Communist tactic that has become the signature of the election. In an example of outright lying, Nixon's ads declared that Voorhis's "voting record in Congress is more Socialistic and Communistic than Democratic." There is no question about the falsity of the charges. There is also no question but that Nixon orchestrated the attack himself. More important, not only was Nixon unbothered by the smear; he later defended it as good politics. As Ambrose notes, Nixon "appear[ed] to have made the transition from nice Quaker boy to ruthless politician without even noticing."[8] What Garry Wills would later label the "denigrative method" of politics—the constant hitting of one's opponents with callous charges, be they fact or fiction, so as keep them on the defensive for the entire campaign—was born.[9]

A common mistake made by Nixon observers is to caricature his entire congressional career as nothing more than a six-year chase after Communists. In fact, Nixon was one of the more moderate freshmen to enter the Eightieth Congress after the Republican sweep of 1946. In foreign policy Nixon showed a streak of internationalism that was more attuned to the followers of Michigan Senator Arthur Vandenberg than it was to the conservative isolationists led by Ohio Senator Robert Taft. Nixon strongly supported the Marshall Plan, and as the most junior member of the House Committee on Un-American Activities (HUAC), he led the successful fight *against* a bill to outlaw the Communist party. He and Karl Mundt of South Dakota responded the following year with a more moderate bill, but it died in Senate committee. When HUAC investigated charges of Communist influence in the Screen Actors Guild, Nixon showed little interest in the witch-hunt, attending only one of the sessions that grilled the "Hollywood Ten." These relatively temperate stands flew in the face of the innate conservatism of southern California. Nixon, however, was both popular and influential in his district, largely because his constituent service was excellent. He was returned to office in 1948 by a resounding margin.

Yet it is the Hiss case by which Nixon's congressional career—and, according to him, his entire career—is ultimately judged. As with most causes célèbres, symbols are more important than facts. Alger Hiss was an urbane, dapper, witty Ivy Leaguer. He had been at the Yalta Conference as a State Department aide, and at the time of his trials he was president of the Carnegie Foundation on World Peace. His adversary was an editor of *Time* magazine, Whittaker Chambers. Earthy, unkempt, yet a superbly thoughtful writer, Chambers was burdened with a single-minded loathing of communism. The antagonists soon came to represent the two sides of the internal cold war that America was fighting with itself. As Americans learned of Chambers's ostensibly patriotic and cathartic charges to HUAC that he and Hiss had participated in a Communist youth group in the 1930s whose primary function was "to infiltrate the government in the interest of the Communist party,"[10] the battle lines were quickly drawn. Depending on one's orientation, Hiss was either a traitor or a persecuted New Deal intellectual and Chambers either a heroic rock turner helping others to find the Communists underneath or a vicious character assassin who had co-opted fear of communism as a tool.

The only thing that can be said of this complex and infuriating case with any certainty is that both men were liars. Hiss lied to HUAC about his relationship with Chambers (he originally insisted that he had never known Chambers, a statement that Hiss himself was soon forced to admit was false), and Chambers lied to HUAC when he said that his cell had not engaged in espionage (if accepted as authentic, classified State Department documents in Chambers's possession—the "Pumpkin Papers"—confirmed the conclusion that both men were traitors). Yet it was Hiss, after one hung jury, who was eventually convicted on two charges of perjury.

Obviously HUAC stood to reap a political windfall from a successful Hiss hunt. To suggest that Nixon had only justice on his mind would be to reconstruct history inaccurately as well as to downplay Nixon's political acumen, which was in an advanced state of development. As he later wrote, "If there turned out to be substance to Chambers' charges, [Harry] Truman would be terribly embarrassed."[11] It would add to the Democratic president's woes in 1948 as he was gearing up for the fight of his political life. Nixon correctly charged that Truman "used the power and prestige of his office to obstruct the Committee's work"; Truman systematically and skillfully suppressed the flow of governmental information to HUAC. Although Nixon's protests did not ultimately cost Truman the election, they did lay the groundwork for charges that would plague Truman through his second term.

Nixon was assisted by a press that had written Truman off as a presidential contender. In his prescient study of the modern press, *The Powers That Be*, David Halberstam observes that Nixon's press relations during the Hiss affair, "contrary to later myth, were quite good." Nixon carefully cultivated newspaper reporters, leaking testimony from HUAC executive sessions and personally calling them to put his particular spin on events. His closest contact in the press was Bert Andrews of the *New York Herald-Tribune*. Andrews gave Nixon a great deal of valuable advice during the hearings, so much that Halberstam considers Andrews "more of a Nixon staff man than a working journalist." Halberstam's conclusion mirrors that of other students of the period: rather than Nixon, it was "Hiss who finally suffered from bad press relations, [because] most [reporters] thought he was guilty of perjury."

The publicity from the Hiss case propelled Nixon into the Senate. His rise had been meteoric. After only two terms in the House, the thirty-six-year-old Nixon had a national reputation, instant name and face recognition, and an issue that continued to make headlines. Indeed, Nixon and others who were stumping on the anti-Communist issue were turned into prophets by the June 1950 invasion of South Korea by the Communists of the North. He was also the unintended beneficiary of a California Democratic party that had split itself wide open with a divisive primary, producing a candidate, Representative Helen Gahagan Douglas, of impeccable liberal credentials. Douglas was opposed by virtually all factions in the state, except those of the Left. She was particularly hated by the oil interests, who were up in arms over her opposition to oil drilling off the California coast (Douglas would later explain her defeat by telling an interviewer that "the oil men could not afford to let me go to the Senate"). Nixon was perceived to be ahead during the entire campaign, and he won with 59.2 percent of the vote.

Despite being the front-runner, Nixon used a strategy in this campaign that would set the standard for all smear campaigns to come. With the help of public relations specialist Murray Chotiner, Nixon turned Red-baiting into an art form, berating Douglas's congressional voting record and labeling her the "Pink Lady" (Douglas retorted with an even more memorable epithet, calling him "Tricky Dick"). In a direct-mail piece that made political history, Nixon blatantly misrepresented Douglas's voting record so that it appeared to coincide with the record of radical Representative Vito Marcantonio of New York. So that the point could not be missed, the mailing was even printed on pink paper. One can salvage little from the 1950 campaign that is of any moral value. It is all the more perplexing because, as in 1946, Nixon would have won the race easily without using smear tactics.

All stratagems aside, Nixon was now a certified Republican superstar. For two years he spent as much time on the road making speeches as he did in the Senate. It was inevitable that his name should emerge as a leading candidate for the vice-presidency in 1952. He was young, articulate, and acceptable to most of the party bosses; most important, he had a positive reputation as a Red-baiter (as compared with Joseph McCarthy, whose attacks were becoming increasingly wild). With Nixon on the ticket, the chances of a flanking attack by McCarthy against a fellow Republican was lessened. Nixon would balance the ticket of either of the two Republican front-runners. Both Robert Taft and Dwight Eisenhower wanted Nixon on their ticket, and both men offered him the second spot well in advance of the party's convention. Taft contacted Nixon personally, and Eisenhower had Thomas Dewey approach him after a May speech in New York.[12]

For his part, Nixon had long since decided where he would place his fortunes. He had written a supporter in October 1951 that he believed it "essential that we put somebody at the top of the ticket who is more sure to win than Taft appears to be at the present time."[13] Nixon told Dewey that he would be "greatly honored" to take the second spot under Ike. With this agreement in hand, Nixon covertly worked for Eisenhower throughout the primary campaign (he was formally sworn to favorite son Governor Earl Warren of California and thus could not openly declare himself for another candidate). After Eisenhower's nomination, a pro forma meeting of the general's staff members in the suite of Herbert Brownell brought unanimous approval of Nixon.*

Nixon's role in the fall campaign was shaped by his 1946 and 1950 victories: he was expected once again to take the offensive. Nixon was quite successful in this role. His campaign speeches slapped at Democrat Adlai E. Stevenson as "Adlai the Appeaser," who had graduated from "Dean Acheson's College of Cowardly Communist Containment." But Nixon's campaign suffered a nearly fatal blow on September 18 when a *New York Post* headline charged that a "Secret Rich Men's Trust Fund Keeps Nixon in Style Far beyond His Salary." The story was, to put it charitably, a gross exaggeration. There *was* a fund, totaling $18,235, set up by Nixon supporters to help him with his senatorial expenses. However, the solicitation of donations to the fund had been a public matter, and the existence of the fund itself was not kept secret (it was kept in a bank account under the name of Nixon's lawyer, Dana Smith, and Nixon did not attempt to hide the fact when first approached about it by reporters). Nor was it very big, even by 1952 standards. It was also quite legal. An independent Price Waterhouse audit, commissioned by the Republican National Committee, made this point clear.[14]

But the Eisenhower campaign could not afford to just let the matter drop. Since the convention, all Republican hands, including Nixon, had been relentlessly attacking the scandals of the Truman administration. Nixon's fund had jeopardized a campaign that Eisenhower himself had dubbed a "crusade" against bad government. Most of Eisenhower's aides wanted Nixon to resign. For his part, Eisenhower distanced himself from the disaster, waiting for two days after the *Post* broke the story before contacting Nixon to discuss the issue. The press, which had been largely pro-Nixon since his entry into Congress, began to savage him. Literally overnight Nixon went from young superstar to being completely expendable.

It was a devastating experience for Nixon. This was the first time he had experienced this kind of political rejection, and it was in the

*In his memoirs Nixon remembers the road to the vice-presidential nomination quite differently. He writes that he first found out that the general wanted him for a running mate on the final day of the convention. Unshaven and unable even to find his wife to tell her the good news, Nixon rushed over to Eisenhower's suite to accept (Nixon, *Memoirs*, pp. 86–87).

midst of his first national campaign. Yet his entire career had prepared him for this moment of emergency. Only a man who had run a campaign like that of 1950 could have survived an attack like that of 1952. As journalist Stewart Alsop later observed, "In these circumstances, to be meek . . . was to commit political suicide."[15] Though he knew that he had little support on the Eisenhower train, Nixon gambled. It is of critical importance that he gambled on television; to that point he had used it very little, and he knew little about it. But he turned out to be a natural.

What became known as the "Checkers speech" was actually two speeches in one. In the first part Nixon spoke directly to the voters who had supported him since 1946—the voters of the Middle. As he bared his financial past to a public unaccustomed to such real-life video drama, Nixon evoked sympathy for his plight as a homeowner. He reminded viewers that he too had a mortgage, he too had bills, and his wife wore not mink but a "respectable Republican cloth coat." He was just like them, even to the point of being hounded and persecuted by authority. Nixon did not deny the fund, correctly insisting that it was "not a secret," not "morally wrong," and that "not one cent of the $18,000 . . . ever went to me for my personal use." He then moaned that his salary was small and that his wife had to work weekends in the office just to make ends meet. But the clincher that equated Nixon with every middle-class family in America was that he owned a dog. No matter that this little black cocker spaniel, Checkers, was a gift to his children from a Texas supporter; "regardless of what they say about it, we are going to keep it."

While the first part of the speech is the most famous, the second part kept Nixon on the ticket. The senator from California directly challenged the hero of World War II to a political showdown. First he demanded that the Democratic candidates release reports on their finances, as Nixon had just done, but certainly Eisenhower could not be left out of the deal. This was not mere spite but a shrewd political judgment, as there had been rumors about the financial arrangements surrounding Eisenhower's wartime memoirs. Next he yanked the decision on his political future out of Eisenhower's hands. Nixon instinctively knew that he was in better shape with the voters than he was with his party's leadership, so he asked his audience to call or write the Republican National Committee. A flood of letters and phone calls somehow found their way there, even though no address had been provided for them (Nixon's paid time ran out before he could finish the last moments of his speech, and the network cut him off). The question of his guilt or innocence was now secondary. He would have to be kept on the ticket—and was.

Despite this victory, the seeds of many of Nixon's future disappointments were sown with the fund crisis. The most important and

longest-lasting effect was the total disintegration of the good press that
Nixon had enjoyed since 1946. With the fund crisis the press had turned
against Nixon and, even more important, he against it. Nixon could
never find it in himself to forgive the press for instantly believing the
fund story. As he later wrote, "I regarded what had been done to me
as character assassination, and the experience permanently and pow-
erfully affected my attitude toward the press."[16] He was particularly
hurt that the newspaper that employed Bert Andrews, the *Herald-Tribune*, was one of the first papers to call for his expulsion from the
ticket. Nixon began to insulate himself from reporters and to develop
a deep and abiding suspicion of their motives.

A second casualty of the Checkers speech was any hope that Nixon
might have had for a close personal relationship with Eisenhower.
Thanks to the challenge issued at the end of the speech, the two men—
despite Nixon's earnest hopes—never became close. This is not to say,
however, that Nixon was a failure as vice-president; quite the contrary.
Appalled by Vice-President Truman's lack of preparation at the time of
President Franklin Roosevelt's death, Eisenhower strengthened both
the office and the expectations of the vice-presidency. By statute Nixon
already sat on the National Security Council; at Eisenhower's request
he also sat with the president's Cabinet, attended most meetings between the president and legislative leaders, and chaired several influential commissions. This expanded activity eventually gave Nixon his
role as political arbitrator of the Eisenhower administration. He acted
as a broker between the Taft wing of the party and the more centrist
administration, deftly handling, for example, negotiations between Joe
McCarthy and the administration while the senator from Wisconsin
was raking the U.S. Army over the coals. Nixon was also a key player
in negotiations that helped to settle the steel strike in 1960, serving as
honest broker between David McDonald of the steelworkers' union
and Roger Blough, chairman of U.S. Steel. Nixon was also the administration's designated campaigner, and he acted as a one-man political
surrogate in the off-year elections.

During Eisenhower's illnesses Nixon set the standard for the vice-
president's role in a time of presidential incapacitation. He acted with
calm and restraint, even refusing to sit in the president's chair during
a Cabinet meeting although it would have been his right by protocol
to do so. Eisenhower's press secretary, Jim Hagerty, would remember
that Nixon was "very conscious of his office as vice-president, very
conscious that he was doing nothing to presume that the president was
overly ill . . . he handled himself beautifully throughout this whole
affair."[17] After Eisenhower's stroke in November 1957, Eisenhower
and Nixon dealt with the problem of the void in the law of presidential
succession. They privately entered into a pact stating that if Eisenhower was incapacitated or for some reason unable to communicate,

Nixon could decide on his own if the president was incapable of carrying out his duties.[18] Clearly one does not venture into hyperbole by stating that Nixon and Eisenhower created the modern vice-presidency.

By 1960 Nixon's star had risen achingly close to its apex. Then it plummeted into free-fall until by 1963 Nixon was treated by most observers as a political has-been. His fall began in 1960 with a presidential campaign whose strategies backfired at almost every turn. A challenge by the young darling of the Republican Left, New York Governor Nelson Rockefeller, forced Nixon to make a humiliating preconvention compact. His liberalization of the party's platform without seeking the advice or consent of the Platform Committee not only angered the party leadership but also cast doubt on Nixon's ability to run an independent campaign. His choice for running mate was also a poor one. Former Senator and United Nations Ambassador Henry Cabot Lodge ran as if he were in no way tied to Nixon, and he made several embarrassing gaffes. Even luck seemed to be against Nixon: a car door slammed on his leg and sent him to the hospital with a wound that would bother him for the rest of the campaign. The biggest strategic blunder, however, was Nixon's decision to campaign in all fifty states, exhausting both himself and his press entourage. The reporters who wrote unkindly about his performance in the first televised presidential debates were already tired and embittered.

The Kennedy-Nixon debates have taken on a mythical quality all their own: John Kennedy won on his looks, while Nixon forgot to shave and sweated away votes under the hot lights; Nixon's Spartan preparation won him the respect of his radio audience, who could not see Kennedy, while Kennedy's self-assurance won him the infinitely larger television audience. Most of this is true. Nixon had forgotten the biggest lesson of the Checkers speech: television works for a politician only if the politician controls it. The Kennedy staff was as concerned about whether the stage background clashed with their candidate's suit and about their candidate's being properly tanned and fit for the occasion (he prepared by taking a brief vacation in Bermuda) as they were with his knowledge of the issues. Nixon prepped himself as he had done for his highly successful debates with Voorhis and Douglas, hiding in a hotel room for several days with his briefing books.

As Americans viewed the debates, the contrast was stark. Kennedy did not look directly at the camera, except in passing. He lunged forward just a bit and had an air of authority in his voice. Nixon, on the other hand, looked directly down the throat of the camera and spoke with a pleading quality in his voice. He looked as tired and as ill as he truly was. His appearance was not helped by a suit jacket that was too big for him, and its dull earth color blended right into the background of the studio set. After watching the debates, Eleanor Roosevelt was worried. She wrote Kennedy that she was afraid that, as with the Checkers speech, Nixon had appealed "to the pity for the underdog which is prevalent in the American people, by seeming to be 'humbler' " than Kennedy.[19] She needn't have worried. On the issues it was almost a draw, but with a slight edge to Nixon. In the hearts of Middle Americans, however, Kennedy was the clear winner.

To put the campaign in its simplest terms, Kennedy offered youth, vigor, and promise for a new decade; Nixon offered four more years of Eisenhowerlike stability. Yet the conclusion that many have drawn—that the nation chose in 1960 to move forward with Kennedy's youth rather than stay put with Nixon's experience—is much too narrow. Indeed, the nation as a whole wasn't quite sure which way it wanted to go. The results of the election were razor close. While Kennedy won 303 electoral votes to Nixon's 219, both men had less than 50 percent of the total, and the margin of Kennedy's total popular victory was one-tenth of one percent. A switch of fewer than 12,000 votes in five states (Hawaii, Illinois, Missouri, New Mexico, and Nevada) would have given Nixon the election. Although the election was, as Theodore White observed, a "personal victory" for Kennedy, it was certainly no mandate. It was also not a victory for Kennedy's party. While Congress had not fallen to the Republicans, the Democrats had nonetheless made a net gain of only two Senate seats and twenty-one House seats.

Nixon has made it clear on several occasions that he felt he was robbed in 1960. Yet after the election Nixon did not retreat into despondence. Nor, in retrospect, was there any need to. Both his party and his career were still intact. He returned to California, joined a law firm, and wrote the first volume of his memoirs, *Six Crises*. But the lure of politics tugged at him. While he had no desire for a rematch against Kennedy in 1964 and his old congressional seat had become safely Democratic, Nixon began to think about running for governor of California. Although he sincerely planned on staying in Sacramento for the entirety of a four-year term, Democrats and anti-Nixon Republicans alike attempted to scare him out of running by charging that he was using the state as a "stepping stone" to a 1964 run for the presidency. The issue would be a gnawing one throughout the campaign. Despite such pressure, the 1962 California gubernatorial race was, as Ambrose puts it, "the only campaign available to him until 1964, and Nixon was hooked on campaigning."[20]

The campaign was a disaster. Incumbent Governor Edmund G. "Pat" Brown did not lend himself to attacks. Neither was he a political neophyte; during the Cuban missile crisis Brown flew to Washington to be seen in his role as vice-chairman of the National Civilian Defense Committee. For his part, Nixon seemed incapable of generating the fire-breathing passion that had typified his earlier campaigns. He was done in by the "stepping stone" issue, the complicated issue of paying for medical care ("socialized medicine") in California, and fallout from a loan given to Nixon's brother Donald by Howard Hughes, ostensibly to start a restaurant—a loan for which Hughes did not demand repayment.* The deciding factor in Nixon's defeat, however, was Kennedy's successful handling of the Cuban missile crisis. After that, as Nixon put it, all he could do was to "play the dreary drama through to its conclusion on election night."[21] The result was the expected resounding defeat.

Two years of exile from power and two political reversals tormented Nixon. The press had been hounding him since Checkers, and although reporters had not caused his loss in 1962, they were certainly reveling in it. Nixon would have done well to heed the advice of his press secretary, Herb Klein, and stay away from reporters the morning after his defeat. But despite Klein's urging, Nixon strode downstairs from his hotel suite and committed what most thought at the time to be political hara-kiri. His opening line—"Now that Mr. Klein has made a statement, now that all the members of the press are so delighted that I lost, I would just like to make a statement of my own"—tipped his hand. The long, rambling talk that followed attempted to explain his defeat and discuss his plans for the future, but its crux was an assault on the press. Nixon claimed that he had "never complained to a publisher, to an editor, about the coverage of a reporter." But he held no hopes that he would be treated fairly that day. "I leave you gentlemen now and you will write it. You will interpret it. That's your right. But as I leave you I want you to know just think how much you're going to be missing—you won't have Nixon to kick around anymore, because, gentlemen, this is my last press conference." It was, of course, never intended to be his last press conference. It was, however, the first time during the campaign of 1962 that Nixon had been on the attack.

It is doubtful that Nixon was thinking about a run for president in 1968 when he packed up his family in early 1963 and moved from California to Manhattan, but his relocation is easily one of the most important events of the 1968 presidential campaign. In light of his distrust, dislike, and awe of the eastern liberal establishment, Nixon's move can be seen as a rare act of personal courage as well as political shrewdness. Not only was he going into a state controlled by his nemesis, Nelson Rockefeller; he was even moving into Rockefeller's neighborhood: he rented an apartment in a building where the governor lived. He was moving into a world unlike any that he had lived in before. In New York the emphasis was not on political power but on wealth. His new law firm gave him the opportunity not only to increase his own income (Nixon's net assets rose from $40,000 in 1952

---

*This loan and its ramifications on what would become known as Watergate are discussed in more detail in chap. 6.

to $515,000 in 1968)[22] but also to meet influential bankers, lawyers, and other men of means who might be potential contributors. Thanks to the generosity of benefactors such as DeWitt Wallace of *Reader's Digest*, Nixon was also able to travel widely, visiting many foreign countries where he was accorded head-of-state status. All this would help Nixon in his drive to convince the party that he was no longer a political albatross.

Perhaps more important was the fact that Nixon learned to truly love New York (he commented to a friend while walking up Park Avenue, "This is where the action is—not with those peasants in California"[23]). He lived for almost three years as a political expatriate, using the temperament of the city to prepare him for his reentry into presidential politics. It matured him. Many of those who observed Nixon during this period have since commented on his tendency to read more, to discuss more, to laugh more, and to listen more. John Sears, who served Nixon as a political strategist from 1966 to 1969, told this author that the New York experience "broadened [Nixon] so that he could take advice from people and not just react to situations." He was more accessible to reporters and, within the bounds of their mutual suspicion, more open with them.

The young minds who surrounded Nixon in New York, of whom Sears is an example, were an integral part of his development. They represented all shades of the political spectrum, from Leonard Garment, Nixon's law partner and a liberal Democrat, to Patrick Buchanan, an editorial writer for the *St. Louis Globe-Democrat*, who offered a blazingly conservative voice to the speech-writing staff. The man who emerged as Nixon's closest political adviser, however, was not a member of this youth movement. Nixon was fascinated by both the meteoric success and the demeanor of the newest member of his law firm, John N. Mitchell. A specialist in municipal bonds, Mitchell had never worked in politics. Nevertheless, Nixon would tell speech-writer William Safire in 1967 that "I've found the heavyweight."[24] Mitchell's success as a bond lawyer had so enthralled Nixon that he would stand outside Mitchell's door at their office just to hear him close a deal over the telephone. At the urging of Walter Williams, who in 1952 had been chairman of Citizens for Eisenhower, Nixon made Mitchell his campaign manager. When it came to his relationship with Nixon, Mitchell pulled no punches. He insisted throughout 1968, to anyone who would listen, that "when I tell Dick Nixon what to do, he listens. I'm in charge." Mitchell quickly professionalized the loosely organized Nixon team, later bragging that the reason the campaign ran so smoothly was that he had gotten rid of all the politicians: "I don't want people who spend most of their time worrying about their own position or image. We're interested in the candidate."[25]

Nixon began his 1968 campaign during the 1966 congressional

campaign. He used the off-year election to begin mending his public image and dealing with the "he can't win" attitude. Nixon traveled over 30,000 miles and visited eighty-two congressional districts in a whirlwind campaign for Republican hopefuls. The ideology of the candidates for whom he was speaking meant less than the fact that he was storing up political IOUs. The perfect example of this was Nixon's vocal support of Rockefeller in his uphill but ultimately successful re-election battle. The 1966 election was a victory both for the party—it picked up forty-seven seats in Congress—and for Nixon. He had helped his entire party, not just one wing of it, and he had received valuable political exposure in the process. The exile had come to an end; Nixon was back.

The presidential campaign of 1968 was violent. The war dominated the primary campaigns, and assassination once again invaded the political process. Small wonder that by the time of the conventions, the nation was already exhausted by the process.

It had long been clear that the financial cost of Johnson's Great Society programs, as well as his single-minded policy of victory in Vietnam, had lost him the support of voters of the Middle. Yet the search for a Democratic candidate who could carry the center was a particularly frustrating one. The doves flocked to the banner of Senator Eugene McCarthy. The soft-spoken Minnesotan was an enigma in politics. On one hand, he was accompanied on his campaign—for no other reason than his own intellectual stimulation—by the poet Robert Lowell, and he continually made It clear that ending the war was more important than his own political fortunes. On the other hand, his drive in New Hampshire and Wisconsin to unseat a sitting president was a thing of political beauty. The organization of his student minions—thousands of clean-cut youngsters (anyone who needed a haircut was firmly asked to leave) pounding on thousands of Democratic doors—gave McCarthy a close runner-up finish in New Hampshire. Polls predicted a clear McCarthy victory over Johnson in Wisconsin. Yet despite these early successes, McCarthy possessed too liberal a reputation to seriously hope to carry the Middle. He had, however, scarred Lyndon Johnson, thus setting the stage for a candidate who had a true chance of carrying the Middle.

Robert F. Kennedy—the epitome of active emotion—entered the race in March because he felt McCarthy was unelectable even if Johnson was toppled. Bobby Kennedy was a human bridge between the doves who supported the antiwar stance that he had been taking since his 1964 election to the Senate and the Cold War hawks who had cut their diplomatic teeth with Harry Truman and perfected their craft with Kennedy's brother John. With enough political skill to avoid being terminally tied to either wing, Kennedy had the best chance of winning the nomination. Johnson saw the handwriting on the wall, and after Kennedy's entry into the race, Johnson withdrew. Like his brother before him, Bobby had a true chance of riding the center to victory. His June 1968 assassination threw the Democrats into turmoil. With McCarthy's campaign disintegrating, the situation was made to order for Vice-President Hubert Humphrey.

During the campaign Nixon would often call Humphrey a "sincere, dedicated radical." Perhaps this description had been true twenty years earlier, but not in 1968. Humphrey, whose virulent pro–civil rights speech to the 1948 Democratic convention had so inflamed the South that its delegates walked out and formed a new party, had mellowed into a man of rather narrow vision. He had been a good party man since 1948 and had been a consistent supporter of Johnson's policies in Vietnam. Throughout the 1968 campaign, Humphrey was perceived, with a great amount of justice, as Lyndon Johnson's candidate. It was the inevitability of his nomination after the Kennedy assassination that played a large role in drawing thousands of disaffected youths to the Chicago convention for a protest, which quickly turned into a bloody street brawl with police. Despite the swirling pace of events around him, Humphrey persisted in calling for an absurd-sounding "politics of joy." The Left despised him. The Right could not forget his past. More than anything in 1968, the Middle wanted to clean house and get rid of any taint of Johnsonism in Washington. That made disaffected Democrat George Wallace surprisingly appealing to the Middle.

Wallace had built for himself a comparatively progressive record during his two terms as governor of Alabama. He had built fourteen junior colleges and fifteen new trade schools, started a $100-million school construction program, and kept taxes down—all with deficit spending. Yet in the true southern demagogic style, he appealed to the fear held by poor whites of being economically strangled by blacks. After being defeated in the 1959 gubernatorial race by John Patterson, who had accepted the support of the Ku Klux Klan, Wallace reportedly told his supporters that he would "not be out-niggered again." He wasn't. During his successful run in 1962, he vowed to place his body in the doorway of any school that was ordered to integrate. In 1963 he made good on his promise, as he physically blocked the entrance to the library at the University of Alabama to demonstrate his disgust at the registration of two black students.

There was no question that Wallace's 1968 candidacy, running at the head of the renegade American Independent Party, had no hope of outright victory. His best hope was to throw a close race into the House of Representatives. This, of course, further endeared him to his home base. As journalist Marshall Frady points out in his prescient biography of Wallace, it mattered little to the sons and daughters of the South that Wallace couldn't win: "What matters is that he fought. . . . He answers the romance of defeat." Nevertheless, Wallace's message was undeniably appealing to much of frustrated Middle America. As he grumbled about students on northern campuses whom he typified as "damn uncultured, ignorant intellectuals," baited those same students into shouting matches during his speeches, and promised that if "some anarchist lies down in front of my automobile, it's going to be the last automobile he lies down in front of," he became a folk hero to blue-collar workers in every part of the nation. Much like Joseph McCarthy in the 1950s, Wallace touched the deep resentment that many workers held for the "big shots." As he fought government, he was fighting the good battle for the little guy. But the violent racial overtones of his rhetoric kept even larger numbers of the Middle outside the South from supporting Wallace. Most could not get past the promise in his 1963 inaugural address to defend "Segregation now! Segregation tomorrow! Segregation forever!" It was this fact that kept Wallace from capturing the Middle; while many privately grumbled in agreement with his histrionics, they would never vote for him.

However, simply because the Democrats could not propose a candidate who excited the Middle did not mean that the Republicans would win it by default. The Goldwater debacle of 1964 had left Republicans with a bad taste in their mouth. More than anything else, they were looking for a man who could win the election. Yet it was soon clear that three of the Republican candidates for the nomination would have no more of a chance of capturing the Middle than did Humphrey or Wallace.

Michigan Governor George Romney was a moderate on most issues, but he was nevertheless held suspect by the Middle because his zealous religious convictions, bland speaking style, and placid temperament made him seem weaker than he in fact was. To make matters worse, his campaign effort was so badly organized that Governor James Rhodes of Ohio was on target when he quipped that watching Romney run was "like watching a duck make love to a football."[26] The press and many party leaders wrote him off when he was quoted out of context as saying that he had been "brainwashed" on the Vietnam War. Romney withdrew just days before the New Hampshire primary, which he surely would have lost.

Nelson Rockefeller was acceptable to the Middle only if no other standard bearer could be found. Elected governor of New York in 1958, he had developed a reputation as a free-spending, progressive executive. His campaign attracted not only liberal Republicans but also disappointed New Deal Democrats who could find no champion in the 1968 field of Democratic contenders. Rockefeller was initially hesitant to make a third run for the presidency. The past eight years had brought the death of his son, a bloody divorce that was exploited by the Goldwater moralists in 1964, and a tough New York reelection campaign in 1966. On March 21 he announced that he would not run in the primaries, then on April 30 he announced that he was in the running, too late to enter any primaries. It is a bit oxymoronish to talk about a Rockefeller campaign in 1968; it was stillborn from the start.

A new entry into presidential politics that year was California Governor Ronald Reagan. Reagan's flip-flop career—from leader of the Screen Actor's Guild and advocate of the leftist Americans for Democratic Action to Republican conservative politician—had captivated Goldwaterites who were looking for a new champion. His 1966 triumph over Governor Pat Brown had been a welcome sign for downtrodden conservatives everywhere. Yet the Middle would not rally around a man who claimed in a speech that dissent in America "is helped along by a force in the world that has followed the Hitlerian technique." Any tinge of reactionism was unwelcome in the Republican party of 1968, and unless Reagan could find an ally with a broader base, he would get nowhere.

In his superb study *The Making of the President, 1968,* Theodore White refers to the "inevitability" of Richard Nixon. Certainly in one sense that is true. The challenges of Romney, Rockefeller, and Reagan were hardly challenges at all. Yet this should not obscure a key point in Nixon's success in 1968: Nixon was the only candidate, except for Robert Kennedy, who seemed to even care about carrying the Middle. In speech after speech he reassured the Middle that he had heard them and was ready to lead their rebellion against the sixties:

> Something is happening . . . a new voice is being heard all over America. It is different from the old voices, the voices of hatred, the voices of dissension, the voices of riot and revolution . . . those who did not indulge in violence, those who did not break the law, people who pay their taxes and go to work. . . . The Forgotten Americans, I call them . . . they cover all spectrums . . . [they] cry out "that is enough, let's get some new leadership." [27]

The Middle heard and heeded. It was ready to flock to the banner of any leader who promised not total victory, not peace at any price, but peace of mind. Despite Nixon lore, he did not *come* back in 1968; he was *brought* back by a massive segment of America that was plotting to overthrow Johnson's Great Society. Nixon would ride the discontent of this group, which he would soon term the "Silent Majority," into the White House.

To be nominated Nixon had to accomplish two things. First he had to win in the primaries so as to erase the image of Nixon the loser. And more important for the long run, he had to win without alienating either the Goldwater Right or the Rockefeller Left. When the primaries finally arrived, they were not a serious problem for Nixon. The only true contest was in Oregon, where an expensive Reagan TV blitz went for nought. Yet, as Nixon feared, Reagan's defeat served not to destroy but to galvanize the remaining members of the Goldwater Right, particularly in the South. There was a very real possibility that Reagan would urge southern conservatives and disaffected Rockefeller liberals to join together to halt his bandwagon.

To counter Reagan, Nixon reached out to Strom Thurmond. The South Carolina legend was more than a power in the Senate; he was the only true Republican presence in the South. Nixon met with Thurmond three times before the convention. During their last meeting, on May 31 in Atlanta, Thurmond quizzed Nixon on many issues, most notably his attitudes on the appointment of conservatives to the Supreme Court and the question of school desegregation. As Thurmond remembered the meeting, "I was satisfied from his answers that he gave me that he was sincere in what he said. . . . I didn't commit myself to him at that time, though. I came back and gave it some more consideration, and several weeks later, I did endorse him." Thurmond's pledge was, as Nixon remembers, "a valuable element in my ability to thwart any moves by Reagan on my right." It turned out to be the key to Nixon's nomination the following month.[28]

Despite Nixon's victory, the possibility of a postconvention ambush from either Rockefeller or Reagan still existed. Nixon protected himself with a shrewd choice for his running mate. The first thing that the country would realize about Spiro T. Agnew was that it didn't know him. Others had been considered besides the Maryland governor, both well known and lesser known.* Agnew was chosen because he held an appeal for both extremes of the party. Until March 21 he had been a sponsor of the National Draft Rockefeller Committee; he was tolerable, for the moment at least, to Rockefeller liberals. Yet it was his rhetoric that endeared Agnew to the Right. A source of eerie entertainment in the fall campaign, Agnew referred to Japanese-American reporter Eugene Oishi as a "fat Jap," to Polish-Americans as "Pollacks," and to Humphrey as "squishy-soft" on communism. Several party moderates, such as Minority Leader Gerald Ford, were disturbed by Agnew's rhetoric and told Nixon so. Their protests were ignored. Agnew served to help keep Wallace at bay and, as Nixon had done for Dwight Eisenhower in 1952, keep the presidential candidate from having to attack along the low road.

---

*Nixon's first choice for his running mate was his close friend Robert Finch. Realizing his limited name recognition, Finch wisely turned Nixon down (Finch would be named secretary of Health, Education, and Welfare in the new Nixon administration). The position was then offered to a man who had an even better chance than Agnew of appealing to both extremes of the party, Congressman Gerald Ford, a choice that, as Finch recalled in an interview with the author, did not cause "pyrotechnics" among the campaign staff. Claiming that he could better serve Nixon in the House of Representatives, Ford also declined.

The war in Vietnam loomed large as an issue that could easily destroy the candidacy of either Nixon or Humphrey. Polls consistently reported an interesting dichotomy. Most Americans disapproved of the way Johnson was handling the war, but at the same time the majority of Americans did not want to stop the bombing of North Vietnam. By 1968 the safest thing that could be said about the Vietnam issue was that it had become completely unpredictable. It had long since defied traditional political or demographic explanation.

Despite the unstable nature of the issue, both Humphrey and Wallace hit Vietnam hard during the campaign. Wallace *wanted* to talk about the war; a strong hawkish line fit in nicely with both his overall strategy and his rhetorical style. Wallace's choice for running mate, former member of the Joint Chiefs of Staff General Curtis LeMay, went even further than Wallace when he advocated "bombing North Vietnam back to the Stone Age." Humphrey, however, *had* to talk about the war. He was faced with the dilemma of having to separate himself from Johnson without losing the support of pro-administration war hawks in the process. The result was a compromise strategy on Vietnam that ended up appealing nicely to the Middle. On September 30 in Salt Lake City, Humphrey pledged that he would end the bombing in the North if the Communists would restore the demilitarized zone between North and South. It was not enough war to satisfy the Right and not enough peace to satisfy the Left. It was, however, the light at the end of the tunnel for the Middle. Immediately after the talk, Humphrey soared in the polls.

Nixon did not have an administration to please; nor did he see any political value in calling for immediate victory. As a result, he took no chances. For all intents and purposes Nixon voiced no Vietnam policy throughout the campaign. When he did talk about it, he hinted that he had a way out but claimed that he should not jeopardize any chance for peace by prematurely discussing his plans. In a 1985 televised interview, Nixon admitted that he actually had no "secret plan" to end the war; it had all been a smokescreen.[29] In the long run, however, it didn't matter. The Middle could not reject Nixon for his stand on the war as it had Johnson—it didn't know what Nixon's stand was.

Instead of Vietnam, Nixon chose to center his campaign on an issue that was by his reading the key concern of the Middle—the question of law and order. Actually, given the events of the sixties, the issue was more a *lack* of law and order. The rioting at the Democratic convention in Chicago had galvanized the issue. Chicago was, in microcosm, the dilemma of violence that the Middle had faced throughout the sixties: blood in the streets, and no one could figure out whom to blame. Perhaps Eugene McCarthy, confronting both police and students on the last night of the convention, was closest to the mark:

"Just what I thought. Nobody's in charge."[30] The Middle had watched both the hippies and the cops run amok for the last time. Eight years of Democratic rule had brought only war and chaos. Wallace was too impulsive to be trusted. The Middle turned to Richard Nixon to be calm but firm.

That he was in 1968, and more. In his acceptance address to the Republican convention, Nixon announced that his attorney general would "open a new front" against crime. After Chicago the strategy was simplified. In a memo to his staff members, Nixon argued that they should emphasize that "a vote for Humphrey is a vote for a policy under which crime will double in the next four years unless we get a change in policy. Sharp. Hard-Hitting."[31] Nixon was on the offensive with the issue from the opening week of the fall campaign. He made his first major speech in Chicago, noting later with some satisfaction that the "contrast with the bitter confrontation that Humphrey was now tied to could not have been greater." As Humphrey struggled with Vietnam, Nixon stepped up his rhetoric on law and order. A key facet of this strategy was a merciless attack on Johnson's attorney general, Ramsey Clark, as being soft on crime to the point of negligence of duty. Another was his subtle slurring of the Warren Supreme Court, which he treated as the ultimate symbol of softness toward alleged criminals. The most effective aspect of this strategy, however, was Nixon's reminiscing about the Eisenhower years, as he did in an oft-repeated passage from his standard stump speech:

> My friends, I was vice-president for eight years, . . . and I am proud that I served in an administration . . . in which we had peace in the United States, in which we did not have this problem of violence and fear which pervades this nation and its cities today.[32]

The law-and-order issue was the one that was helped the most by Nixon's skillful media campaign. Nixon hated the idea of being a packaged candidate, but the experience of 1960 had taught him the value of controlled television exposure. Harry Treleaven, a New York advertising consultant, developed a television campaign that completely ignored Nixon's stands on the issues and concentrated instead on developing an image of the candidate as calm, confident, and thoughtful. Nixon's political advisers disliked this strategy, preferring to show Nixon as having meaningful stands on the issues. John Ehrlichman, then serving as Nixon's chief advance man, later recalled for the author that this preference was based on their feeling that "you just didn't remake Richard Nixon. You tried to get him to be different at the margins, and that was about the best those fellas could do." However, Nixon supported Treleaven, and image won out over substance.[33]

Two of Treleaven's techniques were particularly fruitful. The first was a new twist on a campaign staple: the question-and-answer session. As described to the author by Ehrlichman, "Circular bleachers, basically . . . and he stood right in the middle, with a remote mike . . . to give him maximum freedom. And he just took questions as he went around. Very spontaneous, and he did extremely well." The concept of the "man in the arena" gave the impression that even while surrounded by accusers and questioners, Nixon was calm and thoughtful, the perfect man to deal with chaos. The second method was an imaginative series of television commercials that showed graphic still pictures of horrors in American streets. Nixon narrated the commercial without being seen on screen. The message given was that these scenes were not of Nixon's doing, but his deep baritone voice calmly promised to cure these ills. Humphrey's media campaign, which through September had paled by comparison with Nixon's, got better as the campaign went on. The Salt Lake City speech had cut Nixon's lead in half. On his own, however, Humphrey would never have closed the gap. It took the power of the incumbency to tighten the race into a dead heat.

On October 31 Johnson announced that all bombardment of North Vietnam would cease from 8:00 A.M. the next day and that peace talks would begin in Paris on the day after the elections. The gap between Humphrey and Nixon closed overnight, but Nixon stuck to his strategy of staying away from Vietnam. Instead of attacking Johnson for what was most likely pure political opportunism, Nixon presented himself as a statesman. In a speech at Madison Square Garden the day after Johnson's announcement, Nixon proclaimed that neither he nor Agnew would "say anything that might destroy the chance to have peace." Three days later, after being secretly promised by a Nixon go-between that he would fare better under a Nixon administration than under a Humphrey presidency, South Vietnamese President Nguyen Van Thieu announced that his nation would not participate in Johnson's negotiations. The shift to Humphrey bottomed out, as did the Middle's hopes for an end to the brutality in Vietnam.

In his scathing 1969 essay, *Nixon Agonistes,* journalist and historian Garry Wills postulates that the results of the 1968 election were determined by a "nihilist vote" on the part of an exhausted America. According to Wills, the country had ignored its traditional values and beliefs and had voted *against* Humphrey rather than *for* Nixon. Certainly there was a national sigh of relief that Johnson was leaving the White House. Indeed, 28 percent of Democrats who had voted for Johnson in 1964 voted for Nixon in 1968. Yet the Democratic party as a whole was left unscathed. The election was a hairline decision, with Nixon winning by only 0.7 percent of the popular vote—the smallest percentage of the national vote since Woodrow Wilson's victory in

1912.* Not only was there a gain in Democratic governors; Nixon would be the first president in 120 years to begin his administration with the opposition controlling both houses of Congress.

Yet this should not deny Richard Nixon his victory. As Humphrey talked about the war and Wallace made threats, the law-and-order strategy established Nixon as the candidate of the Middle. The Republicans ran well in the suburbs, the first such showing since Eisenhower. Nixon's campaign was strong enough to survive even the last-minute scare of Johnson's bombing announcement, showing a resilience of planning that it had not shown in 1960. The low-key confidence of the candidate was an unexpected asset.

The difference in Nixon's victory was clearly his surprising success in the South. White southerners deserted the Democratic party in droves. Political scientist Alexander Lamis states the reason for defection simply: "[Nixon] was the major beneficiary of the South's rejection of Humphrey."[34] One might add Johnson to this analysis; by 1968 the South detested Johnson's Great Society and Johnson's war with a virulence that was found in few other areas of the country. It is not surprising that Nixon, whose entire strategy revolved around a promise to reform Johnsonism, did so well in the South, despite the presence of Wallace in the race. Although there was a rise in the number of southern ballots, the Democrats carried only 31.1 percent of the total vote in the South, some two-thirds of which was made up of black voters. In the Deep South Humphrey won only Texas; Wallace captured the rest. Nixon, however, won the border states of Virginia, Tennessee, Kentucky, and North Carolina, and Thurmond's support gave him South Carolina.

The stage was set for the GOP to adopt what Nixon campaign staffer Kevin Phillips, in his influential 1969 book, *The Emerging Republican Majority,* would call "the Southern Strategy." As Phillips described his views to Garry Wills, "Who needs Manhattan when we can get the electoral votes of eleven Southern states? Put those together with the Farm Belt and the Rocky Mountain states and we don't even need the big cities. We don't even want them."[35] Once the Wallace phenomenon had spent itself, as analysts such as Phillips were confident that it would, a major realignment was possible in American politics—a permanent Republican majority.

The task that awaited the new president was hammered home to him on Inauguration Day, 1969. On the way back from the Capitol after Nixon had delivered his Inaugural Address, the presidential parade drove through a throng of protesters some three blocks long. They

*The final vote count gave Nixon 31,785,148 (43.4 percent), Humphrey 31,274,503 (42.7 percent), and Wallace 9,901,151 (13.5 percent). Nixon received 301 electoral votes, Humphrey 191, and Wallace 46.

threw stones at Nixon's car, chanted epithets, and hoisted a North Vietnamese flag. Nixon recalled the scene in his memoirs in words that might well describe his plans for reforming Johnsonism: "I was angered that a group of protesters carrying a Vietcong flag had made us captives inside the car. I told the driver to open the sun roof and to let the other agents know that Pat and I were going to stand up so the people could see us."[36]

CHAPTER TWO

The Rocky Road to a "New Federalism"

NIXON was not about to reverse the trend, begun by Franklin Roosevelt and continued by each of his successors, of keeping Cabinet-level government agencies relatively weak and concentrating the initiation of policy—both domestic and foreign—in the White House. Thus it would be the senior White House staff, not members of the Cabinet, who would guide the Nixon administration. Derisively labeled by two *Washington Post* reporters and ultimately by every history text as "all the president's men," Nixon's staff had become the most famous group of presidential advisers in United States history. What has been lost in the Watergate shuffle is their quiet, ruthless effectiveness. This was a remarkable group of advisers, quite simply the most powerful and efficient presidential staff of the postwar era. They bear close scrutiny.

One of two Harvard University faculty members on the senior staff, National Security Adviser Henry A. Kissinger, will be considered at a later point. The other was, in many ways, both Nixon's biggest surprise in his staff appointments and his greatest coup. The raffish Daniel Patrick Moynihan had long since risen above his difficult childhood in Manhattan's Hell's Kitchen. Trained at Tufts University and the London School of Economics, Pat Moynihan had served as an assistant to Averell Harriman and as John Kennedy's special assistant to the secretary of labor. His national reputation was linked to his publication of the results of a 1965 Labor Department investigation, *The Negro Family: The Case for National Action*. Better known as the Moynihan Report, this study described the problem of single-parent African-American families as a "tangle of pathology" and blamed the disintegrating family for black poverty. Moynihan had been assailed from all sides, and the attacks had ruined his quest for public office in 1965. Embittered, he went back to academe as director of the Harvard–Massachusetts Institute of Technology Joint Center for Urban Studies. It was Bob Finch who brought Moynihan in to see Nixon immediately after the election, and it was Finch who convinced Nixon to take Moynihan into the administration.

Moynihan and Nixon shared a common enemy—the intellectual Left. After leaving the Johnson administration, Moynihan had not, as has been suggested recently by several writers, given up on liberalism. He had, however, given up on liberals. Bruised by his rejection, Moynihan wrote in 1967 that the Left was "as rigid and destructive as any force in American life."[1] Members of Nixon's staff were particularly impressed with a speech Moynihan delivered to a 1967 meeting of the National Board of Americans for Democratic Action. Calling for a "politics of stability," Moynihan argued that "liberals must see more clearly that their essential interest is in the stability of the social order, and given the present threats to that stability, they must seek out and make much more effective alliances with political conservatives who share their interest."[2] If there was such an animal as a Nixon liberal, Moynihan was it.

Added to this ideological harmony was the fact that Nixon sincerely liked Moynihan. It is quite possible, as noted by columnists Rowland Evans and Robert Novak in their useful 1972 book on the Nixon White House, that part of the reason for Moynihan's appointment was that "the idea of this voluble, charming Irishman among the buttoned-up Christian Scientists of the campaign staff appealed to the President-Elect's hunger for novelty." Moynihan also satiated Nixon's love of stimulating intellectual conversation, something that he could not have with many other members of his staff. Thus infatuated, Nixon created a new staff position to suit Moynihan's talents, the Urban Affairs Council, which Nixon described as being comparable in influence to the National Security Council.

Nixon told the press that Moynihan, Kissinger, and his new presidential counselor, Arthur F. Burns, would be equal on the White House pecking order. Few believed him. It was assumed by most observers in early 1969 that Burns was the first among equals. The Austrian immigrant was one of the oldest members of Nixon's staff, and his résumé was truly imposing. As a youth he had learned his father's trade as a house painter; by 1944 he was a full professor at Columbia University. Burns had served as Eisenhower's chairman of the Council of Economic Advisers, and he and Vice-President Nixon had been close friends. Burns had also served on the Advisory Committee on Labor-Management Policy under both Kennedy and Johnson. During the transition, Nixon told Burns that he wanted him to replace William McChesney Martin as chairman of the Federal Reserve Board when Martin retired in 1970, and Nixon was adamant about having Burns in the administration in the interim. For his part, Burns wanted to go to the Fed, but he was not thrilled about serving another stint on the White House staff to get there.

To entice him, Burns was offered a position without precedent. He was made the first counselor to the president and given Cabinet rank—the only Nixon staff member to initially receive that distinction. The scholarly, composed Burns immediately clashed with the puckish Moynihan. Many administration intimates remain convinced that early in the administration, Nixon encouraged their feud as an intellectual exercise designed to provide him with the best range of domestic policy options. No matter what the motive, the fracas between these men and their equally competitive staffs would be one of the major stories of the first term.

Nixon's two key staff assistants, Harry Robbins "Bob" Haldeman and John Ehrlichman, have been linked together by reporter and historian alike: the Axis, the German Shepherds, the Berlin Wall, the men who guarded the Oval Office doors and shielded Richard Nixon from administration and country. The lion's share of the blame for the administration's abuses of power seems to have fallen on Haldeman and Ehrlichman. However, to properly understand the Nixon staff and how the White House worked, it is necessary to separate these Siamese twins of history. They performed vastly different functions for Nixon, and they executed their assigned duties well.

The idea of having a senior staff member who managed both himself and his White House certainly did not originate with Nixon. While Roosevelt, Truman, Kennedy, and Johnson did not have a formal "chief of staff," they nevertheless designated a member of their inner circle who was responsible for day-to-day managerial duties. Eisenhower, on the other hand, utilized his military experience and designated a single aide as chief of staff. As he would in many other areas, Nixon borrowed this idea from his mentor. It is hard to imagine a man more suited to be White House chief of staff than Bob Haldeman. A man of near-genius intelligence, Haldeman was born and reared in California. While he was too young to see active duty during World War II, he took part in the navy's V-1 rocket training program while in college. He received a degree in business administration from UCLA in 1948, then entered the field of advertising. After a short tenure with a smaller firm, in 1949 Haldeman joined the prestigious firm of J. Walter Thompson, where he stayed as an account executive until he was promoted to president and manager of the Los Angeles office in 1959.

It was during this period that Haldeman became fascinated with the politics and style of Richard Nixon. Haldeman worked for the vice-president as an advance man during the 1956 campaign and in several of Nixon's campaign trips during the 1958 off-year elections. These stints led to his taking a leave of absence from Thompson to become

Nixon's chief advance man in 1960. After the defeat, Haldeman stayed on to help Nixon write *Six Crises* and to manage the unsuccessful run for governor of California in 1962 (a race that Haldeman tried to dissuade Nixon from making). Between 1963 and 1967 Haldeman was back at Thompson, where he recruited a young staff from which would eventually be chosen several members of the Nixon White House staff. During the 1968 campaign, while Mitchell mapped out strategy, Haldeman was chiefly responsible for orchestrating the daily schedule and routine of the candidate.

Haldeman was the first and best of a new breed of White House staffer, the managerial assistant. He had no previous government experience, a point which he would later argue was not a "vital factor."[3] He was, however, a born administrator. Rarely if ever did Haldeman concern himself with policymaking in the White House. His function was essentially that of a traffic cop. Haldeman performed this job with extraordinary skill. He would meet with Nixon each morning, and the president would give him a list of people he wanted to see, things that needed to be done, and issues that he wanted to be assigned to a specific member of the staff. Haldeman would write all of these presidential requests on a yellow legal pad and check them off as they were completed during the day.

His single-mindedness in this task of managing Nixon's working day earned for Haldeman the scorn of many, who insisted that he was restricting access to the president. Most who worked in the Nixon White House agree with Haldeman's protest that "there was a screening of who saw the president, but the president himself did the screening. I just carried it out."[4] The daily list of whom Nixon wanted to see is distinguished by its brevity. By most accounts, Haldeman's manipulation of the president's time and schedule was skillful and fair, with complete cognizance of the demands and needs of his boss.

Where Haldeman was lacking was in human relations. Haldeman's duties included being in charge of personnel services, and he ran a tight ship. There was no deviation in uniform (dark suits, white shirt) or demeanor (workaholism expected of all staffers). His acceptance of this role allowed the president to avoid unpleasant face-to-face dismissals or reprimands of employees, which paralyzed him. One rather dramatic example will suffice: Nixon delegated to Haldeman the unpleasant task of informing Secretary of State William Rogers that Kissinger had gone on a secret trip to China, a trip about which Rogers had been neither informed nor consulted.[5] For these efforts Haldeman was as feared as any foreman. He has been depicted as anything from harsh and insensitive to neo-Nazi.

However, despite attempts by contemporary journalists to paint the two men as twins, Ehrlichman's job description was nothing like

Haldeman's. Born and reared in Seattle, Ehrlichman went to UCLA, where his freshman year was interrupted by World War II. He served in the Army Air Corps, flying twenty-six missions over Europe as a B-24 navigator and earning an air medal with clusters. After the war Ehrlichman served as an assistant dean of students at his alma mater while finishing his undergraduate work. He graduated from Stanford Law School in 1951, then entered a Seattle real estate practice. Ehrlichman met Haldeman while both were at UCLA, and it was Haldeman who convinced Ehrlichman to join Nixon's 1960 campaign as a junior advance man (what Ehrlichman gaily called "running away to the circus for a little while"[6]). His experience that year was limited, but he impressed Haldeman, who asked him to return to the 1962 campaign to keep Nixon's schedule. After Nixon's second defeat, Ehrlichman went back to his law practice, pausing only to help coordinate Nixon's speaking role at the 1964 national convention.

It was during the 1968 campaign that Ehrlichman's political stock soared. He and fellow operative William Timmons masterminded a convention operation at Miami Beach that was unparalleled for efficiency and ease of communications. They played a major role in Nixon's ability to blunt the Reagan and Rockefeller bids. After the convention Ehrlichman was put in charge of Nixon's field organization. As tour director he was responsible for everything from transporting reporters' suitcases to packing auditoriums with screaming Nixon faithful. All accounts agree that Ehrlichman's operation was among the most efficient and pleasantly run in memory.

It was inevitable that Ehrlichman would win a key position on the Nixon staff. Ehrlichman was correct, however, when he lamented to the author, with more than a bit of laughter, that "the general perception of my relationship to Nixon is not well understood." The first position given him, that of legal counsel to the president, was an uninteresting hybrid of legal and advisory duties (his first two jobs, for example, were the composition of a conflict-of-interest code for new Nixon appointees and the purchase of two new Nixon homes, one at San Clemente and one on Key Biscayne). During the early months of the administration, Ehrlichman was not even a part of the staff hierarchy. As legal counsel he was a lower-level administrative assistant who reported to Haldeman, and his responsibilities were comparatively narrow. All this would soon change. It was he to whom Nixon would turn to fill the vacuum of power caused by the Burns-Moynihan feud and the general incompetence of the first Cabinet. The difference between Ehrlichman and Haldeman, then, was the difference between policy and administration. From the opening gun, Haldeman took care of Nixon; before the end of 1969, Ehrlichman took care of domestic policy.

Never one for flashy phrases, Nixon took almost eight months to give his domestic program the nickname that the press had been waiting for. He did so in a speech to the National Governor's Conference on September 1, 1969, using a phrase that had been suggested to him by Pat Buchanan:

> If we are to win this race, our first need is to make government governable. . . . The essence of the New Federalism is to help regain control of our national destiny by returning a greater share of control to state and local governments and to the people. . . . We can command the future only if we can manage the present."[7]

To many observers this was merely an exercise in public relations. After all, most presidents of late had had catchy labels for their domestic programs. Announcing that Nixon's was to be called the "New Federalism" caused little stir. The promise to reform the federal government met with an equally lukewarm reception. Every administration had, at some point, promised to make things better—the simplest definition of reform. Yet Nixon clearly saw himself as an enemy of big government in the Jeffersonian tradition, a reformer who wanted to disengage the country from the tentacles of Washington bureaucrats, just as he was going to disengage it from Vietnam. If Nixon had his way, much of the power held by the federal government would be permanently given to the states.

The theoretical explanation of this idea grew to maturity in the intellectual hotbed of the Nixon White House—the speech writers. Holdovers from Nixon's New York years, they represented his desire to staff departments with ideologically competing voices. James Keogh, a former editor of *Time* and author of a 1956 campaign biography of Nixon, was in charge. He coordinated an outstanding trio, chosen to give Nixon the benefit of speeches that spanned the entire scope of the political spectrum. Raymond Price, a former editor of the *New York Herald Tribune,* was the liberal voice; Patrick Buchanan of the *St. Louis Globe-Democrat,* was the conservative (he would also prepare the weekly news summary and briefing books for the press conferences); and William Safire, who had worked for the *Herald-Tribune,* NBC, and a major public relations firm, was the centrist. Safire would take the point on articulating the New Federalism, thus sparking a debate which is described in detail in his 1975 memoirs of the Nixon White House *Before the Fall.*

On October 2, 1969, Haldeman sent Safire a memo asking him to address a looming public relations problem: "Few seem aware of the Nixon political philosophy, or his vision of America—outside of his hope for domestic tranquility." It had been a full month since Nixon's New Federalism speech, and Safire was correct when he later wrote that he was now being called upon to fit "a philosophy to the set of deeds" that had already been announced. He had, in fact, been jotting down ideas even since Nixon's speech in an attempt to find a philosophical common ground for the programs of the administration's first months. In doing so he isolated a key facet of Nixon's thinking. As Safire recalled in his memoirs,

> The reason why political power had been centralizing all our lives was that local government had been unable to meet the crisis of depression and unwilling to adapt to the revolution in civil rights. And the reason the opposite trend—decentralization—was now becoming popular was that the central government had shown itself to be notoriously inefficient, even infuriating, in some of its widely advertised programs. . . .[8]

The result of Safire's thinking on this paradox was a lengthy memo drafted in October 1969, the "New Federalist Paper #1." In the memo Safire argued that the United States government had "a need for both national unity and local diversity . . . a need *both* to establish national goals and to decentralize government services" (emphasis in original). Safire argued that to resolve this dilemma, the administration must use what he called a "standard of fairness," based on the fact that "fairness *in principle* still lies in Federal standards and minimums, but that fairness *in administration* usually lies closest to home." As a result, what Safire called "National Localism" demanded that the position of the localities vis-à-vis the federal government should be strengthened but that the central government was still on top. In the words of Safire, "National Localism says to communities, 'Do it your way . . . but do it.'" Safire signed the memo "Publius," after the pseudonym adopted by Alexander Hamilton, one of the authors of the original *Federalist Papers*.

What Publius argued in a nutshell was that the growth of the central government should be regulated and checked, not reversed, and power and funds that had previously resided in the localities should return there. Safire later described the fundamental tenet of the plan as the belief that "power should be permitted to seek the level where the problem can most fairly and expeditiously be handled." Far from a reversal of the New Deal, the New Federalism singled out areas, particularly Great Society programs, that took the New Deal to excess, and proposed to reverse those tendencies. In a sense it was economic and social containment. The president, obviously affected by Safire's work, kept the memo for a month, then returned it with several comments jotted in the margins. Perhaps the most telling comment: "It is not the middle of an old road. It is a new road."[9]

Publius's theorems were so new that the conservatives on the White House staff hit the roof when they read it. Pat Buchanan turned the document over to Tom Charles Huston for response. Huston's role in formulating the "Huston Plan," one of the first of the White House forays into the abridgment of civil liberties, tends to overshadow his impeccable credentials as a conservative thinker. Huston had taken a bachelor's and a law degree from Indiana University, where he had founded the local chapter of Young Americans for Freedom, a conservative youth group; in 1965, he had been the organization's national chairman. He had served in army intelligence and had worked for Nixon while doing so. When he left the army, he was offered a low-level speech-writer's job in the White House. Huston's mind was that of an ideologue; his was the code of the true philosophical conservative. His response to Publius (appropriately signed "Cato," the Roman moralist), argued that if the New Federalism was adopted, the federal government's power would actually be *increased* to the point of being despotic:

> Throughout the essay by New Publius one catches glimpses of the heavy hand and iron fist. He envisages a New Federalism in which national authority says to local authority, "Do it your way, but do it." Such a political scheme is necessarily authoritarian in implication, if not in practice; it denies discretion and thus denies freedom, for no man is free who lacks the power to say "No." [10]

Perhaps Cato would have muted his comments had he known that Nixon had commented on Publius's earlier drafts; perhaps not. In any case, it was Publius who won the favor of the president. Clearly his memo was the basis for many of the domestic initiatives of the first two years.

The first step in Nixon's plan for reform was to gain a decisive victory over the Democratic-controlled Congress so as to strengthen his hand for future programs. The battle over the antiballistic missile (ABM) program was an inauspicious way to begin. The issue, which mixed domestic and foreign policy, served to forecast the trouble that the administration would have in its dealings with Congress.

In response to the buildup of Soviet offensive weaponry that had occurred since the signing of the Nuclear Test Ban Treaty in 1963, the Johnson administration had authorized the development of the ABM, a defensive weapon designed to intercept and destroy incoming Soviet missiles. As one observer quipped, it was an "antimissile missile." Passage of the ABM program had been a major legislative test for Johnson, who in 1968, despite a defeat on the issue in the Senate Armed Services Committee, had won approval for the first phase of the program. This was the Sentinel system, a missile designed to protect major cities. The next phase of Sentinel was a program designed to prevent the destruction of U.S. missile silos, thus protecting America's second-strike capability.

Nixon was as committed as Johnson to the passage of the entire ABM package. From a political standpoint he had promised Strom Thurmond, as part of their deal in June 1968, that he would back the ABM.[11] More important, Nixon saw passage of the ABM program as an integral first step in forcing the Soviets back to the Strategic Arms Limitations Talks (SALT) bargaining table, a process that had been put on hold since the August 1968 invasion of Czechoslovakia. Congressional Democrats immediately put Nixon on notice that while they had supported the ABM under Johnson, they would not be so easily inclined to do so with a Republican in the White House. Other members who might have been inclined to support Nixon on other defense issues argued that the ABM, which had received mixed reviews after Pentagon testing, probably wouldn't work anyway.

To buttress his case, Nixon ordered Defense Secretary Melvin Laird to announce a temporary halt in construction of the Sentinel system pending a high-level review. When this action did not quiet critics, Nixon announced at a press conference his support of a scaled-down version of Sentinel, which the president said "perhaps best can be described as a Safeguard program." Instead of the massive urban protection system that Sentinel proposed, Safeguard would protect twelve vital metropolitan areas from Soviet missiles. Safeguard was not only cheaper; it also had the political advantage of a "phase system" of slow deployment instead of a fixed schedule. Yet Nixon knew that these concessions would mean little if he could not muster his troops. He admitted as much in answer to a question at the same press conference, when he predicted that the vote in Congress on Safeguard would be "very close."[12]

To try to close the gap, Nixon resurrected a favorite fear of his predecessors: the threat of a Soviet nuclear superiority unchecked by a viable U.S. deterrent. Running concurrently with the ABM debate was an equally ferocious debate over whether to stop the development of another weapon, the multiple independently targeted reentry vehicle (MIRV), an offensive missile that would carry as many as fourteen nuclear warheads into outer space, where each would independently reenter the atmosphere and strike separate targets. This was a ferocious step ahead in nuclear warfare, and one that paled the ABM by comparison. While the United States had first tested MIRVs in 1968, it was a point of debate within the intelligence and defense communities as to whether the Soviets had the technology to be able to produce their own MIRV system. Journalist Seymour Hersh claims in his 1983 book, *The Price of Power*, that a CIA estimate made available to Nixon in June 1969 flatly denied that the Soviets had any such capability. Nixon, however, clearly wanted to believe that the Soviets had their own

MIRVs. Such a threat would make it easier for him to gain congressional support for the ABM. When CIA Director Richard Helms refused to order his staff to change the estimate, Nixon simply ignored it and berated Helms behind his back for disloyalty.[13]

Holding out the threat of Soviet MIRVs, along with exaggerating the national security peril supposedly posed by the shooting down of an American EC-121 jet by the North Koreans in April, the White House staged its first real blitz of Capitol Hill. It was a mixed show from the start. Bryce Harlow, Nixon's chief of congressional relations, had filled the same position in the Eisenhower administration and was one of the most respected and well-liked political operatives in Washington. For public consumption Nixon put Harlow in charge of the ABM lobbying effort. But Harlow ran into constant interference from White House staffers who were running a lobbying effort of their own. Nixon made it clear to Haldeman what he wanted: "This is war—have to get it organized—We've gained the initiative, but have to hold it. . . . Don't worry about country—just Senate. . . ."[14] The pressure put on the Senate was so intense, heavy-handed, and badly coordinated that the White House lost several key congressmen who had previously told Harlow they would vote for the bill.

The result for the administration was an eyelash short of disaster. An amendment to weaken the Safeguard package was proposed by Maine Republican Margaret Chase Smith; it was defeated on August 6 by the closest of margins, a 50–50 tie (enough to kill an amendment). Nixon had his ABM, but senators on both sides of the aisle would not soon forget the White House's approach to vote-getting. They would be less than responsive when Nixon courted them again. Nixon was so incensed by the defections in the Republican ranks that, as he concedes in his memoirs, the vote "confirmed my resolve to pour every possible resource of money and manpower into the congressional elections of 1970 in order to shore up our position in Congress."[15] The clash between Nixon and the Congress had begun, and it was a war that would adversely affect his desire to achieve the New Federalism.

Nowhere did Nixon believe that the federal government had interfered in the rights of the state more than in recent rulings of the Supreme Court. As he would later write, Nixon felt that the Warren Court had been "unprecedentedly politically active . . . too often using their interpretation of the law to remake American society according to their own social, political, and ideological precepts."[16] To Nixon, the justices' decisions had been largely to blame for the social upheaval of the sixties. In this sentiment he was far from alone. The 1966 *Miranda v. Arizona* case, guaranteeing that criminals would be read their rights prior to arraignment, had bred such resentment that court bashing had become a popular topic for the far Right and the Middle alike; in 1968,

75 percent of the public opposed the court's protection for supposed criminals.[17] It was plausible to assume that Nixon planned to refocus the court by appointing more conservative, strict constructionists to each vacancy afforded him.

Seeing the handwriting on the wall, Chief Justice Earl Warren resigned from the court in 1968 in an attempt to allow Johnson to name his successor. In a faux pas of great political impact, Johnson named Associate Justice Abe Fortas to replace Warren. The prospect of the promotion of Fortas, one of Johnson's closest cronies and a member of his Senate staff whom he had named to the court, infuriated lawmakers from both parties. The nomination was filibustered off the table. Reluctantly, Warren agreed to stay on, but he was a lame duck waiting for the opportunity to resign. After Nixon entered office he immediately approached Warren to negotiate a hasty timetable for his resignation.[18]

Even though Fortas's chance to be chief justice was gone, his troubles remained. Soon after Nixon's inauguration, *Life* magazine reported that Fortas had accepted an annual stipend of $20,000 from a family foundation set up by Louis Wolfson and had used the money to supplement his salary. To compound matters, Wolfson was under investigation by the Securities and Exchange Commission; he would eventually go to jail for stock fraud. Despite the subsequent scandal, Fortas dug in his heels and refused to resign from the court. Smelling a second vacancy, Nixon lit the coals under Fortas's feet. During a May 7 meeting, Haldeman's notes show, Nixon ordered his staff to "push on investigation of foundations . . . on Fortas thing—real vendetta— Mitchell, et al., go ahead fast—investigate and prosecute. . . ."[19] John Mitchell, now Nixon's attorney general, personally shared the results of that investigation with Warren, who agreed that Fortas would have to resign. On May 12 Mitchell announced and Warren confirmed that Warren had been informed by the Justice Department that charges were to be brought against Fortas. Fortas resigned two days later, leaving Nixon with his second court vacancy.

The Fortas scandals, coupled with the national law-and-order sentiment, made it the perfect time for Nixon to move the court to the right. All of the men on Nixon's short list for chief justice—Herbert Brownell (his first choice, eliminated because of southern memories of Brownell's role as Eisenhower's attorney general during the Little Rock crisis), Thomas Dewey, Associate Justices Potter Stewart and John Harlan, and John Mitchell—would have done so.[20] When all of the above either declined to be considered or were erased from the competition, Nixon turned to Warren Burger, a justice on the U.S. Court of Appeals for the District of Columbia.

On the surface Burger was well suited for this role of steering the court away from the Warren years. A consistent champion of the rights of victims, he was an outspoken critic of *Miranda*. In a 1967 speech at Ripon College, Burger had charged that criminal trials were often delayed and that the courts had become bogged down with too many appeals, retrials, and delay tactics by defense lawyers. Yet at heart Burger was less a jurist than he was a politician. He had come up through the ranks of Minnesota Republican politics. Working as Harold Stassen's floor manager at the 1952 presidential convention, he was instrumental in convincing Stassen to turn his state's votes over to Eisenhower at the end of the first ballot. Eisenhower had shown his gratitude by naming Burger as an assistant in the Justice Department and by promoting him to the Court of Appeals in 1956.

When it came time for Warren's retirement, Burger's political wiles served him well. There was no question that Burger wanted to be chief justice and openly campaigned for it. On a trip to the White House to swear in several Executive Office appointees, Burger brought along a copy of his Ripon speech and gave it to Nixon. In turn Nixon ordered that the speech be disseminated to the staff. Throughout the next three months Burger flooded the offices of Ehrlichman and Mitchell with handwritten notes, offering unsolicited advice and words of encouragement.[21] He soon had the powerful support of both Mitchell and Rogers, and on May 21 Nixon announced Burger's nomination as chief justice to the nation. The appointment sailed through the Senate Judiciary Committee and the Senate at large with virtually no challenge.

The administration's attempts to fill Fortas's seat fostered a confrontation between the president and Congress that paled the ABM fight. Nixon, looking toward 1972, wanted to appoint a southerner to the Supreme Court, and Nixon's advisers were certain that the appointment would be dictated by Strom Thurmond. On August 18 Nixon nominated Clement F. Haynsworth of Thurmond's home state, South Carolina, to replace Fortas. Haynsworth, chief justice of the Fourth Circuit Court of Appeals, was a conservative, and despite his moderately high overturn rate, he was widely respected. He had also been cleared by Mitchell, and his appointment seemed assured.

Within three weeks, however, the nomination had stalled. Civil rights organizations objected to the appointment of a southerner; organized labor objected to the fact that Haynsworth had been closely connected with cases where labor unions had been big losers. Both groups objected to Haynsworth's passing relationship with convicted Senate lobbyist and ex-Johnson aide Bobby Baker. But the most meddlesome accusation was that he had held stock in a company, Carolina Vend-a-Matic, that had business dealings with a party to a 1965 case before Haynsworth's Fourth Circuit.*

---

*Darlington Manufacturing Co. v. National Labor Relations Board (325 f. 2D 2nd 682).

The conflict had long since been resolved: with the approval of his colleagues, Haynsworth had not recused himself from the case, and a subsequent investigation undertaken by both the sitting head judge of the Fourth Circuit Court and the Justice Department had absolved Haynsworth of any wrongdoing. Attorney General Robert Kennedy himself had written to express his "complete confidence" in Haynsworth.[22]

During his hearings before the Senate Judiciary Committee, Haynsworth produced the investigation report data that had cleared him, but his nomination met stubborn opposition. In an October 8 statement to the press, committee member Birch Bayh, an Indiana Democrat, detailed the story of Carolina Vend-a-Matic without mentioning the favorable results of the subsequent investigation. He also listed other cases that he charged showed conflicts of interest, arguing that Haynsworth had shown a "demonstrated lack of candor" in his testimony before the committee and had shown repeated "violations of the canons of ethics of the ABA."[23] Bayh's attacks were effective. Many moderate Republicans, even those who had supported Nixon on the ABM treaty, abandoned Haynsworth. The two key defections were newly elected Minority Leader Hugh Scott of Pennsylvania and Majority Whip Robert Griffin of Michigan. In October Harlow told Nixon that the probable vote was 52–48 against the nomination, that the situation was "deteriorating," and that Haynsworth should withdraw his name.[24]

Nixon believed that Haynsworth was being unjustly castigated for his conservative beliefs, and he mobilized his forces for the fight. Using the same bludgeoning tactics that had so angered senators during the battle over the ABM, Nixon pulled out all the stops to keep recalcitrant members in line—everything from sending Assistant Attorney General Richard Kleindienst to the hill with orders to "trade judges"[25] to ordering Harlow to "get Murderer's Row in the Senate—need to kick Bayh around."[26] These tactics got Nixon nowhere. He then attempted to mobilize public opinion. On October 20 he met informally with members of the press in the Oval Office to discuss the nomination. After the pleasantries, Nixon drew his knife. In no uncertain terms he made it clear that his choice had been maligned, and he would stick by him:

> When a man has been through the fire, when he has had his entire life and its entire record exposed to the glare of investigation, which, of course, any man who is submitted for confirmation to the Senate should expect to have; and in addition to that, when he has had to go through what I believe to be a vicious character assassination, if after all that he stands up and comes through as a man of integrity, a man of honesty, and a man of qualifications, then that even more indicates that he deserves the sup-

port of the President of the United States who nominated him in the first place."[27]

For Nixon, as he would tell Ehrlichman the next day, the Haynsworth nomination had turned into a "PR Battle" which must be won.[28] This attitude served only to further galvanize Haynsworth's opponents. On November 21 Haynsworth was rejected by the Senate by a 55–45 vote, with seventeen Republicans, including Scott and Griffin, abandoning Nixon and joining thirty-eight Democrats in the nay column.

Furious, Nixon ordered Mitchell to deliver another name that would be acceptable to the South. Mitchell turned to a judge who had previously been suggested by Burger, G. Harrold Carswell of Florida, an associate on the Fifth Circuit Court of Appeals. With minimum fanfare Carswell was nominated on January 19, 1970. Mitchell, who now assumed complete responsibility for the nomination, met with Minority Leader Scott and assured him that Carswell was an "essentially moderate fellow."[29] Satisfied and wishing to make amends with the administration, Scott announced his support for Carswell.

Yet it was quickly clear that using any criterion, Bayh's later assessment that Carswell "made Haynsworth look like Learned Hand" holds true.[30] Carswell's decisions had been reversed at a rate more than twice that of the average federal district judge. Yet even this record might have been defendable had it not been for Carswell's blatantly racist remarks. For example, when speaking to an American Legion group in Georgia in 1948, Carswell had proclaimed that the "segregation of the races is proper and the only practical and correct way of life in our states. I have always so believed, and I shall always so act."[31] When Carswell's background was made public, Scott as well as other moderate Republicans who had announced their support of Carswell were furious. Harlow reported that this nomination was also lost.

Convinced that the Haynsworth debacle had not been Mitchell's fault, Nixon had wanted his friend to take the credit for a successful Carswell nomination. Yet it was soon evident that with Carswell, Mitchell had made a blunder of mammoth proportions. Cutting his losses, Nixon abandoned Carswell several weeks before the floor vote was taken, ordering the staff not to fight for this nomination as they had done for Haynsworth. Even though Carswell was clearly unqualified for the position, Nixon blamed the defeat on the moderate Republicans who had broken with the administration on both nominations. Two weeks before the vote, Nixon ticked off the names of several Republican members—"Mathias, Schweicker, Case, Goodell, Percy"*— and told Haldeman and Ehrlichman that they were never to be invited

*Charles McC. Mathias of Maryland, Richard Schweicker of Pennsylvania, Clifford Case of New Jersey, Charles Goodell of New York, and Charles Percy of Illinois.

to the White House again because they were "never for [the] president on any issue."[32] Nixon also ordered that all senators who had opposed Haynsworth and Carswell should be put to the "Haynsworth Test"—a rigorous check on their character, finances, and club memberships and on racially restrictive covenants in their mortgages.[33]

On April 9 Carswell met the same fate as Haynsworth; despite having his nomination approved by both the ABA Screening Committee and the Senate Judiciary Committee, he was defeated on the floor of the Senate, 51–45. The matter was closed by Nixon with a short, savage statement to the press the same day. In it Nixon said that the Senate had rejected Carswell because of his "philosophy, which I share . . . the South is entitled to proper representation on the court." Once he had completed his statement, Nixon thrust his hands in his pockets and, unsmiling, left the press room without entertaining any questions.

Having made his public display of solidarity with the South, Nixon bowed to the inevitable. On the day after Carswell's defeat, Mitchell was on the phone with Judge Harry Blackmun of Minnesota, an eleven-year veteran of the Eighth Circuit Court of Appeals and a lifelong friend of Burger. Quiet, studious, and a civil rights moderate with an undistinguished record, Blackmun was nominated on April 18, and in confirmation hearings that were overshadowed by the Cambodian crisis and the Kent State shootings, was unanimously confirmed on May 12.

The press trumpeted that Nixon had gone one-for-two with his first two Supreme Court appointments. He had won with Burger, but he had lost his southerner. As he was to soon find out, however, Nixon had made a tremendous mistake with Burger. Primarily a politician, Burger looked not to any ideological preference but to the prevailing political winds as he forged his coalitions on the court. Many observers have noted that he was more concerned with being on the winning side of a decision than with voting his conscience. The first term of the Burger Court would cost the New Federalism dearly, particularly in the area of civil rights.

Nixon's law school days at Duke had given him a good view of how southerners thought. He was against segregation, generally supported the wording of the court in *Brown v. Board of Education of Topeka, Kansas* (1954), and believed that most white southerners supported integrating their schools at the court's "all deliberate speed." In Nixon's view, a speedy, federally forced integration was worse than no integration at all; it would alienate most white southerners and ultimately aggravate racial tensions throughout the country. To Nixon, no panacea of speedy integration was more undesirable than forced busing.

The concept of busing students to school to achieve racial balance, most likely to a school some distance from their own neighborhood, appalled Nixon. At the height of his administration's civil rights crisis, he talked about busing during a lengthy telephone call to Ehrlichman. As Ehrlichman's notes recorded the conversation, the president reflected that "moving by bus to different neighborhood[s] suffer more harm—physical—tearing up neighb[orhood]."[34] Nixon was also struck by the hypocrisy of those in the North who castigated the South while entrenching segregation in their own suburbs. As he mused to Ehrlichman and other staff members in a March 1970 meeting: "White libs condemn South but send kids to private schools—just as wrong as an intractable Southern segregationist."[35] Nixon was ready to approach the issue of civil rights and desegregation from the point of view of a white southerner of the Middle—which he had been while at Duke. That would require a break with recent approaches to civil rights, most notably a reform of what Nixon saw to be the damage done by both Johnson and the Warren Court.

The Civil Rights Act of 1964 had entrusted the enforcement of integration rulings to the Department of Health, Education, and Welfare (HEW) and to the Justice Department. With every passing year since its creation in 1953, HEW had taken on an increasingly assertive and dramatic personality.* As a department, HEW was committed to wholesale civil rights reform on a rapid timetable. Nixon's transition team attempted to clean house at HEW, but it did a poor job. As Frederic Malek, then deputy undersecretary for administration at HEW, told the author, the department continued to "swing far to the left of where the White House was coming from." HEW Secretary Bob Finch, one of Nixon's oldest political friends, did little to help the situation. Finch told the author that he felt that the role of HEW should not be "assertive or dramatic . . . we were trying to pull the country together." Nevertheless, Finch hurt his own cause by appointing an unreconstructed liberal as director of HEW's Office for Civil Rights. Californian Leon Panetta joined the administration believing that Nixon would at least not turn back the clock on civil rights. Panetta began to argue that integration guidelines should be enforced using a method begun by the Johnson administration—denying federal funding to any school district that refused to comply with the guidelines set under Title III.

Personally Finch agreed with the fund cutoff strategy, and he initially supported Panetta's position. Finch was helped by the fact that early in the administration, Nixon had publicly stated, thanks largely to Moynihan, who was privately giving Nixon the same advice, that he also supported the fund cutoffs as a measure to gain compliance. Yet Finch knew Nixon better than almost anyone. He knew that this position was just a starting point so that Nixon could avoid busing, and that cutting off funds was well to the left of where Nixon wanted

*In 1980 HEW was split into two departments, Health and Human Services and Education.

to be on civil rights. Finch also knew that when lobbying from southern congressmen began, Nixon would probably not stick to this position, certainly not if he was offered a more moderate alternative.

Mitchell's Justice Department offered Nixon that alternative. Mitchell argued that if Finch and Panetta had their way, the wrath of southern whites—sure to be furious when federal aid was denied to their children's schools—would come down squarely on the heads of the administration. Instead the Justice Department pushed for enforcement of integration guidelines through the judicial process. Mitchell argued that seeking injunctions and bringing lawsuits was not only a slower, more careful procedure but would place the onus of enforcement on the courts instead of on the White House. Nixon would be shielded from the segregation issue, and it would be buried in the courts until after his reelection. Mitchell quickly began to insist that Finch change his mind on the fund cutoffs.

The issue jumped onto the front burner before the administration was two weeks old. Finch's predecessor at HEW, Wilbur Cohen, had notified five southern school districts that they had lost their federal funding for not complying with integration guidelines. These school districts—two of which were in Thurmond's South Carolina—were scheduled to lose their money on January 29, 1969, a few days after Nixon's inauguration. Thurmond put a great deal of pressure on Harlow and Finch to cancel the cutoffs. Harlow and Mitchell also lobbied Nixon, claiming that if Finch did not reverse the decision, the southern congressional delegation would lose its patience with the administration before there had been a real chance to do business with each other.

Caught up in the infighting, Finch was outgunned and outmatched. He was never particularly strong when it came to resisting pressure from the Nixon staff. Quite aside from that, however, Finch was not about to do something that would cost his friend political capital. Yet he felt a certain loyalty to Panetta as well, and believed that his position had some merit. Finch dealt with his dilemma by negotiating a compromise between Nixon and the five school districts. It was agreed to postpone the fund cutoffs for sixty days, after which the funds would be denied if solid steps toward integration had not been taken. Panetta was furious, but for the moment at least, Thurmond had been mollified.

By July Nixon had had enough of both the bickering in the Cabinet and HEW's strident public appeals for strong enforcement. On July 2 he issued a statement saying that he sided with Mitchell. Nixon announced that the administration was shifting its civil rights strategy into the courts and might ignore other desegregation deadlines set by the previous administration. This statement represented a change in Nixon's earlier public position in favor of the fund cutoffs, a fact not missed by the press, which duly reported the administration's "flip-flop" on civil rights. For its part, HEW was completely caught off guard by the statement. In a press conference Panetta tried to argue that there was really no change in administration emphasis. He quickly received a phone call from Ehrlichman, telling him to "cool it."[36]

Nixon had now changed his civil rights policy to one closer to his own beliefs, closer to the mainstream convictions of the Middle, and more certain to placate the South. In an irony of sorts, Nixon's legal strategy resembled the early strategy of the civil rights crusade in the 1950s, when the National Association for the Advancement of Colored People (NAACP) and other groups had fought the movement's battles in court, their most notable victory being *Brown*. The civil rights movement had long since passed out of its moderate phase, however, and there was no question that Nixon's policy infuriated most black leaders, who saw it as a step backward.

It was not long before political exigencies forced Nixon to change his policy again. Before Nixon had announced his support of Mitchell's court strategy, Finch had approved a desegregation plan for thirty-three school districts in Mississippi. The plan, which included fund cutoffs, had been upheld by the Fifth District Court of Appeals in New Orleans. John Stennis, the crusty conservative senator from Mississippi, let it be known in no uncertain terms that he expected the plan to be scrapped, despite the court's ruling. Stennis held a trump card—his Armed Services Committee held the fate of the ABM. Indeed, in a handwritten note to Nixon, Stennis threatened to sit out the ABM vote if the Mississippi fund cutoffs were not reversed.

Nixon was quick to surrender to Stennis. Under direct orders from the president, Finch wrote a letter to the federal judge in New Orleans reversing HEW's previous stand and asking for a delay in the integration plan. The secretary claimed that it would cause "chaos, confusion, and a catastrophic educational setback." Conveniently ignoring his earlier advice to let the courts handle the issue, Mitchell was quick to support Finch, arguing that it was "simply unreal to talk of instant desegregation." In August the court granted Finch's request, giving the Mississippi school districts an indefinite stay of integration, provided that they took "significant steps" toward integration in the coming year.[37]

But the issue was far from dead. With whiplashlike intensity, a higher court reversed the Mississippi decision. To Nixon's shock and amazement, however, it was the Supreme Court that did the damage, and in a unanimous decision. On October 29, in *Alexander v. Holmes County Board of Education*, the high court ruled that the "all deliberate speed" timeline for integration set out in *Brown* was "no longer constitutionally permissible." The court declared that "the obligation of every school district is to terminate dual school systems at once and to operate now and hereafter only unitary schools," and it instructed the

New Orleans District Court to order the Mississippi school districts to "immediately" integrate. In a statement the next day, Nixon surprised some observers by promising that he intended "to use the leadership resources of the executive branch of government to assist in every way," despite the "practical and human problems involved." [38]

Though he proclaimed publicly that the administration would "carry out the law," [39] Nixon was not about to attack segregation throughout the country, no matter what *Alexander* said. He justified his refusal to move unilaterally as the high court demanded by making a quasi-legal, philosophical distinction. Nixon argued that he was empowered by the U.S. Constitution to address the legal inequities of de jure segregation—the existence of laws that obliged segregation, most notably those Jim Crow laws in southern states and localities, as well as the refusal of many localities to adhere to court demands to integrate their schools. Nixon was ready to fight de jure segregation by using political and legal pressure to change laws, adjust quotas, and redress economic imbalances. Yet Nixon believed that he did not have the constitutional right to attack the de facto segregation of the northern ghettos, where segregation was not legislated but rather a result of custom and mores. To do so would violate not only the right of people to make a free choice with their lives but also the inherent power of the states.

This tactic presented definite political risks: fighting de jure segregation meant risking the wrath of southern whites, while ignoring de facto segregation meant incurring the wrath of northern liberals and blacks. Nixon had long since resigned himself to never having the support of northern blacks, however, and he was convinced that he could enforce the *Alexander*-ordered segregation in the South without jeopardizing his southern base of support. The gamble paid off. Nixon's attack on de jure segregation was the very embodiment of his New Federalism. But for Nixon this volatile issue transcended even Publius's theories; it was personal. Nixon clearly empathized with members of the white southern middle class in this predicament. He made it clear during a staff meeting that the spin from the White House was to be that "we disagree with segregation, not [that] Southerners are morally wrong." [40] This moderate approach would reap a greater integration harvest than had been achieved in any previous administration.

Nixon began by explaining his civil rights stand to the entire nation in a major televised address on March 24, 1970. While he promised that "the constitutional mandate [of *Alexander*] will be enforced," he made it clear that "certain changes are needed in the nation's approach to school desegregation." In terms of de jure segregation, Nixon made it clear that "deliberate segregation of pupils by official action is unlawful" and that "school administrators throughout the nation . . . must move immediately . . . to assure that schools within individual school districts do not discriminate with respect to the quality of the facilities or the quality of the education." Yet he also made it clear that he could do little to combat de facto segregation, as he felt that "we cannot be free, and at the same time be required to fit our lives into prescribed places on a racial grid." For Nixon, one point about de jure and de facto segregation was common and unshakable: "transportation of pupils beyond normal geographic school zones for the purpose of achieving racial balance will not be required."[41] Thanks to *Alexander*, the administration would move forward on civil rights, but the pace and scope of civil rights policy would be dictated by Nixon, not by the court.

Nixon's next step, the February 17, 1970, firing of Leon Panetta, further assured the South that the upcoming changes would be truly as moderate as Nixon had promised in his speech to the nation. An equally important move was to consult his secretary of labor on the problem. George Shultz, former dean of the University of Chicago's Graduate School of Business, was fast emerging as one of Nixon's favorite Cabinet members. With the help of Ehrlichman, Shultz had developed an apparatus through which southern politicians were formally prepared for integration. Shultz set up advisory committees in seven Deep South states to aid with desegregation. He brought these committees to Washington, arranged for them to meet with the president, and even arranged for Nixon to travel to New Orleans to meet with the Louisiana committee, the most intransigent of the lot. This was more consultation than any administration had offered southern politicians on the subject of integration since *Brown*. No longer feeling that they were being completely dictated to by the White House, the southern committees went back to their home districts and pushed for a peaceful integration of their school systems. Shultz and Ehrlichman also convinced Nixon to swallow his convictions on the issue and to let stand an Internal Revenue Service ruling revoking tax exemptions for private (i.e., white) schools.* While this was a noticeable step to the left on the issue, Nixon softened the blow for the South when he stated that he had "no intention . . . of sending vigilante squads . . . of Justice department lawyers . . . to coerce Southern districts to integrate."[42] The specter of Kennedy-Johnson Justice Department representatives who had visited the South during the sixties was missed by no one.

Satisfied, southern politicians began to cooperate. The success of Nixon's post-*Alexander* plans in the South was unquestionable. The South began to integrate peacefully at a rate unseen since *Brown*. At the beginning of his term in office, the percentage of African-American chil-

---

*In a meeting with Ehrlichman and Moynihan, Nixon argued that "Catholics ought not to be dumped on private schools" and admitted that "I'm not a public school man, even though I always went to public schools. [Private schools] bring diversity" (Ehrlichman Notes, February 2, 1970, WHSF-Ehrlichman, box 9).

dren attending segregated schools in the South was 68; by the end of Nixon's tenure, it was down to 8.[43] But Nixon's argument that he was empowered to deal only with de jure segregation effectively ignored half the problem, a fact that Nixon understood and supported. He would not make any serious moves to deal with northern de facto segregation until late in his first term. He needed the votes of southern whites in the upcoming congressional elections, and he needed the votes of southern senators and representatives if he hoped to succeed in his New Federalist reform of that part of the Great Society which the Middle hated the most.

In his memoirs Nixon is clear: "From the first days of my administration I wanted to get rid of the costly failures of the Great Society—and I wanted to do it immediately. . . . The worst offender was the welfare system, and welfare reform was my highest priority."[44] Nonetheless, the anchor of his reform package, the Family Assistance Plan (FAP), dragged welfare reform to a screeching halt before the end of the first term. The story of the FAP is a story of the failure of the most far-reaching, most forward-thinking legislation of the Nixon administration. Its story also reveals a microcosm of staff intrigue and power politics in the Nixon White House, the best example of how Nixon's staff contributed to the failures of the New Federalism.

Ever since the passage of the Social Security Act of 1935, which created what the public refers to as "welfare," politicians of both parties and all ideologies have tried to reform the system. Of the four programs established by the act—Aid to the Blind, Old Age Assistance, Aid to Permanently and Totally Disabled, and Aid to Families with Dependent Children (AFDC)—the latter program drew the most fire. It was easily the most expensive of the programs; the federal share of AFDC was more than 65 percent of the total payment made to each recipient. By 1968 AFDC was costing over two billion dollars, and in that year alone benefit costs had risen by another half-billion dollars. The number of participants in AFDC had risen sharply in the 1960s, bringing with it a corresponding increase in the number of social workers needed to take care of the caseload. The AFDC had created its own bureaucratic jungle.

One suggested solution to the problem was the negative income tax, or guaranteed annual income. First popularized by conservative economist Milton Friedman in 1944, the concept called for replacing welfare payments with a direct payment of cash to persons whose income was so small that they were not required to pay any income taxes. It amounted to a promise to all Americans of a minimum annual income. Friedman argued that the plan would address the problem of poverty while allowing the government to get rid of the AFDC; there would be no need for it if people were simply guaranteed a lump sum.

The idea met with opposition from all directions. Conservatives were so against the idea of welfare that the thought of any program that gave money to the poor was anathema. Liberals also opposed the plan, not only because it threatened the welfare bureaucracy that so many of them had put their faith in but also because labor unions, seeing a threat to their ability to bargain for wages, would oppose it.

There was no reason to believe that any Republican administration in 1969 would sanction the guaranteed annual income as the basis of its welfare reform plan. There was also no question that while Nixon wanted to reform the welfare system, he was not foolish enough to take the Goldwater tack of completely abolishing it. Three weeks after his inauguration, pronouncing that "we *have* to do some new things— can't just keep the same institutions . . . have to show some action— *be different,*" Nixon ordered Haldeman to assign the development of a welfare reform package to the Urban Affairs Council (UAC).[45]

Thus it was Pat Moynihan who assumed the initial responsibility for effecting changes. Originally Moynihan favored only those reforms that did not threaten to destroy AFDC. What changed his mind was a report by Bob Finch, who chaired the UAC's subcommittee on welfare. Finch had been sold on the negative income tax by his undersecretary at HEW, John Veneman. His plan called for a guaranteed annual income of $1,500 for a family of four, with these benefits to be reduced by fifty cents for each dollar of additional income that the recipient earned. Named the Family Security System (FSS), the plan would provide relief for the working poor while eliminating any need for AFDC. With FSS there would also be no need for social workers assessing problems; all that would be needed was to send a poor family a check each month. This idea appealed to Moynihan, who quickly supported FSS, as did Nixon.

Nevertheless, Nixon bemoaned the fact that FSS included no incentive for a poor person to get a job; under FSS a recipient would actually *lose* money if he or she went to work. For this reason, Arthur Burns was adamantly against it. Burns also argued that the plan was political suicide, as a guaranteed income was sure to be rejected by the House Ways and Means Committee, headed by conservative Democrat Wilbur Mills. Burns thus argued for a welfare reform package that included a rigid work requirement.

Burns, a veteran of the Eisenhower White House where political intrigue had been an art form, was a powerful infighter. He quickly recruited other members of the administration, including Harlow and Agnew, to his side. His staff continued the attack, and the fight between Burns and Moynihan was soon the big story among Washington insiders. Moynihan's only ally in the Cabinet, Finch, had lost his influence, being assailed from every direction for HEW's performance on school desegregation. It seemed that FSS—and Moynihan—were destined to early failure.

Yet Moynihan himself was no political neophyte. Having learned early that "proximity is everything," he had made certain that the UAC offices were located in the West Wing of the White House, near the Oval Office. This proximity enabled him to take his case directly to the president without having to make an appointment through Haldeman. Making full use of the fact that Nixon genuinely enjoyed debating with him, Moynihan pressed his case hard to the president. Part of this pressure entailed a deft massaging of Nixon's ego. It was Moynihan who urged Nixon, ever searching for his place in history, to read Robert Blake's biography of Benjamin Disraeli and to see himself, like Disraeli, as a conservative reformer.

For his part, Nixon was leaning toward the idea of Moynihan's grand reform, yet he saw merit in Burns's prudent argument. Typically unable to offend his feuding counselors by rejecting either plan to their faces, Nixon again found his answer through George Shultz. In an off-the-cuff remark made at a UAC meeting (one of the few that Nixon attended), Shultz suggested that while FSS was fine for the unemployed, what it lacked was a provision for the working poor. The observation expressed the obvious. But Nixon was already impressed with Shultz, and he asked him to come up with a welfare plan that would contain work incentives and would also appease both Burns and Moynihan. Shultz's draft plan incorporated the key facets of both arguments. He kept the FSS's $1,500 guaranteed yearly payment as proposed by Moynihan, to assuage Burns, Shultz required that all welfare recipients, except the disabled and mothers with preschool children, would have to go to work if a job was available. Shultz also gave the poor a reason to like this requirement, as he proposed that the first twenty dollars of the person's weekly income be ignored when calculating benefit levels—a twenty-dollar-a-week reason to seek employment while on welfare; if recipients worked, they could pocket that amount and not have it affect their benefit payments.

Tired of the Burns-Moynihan feud, Nixon quickly accepted the package. In late May he told Ehrlichman to draft a bill for Congress based on the Shultz plan. Ehrlichman raised the yearly payment from $1,500 to $1,600 a year and lowered the weekly exemption to approximately $13.85. The key provision remained, however: under the Nixon welfare plan, no longer would a family head automatically be better off taking welfare than working. After heated discussion and lobbying by Cabinet members, Nixon announced to the nation his support of Ehrlichman's bill on August 8, 1969. The sobriquet FSS was dumped because someone protested that it sounded too much like a New Deal program. The package was renamed the Family Assistance Plan.

The in-house struggle over FAP sorely tried Nixon's patience. Already confronted with the Finch-Mitchell feud over civil rights and perhaps seeing the error of his ways in appointing two natural antagonists to slug it out over domestic policy, Nixon separated Burns and Moynihan soon after he announced FAP to the nation. On November 4 Moynihan was "kicked upstairs" to become a counselor to the president, and in December Nixon fulfilled his earlier promise to Burns by nominating him to replace William McChesney Martin as chairman of the Federal Reserve Board. The big winner in the fight to create FAP was John Ehrlichman. Using some of the same tactics Moynihan had used during his battle with Burns—proximity to the president and an endless stream of well-written memoranda—Ehrlichman had positioned himself well. His bill had also given Nixon a workable blueprint to present Shultz's compromise to Congress. On the same day that Moynihan's new position was announced, Nixon made Ehrlichman his new head of domestic policy, and Ehrlichman inherited much of the UAC staff that was cut loose by Moynihan's "promotion." For his part, a dejected Moynihan agreed to stay on with the administration only until FAP had been approved by Congress.

FAP did not fare nearly as well as Ehrlichman. Though the bill was initially quite popular with the public—a Gallup Poll showed that Americans were three to one in favor of it—Congress was openly hostile, particularly (as Burns had predicted) to the sections calling for guaranteed income payments. Wilbur Mills announced in December that "the public isn't ready for [FAP]—and won't be for years."[46] Nevertheless, largely as a result of the close working relationship Moynihan had cultivated with Mills, the Ways and Means Committee finally approved FAP on March 5, 1970, and House Minority Leader Gerald Ford saw the bill through the House, where it passed on April 16 by a vote of 243 to 155.

The Senate, however, was in no mood to look kindly at any administration innovation. It was still smarting from White House tactics on the ABM and Haynsworth and was deep in the mire of the Carswell debate when FAP reached it. Harlow immediately saw that the bill had few solid supporters. It met stiff opposition on Russell Long's Senate Finance Committee that June; after only three days of hearings, the committee sent the bill back to the White House for revisions. Modifications were made, but the guaranteed annual income provision remained. The bill was resubmitted on June 10, and again it was returned to the White House. In July a new HEW secretary, Elliot Richardson, presented a revamped FAP that proved no more acceptable to the Finance Committee than the earlier version.*

In the early months of 1970, Moynihan tried to enlist Nixon's help

---

*Richardson's predecessor, Finch, had collapsed from overwork. He left the department and became the third counselor to the president.

in getting FAP out of committee, but his meetings with the president were now few and far between. Moynihan was receiving little help from past allies; Ehrlichman, with an eye toward consolidating his own position, was doing everything he could to limit Moynihan's influence. Moynihan had compounded his problem with FAP by making several mistakes that resulted in even more disfavor in the West Wing. In December 1969 he called a Conference on Food and Nutrition that ended up being quite vocal in its criticism of Nixon. Two months later a confidential memo that Moynihan had written Nixon calling for a policy of "benign neglect" on the issue of race in the country was leaked to the press. The memo made page one of the *New York Times,* and Moynihan was called in to explain himself before the White House press corps. By the end of spring the access Moynihan once enjoyed had been shut down to a trickle.

It is arguable that even if Moynihan had retained his access, he would not have been successful in marshaling the president's support. Clearly the White House had lost interest in the guaranteed annual income portion of its welfare reform package almost from the moment it began to receive political heat. Hope for its passage by the end of the 1970 session faded. Nixon had truly wanted welfare reform, but now that it was close to impossible, he was more concerned with avoiding a public relations setback. That November he issued a curt order to his staff: "sink FAP."[47] The word was soon out, and the rug was pulled on White House support for the bill in the House. The first battle over FAP had been won by Congress.

Lack of congressional support and bickering among Nixon's Cabinet and staff made it tough going for the New Federalism. Yet there was one area in which Nixon would not be denied—the management crisis in the oversized and poorly administered Executive Office. Nixon put more energy into restructuring the presidency than any other modern president except Franklin Roosevelt, and he met with more success in this regard than anyone had since 1939. Thoroughly revolutionary and far reaching in scope, Nixon's reorganization plan indeed changed the presidency.

By 1969 the size and scope of the federal bureaucracy was such that it gave credence to a later comment by historian Arthur S. Link: "It just seems to me that [the president] needs to keep the numbers down and leave a little breathing space in the executive mansion. You can hardly move around in there for all the people who are in the corridors."[48] Indeed, in 1969 the Executive Office employed more than 4,700 persons. To most of the Republican faithful, including Nixon, what was needed was the application of sound business practices to the White House.

Their ideas were given bureaucratic life in a ten-page memorandum placed on Nixon's desk even before the inauguration and written by Roy L. Ash. Ash was the type of business-savvy professional that Nixon wanted to attract to his team. Originally from Beverly Hills with a master's degree in business administration from Harvard, Ash had worked at Ford Motor Company with Robert McNamara. There, as one set of analysts has observed, he "fell victim to the same affliction" that struck everyone at Ford—"the exclusively analytical approach."[49] Ash had moved on in 1961 to become president of Litton Industries, a high-tech company dealing with advanced electrical engineering, microwave experimentation, and shipbuilding concerns. His pretentious managerial style had led Litton to the brink of financial disaster. As stated by *Fortune* magazine, Ash was "utterly abstract in his view of business. . . . His brilliance led him to think in the most regal of ways: building new cities; creating a shipyard that would roll off the most technically advanced vessels the way that Detroit builds automobiles." Ash's dreams were expensive; as one of his employees put it to the author, he "used today's money [to] live in tomorrowland."[50]

Yet it was precisely Ash's grandiose business style that appealed to Nixon, and it was what prompted him to ask Ash to join his transition team. Ash's strength of personality and devotion to the cause (his favorite maxim was "organization *is* policy") was a great asset. His December 1968 memorandum, "Executive Office Organization," argued that many of the problems that had plagued the presidency of recent years could be traced to the fact that the president himself had become a "domestic desk officer." Ash concluded that a new policymaking structure was necessary for domestic affairs. To this end he recommended the creation of an Office of Executive Management (OEM) that would encompass the responsibilities of the Bureau of the Budget and add three new departments—a Division of Evaluation, a Domestic Policy Council, and a Division of Program Coordination.[51]

Ash had identified an area of perennial concern and had attacked it with the businesslike demeanor and logic that so impressed Nixon. As Ash said in an interview with this author, he believed that the president's time "should be spent in policymaking, not operational activities." This was Nixon's view as well. The idea of streamlining the Executive Office appealed to the chief executive officer in Nixon, who was always looking to tighten his ship, improve productivity, and minimize wasted time. Added to this appeal was the fact that by April Nixon's cabinet and staff were at each other's throats, impeding progress on New Federalist reforms. Nixon asked Ash to chair a presidential council that would streamline the Executive Office.

In April 1969 the President's Advisory Council on Executive Organization (PACEO) was announced. Ash was named as its chairman, and five well-known businessmen made up the committee.* The council met formally one or two days a month for the next two years. It met with Nixon five times during that period and conducted some 1,500 other interviews. A model commission, the Ash Council was known for its efficiency and the general attitude of congeniality that existed among its members. By July they had already submitted to the president two lengthy study plans for their work, and they had decided upon three "high priority areas for council study": social programs, organized crime, and the Executive Office of the President.[52]

While the Ash Council would eventually deal with all three of these issues as well as touching upon many more, it was in the reform of the Executive Office that it made a major contribution. In October 1969 the council submitted what would be known as Reorganization Plan No. 2. This plan called for the creation of a Domestic Policy Council, later to be shortened to the Domestic Council, as an office where the entire scope and range of domestic policy would be formulated. An equally important change came with the development of the OEM. It was the plan of the council to eliminate the Bureau of the Budget (BOB), replacing it with an OEM that would not only prepare the budget but also coordinate programs and become a clearinghouse for legislative proposals initiated in other areas of the executive branch. At the time, the troglodytic BOB was conveniently under fire from many directions, including Capitol Hill. Indeed, Nixon's budget director, Robert Mayo, was never told about the plan for the OEM because the White House felt (with some justification, as events would soon show) that Mayo would oppose any attempt to limit the power of his bureau.

Nixon saw Reorganization Plan No. 2 as a panacea for a host of problems. He eagerly supported the Ash Council's recommendations, which, as he neatly observed, would create "a domestic counterpart to the NSC."[53] He asked the council to prepare the proper legislation, and on March 12, 1970, he asked Congress to approve the measures. The Senate Subcommittee on Executive Reorganization heard all the arguments. Its chairman, Abraham Ribicoff of Connecticut, supported the package, arguing that "the Bureau of the Budget has become power hungry and power crazy."[54] Yet despite a favorable report from the upper chamber, the House subcommittee submitted to considerable pressure exerted by Mayo and the BOB and voted its disapproval of the plan.

Despite that setback, this proved to be Nixon's finest moment on

---

*The other members: Dean George Baker of Harvard University's Graduate School of Business Administration; former Texas Governor John B. Connally; Frederick R. Kappel, chairman of the Executive Committee, American Telephone and Telegraph; Richard M. Paget of the New York management consultant firm of Cresap, McCormick, and Paget; and Walter Thayer, ex-publisher of the *New York Herald Tribune.*

Capitol Hill. Unlike his sharp, antagonistic lobbying effort for the ABM, the fight for the reorganization bill was well coordinated and effectively lobbied, to the point that the White House was able to make some shrewd compromises. One such deal came about when congressional leaders opposed dropping the word *budget*, due in large part to the keen lobbying against the bill by the BOB. The name of the new agency was quickly changed to the Office of Management and Budget (OMB). This effort led the full House to repudiate the subcommittee's disapproval on May 13, and the reorganization plan became effective on July 1, 1970. The OMB and the Domestic Council were in operation, and Nixon had the most significant domestic reform of his administration.

CHAPTER THREE

Radiclibs, Recession, and Revenue Sharing

NIXON'S dreadful relationship with Congress made the stakes for the upcoming off-year election unusually high. While the House of Representatives was certain to remain under Democratic command, a shift of just seven seats in the Senate would give control to the Republicans, with the vice-president then able to create a Republican majority by virtue of his tie-breaking power. Polls showed that there was a strong possibility that Nixon would win those seven seats.

Even though he stood to gain real ground in the fall of 1970, Nixon never intended to campaign for every Republican candidate. Many of them had deserted him on key issues, most notably the ABM, Vietnam, and his Supreme Court appointments. Instead Nixon told his staff that he was not after a majority party but rather an "ideological majority." It would be made up of those legislators who, despite their party affiliation, would support Nixon on the major issues of social and foreign policy—they would be the senators of the Middle.

It was clear that the Middle, recently defined by Nixon as the "Silent Majority," continued to hold the key to electoral success. It was also clear that the same issues that had concerned the Middle in 1968— law and order, disgust with antiwar protest, a return to traditional moral values—continued to concern it in 1970. The Democrats had finally discovered this fact earlier that year, due in large part to the publication of *The Real Majority*. The authors, Richard Scammon, director of the Census Bureau under Kennedy, and Ben Wattenberg, a former speech writer for Johnson and Humphrey, defined these issues in terms of demographic data and called them collectively the "social issue." For Scammon and Wattenberg, the social issue was "a set of public attitudes concerning the more personally frightening aspects of disruptive social change." *The Real Majority* argued that Democrats should abandon their narrow constituencies and, as had Nixon in 1968, start playing to the social issue.

Scammon and Wattenberg's national best-seller was widely read at the White House, championed by Buchanan, and accepted by Nixon. This was no great surprise; Nixon had recognized the plight of the Middle two years before the book's publication. Nixon also appreciated the fact that he had in his administration a man whom he viewed at the time as "the perfect spokesman to reach the Silent Majority on the social issue."[1] In 1970 no one—not even the president himself—could galvanize the Middle and attack administration opponents like Spiro Agnew.

During the first half of 1969 Spiro Agnew's political stock had never been lower. Simply put, Nixon was not about to give Agnew either the freedom or the influence that Eisenhower had given Nixon. After the inauguration Nixon attempted to play to Agnew's strength by creating the Office of Intergovernmental Relations as a part of the Office of the Vice-President and by naming Agnew as his liaison to state and local governments (a small part of the evolving New Federalism). This experiment, however, was shortlived. By fall Nixon was moaning that Agnew "does not play [the Governors] well," and this area of responsibility was slowly transferred, de facto, to others on the staff (for example, Nixon ordered that no member of the staff was to call Rockefeller except Kissinger).[2] Throughout his tenure as vice-president, Agnew was never consulted on political matters and was specifically instructed by Nixon not to propose policy.

Forced out of the power loop, Agnew developed into a traveling road show of some significance. His speeches were manna for the Middle, as the vice-president used his national forum to lash out at the nation's intellectuals, whom Agnew held personally responsible for most of the nation's troubles. Agnew's attack opened on May 8, 1969, at the University of Utah, where he reprimanded long-haired students ("I didn't raise my son to be a daughter") who were "hell-bent on non-negotiable destruction." Agnew concentrated his criticism, however, not on the students but on the adults in academe, whom he depicted as "college administrators [who are] confused and capitulating. We have sophisticated faculties distraught and divided over issues as basic as assault and battery, breaking and entering."[3] His assault was broadened on June 7 to include the entire liberal bureaucracy. Delivering the commencement address at Ohio State University, Agnew snarled that the "snivelling, hand-wringing power structure . . . deserves the violent rebellion it encourages." On October 19, at a fund-raising dinner in New Orleans, Agnew gave a label to these liberals that would become part of the national vocabulary: an "effete corps of impudent snobs."

Agnew was beginning to carve a niche for himself by saying things that other members of the administration wanted to be said but could not say on their own. He was a George Wallace without the integration baggage, speaking directly to the Middle. His most famous attack against highbrows came on November 13, when he broadened his criticism to include a specific subgroup of "effete snobs"—the national political press. On November 2 Nixon had delivered a televised speech on the Vietnam War, which had been skewered by postspeech analysts. Two weeks later Agnew was scheduled to speak at the Midwest Republican Committee meeting at Des Moines. When his text was released to the press, there was a flurry of activity, with the networks jumping over each other to cover the speech live. Small wonder; the Des Moines speech was one of the most savage attacks against the media in modern political history. Agnew first assailed the "small band of network commentators and self-appointed analysts" whose "minds were made up in advance" about Nixon's speech. He then charged that "a form of censorship already exists when the news that forty million Americans receive each night is determined by a handful of men responsible only to their corporate employers and filtered through a handful of commentators who admit their own set of biases." Agnew concluded his talk by borrowing a page from the Checkers speech. He asked his audience to "register their complaints on bias through mail to the networks and calls to the local stations." Like Checkers, the gambit worked. Within hours of the speech, stations all over the country were flooded with calls, the overwhelming majority of them in favor of the vice-president.

The reaction to the speech from the media was just as swift. Dr. Frank Stanton, president of CBS, called it "an unprecedented attempt by the Vice-President of the United States to intimidate a news medium which depends for its existence upon government license."[4] Walter Cronkite criticized it as "an implied threat to freedom of speech in this country."[5] The criticism confirmed Agnew's new status in national political affairs. He had moved from the obscurity of the vice-presidency to the role of defender of the Middle as he attacked the powerful with reckless abandon. He was in demand everywhere. Copies of his speeches were published and quickly sold, and recordings of those speeches were being played on radio stations.

None of this, of course, was lost on Nixon. The White House had been carefully monitoring the progress of the vice-president's speeches throughout 1969, and what they heard they liked. The day after the Des Moines speech, Nixon observed to Haldeman that Agnew was "a good property" and ordered his staff to "keep building him." Agnew was soon the darling of the Republican fund-raising circuit, for a time supplanting Ronald Reagan and raising some two million dollars for the party coffers in about a month's time. As the vice-president gained in national prominence, Nixon began to get questions from the press about whether Agnew would be kept on the ticket in 1972. Nixon was noncommittal on this point. Despite Agnew's performance on behalf of the administration, Nixon had grave doubts about his abilities as vice-president, telling Ehrlichman, for example, to make sure he stayed out of the loop on busing because "Agnew can go too far—with [a] McCarthyite tinge."[6] But this concern did not keep Nixon from appreciating Agnew's value on the hustings and deciding to make Agnew his point man for the 1970 congressional campaign.

The decision was a logical one; had it not been tampered with by the White House in midcampaign, Agnew's campaigning might well have led to more successes for both the GOP and the White House. The vice-president galvanized the Middle by painting both the Democrats and several anti-Nixon Republicans as permissive liberals who had countenanced all the disruption of the sixties and were obstructing Nixon's attempts to reform the excesses of that era. They were lumped together into a new "party" that Agnew called the "Radiclibs," defined during the campaign as members of Congress who "applaud our enemies and castigate our friends and run down the capacity of the American government . . . and so I call on the majority of people to turn them out of office."[7] It was, no more and no less, an attempted purge.

Putting Agnew on the campaign trail was like unleashing a hungry Doberman. In Illinois, campaigning for Governor Ralph Smith (who was being challenged by Adlai Stevenson III), Agnew lashed out at "the troglodytic leftists who dominate Congress" and "the tired, irrelevant liberalism that made the Ninety-First Congress a citadel of reaction." In San Diego he lumped together four leading paragons of Democratic liberalism—Senators William Fulbright of Arkansas, Ted Kennedy of Massachusetts, and Joseph Montoya of New Mexico, and Democratic National Committee Chairman Larry O'Brien—as "nattering nabobs of negativism" who "have formed their own 4-H Club—the hopeless, hysterical hypochondriacs of history." In Tennessee he referred to Senator Albert Gore, Sr. (who had voted against Haynsworth and Carswell and had referred to Agnew as "our greatest disaster next to Vietnam"), as "the Southern regional chairman of the Eastern liberal establishment."

But this was Nixon's purge, not a mindless Agnew vendetta. Where the administration had marked a conservative Democrat to be spared, Agnew tread more lightly. For example, Wyoming Republican John Wold was virtually ignored by Agnew during a trip to Casper; his Democratic opponent, Gale McGee, was a consistently strong supporter of Nixon's stand on Vietnam. Several key conservative Democrats, such as Robert Byrd of West Virginia and Henry "Scoop" Jackson of Washington, were already considered to be part of this majority. They were helped in every way by the White House, short of an overt public endorsement.

The primary target for the purge of the Radiclibs was Senator Charles Goodell of New York. Goodell had been appointed to serve the unexpired term of Robert Kennedy following his assassination. He quickly earned the wrath of the White House by emerging as one of the most vocal Republican critics of the administration, refusing to support either the Haynsworth or the Carswell nomination. Goodell was also a leading Republican voice against the war, as evidenced by his April 1970 introduction of the first Vietnam disengagement bill, calling for the withdrawal of all troops from Southeast Asia by the end of 1970. That fall Goodell was being challenged not only by Democrat Richard Ottinger but also by Conservative party candidate James Buckley, who was running a Nixonlike law-and-order campaign. Agnew began his assault with a few days of sniping at Goodell from campaign stops in other states, where he called him the "Christine Jorgensen of the Republican party"—a brutal reference to the first person who had undergone a sex-change operation. Agnew made no attempt to hide this anti-Goodell campaign, observing in a Minot, North Dakota, interview that while he was not endorsing Buckley, "I'm merely saying that I'm not supporting Senator Goodell." The clincher was Agnew's attendance at an October 5 Buckley fund-raiser in New York City. Despite grumbling from within the party, the anti-Goodell attack was supported wholeheartedly by the White House, and Nixon gave the matter his personal attention. On November 1, two days before the election, Nixon ordered Ehrlichman to authorize the use of a four-minute television spot, an advertisement that all but gave the blessing of the White House to Buckley.[8]

With Nixon's full support, the vice-president had succeeded in taking the offensive, and he had done so with a vengeance that sent the "Radiclibs" reeling. His blows on the social issue were stinging. As a result, on the advice of shrewd observers such as Hubert Humphrey, the Democrats decided to counterattack with an issue that would be much harder for anyone in the administration to defend—the sagging economy. Their timing was perfect. The papers were full of statistics on inflation and the impending recession, and a massive three-state strike at General Motors helped hammer the point home. By the end of September the polls showed that the Republicans stood to lose all of the key Senate races and to take an unexpectedly hard pounding in the House. Several White House politicos, most notably Bob Finch, begged Nixon to deal with the economic issue, which had clearly supplanted the social issue as the chief concern of the Middle. Nixon, however, was convinced that playing to the social issue was still the right strategy. He would not shift tactics; he would merely shift principals. After returning from his second European trip, Nixon went out on the campaign trail himself. Between October 7 and election eve he visited twenty-three states. Coinciding with this campaign blitz was a torrent of legislation from the White House, all designed to appeal to the voters of the Middle.* Agnew found himself relegated to the background—the president was now the issue.

Nixon's campaign raised Republican hopes, and the polls showed an improvement in GOP chances after the president entered the fray. These gains, however, were thrown away by the Nixon staff during the final week of the campaign. The unraveling began on October 29 as Nixon drove into San Jose for a rally. The presidential entourage met a riot of some proportions (the police guesstimate was 5,000 demonstrators). Bill Safire, who was there, described it as "a lynch mob, no cause or ideology involved, only an orgy of generalized hate."[9] Cars were assaulted, rocks thrown, and when the entourage finally got inside the Municipal Auditorium the hall was attacked with a battering ram. After the rally Nixon appeared to the crowd and, in what appeared to be a completely spontaneous gesture, climbed on top of his car and flashed his trademark "V for Victory" sign. The gesture was followed by a pelting of rocks and vegetables, one missile just missing the president's head. The Secret Service initiated emergency evacuation procedures, and although the motorcade finally made its exit, windows in the cars that trailed Nixon's, as well as in the press bus, were smashed.

Sensing the opportunity to make political mileage out of the close-to-tragic event, Haldeman ordered Safire to write a tough law-and-order speech for the president to deliver the next day in Phoenix. The speech was Nixon at his most severe:

> For too long, we have appeased aggression here at home, and, as with all appeasement, the result has been more aggression and more violence. The time has come to draw the line. The time has come for the great silent majority of Americans of all ages, of every political persuasion, to stand up and be counted against appeasement of the rock throwers and obscenity shouters in America.

Nixon ended his speech with a promise: "As long as I am president, no band of violent thugs is going to keep me from going out and speaking with the American people wherever they want to hear me and wherever I want to go. This president is not going to be cooped up in the White House."[10]

The Phoenix speech was Nixon the campaigner at his best, but the White House was unable to exploit its success. The speech had not been televised, but it had been videotaped. However, it was videotaped in black and white, and the audio was terrible. In addition, several

---

*Some examples: On October 15, Nixon signed the Organized Crime Control Act; on the same day, he signed the Urban Mass Transportation Act; still on the same day, he announced the Jobs for Veterans Program.

advisers argued that election eve, when many members of the staff wanted to have the speech broadcast, called for a conciliatory, "everybody go out and vote" speech rather than for the fire that Nixon had emitted in Phoenix. Nevertheless, Nixon told Haldeman that he wanted the speech broadcast on election eve during halftime of the regionally telecast Monday night football game. It was, as Nixon wrote in his memoirs, "a disaster." [11] The already miserable videotape had been edited to fifteen minutes of pathetic technical quality; after its broadcast, several local GOP groups called television stations and charged that the program was Democratic sabotage. To complete the rout, it was immediately followed by a superbly produced Democratic party speech delivered with soothing skill by Senator Edmund Muskie. Once again, as in 1960, Nixon suffered on television by comparison to an opponent who looked more presidential than he.

Safire was close to correct when he sarcastically recalled that the speech "only cost us a couple of hundred thousand dollars and two or three Senate seats." [12] Certainly the contrast to Muskie's speech led many undecided voters to vote against Republican candidates. The results of the election were too mixed, however, to attribute them to any one cause. The Republicans lost only nine seats in the House, a good record for the White House party in an off-year election; yet the Democrats still enjoyed a large majority of 254 to 181. In the Senate the Republicans actually picked up two seats, and that figure looked even better to Nixon when he saw that Gore was beaten in Tennessee and Goodell in New York. But the Democrats still controlled that body, 55 to 45. It was a draw.

Nevertheless, Agnew was ecstatic. Secretary of the Interior Walter Hickel recalled that when Agnew heard the first report of Goodell's defeat, he strutted over to the television set and announced, "We *got* that son of a bitch!" [13] They had defeated several of those whom they had wanted to defeat. To the press Nixon took the politic stance that "when the party in power loses little or anything in an off-year election, it has to be called a victory." In his memoirs Nixon shares Agnew's glee, writing that "it was . . . particularly gratifying to me that some extreme liberals were among those senators retired by the voters." [14]

Nixon's delight with the success of his purge was indicative of just how bad the relationship between president and Congress had become. Not since Harry Truman's 1948 campaign against the "do-nothing 80th Congress" had a president attacked Congress as a whole in quite the manner Nixon and Agnew had in the fall of 1970. Nixon and Capitol Hill were no longer political adversaries; they were blood enemies. Several analysts have concluded that Nixon abandoned domestic policy after 1970. Nixon still had domestic reforms on his agenda, but for all intents and purposes he had no relation with Congress. As a result, much of Nixon's agenda was either defeated or begrudgingly abandoned—as noted in the preceding chapter, this was the fate of FAP. There were a few legislative successes. They were not, however, achieved by compromise—after 1970, the administration refused to compromise with Congress, and vice versa. They were achieved through the intercession of someone outside the administration whom Congress respected. Revenue sharing, long a priority of both parties, is an excellent case in point.

Although strains of the New Federalism were running through all of Nixon's domestic policies, none were more indicative of the new governmental relationship that Nixon hoped to create than was revenue sharing—a program in which the federal government would allocate funds to states and cities without any restrictions on how that money might be spent. There was, of course, money already going to the states. Most of it, however, was tied into specific programs and could only be used for specific purposes. As the expenses of the Great Society had piled up and the problems of the cities mounted, demand had increased for more unrestricted funding to be channeled to localities. Republican governors and mayors, most notably Nelson Rockefeller and George Romney, had begun to press Johnson to "share the wealth," but to no avail. During the 1968 election both Nixon and Humphrey had supported the concept of revenue sharing.

Although Arthur Burns was fundamentally in favor of some sort of new revenue-sharing package, he counseled Nixon to move cautiously. However, as FAP picked up steam within the administration, so did revenue sharing. In the August 6, 1969, speech that announced FAP to the nation, Nixon also announced that he was sending a revenue-sharing plan to Congress. Five days later Nixon sent that proposal to the Hill. In it he proposed that one-third of one percent of all monies raised from personal income taxes (approximately $500 million) be immediately sent back to state and local governments with no strings attached. The initial plan favored the large states, as "the allocation of the total annual fund among the 50 states and the District of Columbia will be made on the basis of each state's share of national population." This percentage would steadily rise, until by 1976 a full one percent of all taxes collected would be returned to the states.[15]

Revenue sharing excited the president as FAP had not. Nixon's support for the plan stemmed not only from his dream of emasculating the Great Society but also from a belief in the tenets of the New Federalism. He told his staff to "talk it up,"[16] which they did. More important, Nixon himself took to the stump for revenue sharing—it was the only major piece of domestic legislation that Nixon personally campaigned for. In a February 1970 speech at City Hall in Indianapolis, Nixon synthesized his support for the bill:

Here we are, bringing Washington to Indianapolis and the cities. And this
is a theme I wish to emphasize. . . . let's get it [power] back to the people
and to the cities and to the States where it belongs . . . because I very
firmly believe that the people know best.[17]

Congress, however, disagreed, declining to consider revenue sharing
before the end of the 1970 session. Refusing to abandon revenue sharing as he had abandoned welfare reform, Nixon pushed the program
to the head of his 1971 domestic package. In his second revenue-sharing proposal, announced during his January 1971 State of the Union
message, Nixon proposed to increase the general revenue sharing to
the states to $5 billion. He had, however, added a component to the
proposal designed to appeal to the more fiscally austere in his party. A
second program, to be called "special" revenue sharing, would send a
total of $11 billion more to the states, paid for through $10 billion in
spending cuts from existing federal programs.

Despite the inclusion of special revenue sharing, Congress continued to be largely against turning any of the federal monies to the states,
at least not without restrictions. Both Wilbur Mills and John Byrnes,
respectively the chairman and the ranking Republican on the House
Ways and Means Committee, were strongly against the administration's package. After meeting with the president in January, Mills told
the press that he would hold hearings on revenue sharing "for the
purpose of killing it."[18] Nixon was prepared for this and, unlike his
action in the fight over FAP, responded with a cogent plan and strove
to put the onus of blame for resistance to social reform onto the backs
of Congress. During a February 17 press conference, Nixon said that
"when we consider reforms, we must remember that they are always
opposed by the establishment . . . the establishment of Congress, the
establishment of the federal bureaucracy, and also great organizations."*[19] He also inundated Mills with a host of special revenue-sharing proposals, all designed to send monies to a specific constituency,
thus making it politically difficult for the chairman to ignore them.†
Added to this White House pressure was Mills's own desire to run for
the Democratic presidential nomination in 1972. But Mills did not cave
in. Nixon's relationship with Congress was so bad that he could not
even muster the votes to get revenue sharing voted out of committee,
where it languished through the summer and fall of 1971.

Beleaguered state officials could wait no longer. Nelson Rockefeller

---

*Nixon had another suggestion for dealing with the situation. During a February 5
meeting, Ehrlichman's notes recall, Nixon mused: "[Mills] to the Supreme Court? Roll
him on his committee?"

†On March 4 Nixon asked for $2 billion for manpower revenue sharing; on March
5, $2 billion for urban community development; on March 10, $1 billion for rural community development; on March 18, $2.6 billion for transportation; and on April 3, $2.8
billion for education.

had been a vocal supporter of revenue sharing from the start. Small wonder; his building program in New York had resulted in a 1972 budget that called for $7.9 billion in expenditures and only $7.5 billion in revenues. The funds from revenue sharing were a necessity if Rockefeller was to avoid raising taxes in an election year. Indeed, Rockefeller had taken the colossal gamble of including revenue-sharing funds in his 1973 budget before the bill was even reported out of the Ways and Means Committee. There was an air of desperation in the way the governor buttonholed congressmen and pestered Mills, but his entreaties worked. During a meeting between Nixon and the congressional leadership on September 28, Minority Leader Gerald Ford was able to tell the president that Mills was "close to on the ropes" over the issue.[20] Mills's compromise package called for a five-year revenue-sharing plan, authorizing $5.3 billion during the first year, with two-thirds of the monies going to the local governments and one-third to the states. That figure would rise over the five years until the states would be receiving $3 billion a year and the local governments $3.5 billion. The states' money would be divided according to state income tax collections and the combined general tax contribution of the state and local governments, a formula that continued to benefit the large urban states (such as New York). The local government's share would then be awarded based on general population, urban population, and population inversely weighted for per capita income.

It was largely through Rockefeller's efforts that revenue sharing was passed in any form. When Mills's bill came to the floor of the House, Rockefeller was very much in evidence, along with Mayors Moon Landrieu of New Orleans and Henry Maier of Milwaukee. Mills had obtained a closed rule for the bill from the House Rules Committee (no amendments could be added to it on the floor), but that ruling was challenged. For three weeks the bipartisan coalition of mayors lobbied the membership, finally securing on June 21 a vote of 223–185 sustaining the Rules Committee's decision. Quick passage of the bill followed. Thanks not to the efforts of the administration but to those of Rockefeller, Nixon signed revenue sharing into law on October 20, 1972.

Poor congressional relations was not the only problem that continued to plague Nixon's domestic policies. The Burger Court had been the source of several unpleasant surprises for the Nixon administration. The *Alexander* ruling had ordered Nixon to speed up integration; he had done so in the South, and with much success. However, for many reasons, Nixon had ignored the problem of civil rights in the North. As it had done with *Alexander*, the Burger Court would once again attempt to force his hand.

Nixon's refusal to deal effectively with the problems of the northern ghettos was shaped by a number of forces. Constitutionally, Nixon sincerely believed, the president did not have the authority to challenge de facto segregation anywhere in the country. This belief fit in with Nixon's reading of the political situation—he had long since conceded the northern black vote to the Democrats, and he was busy working on the white vote by spreading his antibusing stand. It was poor politics, however, to be seen as completely ignoring northern blacks. On March 3, 1969, an executive order created the Office of Minority Business Enterprise (OMBE) in the Department of Commerce. The plan was to use tools that were already on hand to increase the percentage of minority-owned small businesses, which was less than one percent. OMBE was the personal project of Commerce Secretary Maurice Stans, who spent a considerable amount of time holding meetings with minority business persons. In the public sector Stans urged the Small Business Administration to give minorities more loans. He also urged that franchise businesses hire and train more minority workers. To its critics, particularly in the civil rights leadership, OMBE was mere window dressing, another government agency that missed the point. As Stans recalled for the author, however, the attitude of minorities "changed 180 degrees in the first six months. . . . [OMBE] extended for the first time an inviting hand . . . to open for them the process of ownership."

Nevertheless, despite Stans's zeal, it is clear that OMBE was not high on Nixon's list of priorities; it was never an integral part of Nixon's civil rights package in the North. Nixon demanded that his administration refrain from meeting the issue head on. He ordered the Justice Department to keep integration bottled up in a few northern courtrooms. He made this clear in a February 4, 1970, meeting, where he ordered Ehrlichman to tell Mitchell that "no more suits [were] to be filed in North (Ill., Calif.)," but to immediately file suits in New York and Boston (Justice concentrated throughout 1970 and early 1971 on litigation in those two cities; predictably, the suits did not get very far).[21] This was one order that Nixon expected to be carried out. In the summer of 1971, Ed Morgan, the Domestic Council staffer in charge of minority issues, wrote Nixon a memo reporting that in some sections of the country HEW and Justice were overenforcing the integration laws. Nixon was infuriated. He wrote a note to Ehrlichman in the margin of Morgan's memo: "E: I want you personally to jump Richardson and Justice and tell them to *knock off this crap.* I hold them personally accountable to keep left wingers in step with my express [sic] policy—do what the law requires and not *one bit* more."[22]

Yet once again, as it had done with *Alexander,* the Burger Court intervened with a decision that forced Nixon to reevaluate his policy. On April 20, 1971, in *Swann v. Charlotte–Mecklenburg County School District,* the court held that busing to achieve racial integration in schools was constitutional. It also accepted a plan that provided for roughly equal ratios of black and white students in each public school. *Charlotte* shook the Nixon administration to its foundations. It would now be impossible to ignore de facto segregation in the North without openly defying the court. Privately Nixon fumed at the audacity of Burger and his court. There would be no blanket statement, as he had made after *Alexander,* saying that the administration would obey the decision of the court. Instead Nixon concocted a halfway measure designed to leave him some room to breathe. Ehrlichman's notes show that in a meeting the day after the decision, Nixon ordered his staff not to "admit racial balance and busing are required at *all levels*—eg: age makes a difference."[23] The administration's position would now be that since *Charlotte* had not made an age distinction clear, it continued to be unconstitutional to bus elementary school students despite the ruling.

George Wallace, however, abhorred halfway measures. Making his second run for the presidency, Wallace denounced busing as a societal evil, *Charlotte* as unconstitutional, and Nixon's stand on the issue as spineless. With the exception of the last point, Nixon wholeheartedly agreed with Wallace, yet was unable to say so in public. That made it particularly galling for members of the administration, as they were forced to watch Wallace slice into Nixon's support among the Middle. The busing issue was the key factor in Wallace's March 14 victory in the Florida primary, where he handily defeated six other Democratic contenders (including George McGovern, who came in last).

Sensing that he was losing control over the issue, Nixon could wait no longer. Three days after the Florida primary he proposed a "moratorium" on all court orders requiring new busing until June 1, 1973, or until Congress passed his equal educational opportunities bill which asked for $2.5 billion for improvement of education in the ghettos.[24] This, of course, was an unrealistic scenario—Congress could never move that quickly on the issue. However, the real crux of the plan was that Nixon was going to hold busing hostage; if Congress came up with the money, he would loosen the strings. Nixon was simply ignoring *Charlotte* and acting as if he could decree busing out of existence for as long as he liked. Senate liberals—both Republican and Democrat—would have none of it, resorting to filibuster. The bill was killed in October 1972.

Recognizing that Nixon never intended to be bound by *Charlotte,* in March 1973 the court recommitted itself in *Keyes v. Denver School District* to extending integration in the North. But by that point Watergate had relegated all domestic concerns to the back burner. When Nixon resigned in 1974, he left behind a powder keg in the North. His refusal even to consider busing as an option, followed by his noncompliance with the *Charlotte* decision, had lit the fuse. His successors would have to deal with the explosion.

Despite the Supreme Court's unanimity on *Charlotte*, the administration suspected that Burger's coalitions on the busing cases were shaky. Nixon was convinced that given another chance he would be able to shift the court to the right and affect subsequent civil rights decisions. In October 1971 he got his chance as, within six days of each other, liberal luminaries Hugo Black and John Harlan resigned from the court.* Memory of the Haynsworth-Carswell debacle was still fresh, and Nixon ignored advice such as that from speechwriter Pat Buchanan that "we ought to get the most brilliant and qualified Italian-American strict constructionist jurist . . . and then play up his Italian background— and let the Democrats chop him up if they want."[25] Nixon made it clear in his memoirs that "above all, I wanted my nominees to be confirmed."[26] Perhaps, but the evidence suggests that Nixon was once again more interested in confirming a southerner. After he had settled that political score with Strom Thurmond, Nixon would make history—he would nominate a woman.

Nixon's first choice for his southern seat, Congressman Richard Poff of Virginia, was instantly accused in the press of being a racist. Poff quickly withdrew his name from contention. Nixon then tried another tactic. At an October 12 press conference he announced that he was considering several candidates for Harlan's seat, including Senator Robert Byrd of West Virginia, a southern Democrat who had been sympathetic to the administration, and "at least two women." The strategy of the Byrd trial balloon was sound. Like Poff, Byrd would satisfy the South, and the quick confirmation that would be afforded him as a member of the Senate club would help the nomination of the woman whose name went in with his. Byrd's appointment, however, was savaged by critics when it was learned that he had finished law school at night, had never been admitted to the bar, and had never tried a case. Mitchell suggested the name of Herschel Friday, a municipal bond lawyer from Arkansas, as an alternative. Nixon reluctantly dropped Byrd, but his hopes for confirming a woman remained.

Nixon had toyed with the idea of appointing a woman to the Supreme Court for some time. One under consideration was Rita Hauser, a New York attorney. But after Hauser made a public comment that persons of the same gender should be allowed to marry legally, Nixon told Ehrlichman and Shultz, "There goes a Supreme Court Justice—I can't go that far—that's the year 2000! Negroes, OK, but that's too far!"[27] A more moderate jurist was necessary if a woman was to be confirmed; Mitchell submitted the name of Mildred Lillie, a California Court of Appeals judge.

Nixon was pleased with both Friday and Lillie, but he was not about to entrust the fate of these nominations to the Justice Depart-

---

*Black died two weeks after his resignation, on October 25.

ment. Thanks to the Haynsworth and Carswell defeats, John Mitchell's star had fallen to the point where Nixon had even mused about the possibility of removing him from the Cabinet and appointing him to the next available circuit or district judgeship.[28] Notes taken during meetings held to discuss the new nominations clearly show that Nixon was taking more personal command of this nomination than he had with either Haynsworth or Carswell. He ordered Ehrlichman to send two staffers, presidential Counsel John W. Dean III and Domestic Council member David Young, to interview the candidates. They flew to Little Rock, and Dean phoned Ehrlichman with disappointing news. Friday was young (forty-nine years old) and smart, but his lack of knowledge of constitutional law was disturbing. Dean concluded that "he would probably make Carswell look good as a witness."[29] Ehrlichman quickly convinced Nixon to drop Friday from the list.

Lillie was a better candidate, but her lack of experience on the bench would still hurt her chances. To try to ensure her confirmation, Lillie's name was secretly submitted to the review of a committee of the American Bar Association. The process was compromised, however, when her name was prematurely leaked to the press, and Lillie was brutalized by reporters for her lack of experience. The pressure from the press ensured a negative review from the ABA, although the committee also cited her high rate of reversal. Furious, Nixon called Ehrlichman on the phone, ordering him to find out who leaked the story; Ehrlichman's notes of the conversation contain Nixon's order: "Tell your boys to get going—kick their ass."*[30] Once again Mitchell had disappointed Nixon; once again Nixon turned to Ehrlichman for ideas. Ehrlichman suggested Lewis F. Powell, Jr., a moderate Virginia lawyer of no established reputation. After expressing an initial reluctance to take the job because of his age (sixty-four), Powell gave in to Nixon's persistence and accepted. Nixon had his southerner, but he had lost his woman.

For the second vacancy Nixon completely ignored Mitchell's counsel. He considered William French Smith, then legal counsel to Ronald Reagan,* and even Spiro Agnew, so that he might be able to name a new running mate in 1972, but both men were unconfirmable. Richard Moore, a sometime speech writer and member of Nixon's staff, submitted the name of Assistant Attorney General William Rehnquist. Born in Wisconsin and educated at Stanford Law School (a classmate of both John Ehrlichman and future Justice Sandra Day O'Connor), Rehnquist had been on no one's list immediately after Harlan's and Black's retirement; indeed, in his role as head of the Justice Depart-

*It is likely that the "boys" Nixon was referring to were the "Plumbers," who had been in business for several months. Co-commanded by David Young, they were directly responsible to Ehrlichman. For more detail on the "plumbers," see chap. 6.

*Smith would become the first attorney general in the Reagan administration.

ment's Office of Legal Counsel, he had helped to draw up the lists that were submitted by Mitchell. Nevertheless, Moore and Ehrlichman now argued that Rehnquist's conservative credentials would help Nixon in his goal toward a law-and-order court.

Rehnquist's nomination was by no means a cinch; he had been too visible an ally of the administration. But Nixon used the novel tactic of sending the Powell and Rehnquist nominations to both the Senate and the American Bar Association Screening Committee (a step that had become more important since the ABA's skewering of Carswell and Lillie) as a "package." With Powell's nomination all but assured, Rehnquist profited from this strategy, as well as from the exhaustion that was felt by all concerned after dealing with Haynsworth, Carswell, Friday, and Lillie. Indeed, Rehnquist's confirmation process was surprisingly easy, given that an investigation of his background revealed many of the same types of reactionary beliefs that had destroyed Carswell.* No longer in a mood to challenge Nixon on his court appointments, the Senate quickly confirmed Powell and Rehnquist.

After 1970 no facet of domestic policy received more attention than the problem of the sagging economy. Nixon struck out at inflation and recession in a way that led him to make the most drastic changes in the economy since 1944. These were reforms that Nixon had hoped to avoid. His grudging moves toward a controlled economy were so poorly conceived that he left his successor with a spiraling inflation that would become the key domestic crisis of the Ford years.

Inflation—persistently rising prices—had been a part of life in the United States since the mid-1950s. The average price level as measured by the Consumer Price Index (CPI) had steadily increased since 1955. Yet between 1965 and 1968 the CPI had risen 10 percent, its sharpest rise since 1953. This jump in inflation was caused by several factors: spending on Great Society programs without a corresponding rise in taxes (indeed, taxes had been cut in 1964), an overstimulation of investment as a result of the tax cut, and the expenses of the Vietnam War. Congress had attempted to stem inflation in 1968 by passing a

---

*As a law clerk for Justice Robert H. Jackson in 1952–1953, Rehnquist wrote a memo arguing that Julius and Ethel Rosenberg were "fitting candidates" for execution and that in their case, "it's too bad that drawing and quartering had been abolished." He also wrote memos on racial issues; one contended that the separate-but-equal doctrine was right ("Plessy was right, and should be affirmed") and another asserted that "it is about time that the Court faced the fact that the white people in the South don't like the colored people." It was also revealed that in testimony given in 1964 at an informal public hearing in Phoenix, Rehnquist had been an open proponent of racial zoning covenants for private businesses. During his confirmation hearings, Rehnquist brushed aside this criticism, saying that "I think I have come to realize since . . . the strong concern that minorities have for the recognition of these rights. I would not feel the same way today about it as I did then" (*Washington Post*, July 6 and 7, 1986; Rehnquist testimony, June 15, 1964, Ervin Papers, series 2, Supreme Court Nominations, box 114, folder 568).

10 percent income tax surcharge to help pay for the war effort, but it was too little too late. The new administration faced an annual inflation rate of 4.7 percent. There was, however, some good news. The Democratic spending spree had kept business from sagging into the abyss; unemployment in the last years of the Johnson administration had dropped to 3.3 percent, its lowest level since 1953. Nixon, then, faced a pitiless economic dilemma: how to lower inflation without placing so many restraints on the economy that the nation's business activity was slowed, thus causing a recession that would lead to political disaster.

Nixon did not like economics, and discussions of the "dismal science" usually wearied him. On the whole, Nixon also did not like to listen to his economic advisers. Paul McCracken, Nixon's chairman of the Council of Economic Advisers until 1973, had a Ph.D. in economics from Harvard and had taught at the University of Michigan's School of Business Administration. He had also served on the CEA during Eisenhower's second term. Nixon respected McCracken's advice, particularly his ability to boil often complicated ideas down into readable memo form (virtually every available memo from McCracken has "excellent" scribbled in the margin by Nixon). Yet with a professorial demeanor that often drifted into lecturelike diatribes, McCracken often bored Nixon in meetings. Nixon also respected Arthur Burns's knowledge of economics (on September 11, in a meeting with Ehrlichman and Burns, Nixon turned to Burns and said, "Arthur, watch the economy for me. Let us know when we need to [do] something rough"[31]), but he was impatient with his inability to compromise for the political good. Nixon usually preferred to get his economic advice from politicians; his favorite source for that advice was a Democrat.

Early in 1970 Nixon had hosted a dinner for French President Georges Pompidou in New York. A guest at that dinner was a former Democratic governor of Texas, John Connally. As he passed through the receiving line, Connally told Nixon that he would be "happy to do something for the administration at any time." Nixon was sufficiently impressed with the Texan's offer that later that same evening he dictated a memo to Haldeman, directing him to "pass this on . . . [Connally] is a top property and would be excellent in the Cabinet or in any other position of significant importance requiring him to do something."[32] On December 14 Nixon announced that Connally would replace David Kennedy as secretary of the treasury.

There was no Cabinet member who served during the Nixon tenure to whom the president felt closer than he did to John Connally. The Cabinet was not Connally's first service for the administration. He had been a member of the Ash Council, and during a particularly violent meeting with the Cabinet, Connally had personally saved the plan from emaciation. Called "Big John" by friend and foe alike, Connally was big in size, stature, and opinion. His larger-than-life attitude combined political savvy with Texas showmanship. His was not a moderating voice in the inner circle, but the voice of action ("Sometimes it's not *what* you decide, but *that* you decide"). Observing the relationship between Nixon and Connally, the staff began to whisper, "The boss is in love." [33] It was Connally who pushed the hardest for Nixon to adopt radical methods for dealing with the economic mess; it was Connally who called the loudest for wage and price controls.

Nixon's fundamental economic conviction was a pillar of the conservative's credo—the free market economy. His World War II experience at the Office of Price Administration had taught him to abhor any government controls on the economy, particularly those on wages and prices known collectively as "incomes policy." Early in the administration he emphatically rejected any proposals for any such controls, voluntary or otherwise. However, closer to Nixon's heart than any economic philosophy was his political sixth sense. He had always believed that the dip that the economy took in 1958–1959 and Eisenhower's delay in dealing with it were major factors in his own loss to Kennedy. With his reelection in mind, Nixon did not want to make the same mistake.

His initial steps, what he called his economic "game plan," were predictably conservative. First, in terms of monetary policy, he announced that the administration would cut government spending. In a March 26, 1969, message to Congress on fiscal policy, Nixon warned the legislators to expect deep budget cuts. On April 14 Nixon announced that he had made several cuts in the fiscal 1970 budget submitted by Johnson, to bring it down from $196.9 billion to $192.9 billion. While the rhetoric made for good politics, Nixon did not follow through with his threats. When forced to plan his own budget for the following year, the president could not bring himself to slash projects that were close either to his heart or to the hearts of his supporters. He would not, for example, cut out the Family Assistance Plan or the Supersonic Transport (SST) System, two programs that Budget Director Robert Mayo had marked for extraction from the fiscal 1971 plan. Nixon also refused to approve cuts for defense spending as large as Mayo recommended. As a result, government spending actually increased through Nixon's first term, jumping from $194.6 billion in FY 1968–1969 to $250 billion in FY 1972–1973.

In terms of monetary policy, Nixon promised to continue the tight money policy that the Federal Reserve had held since the 1968 appointment of William McChesney Martin as its chairman. Concerned with inflation, Martin discouraged borrowing by keeping interest rates high. Despite his efforts, inflation continued to skyrocket. Many of Nixon's advisers, including Shultz and McCracken, lobbied hard for a return to a looser credit before business was irredeemably hurt. As a result, once again Nixon backed down. Under pressure from the White House, the Fed's tight money policy was eased by fall. Borrowing increased; thus inflation continued to rise.

By mid-1969, then, the game plan was not working. Nixon had succeeded only in slowing the economy, increasing unemployment, and leaving inflation virtually untouched. It was clear that Nixon would not be able to balance the budget, and to the horror of conservatives, he didn't seem to want to. The economy was moving toward the worst of both possible worlds: stagnant business activity with its accompanying unemployment, and inflation with its accompanying high prices—the textbook definition of stagflation.

Key members of the administration's economic team began to worry out loud. Burns became the most persistent voice of protest. He was disgusted with Nixon's unbalanced budget and disappointed in his friend McCracken, whom he felt was more concerned about inflation than cutting back on spending. Burns was coming to believe that an income policy would be necessary. He began to voice his opinion in meetings, to the dismay of the rest of the economic team. Burns's criticisms, coupled with his feud with Moynihan over FAP, helped lead to the nomination of Burns to replace Martin at the Fed, an appointment that was formalized on January 31, 1970. The move was to serve a dual purpose: to farm Burns out of the White House and hopefully to put a man at the Fed who would be more prone to cooperate with the administration's views on monetary policy than Martin had been. This, however, was not to be. At the Fed Burns continued to speak out in opposition to the administration's economic policy. As Nixon continued to balk at making substantive cuts in the fiscal 1971 budget, Burns refused to loosen money any further unless deeper cuts were made in the budget. Nixon blinked, cutting back on federally financed construction projects and vetoing several large appropriations bills. As a result, the budget sent to Congress by the administration on February 2 projected a $1.3-billion surplus, and Burns lowered interest rates again.

It was far from enough to reverse the downward spiral. Government spending had already accelerated so far beyond collectible revenues that despite the rosy projections in the budget, the government had long since spent more than it had been allotted. At fiscal year's end on July 1, 1970, there would be a $2.8-billion deficit. The same fate awaited Nixon's FY 1972 budget; by early spring, officials were predicting a $23-billion deficit. The cycle of deficit spending had begun, a cycle that neither Nixon nor any of his successors could break.

Not surprisingly, Nixon blamed Congress. On July 18 he charged that there was a "persistent and growing tendency on Capitol Hill to approve increases in expenditures without providing the revenue to pay for the costs."[34] This was true, but it was only a small part of the problem. The administration could not bring itself to make cuts that might balance the budget. Recognizing that Nixon would never make the necessary cuts, Burns had decided that economic controls were now necessary. He went public with his views on December 7 in a speech at Pepperdine College, where he declared that the time had arrived to "supplement our monetary and fiscal policies with an incomes policy."[35] Nixon was furious. According to Ehrlichman, he reacted wildly: "Burns will get it right in the chops! Is it time to take the Fed on in public? We won't take this! Is it time to give the Fed a good kick now?"[36] Characteristically, after this diatribe Nixon did nothing.

Despite pressure from Burns, Nixon refused to admit that controls were either necessary or inevitable. Shultz and McCracken both agreed with him. Yet a new strategy was necessary before the country plunged head first into economic anarchy. What Nixon offered to the nation on June 17, 1970, was at best a half measure. Nixon announced that he was beginning a program of "inflation alerts." When an industry's wages or prices were at a proper level, that fact would be publicized. He made it clear that if industry cooperated, this would be enough. In any case, he promised that "I will not take this nation down the road of wage and price controls."[37] It was, of course, not enough. The inflation alerts program was a public relations gimmick with no teeth. As reporters Evans and Novak caustically observed, Nixon was acting "as if the past eighteen months of deepening failure had not occurred."[38]

Nixon's next move was to further shake up his economic team. On July 2 he fired Mayo and promoted Shultz to head of the Office of Management and Budget. Shultz began his tenure by suggesting that Nixon accept a rather novel idea: a budget balanced at full employment—a budget that was temporarily unbalanced, but which *would* be balanced when new employment produced expected new revenues. This was, in many ways, playing with mirrors. The budget deficit was still huge, but it was justified by the belief that revenues would soon catch up. When Nixon accepted Shultz's finagling, he had accepted the inevitability of both deficit spending and an unbalanced budget.

As the economy went into fiscal free-fall through the summer of 1970 and as the off-year elections approached, Congress attempted to force Nixon's hand. On August 17 Nixon reluctantly signed an extension of the Defense Production Act of 1950, which contained an amendment giving the president authority to freeze wages, salaries, prices, and rents. In a statement following the signing, Nixon made it clear that he knew what Congress was up to:

"Were it not for the need to extend the basic law, I would withhold my approval. . . . This bill contains three provisions which in my view are objectionable. First, the bill gives the president authority to establish controls on prices, rents, wages, and salaries at levels not less than those prevailing on May 25, 1970, and they enforce those controls by fines and injunctions. I have previously indicated that I did not intend to exercise such authority if it were given to me. Price and wage controls simply do not fit the economic conditions which exist today."[39]

That was but the opening salvo in the congressional elections of 1970, in which, as noted earlier, the economy was a featured issue. It was clear from even a surface analysis of the electoral results that the recession was the key factor in explaining the Republican losses.

After the election, legislators began to scream for an all-out presidential attack on inflation. On January 12 Nixon publicly denounced price hikes by Bethlehem Steel, a condemnation that eventually resulted in a rollback of prices. On February 23 he suspended the Davis-Bacon Act, which had required contractors to pay prevailing wage rates to all workers in a given area. The suspension of the bill amounted to freezing of wages in the construction industry for one month. Yet these were but warnings. As soon as the demands of both labor and industry moderated, Nixon once again backed off, telling Safire that he would "let them have their cherished Davis-Bacon back later on."[40] Nixon reinstated the act on March 29 after the creation of a commission that would mediate future wage movements. These actions did absolutely nothing to improve the economic situation. The Consumer Price Index had risen almost four points in the first six months of 1971, and there was no accompanying prosperity—unemployment was up to 6.1 percent.

Despite his anger over Burns's public demands for a wage and price freeze, Nixon had privately come to the conclusion that he would have to take more drastic measures than he had ever deemed necessary. On October 23 Nixon met with Shultz and Ehrlichman, suggesting that they "do it [wage and price controls] after the election, maybe?" Shultz, who at that point was still arguing against controls, replied that it would be a "shock effort." Nixon then ordered both of his aides to "work on it with [a] restricted staff."[41] John Connally, who had been a persistent and effective proponent of an incomes policy from the moment he walked in the door at the Treasury Department, worked on Nixon through the spring and summer of 1971, and Nixon finally was ready to accept wage and price controls. But before he stopped the economy from moving for any period of time, he had to decide what to do about the dollar.

The complex issue of the dollar was, at its heart, one of the foundations of the nation's growth as a postwar world power. In July 1944 at Bretton Woods, New Hampshire, forty-four nations had decided to fix the price of gold at thirty-five dollars an ounce and to tie their individual currencies to the U.S. dollar. The move was justified by all participants as one that would prevent another postwar depression.

In reality, the system was but another example of U.S. hegemony in the new world marketplace. The dollar was now the world's currency. The United States controlled both the International Monetary Fund and the World Bank—organizations set up at Bretton Woods to monitor the world's monetary situation—and stood to profit greatly from the increased trade and direct investment that the situation proffered.

By the late 1960s, however, the world economic situation had deteriorated greatly. With the onset of inflation in the United States, gold looked much better to Europeans than the dollar. European countries began to increase their money supply, stocking up on their own "Eurodollars"; that forced the United States to release more of its own dollars to keep up. The increased printing of U.S. dollars only served to feed inflation. U.S. economists began to warn that European bankers, wary of the stability of the dollar, would soon demand to have their dollars redeemed for gold. Conventional economic wisdom predicted that if there was a worldwide run on gold, with everyone demanding an ounce of the metal for thirty-five dollars, chaos would quickly follow. But, if Nixon ordered an end to the convertibility of dollars into gold and allowed the dollar to "float" against other currencies on the world market—what economists called "closing the gold window"—a whole new set of world economic rules would result, rules under which the United States might not be the predominant player.

Nixon was fundamentally opposed to closing the gold window. It would be an irreversible decision, ending the nation's unchallenged hegemony in the world marketplace. By 1971, however, it was clear that the dollar was so unstable abroad and inflation so bad at home that to continue to print dollars simply to keep up with Europe was a ludicrous cycle. Nixon begrudgingly agreed with Connally that the gold window must be closed. The best that could be hoped for was to hold out for a favorable political time—perhaps after the presidential election of 1972. The British denied Nixon this luxury, demanding in early August 1971 that the United States guarantee the convertibility of the dollar holdings of the Bank of England into gold. A worldwide economic crisis was but a decision away.

On Friday, August 13, Nixon ordered all of his economic advisers to Camp David. It was less a summit than a briefing. The president had decided to use the authority granted him by Congress, which he had said he would never use, to impose wage, price, and rent controls for ninety days. He also told his advisers that he was closing the gold window and imposing a 10 percent tariff on a long list of imports. To try to stimulate the domestic economy, Nixon would also ask Congress to repeal the 7 percent excise tax on automobiles, grant a 10 percent tax cut for new investments, and grant more personal exemptions. A Cost of Living Council, headed by Connally, would be formed to oversee the program. The plan, which Nixon entitled the "New Economic Plan" but which was quickly dubbed "Phase I," was announced to the nation on Sunday evening, August 15.

Herbert Stein, a member of Nixon's Council of Economic Advisers who was present at the Camp David meetings, recalled that the imposition of controls "was the most popular move in economic policy that anyone could remember."[42] That was true for Americans of the Middle, who overwhelmingly supported the move. On the surface, Phase I certainly seemed to be holding the economy steady. To the end of 1971, unemployment stayed at about 6 percent, while inflation declined slightly to about 3.2 percent. That was enough of a success to encourage Nixon, urged on by Defense Secretary Melvin Laird, to ask for an extension of the controls past the November 13 deadline. The new program, known as "Phase II," extended controls to April 30, 1972, and appeased labor by allowing modest wage increases of up to 5.5 percent.

Speaking with the author, Stein was uncompromising in his criticism of the move, calling Phase II "just ridiculous . . . absurd." Stein believes that the biggest problem was that "we had no plan for getting out of . . . the ninety-day freeze." The evidence leads one to conclude that the administration expected Phase I to markedly lower both inflation and unemployment, and that once that occurred, the controls could be dropped. But when conditions did not markedly improve as a result of Phase I, the administration had no real plan of action. In fact, no strategy had been set for what would happen after Phase I even under the best of conditions. Phase II was a poorly thought out, hastily implemented program.

Economic considerations aside, presidential politics doomed Phase II. Nixon was infinitely more concerned with lowering the unemployment rate before the election than he was with finding a long-term cure for inflation. As a result, in early 1972 Nixon ordered his Cabinet to spend money so as to produce a boom in the economy, new jobs in newly funded programs, and a corresponding rise in the employment rate. During 1972 federal spending increased by a gigantic 10.2 percent. Burns's Fed cooperated by loosening the money supply to meet the needs of the spending spree. The result was predictable even to a freshman economics major. Inflation skyrocketed, and the weakly enforced Phase II controls could not keep consumer prices from rising as a result. Mismanagement was the byword, and the public panicked. Many stores reported a run on goods, purchased by people who did not know what to expect from their president next.

Phase II was clearly a disaster, and none of Nixon's economic advisers wanted to see any further kneejerk reactions to the economy that might make things worse. On October 12 Stein wrote Nixon a lengthy memo on the state of the economy. He concluded that he "wouldn't try to tighten policy beyond our present plans."[43] Such counsel finally prevailed. In May 1972 the administration abruptly stopped the expansion and launched a budget-cutting spree for FY 1974 every bit as wild as the economic stimulation that had preceded it.

At first glance it would seem safe to assume that Nixon had caused this wild manipulation of the economy simply out of a desire to make the economy appear stronger in time to help his reelection chances. Laird, for example, was quoted as saying that "every effort was made to create an economic boom for the 1972 election" and that he had ordered the purchase of a two-year supply of toilet paper just to pad his budget.[44] However, the overwhelming majority of Nixon staffers, particularly his economic advisers, have virulently denied the charges. Stein, for example, has argued that since the FY 1973 budget was going to be out of balance anyway—a result of Nixon's acceptance of balancing the budget at full employment—it was the right time to try to stimulate the economy.*[45]

This is an unresolved point. On one hand, it is easy to accept that Nixon would attempt to gain every possible advantage for an upcoming political battle in which the polls had him trailing, largely because of the economy. Yet it is difficult to believe that Nixon would have stimulated the economy, for whatever reason, had he been aware of the frenzied inflation that would follow, a development that could also hurt his electoral chances. A more likely conclusion is that no one—not Nixon, not his advisers, and not the country—was thinking beyond the immediate success of the controls. The chance to lower unemployment was there, and the political Nixon acted hastily, without fully analyzing the economic consequences of his actions.

Phase II was allowed to expire on April 30, 1972, but the damage had long been done. Phase II had effectively killed the gains of Phase I. The economy was no better off than it had been before, and in some quarters, notably the area of consumer prices, it was even worse. By early 1972 buttons appeared with the threat, "Phase III: Dump Nixon." As the 1972 election approached, Nixon had learned the lesson that Arthur Burns would acerbically tell *Time* in a 1987 interview: "Anyone who is convinced that he can fine-tune the economy doesn't know what he is talking about."[46]

---

*At the 1987 meeting on the Nixon presidency held at Hofstra University, Stein and Maurice Stans were sitting on a panel dealing with Nixon's economic and monetary policy. One of the academic papers charged that Nixon manipulated both wage and price controls and the following economic stimulation in order to strengthen his hand in 1972. When the point was made, both Stans and Stein rolled their eyes and smiled; they both laughed through the conclusions of the paper. When it was Stein's turn to respond, he chided that "I do not recognize in [the papers] the five and a half years that I spent in the Old Executive Office Building." He also observed that "what is especially amusing is the picture of Richard Nixon lecturing Arthur Burns on monetary policy. That's not the direction that the [lecturing] began."

CHAPTER FOUR

"Peace with Honor"

R ICHARD Nixon came to the White House the best prepared of any president in the twentieth century to conduct foreign policy (except, perhaps, George Bush). As congressman and vice-president, Nixon had traveled to over eighty countries. His travel for Eisenhower had included a 1953 trip to Asia and the Far East, with six days touring Cambodia, Laos, and Vietnam; an April 1958 visit to South America, where in Venezuela his entourage was attacked by leftist mobs; and a July 1959 trip to Moscow, where he had engaged in a heated argument with Nikita Khrushchev in the middle of a model of a modern American kitchen in the new American Exhibition (at that meeting, Nixon had met Leonid Brezhnev for the first time). Even while out of office, Nixon had continued to travel extensively. He had met with Romania's Secretary General Nicolae Ceausescu, again visited Vietnam, and summited with Chiang Kai-shek, Eisaku Sato, and Yitzak Rabin. When he observed during his July 1967 lakeside speech at California's Bohemian Grove that "never in human history have more changes taken place in the world in one generation,"[1] Nixon was correct, and he himself had built firsthand relationships with most of the world leaders who had effected those changes.

Nixon's stand on foreign policy was, as has been noted, nowhere near as dogmatic as myth would have it. While he was one of the loudest voices of protest against Truman's "loss of China," he supported the Marshall Plan as well as the president's decision to send troops to Korea (however, during the campaign of 1952 he charged Truman with negligence that invited the North Korean invasion). As vice-president Nixon disliked John Foster Dulles's confrontational attitude, and in a 1958 interview with C. L. Sulzberger of the *New York Times* he criticized the foreign policy of the Eisenhower administration as "inept in presenting a true picture, even of ourselves."[2] In a November 1958 speech before the English-Speaking Union at London's

Guildhall, Nixon concluded by saying that "we should speak less of the threat of communism and more of the promise of freedom; that we should adopt as our primary objective not the defeat of communism but the victory of plenty over want, of health over disease, and of freedom over tyranny."[3] Nevertheless, he counseled Eisenhower to send United States troops into French Indochina. Though viewing John Kennedy to the end as a weakling, Nixon privately supported Kennedy's decision to invade Cuba at the Bay of Pigs and just as privately derided the young president for refusing to give the invading troops any air cover. He also counseled Kennedy during the Cuban missile crisis to seek some pretense for a second invasion and put an end to the Cuban menace once and for all.

Far from being a myopic cold warrior like his four immediate predecessors in the White House, Nixon held a world view that was more pragmatic and flexible than analysts have credited him with. Clearly these views were based in part on his reading of the political winds. At their core, however, was an acceptance that over the preceding decade the world had changed from a bipolar one to a multipolar one, with several seats of power emerging to challenge the American-Soviet hegemony. The war in Korea had been lost. By 1968 the United States was also losing in Vietnam. China was challenging the Soviets for control in the Far East as well as for the title of the true ideological heir to Marx. The Soviets were gaining a solid beachhead in the Middle East, and several nationalist movements had changed the already complex nature of that region's politics. The 1960s, then, brought with it a changed superpower relationship in which both the Soviets and the Americans were limited in the extent of their worldwide influence. Continuing the ideologically rabid rhetoric of the early Cold War, as Goldwater conservatives were wont to do, could not mask the fact that U.S. power could no longer be counted upon to check these developments around the world.

Nixon understood—and to the consternation of the Republican Right, *accepted*—the new limits on U.S. power and the reality of the new multipolar world. He proposed a foreign policy emphasizing two ends that would deal with these developments. The first was a rapprochement—"détente"—with the two major Communist powers. The second goal, the subject of this chapter, was a withdrawal of U.S. forces from areas of foreign entanglement that strained the nation's interests and resources. "Devolution," a breaking apart, would be evidenced by Nixon's withdrawal from Vietnam and his espousal of Vietnamization.

The two goals were complementary. As the United States backed off on its military intervention, it would present itself as a more credible ally to the Communist powers; as détente was achieved, so would come the balance and stability that would make devolution all the easier. All other initiatives in foreign policy, in whatever part of the

world, would be considered by Nixon in light of how they would help
to achieve these two goals. All of Nixon's foreign policy, then, was
linked to the goals of détente and devolution.*

Of all the people interviewed for this book, only a handful disputed
a description of Henry Alfred Kissinger as a "genius." Despite their
wariness of his duplicity, his contacts with the press, and his pragmatic—nay, his amoral—approach to his job, the sheer force of his
intellect impressed all around him. Clearly Kissinger played a key role
in Nixon's attempt to reform foreign policy to meet the new needs of
a multipolar world. But to argue, as have many scholars, that it was
Kissinger's foreign policy and not Nixon's is to give infinitely more
credit to Kissinger than he is due.

Born in Fuerth, Germany, in 1923, Heinz Kissinger grew up an
Orthodox Jew in the midst of Adolf Hitler's Nazi nightmare. As a boy
Kissinger saw the rampages of the Brownshirts and was beaten by his
classmates as the youngsters registered their own feelings about his
faith. His concentrated and accelerated education began in 1935, when
the Reich expelled all Jewish children from public schools. Freed from
the confines of a set curriculum and now under the tutelage of religious masters, Kissinger began a study of history that was advanced
far beyond his years. When his father, a public schoolteacher, was dismissed from his job, the family could foresee their fate. The Kissingers
were one of the lucky Jewish families who were able to emigrate to
the United States, arriving in the Washington Heights section of New
York in August 1938. Far from a flamboyant teenager, young Heinz—
now known as Henry—earned honor roll grades during his last two
years of public high school while working a full-time job at a nearby
shaving brush factory. He began his college career in 1941 at the tui-
tion-free City College of New York, but World War II intervened.

Like Nixon, Kissinger saw active duty during the war. Kissinger
returned to Germany, where the anti-Semitism of his youth had been
played out on a monstrous scale. He worked for Division Intelligence
(G-2), first as an interpreter, then in the Counterintelligence Corps,
then in the military government of occupied Germany. One might expect that such assignments, in which he was either ferreting out Nazis
or governing ex-Nazis, would be a highly emotional experience for a
young Jewish emigrant. But Kissinger, unlike Nixon, seems to have
been little changed or emotionally affected by his military service. Most
who served with Kissinger recall how he was able to make himself

*This is not an original thesis of this author. The dual goal of détente and devolution
is a key theme in Robert Litwak's outstanding analysis of the Nixon and Ford foreign
policy, *Detente and the Nixon Doctrine: American Foreign Policy and the Pursuit of Stability,
1969–1976* (Cambridge, Mass., 1984).

detached from the emotional quality of his work. As one recalled, "He can forget, to some extent. Moreover, this is a technical man."[4]

In 1947 Kissinger entered Harvard (he would later recall that "I felt like an immigrant again"[5]). He studied in the Government Department, taking his undergraduate degree, Phi Beta Kappa, in 1950. His honors thesis, "The Meaning of History," was a 377-page opus that concentrated on the intertwining of the works of Kant, Hegel, and Spengler. As a graduate student Kissinger worked at his first teaching position in the experimental Harvard International Seminar. After he completed his Ph.D. in 1954, he turned down several tenured faculty offers to sign on with Nelson Rockefeller, who in 1955 was serving as President Eisenhower's special assistant for international affairs. When Rockefeller resigned, differing with the administration over the course of its foreign policies, he kept Kissinger on as executive director of the special studies project of the Rockefeller Brothers Fund. A think-tank project created by Nelson, its purpose was to write option papers on a multitude of issues, discuss those drafts in seminars and subpanels, and present a published series of final reports. As director Kissinger worked with and commented on the papers of many of the nation's intellectuals. He also adopted a herculean work schedule to get the project completed on time and began a pattern of ruthlessness with his staff that would stay with him for the rest of his career. The final published result, *Prospect for America: The Rockefeller Panel Reports* (1958), was impressive.[6]

Kissinger stayed on as a paid consultant to the Rockefeller family for the next dozen years, but the prospect of following his patron to Albany in 1958 was unappealing. Kissinger opted to return to the faculty at Harvard, where he would serve until leaving to join the Nixon administration. With the tenure he was awarded in 1962, Kissinger finally felt free to dabble in politics. He served as an outside consultant to the Kennedy administration, but his advice, primarily on German policy, was ignored. In 1964, while continuing a full-time teaching load, he replaced Emmet Hughes as Rockefeller's foreign affairs consultant during the governor's run for the presidency.

Despite Rockefeller's defeat, Kissinger had impressed fellow Harvard alumnus Dean Rusk, who asked him to send briefings to the Johnson administration on Vietnam. This was a subject on which Kissinger had virtually no experience. However, he was a quick study (he hurriedly enlisted the help of two Harvard graduate students to help him research the background of the war, pleading with one to "please tell me anything you know about Vietnam, because I don't know anything before 1963"[7]). Kissinger was far from a dove on the war, supporting Johnson's bombing strategy, but he was perplexed by the lack of planned options available if military victory did not immediately occur. To try to fill this gap, in 1967 Kissinger tried to arrange a meeting in Paris between two Frenchmen and a member of the North Vietnamese government. Code-named Operation Pennsylvania, the attempt failed.[8] In the eyes of the administration's many critics, however, Kissinger's star rose.

Signing on again with Rockefeller in 1968, Kissinger publicly described Nixon as "the most dangerous, of all the men running, to have as president."[9] After Nixon's victory in Miami Beach, one observer recalls, a drunken Kissinger flew back to New York cursing Nixon's name to all who would listen to him.[10] His outrage was short-lived. Journalist Seymour Hersh's revelations of Kissinger's song-and-dance during the 1968 campaign, found in his influential book on Kissinger's years in the Nixon White House, *The Price of Power*, provide an amazing display of political fortitude and chutzpah. Hersh charges that Kissinger continued to send advice to the Johnson administration while also providing both the Nixon and the Humphrey campaigns with information.* According to Hersh, the information brought him to the attention of Richard Allen, Nixon's director for foreign policy research, who paved the way for Kissinger's appointment as special assistant for national security affairs.

Kissinger's shift from Rockefeller to Nixon was not as abrupt as it seems on the surface. In his doctoral dissertation, published in 1957 under the title *A World Restored: The Politics of Conservatism in a Revolutionary Era,* Kissinger argued, as had Metternich, that while nations could profit from an adroit use of force, they must keep in mind that they would ultimately encounter limits to the extent of their power. Yet, according to Kissinger, in the hands of an enlightened leader such as Bismarck these limits could be transcended. The true statesman, for Kissinger, was the man who could fuse the caution of Metternich with the activism of Bismarck. Clearly Kissinger believed he had found such a leader in Richard Nixon.

The Kissinger appointment was more than just a quid pro quo to the Rockefeller wing of the party. Kissinger was the epitome of what Nixon was looking for in his appointments. He was as much the technocrat as Roy Ash, as much the savvy politician as John Connally, as much the conceptual thinker as Daniel Patrick Moynihan, as much the bureaucrat as Bob Haldeman. As Nixon would soon find out, he was also as conceptual a thinker, as paranoiac, and as secretive as Richard Nixon. It was this broad range of personality and the ability to adapt to Nixon's whims and moods—some at the time called it pandering— that made Kissinger so invaluable to Nixon.

There can be no question, however; despite Kissinger's own proclamations in his mammoth memoirs, the foreign policy of the Nixon

---

*In his memoirs Kissinger denies any contact with the Nixon campaign during the election.

administration was Nixon's creation, not Kissinger's. There was no sycophantic trust between these two men. David Eisenhower, Nixon's son-in-law, was close to the mark when he told this author that there was a "coalition effect" between Nixon and Kissinger, wryly noting that "you don't function with a stranger the way you do with a Haldeman or an Ehrlichman." Kissinger was the perfect technocrat to put into play the secret diplomacy that would link foreign policy concerns to each other and allow Nixon to acquire both détente and devolution. While the only person whom Nixon completely trusted with the creation of foreign policy was himself, the only one he trusted with its execution was Kissinger.

In July 1969 Nixon made his first foreign trip as president. His first stop was the aircraft carrier *Hornet,* stationed about a thousand miles southwest of Hawaii. There the president welcomed home the *Apollo XI* astronauts from their successful maiden voyage to the moon. The next stop was Guam, where Nixon made some informal comments to newsmen at the Naval Air Station. The interrogation eventually turned into a lengthy Nixon monologue on the U.S. role in Asia. Toward the end Nixon articulated what would soon be dubbed the Nixon Doctrine:

> [We must] be quite emphatic on two points: One, that we will keep our treaty commitments, our treaty commitments, for example, with Thailand under SEATO; but, two, that as far as the problems of internal security are concerned, as far as the problems of a military defense, except for the threat of a major power involving nuclear weapons, that the United States is going to encourage and has a right to expect that this problem will be increasingly handled by, and the responsibility for it taken by, the Asian nations themselves.[11]

For those expecting Nixon to be an international gunslinger, this was a startling admission of the limited role that the United States would now play in the new multipolar world. Treaties would be kept, and our allies would continue to be shielded by our nuclear arsenal. However, the nation involved would be expected to bear the brunt of any military intervention that might be necessary to help solve its problems. The Nixon Doctrine put the world on notice that after extricating itself from Vietnam the United States was no longer the world's policeman. It was Nixon's public justification for devolution.

Clearly Nixon had come to believe that a withdrawal of U.S. troops from Vietnam was the only practical political and military option open to his administration. After Tet he and Kissinger had both given up any hope for a military victory. According to Haldeman, Nixon told him that "I'm not going to end up like LBJ—holed up in the White House afraid to show my face on the street. I'm going to stop that war.

Fast."[12] However, devolution was not going to happen overnight. A precipitate withdrawal would, in Nixon's mind, eliminate any reason for the North Vietnamese to negotiate and would bring an effective end to the Thieu regime in South Vietnam. Nixon's solution to this dilemma of devolution was a two-pronged strategy of attack and withdrawal. He would initiate a gradual withdrawal of troops, yet in large enough numbers so that the pullout would be complete before the 1972 election. He would protect that withdrawal with military operations along Vietnam's periphery, attacks that would involve an increasing number of South Vietnamese troops as Americans were withdrawn.

These actions were not, as many have interpreted them, an attempt to win the war in one grand stroke. A successful war on the periphery would protect the process of devolution, destroy Communist enclaves in Cambodia and Laos, and, as a collateral benefit, scare the North Vietnamese back to the peace table. This combination of devolution and war on the periphery was Nixon's oft-cited concept of "peace with honor," a withdrawal that was not—or, in the worst-case scenario, did not resemble—an American defeat. The key to this plan lay with the fate of the neutral nation of Cambodia.

Located to the immediate west of South Vietnam, Cambodia was led by Prince Norodom Sihanouk's corrupt, opulent regime, which had grown fat on the U.S. aid begun in 1955. Few persons in the U.S. military or diplomatic corps considered Sihanouk a trustworthy ally. This was with good reason; American money had not kept Sihanouk from concluding that the North Vietnamese would eventually defeat the Americans. In December 1963 he canceled all U.S. aid, and in 1965 he ended diplomatic relations with the United States. That done, Sihanouk virtually opened his doors to the North Vietnamese. By 1966 they had set up hundreds of camps along the South Vietnamese–Cambodian border, soon to be called "sanctuaries." They had also increased their use of the Ho Chi Minh Trail, which wound through Laos into northern Cambodia, to run supplies into South Vietnam. By 1966 the North Vietnamese had also begun to ship supplies by water into Cambodia, running them through the southern port cities of Ream and Sihanoukville. For all intents and purposes, North Vietnam had become an army of occupation in Cambodia.

Sihanouk quickly regretted his decision and secretly moved to have the Americans expel the North Vietnamese from his nation. As he continued to profit from the North Vietnamese presence, he welcomed secret search-and-destroy missions by the Americans across his border (the Salem House and Daniel Boone missions). By 1967 he was also accepting United States intelligence on the existence of the Communist sanctuaries within his borders (code-named Vesuvius), proffered with American hopes that the prince would use the information to help him expel the Communists. In an interview with Stanley Karnow of the *Washington Post*, published on December 29, 1967, Sihanouk revealed that he would grant the United States the right of "hot pursuit" against the North Vietnamese in Cambodia, so long as no Cambodians were drawn into the fray. Already the target of antiwar vitriol, Johnson could not jeopardize his administration further by publicly invading a neutral nation or by revealing the nature of previous covert missions. He firmly rejected Sihanouk's "offer."

In February 1969 General Creighton Abrams, who had replaced William Westmoreland as the commander of U.S. forces in Vietnam, requested a single attack on Communist sanctuaries located in Cambodia's Parrot's Beak region, an area of dense jungle some thirty-three miles due west of Saigon. To strengthen his case, Abrams cited recent intelligence reports concluding that the North Vietnamese headquarters for the entire South Vietnamese theater, the Central Office for South Vietnam (COSVN), was located there. Abrams's plan received the enthusiastic support of General Earle Wheeler, chairman of the Joint Chiefs of Staff. Yet undertaking such an operation was risky. Even though recent events suggested that Sihanouk would probably look the other way in order to rid himself of his North Vietnamese squatters, Cambodia was technically a neutral nation. Any attack was sure to bring widespread condemnation.

These problems did not cause Nixon the concern that they had caused Johnson. There is little question but that Nixon was in favor of the plan from the start. To skirt the neutrality issue, Nixon authorized the bombing of the sanctuaries, code-named Operation BREAKFAST, but ordered that it be kept secret. Pilots were not to be told where they were going for their missions, and their navigation was completely controlled by radar. Their sorties were reported by the Pentagon as being in South Vietnam. Nixon's decision was not without its opponents. Secretary of Defense Melvin Laird and Secretary of State William Rogers supported the bombing but were against the secrecy aspect from the start, although Laird moderated his stand by March. To circumvent the continuing opposition, Nixon simply did not tell either Rogers or Laird when BREAKFAST was to begin.[13]

The BREAKFAST bombing of Parrot's Beak began in late February. Initially Abrams had proposed only one strike, designed to knock out COSVN. Once that first strike was made, however, it was impossible to turn back. The program was immediately extended to include the bombing of other sanctuaries, code-named (most likely with a smirk by someone in the high command) LUNCH, SNACK, DESSERT, DINNER, and SUPPER. The bombing program, now known collectively as Operation MENU, began on March 18, 1969, and continued until April 1970.

Hersh is not far from wrong when he notes that "eventually, the secret became more important to the White House than the bombing."[14] On March 26, one week after the first BREAKFAST mission, the *New York Times* ran a story by Pentagon correspondent William Beecher which accurately charged that Abrams had requested the bombing of Communist sanctuaries in Cambodia. On May 9 Beecher again wrote that Americans were making bombing runs inside the Cambodian border. That the story was virtually ignored by the public did not mean that it went unnoticed in the White House. A furious Kissinger called J. Edgar Hoover, director of the Federal Bureau of Investigation, and pleaded with him to find the source of Beecher's story. Hoover told Kissinger that the source was probably a National Security Council staffer, Morton Halperin. Halperin had long been under suspicion by the White House. He was a Johnson holdover, had argued for the bombing halt in 1968, and had even participated in an antiwar teach-in at Harvard. Convinced on the barest of evidence that Halperin was the culprit, Kissinger ordered a wiretap put on his aide's home telephone. More taps would follow.* The abuses of power had begun—in 1969.

Those who hoped that MENU would deliver a knockout blow to the North Vietnamese received a case of military indigestion. To avoid the bombing, the North Vietnamese simply moved deeper into Cambodia, thus increasing the problem for both the Americans and Sihanouk. In his critical study of Nixon's policy toward Cambodia, William Shawcross offers overwhelming evidence that rather than bombing Communist sanctuaries, the B-52s were actually leveling villages of Cambodian civilians. Most important, COSVN was never found, much less destroyed. Nixon argues that "soon after Operation BREAKFAST began, there was a steady decline in casualties in Vietnam."[15] That is true, but it was less a result of BREAKFAST than of the fact that simultaneously with MENU Nixon was beginning to withdraw troops from Vietnam.

The idea of turning the war over to the South Vietnamese was certainly not new. It had been the goal of U.S. "military advisers" under Kennedy to do just that, and Johnson, when his escalation failed, had toyed again with such a program. Yet Nixon made it his own. Defense Secretary Laird gave the program its snappy name, and "Vietnamization," the next logical step after "nation-building," was soon the centerpiece of devolution. It would be a withdrawal with honor, leaving behind a well-trained South Vietnamese army to protect the integrity of the Thieu regime. The first step came on May 13, 1969, when Nixon asked Congress to reform the military draft by shortening the period of a young man's vulnerability and initiating a lottery system. The next day Nixon announced to the nation an eight-point plan

---

*Halperin told the author that he believed "the story came out of the Air Force people . . . those people who thought [the bombing] was a good thing and wanted people to know that, or who were disturbed about the excessive secrecy."

for peace that centered on a mutual troop withdrawal over a twelve-month period with the establishment of an international body to verify the withdrawals. Three weeks later, on June 8, Nixon met with Thieu on Midway Island and, despite the vociferous objections of the South Vietnamese leader, announced the first of his troop withdrawals—the immediate pullout of 25,000 U.S. combat forces, to begin in the next thirty days and be completed by the end of August.

Nixon continually took the public position that Vietnamization was working and that he had now bent as far as he intended to bend. After a second meeting with Thieu on August 30 in Saigon (the meeting was part of his world tour, which included the stop in Guam where he pronounced the Nixon Doctrine), Nixon told reporters that since the Midway meeting there had been "steady progress in pacification . . . the elections of village and hamlet officials . . . [and] the improving performance of the Vietnamese armed forces." He also made it clear that "I believe the record is clear as to which side has gone the extra mile in behalf of peace. . . . We have gone as far as we can or should go in opening the door to peace, and now it is time for the other side to respond."[16] However, Nixon's moves in early 1969 failed to mollify any of his three enemies in the Vietnam War. Despite direct written entreaties from Nixon to Ho Chi Minh and promises of Romanian dictator Nicolae Ceausescu to intervene on Nixon's behalf,* the North Vietnamese refused to be pushed back to the Paris peace table. All Nixon got was an agreement for the head of the North Vietnamese delegation in Paris, Xuan Thuy, to meet secretly with Kissinger. The meeting on August 4 was counterproductive. Xuan refused to budge on his country's two preconditions for reconvening serious negotiations: the Americans must withdraw all their forces and depose Thieu. Kissinger delivered Nixon's response: unless some progress toward peace was made by November 1, the one-year anniversary of Johnson's bombing halt, Nixon would "take measures of the greatest consequences."[17]

As Nixon's secret deadline approached, it became clear that Vietnamization had also failed to mollify Congress. In fact, opposition to the war in Congress had steadily increased since the beginning of the year and had become bipartisan. In an interview given to the Lyndon B. Johnson Library Oral History Project at about this time, Democratic Senator Frank Church was scalding in his criticism of Vietnamization: "I wonder how gullible we Americans can become, when these many years later, we're still being told that we must equip and train these South Vietnamese to fight, that it is now the new mission. . . . I wonder how long it must take. I suppose we'll have to send them all to West Point."[18] On September 25 Senator Goodell introduced the first

*Nixon visited Romania as part of his summer 1969 world trip, becoming the first U.S. president to visit a Communist satellite country.

Vietnam disengagement bill, which called for withdrawal of all U.S. troops from Vietnam by the end of the next year. Ten such resolutions were introduced in Congress over the next three weeks, resolutions which Nixon denounced as making it impossible for him to carry on meaningful negotiations.

Most baffling to Nixon was that Vietnamization had quite the opposite effect on the antiwar movement than he had intended: it stoked the flames. Sam Brown, a former McCarthy volunteer, had come to the conclusion that it was time to move the protests off campuses, where they had become increasingly violent. His plan was to broaden the base of the antiwar movement by moving into the communities to capitalize on the growing resentment to the war among Middle Americans. Brown wanted a nationwide series of demonstrations that would emphasize solemnity and peace rather than violent confrontation. The result was a call for two nationwide "moratoria" against the war, scheduled for October 15 and November 15, 1969. Despite Nixon's attempts to blunt the effect of the announcement with an increase in the pace of withdrawals and a defiant message that "under no circumstances will I be affected" by the protests,[19] the First Moratorium against the War was a spectacular success. All over the country protesters gathered peacefully. Some 250,000 went to Washington; in Boston, close to 100,000 gathered on the Boston Common. The antiwar movement had been revived, but it had not yet reached out to the Middle, as it had hoped to do by keeping the moratoria peaceful and including a wide range of participants. Largely responsible for this was a letter to the protesters from Ho's successor as leader of North Vietnam, Pham Van Dong. Broadcast on Radio Hanoi, the letter applauded the "broad and powerful offensive . . . to demand that the Nixon administration put an end to the Vietnam aggressive war" and cheered: "May your fall offensive succeed splendidly." Although Brown tried to distance himself from the message, many in the Middle saw the moratorium as the work of Communist sympathizers. For his part, Nixon maintained a public stoicism. On the day of the first moratorium he issued a defiant press release describing himself as going about "business as usual."[20]

Despite his bravado, Nixon's Vietnam policy was only partially successful. While the troops were coming home, the war on the periphery had not scared the North back to the peace table, and the White House was clearly convinced that the antiwar demonstrators were having a direct effect on North Vietnamese intransigence. Despite his October 20 warning to Soviet Ambassador Anatoly Dobrynin that "we will not hold still for being diddled to death in Vietnam,"[21] Nixon was forced to allow his November 1 ultimatum date to pass by without any military response. In an attempt to blunt the effect of the upcoming second moratorium, Nixon decided to turn his previously announced speech on the conduct of the war into an impassioned plea for the Middle to take control of their children.

Nixon's speech, delivered to a live television audience on the evening of November 3, was the most eloquent of his administration. He began with a defense of America's responsibility to South Vietnam, a commitment which he was quick to state he had inherited from Kennedy and Johnson. Nevertheless, he made it clear that he "rejected the recommendation that I should end the war by immediately withdrawing our forces. I chose instead to change American policy on both the negotiating front and the battlefront." To make clear his dedication to negotiation, Nixon made public his secret July-August correspondence with Ho, emphasizing its unfavorable reply. He explained his Vietnamization program, noting that he had ordered General Abrams "to enable the South Vietnamese forces to assume the full responsibility for the security of South Vietnam," but that "I have not and do not intend to announce the timetable for our program." He closed with a plea for the support of the Middle, and in doing so he gave them a name:

I have chosen a plan for peace. I believe it will succeed. . . . And so tonight—to you, the great silent majority of my fellow Americans—I ask for your support. I pledged in my campaign for the presidency to end the war in a way that we could win the peace. I have initiated a plan of action which will enable me to keep that pledge. The more support I can have from the American people, the sooner that pledge can be redeemed; for the more divided we are at home, the less likely the enemy is to negotiate at Paris. Let us be united for peace. Let us also be united against defeat. Because let us understand: North Vietnam cannot defeat or humiliate the United States. Only Americans can do that.[22]

The speech was selective in its truths but not in its message. Nixon laid the blame for the longevity of the war squarely at the feet of the Left. While he claimed that he had changed U.S. policy, he did not, of course, reveal the bombing of Cambodia. Yet, as he had done in 1952 during his Checkers speech, Nixon weathered a time of crisis by appealing to the Middle for help. As had occurred then, the support he received was both immediate and overwhelming. The White House switchboard was flooded with calls and telegrams. Nixon's remembrance is of more than 50,000 telegrams and 30,000 letters coming in. At a Cabinet meeting two days later, it was noted that 40 percent of the wires used the phrase "I am a member of the Silent Majority,"[23] and the Gallup Poll taken immediately after the speech showed 70 percent approval.

The silent majority speech had galvanized the Middle. As Nixon recalled in his memoirs, "I had never imagined that at the end of my first year as president I would be contemplating two more years of fighting in Vietnam. But the success of the November 3 speech had bought me more time."[24] Still, the speech did not isolate the antiwar movement, as Nixon had hoped. The November 15 moratorium went ahead and was as successful as its predecessor. The highlight was a three-day march against death, in which some 40,000 people marched from Arlington Cemetery to Capitol Hill. An estimated 250,000 attended the rally that followed.

The impact of the second moratorium was intensified by a November 13 reminder, published in the *New York Times*, of the brutality and inhumanity of the war. The *Times* reported that on March 16, 1968, Company C, 1st Battalion, 20th Infantry, had moved into a village in the northeastern province of Quang Ngai that the army had christened "Pinkville" because of the color used to highlight the area on military maps. The soldiers had found no Vietcong, only a village of civilians. The company's commander, Second Lieutenant William Calley of Palm Springs, Florida, had ordered his men to round up the civilians into the center of the village and had given an order to his second in command, Paul Meadlo: "You know what to do with them, don't you?" Meadlo, thinking he was to guard the villagers, had answered in the affirmative. Calley had returned fifteen minutes later, furious with Meadlo. "How come you haven't gotten rid of them yet?" Calley had shouted. Meadlo had replied, "I didn't think you wanted us to kill them, just wanted us to guard them." Calley had answered, "I want them dead," stood back, and started shooting. After being commanded by Calley to follow suit, Meadlo had emptied four M-16 clips into the screaming mass of humanity. Depending on whose figures are believed, between 370 and 567 villagers were murdered by Company C in the hamlet of My Lai 4.[25]

Even though the atrocity had occurred before Nixon took office, the potential for political fallout from My Lai was grave. Nixon gave Haldeman the party line during their morning meeting of November 25: "re atrocities . . . make point it was done before RN—this is in total violation of direct national policy and prosecution will be pursued properly."[26] Nixon carried the spin to the public during a December 8 press conference, lamenting that My Lai, although "certainly a massacre, and under no circumstances was it justified . . . [was] an isolated incident." Nevertheless, Americans were forced to come to grips with the brutality of the war in a new way: civilian deaths at the hands of U.S. soldiers.

For his part, Nixon would not allow himself to be pushed by My Lai or Congress, any more than he would allow himself to be pushed by the moratoria. Vietnamization continued at Nixon's pace. On November 26 the draft reform bill was signed into law, and on December 1 the first draft lottery since 1942 was held at Selective Service headquarters. Two weeks later, on December 15, Nixon announced a further reduction of 50,000 more U.S. troops by April 15 of the next year.

It was clear that the events of 1969 had done nothing to dissuade Nixon from the belief that gradual withdrawal, coupled with shows of military force, would eventually bring his "peace with honor." It was also clear that this devolution was way behind schedule. When asked during a December 8 press conference to assess the chances for a negotiated end to the war, Nixon glumly responded, "Not good."

At the beginning of 1970, then, Nixon faced a double-edged sword. Domestic politics demanded that he do something to bring the war to an end before he was held politically accountable, most immediately in the upcoming congressional elections. Yet Nixon's own view of the situation kept him from supporting the calls for instant withdrawal, and the complexities of an evolving détente demanded that he show strength to our potential new allies. When it presented itself to the administration in March 1970, the new situation in Cambodia seemed perfectly suited to deal with this dilemma.

Sihanouk's position had badly deteriorated over the past year. He had alienated both his own middle class and his army by refusing to share with them the wealth of U.S. aid. He also had a serious problem with the North Vietnamese. The secret bombing of Cambodia had, as noted, pushed them farther into Cambodia, and their presence terrorized the people. Also, Hanoi had exploited Sihanouk's domestic problems by subsidizing a Khmer Rouge (Cambodian Communist) force and sneaking it back into Cambodia to foment civil war. A cadre within the Sihanouk government, led by Prime Minister Lon Nol, seized upon the unrest, and on March 11 Sihanouk's government was overthrown. The phlegmatic Sihanouk, now in exile in China, received no sympathy from the United States. Lon Nol, on the other hand, worked hard to become a more staunchly pro-American ally. His public support of U.S. efforts in South Vietnam earned Lon Nol's government the immediate recognition of the United States. One of the first acts of his new government was to ask the South Vietnamese for military help in ridding his country of the Communists; the reply quickly came in the affirmative.

Three days after the coup, Nixon told a press conference that "I will simply say that we respect Cambodia's neutrality."* The MENU bombings make this statement laughable; the administration never held Cambodia's neutrality in high regard. Of far greater concern were the Communist sanctuaries, including COSVN, which had escaped a full year

*Sihanouk remains convinced that Lon Nol was helped in the coup by the CIA (the title of his memoir is *My War with the CIA*, New York, 1972). All involved, in interviews with this author and in previous interviews, vehemently deny any U.S. role in the coup, while they do not attempt to hide their satisfaction with the coup's results. Despite the rather flimsy scenarios presented by later writers (whose sources are particularly contradictory on this point), there is to date no hard evidence of any CIA role in the Lon Nol coup.

of MENU bombing, and the prospect that the North Vietnamese would take advantage of the unrest in Cambodia by moving to overthrow the Lon Nol government. Nixon was besieged with requests from his military advisers to invade Cambodia and destroy the sanctuaries once and for all. Nixon's and Kissinger's protests in their memoirs that the decision to invade was a long and difficult one rings hollow. As with the decision to bomb, Nixon was in favor of attacking the sanctuaries as soon as Lon Nol's coup was a success. Pleas from Rogers, Laird, and several of the more liberal members of the NSC to reconsider were left unheeded; Nixon again took the advice of his generals. Nixon quotes a joint response from Ambassador to Vietnam Ellsworth Bunker and General Abrams in his memoirs: "We both agree that attack on this area should have maximum unsettling effect on the enemy, who has considered until now his sanctuaries immune to ground attack."[27] Speech writer Bill Safire asked if the decision contradicted the Nixon Doctrine; Kissinger bellowed, "We wrote the goddam doctrine, we can change it!"[28]

On March 26 Nixon ordered an invasion of Cambodia. South Vietnamese (ARVN) forces would invade at Parrot's Beak, still reported to host COSVN. A joint ARVN and U.S. force would attack at the Fishhook, the North Vietnamese base some fifty miles northwest of Saigon. Several NSC staffers observed that after the incredible amount of MENU bombing that the Parrot's Beak area had absorbed, if COSVN had ever been there, it couldn't be there now. Nixon and Kissinger weren't listening.

The reasons for the invasion of Cambodia are still a topic for heated debate. It bears repeating that it was never expected by anyone, not in the White House nor in the military, that this action would be the great surprise attack that would destroy the North Vietnamese and "win the war." Yet a clear victory would bear much fruit. It would do much toward scaring North Vietnam back into serious negotiations. The inclusion of ARVN troops would help demonstrate the success of Vietnamization, thus silencing many of the administration's domestic critics. Most important, the incursion was a direct message to both the Soviet Union and China, who were quick to publicly censure the United States for the invasion, that the United States was still a military power to be reckoned with.

This was the message in Nixon's speech to the nation on the evening of April 30. After justifying what he termed the "incursion" into Cambodia as a reaction to North Vietnamese "aggression" (Nixon would later write that calling the operation an invasion "would be like accusing the Allies of 'invading' German-occupied France in 1944"), Nixon defended his actions with rhetoric that brought back memories of Cold War bellicosity: "If, when the chips are down, the world's most powerful nation acts like a pitiful, helpless giant, the forces of totalitarianism and anarchy will threaten free nations and free institutions throughout the world."

Nixon contends in his 1990 memoirs *In the Arena* what he has consistently argued since 1970: "The [Cambodian] operation was completely successful. The Communists dropped their plans for another offensive that year, thousands of American and allied lives were saved, and our withdrawal program went forward on schedule."[29] This is correct only in a very limited sense. ARVN forces entered Cambodia on April 28; American forces were crossing the border as Nixon spoke to the nation. COSVN was located, but as Stanley Karnow drolly observed, "instead of an Asian Pentagon, COSVN turned out to be little more than a scattering of empty huts."[30] U.S. troops thrust into Cambodia some twenty miles, and ARVN moved even farther, encountering areas populated with civilians. The sanctuaries were rendered useless for a time, and that triumph did give some credence to those who argued that Vietnamization, given more time, would work.

Shawcross, however, argues that the real catastrophe brought about by the Cambodian incursion was a long-term one. The tragedy of the Cambodian refugees of this new war, driven into the arms of an unsympathetic South Vietnam, is one of the most gruesome stories of modern history. The new war between the North Vietnamese, their Cambodian Communist allies, the Khmer Rouge, and Lon Nol's army was a cataclysm for the Cambodian people. The ultimate victory of the Khmer Rouge, the ensuing regime of the sadomasochistic Pol Pot, and the genocide of a Cambodian generation was the final result. Yet despite Shawcross's passion, this disaster was related to, but not directly caused by, Nixon's "incursion."

From a political point of view the Cambodian incursion was unquestionably the biggest disaster of the Nixon administration. Nixon had attempted to deflect some of the expected criticism by announcing on April 20 the withdrawal of 60,000 more troops from South Vietnam in 1970 and another 90,000 in 1971. However, no olive branch could stem the reaction. The press immediately began to gouge at the administration, the most famous example being a *New York Times* editorial pronouncing that "presidential assurances can no longer be accepted."[31] Few in the administration could bring themselves to agree with the dire prediction of Safire, who foresaw that the announcement of the incursion would "blow the lid off campuses from Yale to Berkeley."[32] Within hours of Nixon's April 30 speech, students were electrified into action, and plans were quickly made to descend upon Washington to protest the incursion. The peaceful and broad-based goals of the moratoria were forgotten; faced with this new proof of Nixon's deception, the movement was furious and poised for action. Nixon's off-the-cuff comment on the situation, made to reporters while visiting the Pentagon the next day, has been interpreted by many to the author as a sign of his stress over the preceding twenty-four hours. It can just as easily be seen as a clear synopsis of Nixon's view of the antiwar movement as a whole:

> You see these bums, you know, blowing up the campuses. Listen, the boys that are on the college campuses today are the luckiest people in the world, going to the greatest universities, and here they are storming around about this issue. You name it. Get rid of the war, there will be another one.[33]

The "bums" remark inflamed an already smoldering situation. The bloodiest and most consequential explosion occurred at Ohio's Kent State University. Immediately upon hearing of the incursion, a group of graduate students who called themselves World Historians Opposed to Racism and Exploitation (w.h.o.r.e.) buried a copy of the U.S. Constitution that had been ripped from a textbook. Their actions were followed by a hastily announced "street festival," which quickly turned violent. Ohio Governor James Rhodes imposed a curfew and called in the National Guard. Before the Guard arrived, students burned a shed that housed the ROTC program. Compromise was impossible; when a delegation tried to approach the commander of the Guard, he ordered his men to march on the students with bayonets. The Guard's weapon of choice was the M-1, a devastating weapon whose bullets could travel wildly for almost two miles.

On Monday, May 4, the Guard struck. At about 11:00 A.M. a bell began to toll, and students left their classes for a rally that had been announced the previous Friday. The Guard used the campus radio station to announce that the rally had been banned by the administration and that Rhodes had given guardsmen the power of arrest, but the students ignored the warning. Estimates of the number of students who eventually faced the Guard vary; James Michener, author of the best book on the tragedy, says that the students numbered about 2,500. Troops began what the students interpreted as a withdrawal up Blanket Hill; students chased them with rocks. The Guard wheeled around and assumed a firing position. Michener describes the next horrifying thirteen seconds:

> There was a single shot . . . then a period of silence lasting almost two seconds, then a prolonged but thin fusillade, not a single angry burst, lasting about eight seconds, then another silence, and two final shots. . . . Twenty-eight different guardsmen did the firing . . . some guardsmen, fed up with the riotous behavior of the students and in fear of their lives did fire directly into the crowd . . . when the volley ended, thirteen bodies were scattered over the grass and the distant parking area. Four were dead, and nine were wounded more or less severely.[34]

The huge picture on the front page of the *New York Times* the next day was as grotesque as any that had returned from a battle zone: a young woman kneeling over the bleeding body of a downed student, with her outstretched arms pleading for help. The response of the administration was nothing short of callous. Vice-President Agnew called the deaths "predictable and avoidable"; the president warned that the episode "should remind us all once again that when dissent turns to violence, it invites tragedy."[35]

The catastrophe at Kent State was immediately followed by other acts of resistance. Across the country students went out "on strike," and many colleges closed to avoid any further violence. The brutality repeated itself in an attack that received comparatively little press coverage. On May 14 at predominantly black Jackson State University in Mississippi, following two nights of unrest, a force of National Guardsmen, highway patrolmen, and city police fired, according to a report, almost "400 bullets or pieces of buckshot" into a girls' dormitory in a twenty-eight-second period. Two students were killed, and twelve were wounded.*

The extent of the reaction to Cambodia caught the entire administration off guard. It adopted a bunker mentality; officials spent several nights in the War Situation Room in the White House basement.[36] Secretary of the Interior Walter Hickel tried to get Nixon to open the doors. Denied an appointment with either Ehrlichman, who was coordinating the response to the protesters, or Nixon, Hickel sent a letter of concern to the president on May 6:

Addressed either politically or philosophically, I believe we are in error if we set out consciously to alienate those who could be our friends. Today our young people, or at least a vast segment of them, believe they have no opportunity to communicate with government . . . other than through violent confrontation . . . we have an obligation as leaders to communicate with our youth and listen to their ideas and problems.[37]

Hickel's letter would simply have been ignored had events not taken a twist that sent the White House into fits of apoplexy. That evening portions of the letter were leaked to the Associated Press. Hickel argues that he was just careless with the delivery of the letter;[38] Ehrlichman contends that the letter was deliberately leaked by a Hickel staff member to a reporter on the *Washington Star*.[39] Regardless, Nixon immedi-

*New York Times, May 15, 1970. Following the protests against the Cambodian incursion, Nixon appointed a Presidential Commission on Campus Unrest headed by former Pennsylvania Governor William Scranton. Its report, released on September 26, found "unparalleled crisis" on college campuses. Three days after its release, during a speech in Sioux Falls, South Dakota, Vice-President Agnew attacked the report, calling it "truncated . . . distorted, [and] contrived," offering more "pabulum for the permissivists" (*Collected Speeches of Agnew*, 227–229).

ately decided to fire Hickel, but fear of inciting more violence on the campuses and making Hickel a political martyr postponed the deed until after that fall's congressional elections.

Yet for the long term the most important reaction to the Cambodian incursion came from the halls of Congress. Nixon had taken his disdain for Congress to a new level. As he had done with the nation at large, Nixon had deliberately deceived Congress on Cambodia (indeed, he continued to mislead it on the bombing of that country). He had misinformed not only the Democratic leadership but the leadership of his own party as well. The mood in Congress was quietly ugly on the minority side and publicly vengeful on the Democratic side. The McGovern-Hatfield amendment, demanding complete withdrawal of all U.S. forces from Vietnam by the end of 1970, and the presentation of the second Cooper-Church amendment calling for limiting U.S. involvement in Cambodia, indicated the nasty attitude on the Hill. These were primarily partisan moves, and the time was not yet ripe for the legislative revolution that would occur in 1973—both pieces of legislation were defeated before year's end. However, it is clear that Cambodia crippled Richard Nixon's hopes of ever having any substantive relations with Congress, a situation that his actions in that fall's congressional elections, already discussed, made irreversible.

It was undebatable that in terms of the number of combat troops in the field, U.S. commitment had dropped significantly since 1969. The Cambodian incursion, however, had done little to advance Nixon's goal of "peace with honor" and much to frustrate it. The incursion clearly showed that ARVN forces were not prepared to handle the war on their own. Nixon's capability of conducting a secret military strategy, seen by Nixon and Kissinger to be crucial toward a successful conduct of the war, had been damaged beyond repair. A new life had been breathed into the antiwar movement, particularly within the halls of a Democratic Congress which, after the recent congressional elections, was breathing fire anew. A Gallup Poll taken in mid-February 1971 would show that 66 percent of those asked wanted to have their congressman vote for a proposal then pending that called for bringing all U.S. troops home before the end of the year. Most important, the resolve of the North Vietnamese to win without the peace table had been stiffened. All of these factors combined to force Nixon into taking a step away from "peace with honor" in an October 7, 1970, speech, as he floated the idea of a "standstill cease-fire." As 1971 began, devolution was no closer, and in many ways further away, than it had been in January 1969.

Despite the muddy nature of the situation in 1971, Nixon deviated little from his policies of the previous year. On January 28 he sent a special message to Congress on draft reform in which he announced that his goal was to move toward an all-volunteer army and proposed "an additional $1.5 billion in making military service more attractive to present and potential members, with most of this used to provide a pay raise for enlisted men."[40] At the same moment, however, he was planning another "big play." This one, however, would not repeat the mistake of involving U.S. ground troops.

Nixon and his advisers feared a North Vietnamese offensive in 1972 designed to affect the outcome of the presidential election in the United States. They believed that they could halt such an invasion by cutting off the Ho Chi Minh Trail at its Laotian starting point. On February 8, using U.S. air cover, South Vietnamese troops invaded Laos (mission code name: Lamson 719), thus violating the neutrality of a second nation. From the start it was clear that ARVN met much heavier resistance than had been anticipated. One source reports that the South Vietnamese forces suffered a casualty rate as high as 50 percent, with some 2,000 dead. The Ho Chi Minh Trail easily survived the hapless operation, and within six weeks ARVN troops were forced to withdraw back inside the borders of South Vietnam. Laos had been the first dry run of the success of Vietnamization; it was a complete failure.

The Laotian disaster did nothing to help devolution. Immediately after the invasion, Kissinger's secret talks with Le Duc Tho of North Vietnam reached an impasse. Kissinger offered his counterpart his most comprehensive peace offer to date; in exchange for all U.S. POWs, Nixon would agree to withdraw all American troops within seven months of a cease-fire. As he had hinted he would do in his October 7, 1970, speech, Nixon had now completely abandoned his demand for mutual withdrawal, the backbone of U.S. negotiations since 1969. This was also a tacit abandonment of the Thieu regime, leaving it to fend for itself after the withdrawal. By this point Nixon's courting of China had begun to pay off, as Premier Chou En-lai informed Hanoi that in case of an American ground invasion of the North, China would not intervene. Tho refused to budge. He countermanded that any settlement must include a formal agreement by the United States to abandon the Thieu regime. Nixon was unwilling to go this far, and the talks were once again suspended.

As expected, the events of the spring of 1971 exacerbated the demands from the American Left for an immediate pullout. Senator Jacob Javits of New York sponsored a resolution immediately after the invasion stating that it was the nation's intention to withdraw all its troops from South Vietnam; Nixon publicly opposed the measure. It was now clear, however, that the Middle was losing its patience with Nixon's search for "peace with honor." Even those who had supported Nixon on the war found it difficult to explain away the deceit over Cambodia and the failure in Laos. A Gallup Poll taken February 19–21 showed that 49 percent of those surveyed believed that the Laotian initiative would lengthen the war, as opposed to only 19 percent who believed it would shorten it. On the left, the student movement had been revitalized in the preceding year. On April 24 demonstrations were held all over the country that eclipsed the 1969 protests in both size and spirit. During May Day protests in Washington, District police arrested 12,614 people in four days, keeping them in huge holding areas such as Robert F. Kennedy Stadium. The courts eventually threw out the majority of the arrests, charging that the administration had violated the civil rights of the protesters.

At the beginning of June a Gallup Poll told the bleak story of the chasm of the credibility gap: 67 percent of those polled believed that the Nixon administration was not telling the public all it knew about Vietnam. The summer showed little respite from the raging criticism of the war. Little wonder that the June 15 publication by the *New York Times* of a secret Defense Department study that came to be known as the Pentagon Papers sent the administration into another apoplectic fit.

The study had been commissioned by Secretary of Defense Robert McNamara in June 1967, largely as a result of his growing disenchantment with Johnson's preoccupation with the war.* It was to be, according to the secretary, an "encyclopedic and objective" history of U.S. involvement in Indochina since World War II.[41] The committee that McNamara assigned to work on the project (the "Group of Thirty-Six") included several analysts whom Kissinger would eventually bring onto the NSC and whom the administration would eventually target as being unreliable liberals—Leslie Gelb, Morton Halperin, and Daniel Ellsberg. Assured that the project would remain completely secret for their lifetimes, the group was given unlimited access to Defense Department files. They were also given quiet access to a great deal of CIA material as well. The group collected documents and prepared narrative analyses based upon their interpretation of those documents. They worked through to early 1969, when Gelb delivered a copy of the final study to outgoing Defense Secretary Clark Clifford, who had replaced McNamara in 1967. A copy was also given to Johnson, McNamara, and President-elect Nixon.

Most important, one copy of the report went with Ellsberg when he left the NSC to join the Rand Corporation. Ellsberg leaked the papers to Neil Sheehan of the *New York Times* in April 1971 (he had tried to get Senator William Fulbright to make the papers public, but Fulbright refused).[42] For two months staff members of the *Times* studied the documents in New York's Hilton Hotel, arguing among themselves whether the publication of the report would violate the Espionage Act and whether publisher A. O. ("Punch") Sulzberger would allow the

*Several sources have suggested that McNamara was planning to give the secret report to his friend Robert Kennedy for use in his upcoming presidential campaign in 1968.

paper to print the report. He did, and on June 13 and 14 the first two installments were run.

"The History of United States Decision Making Process on Vietnam Policy," soon to be dubbed the Pentagon Papers by the press, consisted of forty-seven book-length volumes, 3,000 pages of narrative history, and 4,000 pages of documents. The report is by no means a history of the Vietnam War. It is a rather narrow study of the role that presidential decision making played in the escalation of that war. As a whole the Pentagon Papers ended the popular "quagmire myth" of the time, which argued that the United States had been drawn into the Vietnam mess against its will. Indeed, the study left the distinct impression of presidential premeditation, deceit, short-sightedness, and failure. Four revelations out of the many in the project—revelations long assumed by those in power, but now supported by documented evidence—made the greatest impression in the public mind when the project appeared in the press. First, Truman had begun the commitment in Vietnam with his financial largess to the beleaguered French. Second, John Kennedy had looked the other way and could easily be seen as having given his tacit approval to the November 1963 coup that led to the assassination of President Ngo Dihn Diem. Third, a covert war had begun under Kennedy, had been intensified under Johnson, and had been hidden from the American people. And fourth, the decisions to commit U.S. ground troops and to begin the bombing of the North had been made long before either of the attacks that officially promoted them—at the Pleiku army barracks and in the Gulf of Tonkin. Clearly the findings of the project weakened the public's already melting respect for the office of the presidency. Yet in the long run the revelations of the Pentagon Papers stood to do Nixon no real harm, and it is extremely doubtful that they compromised national security in any significant way.

In a later interview with this author, Ehrlichman moaned that "we should have let them print the stuff on page one." Yet this was not the type of transgression that Richard Nixon could let go unchallenged. His belief in the ability of a president to conduct his foreign policy in secrecy transcended every other maxim of his administration. On June 14 Mitchell sent a telegram to the *Times* demanding that it stop publication. The next day, along with running a third installment of the study, the *Times* printed Mitchell's letter on page one. That afternoon the *Times* was temporarily enjoined by a U.S. district judge from further publication of the Pentagon Papers, pending a court hearing. By then, four other papers had begun to publish excerpts, and three of them were similarly enjoined from publication by the court. This was fuel for the demand by both sides that the case be sent immediately to the Supreme Court before receiving a lower court review.

On June 30, by a six-to-three margin, the Burger Court once again ruled against the Nixon administration. The decision in *New York Times v. U.S.* freed the press to continue publication of the report. In defense of the First Amendment right of the *Times* to publish, Justice Potter Stewart wrote in the majority opinion that "the only effective restraint upon executive policy and power . . . may lie in an informed and enlightened citizenry . . . it is perhaps here that a press that is alert, aware, and free most vitally serves the basic purpose of the First Amendment." In his last opinion, Justice Hugo Black concurred, noting that "only a free and unrestrained press can effectively oppose deception in government."[43] By and large, the public agreed with the court; in a Gallup Poll taken the week of the decision, 58 percent believed that the publication of the papers was "the right thing to do."

Seething with anger, Nixon centered his wrath on the leaker. Ellsberg represented everything that was abhorrent to Nixon and his White House; any thought that he might have acted out of a call from his conscience was lost upon a White House hell-bent on revenge. Ellsberg was indicted by a Los Angeles grand jury and charged with unauthorized possession of "documents and writings related to the national defense." The mission of the White House was clearly to see to his conviction. The story of how the White House "Plumbers" were formed to react to this crisis is told in a later chapter; it was clearly the step that sealed the fate of Nixon's administration.

The latter part of 1971 was spent in a whirlwind of negotiations that led to disclosure of the China and Soviet summits. Attempting to exploit what would be billed as the year of détente, Nixon announced in his State of the Union Address on January 25, 1972, that "Vietnam no longer distracts our attention from the fundamental issues of global diplomacy or diverts our energies from priorities at home."[44] This was, of course, nonsense. Despite progress with détente, the American people clearly believed that the war was still the nation's number one problem. The administration was justifiably concerned that continued failure to completely withdraw from Vietnam would cost it both the Soviet summit and the 1972 election.

Nixon had moved quickly to regain the initiative. In November 1971 he had withdrawn 45,000 troops; on January 6 he had announced his intention to recall an additional 70,000 troops over the next three months. That would lower the U.S. presence in Vietnam to 95,000, of whom some 6,000 were combat troops. One week earlier the Paris peace talks had once again come to life. To force the hand of the North Vietnamese at the peace table, Nixon took a calculated diplomatic gamble in his State of the Union message. He revealed the record of Kissinger's twelve secret sessions with Le Duc Tho. He also warned that "if the enemy wants peace, it will have to recognize the important difference between settlement and surrender."[45] For the fourth straight year, however, the North Vietnamese did not bow to Nixon's threats. On March 30 they launched their largest conventional attack of the war. The offensive was aimed at ARVN units in an obvious attempt to destroy Vietnamization before the presidential election. Even though the South Vietnamese outnumbered the Communists some five to one, the early going of the offensive was a North Vietnamese success. The only factor that saved much of ARVN was the U.S. air cover it received.

The option of renewing the bombing of the North, which Johnson had ended in October 1968, had been on the table since 1969. Nixon had consistently resisted such a move, preferring to give the war on the periphery a chance. Aside from this, the bombing of the capital city of Hanoi and the key port of Haiphong had always been off limits, a concession to the fear of inflicting civilian fatalities and the worldwide revulsion that such an attack would bring. Yet by the spring of 1972 Nixon believed that he had run out of diplomatic and covert options. On April 1, two days after the spring offensive began, Nixon ordered the bombing of North Vietnamese territory within twenty-five miles of the demilitarized zone as well as B-52 strikes on fuel depots around Hanoi. Stopping just short of ordering the renewal of bombing throughout the North, Nixon clearly hoped that this decision would scare the North Vietnamese back into serious negotiations. Once again, however, the North Vietnamese read Nixon's situation well. They continued their offensive and spurned the peace table.

With his threats ignored, Nixon was left only with options that were personally repulsive to him—do nothing or renew the bombing of the entire North. Rogers and Laird counseled against any further escalation because the domestic uproar would transcend that which followed the Cambodian incursion. Kissinger also argued against it, but because he believed that the Soviets would cancel the summit in protest. The threat was a real one; throughout the month of April, Brezhnev had, as Nixon later wrote, "bluntly asked me to refrain from further actions."[46] But the military, contending that the entire South Vietnamese defense perimeter was in jeopardy of being lost, pleaded for increased bombing. Taking a chance on ending détente, Nixon once again sided with his generals. On May 8 he announced to the American people that he had ordered the mining of Haiphong harbor as well as other North Vietnamese harbors, a naval blockade of North Vietnam, and a renewal of the bombing of the North.

Observations such as that made by historian George Herring, who noted that the decision "raised the stalemate to new forms of violence,"[47] speak the obvious but downplay the fact that unlike his previous military moves, the renewal of the bombing accomplished all that Nixon hoped for at the time. Code-named Operation LINEBACKER, the June 1972 bombing dropped some 112,000 tons of bombs on the North and wreaked havoc on both North Vietnamese property and morale. Thanks most probably to the fact that the public was détente dizzy after Nixon's China trip, the decision met with a lower than expected amount of domestic and congressional rage. On the political front it strengthened Nixon's credentials, particularly with the Middle, as a man who would try negotiation but not be afraid to resort to shows of strength—a key part of the positioning of the president for the upcoming election. In fact, opinion polls showed Nixon's approval rating at a whopping 60 percent. The move was also the spear that prodded the North Vietnamese back to the peace table, as Kissinger and Le Duc Tho rekindled their talks the following month. Most important, as Nixon had correctly guessed, the trade-hungry Soviets did not cancel the summit. In short, from the White House point of view, LINEBACKER was a success; indeed, it was Nixon's first true success of the war.

On July 19 Kissinger began what was to be the final stage of his secret negotiations with Le Duc Tho. The pace was maddening. Throughout the summer and early fall, both sides abandoned many of their most cherished demands. The United States formalized its decision to back off on its commitment to Thieu. Nixon also agreed to accept North Vietnamese military presence in South Vietnam after the cease-fire (to be confined to territory held at the time of the armistice— the so-called "leopard-spot" agreement). The North Vietnamese had dropped their insistence on a completely new government in Saigon and promised the release of all U.S. POWs, all in exchange for complete U.S. military withdrawal. Both sides agreed to the formation of a tripartite electoral commission, including the Vietcong, which would oversee the cease-fire.[48] On October 11 Kissinger and Tho worked out a draft treaty. All that remained was to obtain the agreement of the Thieu regime.

Thieu, however, reacted with disdain to an accord that had as one of its key planks the destruction of his government. To gain Thieu's compliance, Nixon ordered a flood of both financial and military aid to South Vietnam—Operation ENHANCE PLUS—which, among other benefits, provided Thieu with the fourth largest air force in the world.[49] Yet Thieu remained outraged by the draft agreement. On October 21 Kissinger flew to Saigon to coax Thieu into accepting the accord. It was not to be. A hysterical Thieu charged Kissinger with double-crossing South Vietnam in order to gain favor with the Soviets and Chinese. Kissinger cabled Nixon that Thieu's terms, which included having South Vietnam recognized as a sovereign state, "verge on insanity."[50] Kissinger counseled Nixon to go ahead with the treaty despite Thieu's resistance. On October 24 Thieu publicly denounced the treaty and called for the quick annihilation of all Communist influence in the South. Furious with this intransigence, Hanoi accused the Americans of trying to destroy the treaty and demanded that it be signed by October 31.

This, Thieu would never agree to do. More important, thanks to the newly strident tone in North Vietnam's demands, Nixon now refused to sign.

Despite all this, Kissinger shocked the world—and the White House—with his October 31 announcement to the press that "peace is at hand." Peace was no closer on October 31 than it had been four months earlier. Kissinger knew this; Nixon did as well, and the president had not authorized the statement. Designed to force some movement in the stalemate, Kissinger's announcement could eventually make the president look foolish as well as weaken his bargaining position by increasing Thieu's intransigence. This was no election ploy; Nixon was furious with his aide. The president quickly released what amounted to a retraction of Kissinger's pronouncement, saying that the draft treaty still contained "differences that must be resolved."[51] Within a little over twenty days the administration—and most of the blame must lie with Kissinger—had squandered away all that had been gained by the May decision to escalate. While the announcement made no appreciable impact upon the presidential election, there would be no peace in November.

Once freed of the election, Nixon became obsessed with ending the Vietnam War before the new year. The first step necessitated beating Thieu into submission. On November 9, only two days after the election, Nixon dispatched Alexander Haig, Kissinger's adjutant on the National Security Council, to visit the South Vietnamese leader. Haig delivered a letter from Nixon that bluntly stated the facts of life: "We will use our maximum efforts to effect these changes in the agreement. I wish to leave you under no illusion, however, that we can or will go beyond these changes in seeking to improve an agreement that we already consider to be excellent."[52] Five days later Nixon sweetened the pot by promising Thieu in a second letter that "you have my absolute assurance that if Hanoi fails to abide by the terms of this agreement it is my intention to take swift and severe retaliatory action."[53] Despite Nixon's best efforts, Thieu would not budge. The North Vietnamese, sensing that the time was ripe for an even better deal, were also intransigent. On November 20–21 Kissinger and Le Duc Tho held private conversations to work out the problems of the previous month. The talks lasted through to the middle of December, with little appreciable progress. After an impasse was reached on December 13, the talks were once again suspended.

It is clear from a reading of recently declassified material, as well as from the notes of participants in meetings at Camp David to consider the available military options, that Nixon had finally reached the end of his rope on Vietnam. Nixon told his chairman of the Joint Chiefs of Staff, Admiral Thomas Moorer: "I don't want any more of this crap about the fact that we couldn't hit this target or that one. This is your chance to use military power effectively to win the war, and if you don't, I'll consider you responsible."[54] Nixon's order to increase the bombing of the city of Hanoi was a direct result of the frustration of the previous month. The "Christmas bombing," (code-named LINE-BACKER TWO) began on December 18 and lasted, with a break on Christmas day, until December 28. It was the most devastating U.S. offensive of the war. Some 36,000 tons of bombs were dropped over the eleven-day period, from approximately 3,000 B-52 sorties. That exceeded the entire total of tonnage dropped between 1969 and 1971. The Christmas bombing left the North Vietnamese staggering. On December 26 they sent a signal about resuming negotiations, and two days later, Nixon suspended the bombing.

On January 8 Tho and Kissinger met again in Paris; Kissinger would later recall that when he saw the North Vietnamese delegation enter the room, "it was absolutely clear that they had come to settle."[55] The next day Tho withdrew demands that he had made since their last meeting. Three days later negotiations were concluded, and the treaty was signed in Paris on January 27, one week after Nixon's inauguration for a second term. It recognized the Thieu regime and the Provisional Revolutionary Government (PRG) as coequal administrators of South Vietnam and called for an exchange of POWs and an in-place cease-fire. Article Four of the treaty made it clear that "the United States will not continue its military involvement or intervene in the external affairs of South Vietnam"; Article Five stipulated that the United States agreed to withdraw all its forces. Kissinger called Nixon to tell him that the agreement had been accepted; it was the president's sixtieth birthday.

Nixon did not, however, intend for this to be the end. In direct violation of Articles Four and Five but in agreement with the spirit of his secret promise to Thieu, Nixon continued financial support of South Vietnam. He sent South Vietnam at least $813 million in military aid and planned an additional appropriation of $1 billion in aid to increase the size of Thieu's army. The administration also sent approximately 8,000 "civilian" advisers and technicians to South Vietnam. As the *Washington Post* observed on February 18, 1973, "Thieu is continuing to run South Vietnam almost as if the Paris cease-fire agreement had never been signed." Oblivious to the criticism, during a March meeting at San Clemente Nixon promised Thieu that the aid would continue.

Thieu used the aid to once again take the offensive in an attempt to capture as much territory as he could before the expected Communist overrun of the South. ARVN units attacked villages that were under PRG control, at a loss of some 6,000 men during the first months of the peace. U.S. military attention was concentrated on Cambodia, specifically the saving of Lon Nol's government from the onrushing Khmer Rouge, who had their new ally, Prince Sihanouk, closely in tow. In mid-March the United States reinstated bombing runs over Cambodia. From March to May 1973 U.S. B-52s dropped some 95,000 tons of bombs on Cambodia, three times as much as they had dropped in the whole of 1972. The public justifications were familiar enough: without the bombing, Lon Nol's government would fall to the Communists, and that must not happen. Congress had originally acquiesced to Nixon's initiatives, but as Watergate grew more sordid, it began to balk. On May 1 the House voted to cut off all funding for the bombing, compromising with the administration on June 30 and agreeing to let the bombing in Cambodia run until August 15.

It seemed as if the same play was appearing on the Southeast Asian stage, only with a smaller cast. But for now Nixon had proclaimed the war to be over. Two weeks after the cease-fire was signed, during a meeting of the Foreign Relations Committee, Hugh Scott jotted down in his notes what might well be an appropriate epitaph for the Nixon Vietnam experience: "Where ideology and national interest conflict, ideology gives way."[56]

CHAPTER FIVE

''Hard-Headed Détente''

NIXON'S understanding of the limits placed on America's power by the new world order is seen no more clearly than in two remarkable 1967 exchanges. In July Nixon was asked to deliver the main address at California's Bohemian Grove in honor of Herbert Hoover. The talk was off the record, but its message quickly filtered down through the ranks of the Republican faithful. Nixon urged that the United States encourage trade with the Soviet Union and that "diplomatically we should have discussions with the Soviet leaders at all levels to reduce the possibility of miscalculation and to explore the areas where bilateral agreements would reduce tensions."[1] Nixon expanded on this theme in an October 1967 article for the influential journal *Foreign Affairs*. Entitled "Asia after Vietnam," the article observed that "the role of the United States as a policeman is likely to be limited in the future" and "we simply cannot afford to leave China outside the family of nations." Clearly Nixon's views had developed beyond the Cold War rhetoric of previous administrations. His was now the voice of progressivism in foreign policy, as he advocated a more secure relationship with both of the major Communist powers.

Kissinger's explanation of détente as "an attempt to work out ground rules and agreed restraints in our relations"[2] certainly sums up the hopes of the administration. It would soon be clear that the administration viewed the normalization of relations with the People's Republic of China (PRC) as the primary goal of détente, one that would both support devolution from Vietnam and lead to a new relationship with Leonid Brezhnev's Soviet Union. Such a plan terrified conservatives, who had not yet come to grips with the fact that America's power had been limited in any way since 1945 and refused to accept the need for "dealing" with the Chinese or the Soviets.

Despite the fears of the Right, however, Nixon never intended—nor did he ever portray—détente to mean the development of an un-

checked trust of the two largest Communist powers. Nixon's most cogent explanation of his ideas on détente are found in his 1980 book,
The Real War. There he views the concept in typically realistic terms:

> We must understand that détente is not a love feast. It is an understanding
> between nations that have opposite purposes, but which share common
> interests, including the avoidance of a nuclear war. Such an understand-
> ing can work—that is, restrain aggression and deter war—only as long as
> the potential aggressor is made to recognize that neither aggression nor
> war will be profitable.[3]

In later writings Nixon would label this approach as "hard-headed détente." For him this was not a philosophical ideal; he had not accepted
détente because of the liberal ideal of acceptance of other nations as
equals. For Nixon détente was a diplomatic necessity based on a pragmatic reading of the post-Vietnam world order. If the United States
was going to continue to play a dominant role in the new multipolar
world, a working relationship had to be achieved with the two nations
that stood to gain the most if America faltered any further on the world
scene. It can be boiled down to a simple phrase—trite, but incredibly
close to the mark: "If you can't beat 'em, join 'em."

Conservatives had been judged in the 1950s by the strength of their
defense of Taiwan. The always vocal "China Lobby" charged that Harry
Truman had "lost" China to the Communist forces of Mao Tse-tung in
1949 by withdrawing U.S. aid from Chiang Kai-shek's Nationalist forces,
thus hastening their defeat at the hands of Mao and their eventual
banishment to their island prison. Despite the argument by many ex-
perts that the people of China *followed* Mao and the Truman administration simply accepted this fait accompli, criticism of Truman raged
during the last two years of his administration. This criticism had been
eagerly joined by an upwardly mobile Senator Richard Nixon.

The relationship between the PRC and the United States after Mao's
1949 victory was virtually nonexistent. Until the time of Nixon's dramatic approach, it was darkened by the Chinese role in the Korean
War and colored by Cold War rhetoric, which painted the PRC as one
more member of an ideologically solid Communist bloc. However, cracks
began to appear in this "bloc" as early as 1961, when the first dispute
between the Soviet Union and the PRC over their lengthy shared border was reportedly threatening their 1950 military alliance. Few in the
PRC hierarchy could miss the import of Soviet Premier Leonid Brezhnev's proclamation, following his August 1968 invasion of Czechoslovakia, that the Soviet Union had a duty to invade other "deficient"
Communist nations and bring them back into the world order.

Nixon, who saw the importance of the Sino-Soviet split faster than

most in his party, has since argued that the split was the most important political event of the time. The split certainly was a key factor in
Nixon's developing political ideology, as he began to consider the pos-
sibilities of playing the Soviets against the Chinese to benefit the United
States. The internal politics of the PRC in 1969 were perfect for such
an overture. The Cultural Revolution of 1966 had only momentarily
cemented Mao's grip on his country. As his revolution soured, which
it did almost immediately, Chinese politics began to fragment. Mao's
life was threatened by members of the very Red Guard that had promoted his revolution, and he was forced to move out of Peking. He
would return there only to meet with Nixon in 1972. As Mao withdrew, so did China, adopting an isolationist foreign policy that culmi-
nated in the 1967 decision to withdraw its ambassadors from every
nation in the world except Egypt. This policy only strengthened world
opinion against the Chinese. In addition, the Chinese economy was
beginning to show the strain of supporting North Vietnam, and by
decade's end the winds of change had begun to stir. PRC politics slowly
began to reflect a desire to moderate the country's isolationism and to
bring China into the light of modernism.

There was a fierce internal debate, however, as to how the PRC
should move forward. One group, led by Lin Piao, argued that China
should ally itself with the Soviet Union and combine forces to drive
the United States from the Far East. A second group, spearheaded by
Premier Chou En-lai, claimed that Washington had been so weakened
by its involvement in Vietnam that the PRC could safely begin to negotiate with the Americans. Chou further contended that such negotiations would serve the dual purpose of infuriating the Soviets, perhaps
to the point of making concessions to the PRC to keep it from joining
the American camp. Like Nixon, Chou was a broad, conceptual thinker
who was taking an internationalist stance in a nation whose people
had traditionally been isolationist. He was also pursuing a policy of
diplomatic linkage which in many ways resembled that of Nixon.

Next to disengagement from Vietnam, normalization of relations
with the PRC was the cornerstone of Nixon's foreign policy. As "Asia
after Vietnam" suggests, Nixon had decided upon the move several
years before he entered the White House. He had bounced the idea off
several of the world leaders between 1964 and 1967, most notably
Romania's Nicolae Ceausescu and France's Charles de Gaulle. Both
were strongly in favor of the move; de Gaulle went so far as to counsel
Nixon to recognize China before events forced him to do so.[4] Such a
venture was high-risk. If word of the overture leaked prematurely, Nixon
stood the chance of having the venture scuttled by protests from the
conservative wing of his own party. Secrecy was also necessary to keep
the Soviets from making a precipitate reaction to the overture. This
approach was supported by a 1968 transition team report from a num-

ber of academics who called for "secret, even deniable" talks with the PRC.[5]

Nixon was convinced, however, that the diplomatic advantages that would accrue from a normalization of relations with the PRC was worth any risk. Aside from Nixon's belief that an increased role for China was inevitable, there were two other reasons for him to seek détente with the PRC. The first involved his philosophy of diplomatic linkage. As he would write in his memoirs, Nixon "doubted that any true détente with the Soviets could be achieved until some kind of rapprochement could be reached with Communist China."[6] Any U.S. overture to China would be of sufficient concern to the Soviet Union that the Soviets would be more willing to negotiate with the United States. The second reason involved Nixon's hope that the PRC would be so grateful for U.S. advances that it would be willing to put pressure on its client state, North Vietnam, to return to the Paris peace table. The political windfall would also be well worth the effort, as Nixon could take credit for the biggest coup of the postwar era immediately before the 1972 election. For several reasons, then, Nixon's move toward normalization of relations with China was the most complicated clandestine adventure of the Nixon years.

As the administration began, outsiders could see little to warn them that a change was in the air. On February 18 the PRC canceled the resumption of its fifteen-year-old ambassadorial talks with the United States, scheduled to reconvene that month in Warsaw. When Nixon returned from his first European trip, he told the press that in Chinese relations he was "being very realistic, in view of Red China's breaking off the rather limited Warsaw talks that were planned, [and] I do not think that we should hold out any great optimism for any great breakthroughs in that direction at this time."[7] Throughout that spring's debate over the ABM, the administration contended that while the missile system was not solely intended to protect the United States from an attack by the Chinese, that would certainly be one benefit of its approval.

Despite administration rhetoric to the contrary, Nixon began his move toward China before his seat in the Oval Office was warm. On February 1, in one of the first directives to his National Security Council staff, Nixon ordered a preliminary exploration of the chances for a rapprochement with the PRC.[8] Events in Vietnam pushed this exploration along; the Soviets were growing closer to the North Vietnamese by the day, and the Chinese seemed to want to back away from their involvement. Tension between the PRC and the Soviets had also escalated, and by the summer of 1969 the world was learning of bloody clashes along the Sino-Soviet border. Kissinger later told an academic audience that by that summer Nixon was convinced the Soviets were preparing for an all-out attack on the PRC.[9]

During his trip to Europe and the Pacific late in the summer, Nixon began to test the diplomatic waters. His announcement of the Nixon Doctrine early in that trip made it clear to the world that the focus of U.S. foreign policy was changing, possibly leaving room for a PRC role in Far Eastern affairs after a U.S. withdrawal from Vietnam. Nixon also talked with Ceausescu and Pakistan's Yahya Khan, obtaining their cooperation in his venture. Both were dictatorial strongmen who had pummeled their people into submission. But both were close to Mao, and they agreed to use their offices as back channels to carry messages from the Americans to the Chinese. Soon after his return, Nixon instructed the U.S. ambassador to Poland to initiate talks with his Chinese counterpart in Warsaw. His moves paid off: that December the Chinese agreed to reinstate ambassadorial-level talks.

The major bone of contention throughout this early maneuvering was Taiwan. Chou had insisted during the Warsaw talks, and would continue to insist through Nixon's backchannels, that the one unshakable prerequisite for opening negotiations with the United States was that the Americans renounce their commitment to the Nationalist Chinese. The PRC saw itself as the one legal government of the Chinese people and the Nationalist regime on Taiwan as an outlaw. Chou publicly denounced any attempt by Nixon to come to a "two Chinas" policy. Yet this was not a barrier that Nixon, despite his bombast on the side of the China lobby while he was in Congress, intended to let stand in his way: the Taiwan relationship was expendable from the start.

All these plans almost went for naught. With the April announcement of the Cambodian incursion, both the Soviet Union and the PRC publicly denounced the United States and, more important, once again canceled the Warsaw talks. Through the latter half of 1970 Cambodia brought progress toward a China rapprochement to a screeching halt. Nixon, however, refused to abandon the initiative. On October 26 he welcomed Ceausescu to the United States. In his toast at the state dinner that evening, Nixon referred to Communist China as the People's Republic.[10] It was the first time that an American president had ever used that term, and the message it sent through the diplomatic world was unmistakable.

Once the election campaign was over, Nixon was free to unleash his final drive for the China opening. The offensive was twofold. The first tactic centered on an assault against Taiwan at the United Nations. In a secret memo to Kissinger dated November 22, Nixon asked his security adviser

on a very confidential basis . . . to have prepared in your staff—without any notice to people who might leak—a study of where we are to go with regard to admission of Red China to UN. It seems to me that the time is approaching sooner than we might think when we will not have the votes to block admission. The question we really need an answer to is how we can develop a position in which we can keep our commitments to Taiwan and yet will not be rolled by those who favor admission to Red China.[11]

Despite consistent denials to the press, policy had clearly changed. Taiwan's membership in the United Nations would now be sacrificed, and the United States would support the PRC's application for admission to that body. The second strategem was a frantic increase in communications sent through the diplomatic backchannel. On November 5, 1970, American journalist Edgar Snow met in Peking with Chou. During the week of November 12 Pakistan's Yahya Khan met with both Chou and Mao Tse-tung, also pressing the U.S. case. On December 18 Mao met personally with Snow. According to Seymour Hersh, it was during this meeting that the leader of the PRC made it clear that Nixon would be welcome to visit China.[12]

Nevertheless, détente would once again be threatened by devolution. During the January 1971 invasion of Laos, the press ran stories speculating that the PRC was about to intervene, as it had done during the Korean War. Ironically, the invasion's complete failure and the few U.S. ground troops utilized saved the Nixon trip to China by making a strong Chinese protest unnecessary. In fact, quite the opposite reaction occurred. In early March Chou visited Hanoi, where he refused to make a commitment to intervene if the United States decided to invade North Vietnam on the ground.[13] That the North Vietnamese ignored the threat and walked out of their talks with Kissinger (China, too, was learning its limits on the world stage) did not sour the PRC's budding relations with the Americans. An April invitation for a U.S. ping-pong team to play in China and relaxation by the United States of its twenty-one-year-old trade embargo with the PRC were the first public signs of the new relationship, and speculation regarding a summit ran rampant. The actual planning of the trip needed to be done before the press stole Nixon's surprise.

Despite the drama of Henry Kissinger's secret visit to China the week before the announcement of the summit, Kissinger did little haggling with Chou. The lengthy chapter in his memoirs treating the trip as a triumph of his negotiating skills is correctly dismissed by Nixon as "fascinating."[14] Kissinger's task was to communicate Nixon's concession on Taiwan and to confirm the details of a meeting that had already been agreed upon by all parties. Nevertheless, when the White House announced on July 15 that Nixon would visit the PRC sometime before May 1972, the press gave Kissinger the lion's share of the credit. His image had become that of Nixon's indispensable superman. He was now depicted on magazine covers as "Henry the K" and "SuperKraut." Clearly Kissinger's influence had surpassed that of the secretary of state—Rogers was not told about Kissinger's trip until after he was in the air (true to form, Nixon couldn't break the news; as noted earlier, he left that job to Haldeman). Yet this says little, as Rogers was always a secondary player in foreign policy. Nixon clearly felt that he needed Kissinger's diplomatic skills to make détente work. Nevertheless, he was visibly angered by the vast amount of press accorded to Kissinger, much of which was generated by Kissinger's own prodigious public relations machinery and his constant leaks to friendly reporters. Press reports and memoirs to the contrary, the China opening simply was not Kissinger's accomplishment. It was Nixon's.

The announcement of the trip was not welcome news for all of America's allies. Japan felt particularly betrayed. A November 1969 meeting between Prime Minister Eisaku Sato and Nixon had produced a communiqué promising that the United States would uphold its treaty commitments in the Pacific. The Japanese now believed that Nixon was consorting with the enemy, an act of treachery that would be compounded only one month later by his closing of the international gold window. Relations with India were also hurt; in return for Yahya Khan's acting as one of Nixon's back-channel negotiators with Chou, Nixon threw his administration's support behind the brutal Khan regime during its December 1971 war with India. The shift was decried as an abandonment of a treatied ally and a "tilt" toward Pakistan; it was but one further step in the policy of linkage to achieve détente.

At home Nixon instantly lost the support of conservatives whose backing of Taiwan and opposition to the abandonment of Chiang Kai-shek to the Communists had been a backbone of ideology since 1949.* Coupled with Nixon's acceptance of wage and price controls, the China move convinced conservatives that Nixon was not one of them. However, their cries of dissent were largely lost in the screams of approval that came from Middle America. Even the Democrats in Congress were forced to grumble their approval. For the White House, a particularly satisfying message of congratulations came from Ted Kennedy; with some glee, Nixon aide Chuck Colson wrote that "it must have pained him to do it."[15] Through the last months of 1971 Nixon's diplomatic juggling act was the world's hottest story.

Unlike the China initiative, summitry with the Soviets was nothing new. Eisenhower, Kennedy, and Johnson had all met with their Soviet counterparts. Eisenhower and Kennedy had traveled to Vienna for their summits, and in 1965 Alexei Kosygin had visited Johnson in the United States. For the most part these meetings had been staged affairs, with little of substance to show for the effort. Nixon certainly understood the political value of such a sideshow in 1972, particularly if it in-

---

*On October 25, 1971, the United Nations, with the support of the United States, voted to expel Taiwan and admit the PRC.

volved the first trip by an American president to the Soviet Union. As former NSC staffer Roger Morris has written, "if China was a wholly novel and only potentially winning issue, summitry with the Russians was sure-fire presidential politics."[16] However, Nixon approached the Soviets and their general secretary, Leonid Brezhnev, with a whole new agenda in mind.

Only weeks before his death in 1963, Kennedy had made embryonic moves toward de-escalating the Cold War, using the scare of the Cuban missile crisis to get a nuclear test ban treaty. Johnson, even as he was planning to escalate the war in Vietnam, hoped to continue this diplomatic warming. However, the tension between the United States and the Soviet Union was not assuaged under Johnson; indeed, it was worsened. Johnson had originally hoped that the brief thaw which followed the test ban treaty would bring about a situation in which he could ask the Soviets to put pressure on the North Vietnamese to come to the peace table. There were several reasons for this belief, not the least of which was that U.S. presidents from Truman to Ford had consistently overstated the extent to which the Soviets had control over the North Vietnamese. For their part, the Soviets had no intention of solving this problem for the United States. They had used the period from 1963 to 1967 to come close to reaching a military parity with the United States; Kosygin was all too pleased to keep U.S. troops tied up during this period of Soviet military growth.

Johnson was also unsuccessful in extending Kennedy's initiative in nuclear control. In June 1967, only two weeks after the world had been staggered by the Six-Day War in the Middle East, Johnson and Kosygin were unable to conclude an agreement limiting ABMs during a summit held at New Jersey's Glassboro State College. They did sign an agreement to stop the proliferation of nuclear weapons (an agreement not joined by the PRC) but not their development. As a result, the United States was able to continue both the development and testing of ABMs and MIRVs. Throughout 1968, events transpired at a frenzied pace—the brutal repression of the 1968 "Prague Spring" in Czechoslovakia, the Brezhnev Doctrine that followed, and the increased brutality of the Soviet state, with its escalated repression of both intellectuals and Jews. By the time Nixon took office, relations between the two nations were worse than they had been since 1962.

For both the Republican Right and Middle America, Nixon was the perfect man to step into this breach. The mellowing of Nixon during the 1968 campaign had done nothing to fundamentally change his image in the minds of the public as America's number one Soviet baiter; memories of the 1959 kitchen debate with Khrushchev were fresh. Yet, as noted earlier, Nixon was less of an ideologue and more of a pragmatist on this issue. Unencumbered by constricting convictions, Nixon saw U.S.-Soviet relations through the same realistic prism with which he looked at China. For him the key development was the Sino-Soviet split, which he believed would eventually force the Soviets to look elsewhere for the trade that their crumbling economy so badly needed. As he had done with China, Nixon concluded that the Soviets needed détente with the Americans as much as Nixon wanted détente with the Soviets.

The Soviets, surprised to sense a change of both tone and rhetoric under Nixon, were nevertheless quick to respond. They called early for talks to limit the development of strategic arms (SALT). In fact, Seymour Hersh reported that as early as Nixon's inauguration day the Soviet Foreign Ministry announced that "when the Nixon administration is ready to sit down at the negotiating table, we are ready to do so, too." [17] On the surface, Nixon looked ready to accommodate the Soviets. He reversed his earlier opposition to the nonproliferation treaty, an agreement to halt the spread of nuclear weapons that had been stalled in the Senate since the Czechoslovakian invasion. With Nixon's support, the treaty was approved by the Senate on March 13, 1969.

Nixon, however, wanted much more than another test-ban treaty. He made this clear during his very first press conference:

> What I want to do is to see to it that we have strategic arms talks in a way and at a time that will promote, if possible, progress on outstanding political problems at the same time—for example, on the problem of the Mideast and on other outstanding problems in which the United States and the Soviet Union acting together can serve the cause of peace.[18]

The "outstanding problem" to which Nixon referred was Vietnam. What he wanted was the same thing that Johnson had wanted: to tie the beginning of any SALT talks to Soviet willingness to put pressure on the North Vietnamese. Yet like Johnson, Nixon could not make it work. In April 1969 Cyrus Vance, then deputy chief of the Paris peace talks delegation, went to Moscow to propose that any start of SALT talks be predicated on Soviet willingness to sit on the North Vietnamese. Brezhnev scuttled the initiative by simply ignoring Vance.[19] During a series of secret White House meetings with Kissinger in early 1969, Ambassador Anatoly Dobrynin begged Kissinger to believe that Moscow did not have the pull to pressure North Vietnam into negotiations.[20] Nixon never stopped asking the Soviets to sit on the North Vietnamese, even during the May 1972 summit, but he was always rebuffed. Nixon quickly concluded that if he waited for the desired breakthrough on Vietnam, he might easily miss the boat on détente. The Soviets were informed in June 1969 that the Americans were ready to begin the SALT talks; the opening session was set for that November.

Nixon was convinced that a key to getting an acceptable SALT treaty lay in his having the ABM to bargain with. Even though his own intelligence told him that the ABM probably wouldn't work, Nixon was willing to fight for the system so that he could present the Soviets with a solid chit to begin the haggling. Despite Nixon's strong denial in his memoirs,* he was clearly ready to bargain away part of his ABMs, and, as will be seen, he did so. He was not, however, willing to give up U.S. superiority in offensive weaponry, particularly MIRVs. On that point the Soviets were just as stubborn. They too would not consider limits on their own offensive weaponry unless the United States agreed to reduce its fighter-bomber aircraft, a concession that was not forthcoming.

Throughout the spring of 1970, then, the SALT talks stalled, and the administration did little to speed their progress. As the negotiations dragged on and as the administration faced crises of more immediate import, Nixon lost some of his interest in SALT. He grew bored with the minutiae of technical talk that accompanied the seemingly endless briefings on the issue. The deadlock, however, could not be tolerated much longer. The national reaction to the Cambodian incursion made it clear to the administration that a SALT agreement would be a major weapon in its holster as it geared up for both the 1970 and the 1972 campaigns. It was also faced with a renewed congressional threat to the life of the ABM program. New studies had indeed shown that the system was untrustworthy, and in several key votes Congress had come within an eyelash of cutting off all funding for the project. If Nixon did not show substantial gains in the congressional elections, his staff predicted, the ABM would be terminated.

Adding to the concern was a crisis that threatened to destroy the SALT talks altogether. On September 15, 1970, in an eerie jolt from the past, a U-2 reconnaissance mission over Cuba revealed that troop barracks and other facilities had been constructed recently near the southern naval base of Cienfuegos. Along with this information came evidence suggesting that the Soviets were constructing strategic air missile (SAM) batteries at the same spot. If this was true, it was in direct violation of the 1962 agreement between the Soviets and the Americans that had ended the Cuban missile crisis. Talks with Ambassador Dobrynin brought official assurances that no offensive military installation was under construction in Cuba, and the crisis passed. As has been charged of Kennedy during the Cuban missile crisis, several observers have publicly and privately accused Kissinger of deliberately exaggerating the crisis in Cuba during the congressional election campaign, simply to prove to Nixon that he could handle a crisis.[21] Never-

---

*Nixon: "Stated in its simplest form, the Soviets wanted to conclude an agreement dealing only with the limitation of defensive ABM systems. We, however, wanted to conclude a comprehensive agreement covering not only defensive systems like the ABM's, but also offensive weapons like . . . ICBM's and . . . MIRV's" (*Memoirs*, p. 523).

theless, Cienfuegos unquestionably left the pall of nuclear confrontation hanging over the White House and sparked renewed interest in a SALT treaty.

As soon as the congressional elections were over, Nixon moved quickly to end the stalemate over SALT. As was the administration's style, Nixon moved not through the talks in Helsinki* but rather through a diplomatic back channel. In December 1970 Kissinger began a series of meetings with Dobrynin. According to Hersh, who uncovered the top-secret negotiations, linkage was once again the key to success: "Nixon . . . accomplished his backchannel SALT breakthrough only after assuring Moscow that he would end the grain embargo and once again sell American wheat to the Soviet Union."[22] Soviet acquiescence to this proposal resulted in the startling announcement on May 20, 1971, of a "major breakthrough" on SALT. The Soviets agreed to discuss "certain measures" regarding the limitation of defensive weaponry. While both sides agreed to an interim freeze on ICBM launchers, the Soviets acknowledged that U.S. aircraft already in Europe would be excluded from consideration and the Americans conceded a Soviet demand to exclude submarine-launched ballistic missiles as well as Soviet land-based missile systems from the conversations. The talks would now center solely on ABMs.

In his speed to get a SALT agreement in time for a preelection summit and before the Democratic Congress finally killed the ABM, Nixon gave away infinitely more than he got. The Republican Right was enraged at the announcement of the "major breakthrough," observing that Nixon had limited ABMs before even beginning to negotiate a bilateral agreement to reduce offensive weapons. The Right was also furious over American acquiescence in keeping Soviet MIRVs completely out of the discussions. Nixon was clearly heading toward a SALT agreement that would ignore the fact that the Soviets had surpassed the United States in offensive capability. But in the heady climate of détente, such details took a back seat to what Nixon liked to call "the big picture." In that picture, China loomed large.

Mao Tse-tung seems to have eerily predicted the Nixon visit to China in a 1956 poem:[23]

> Great plans are being made.
> A bridge will fly to the north and south,
> A deep chasm becomes a thoroughfare.
> The mountain goddess, if she is still there,
> Will be startled to find her world so changed.

---

*The president had run out of patience with Gerard Smith, his chief arms negotiator, who was publicly calling for an end to the development of MIRVs.

The planning of the China trip showed the Nixon staff system at its finest. Everything from the building of satellite dishes so that the American public could follow the drama live to meticulous arrangements for photo opportunities at sites such as the Great Wall were planned to the most minute detail. Americans watched with almost reverential awe as Nixon strode jauntily from Air Force One on February 21 to meet Chou En-lai with a handshake that came to represent détente. Nixon's visit with Mao Tse-tung, which he did not learn had actually been granted until he was in the air to China,[24] was the crowning moment of the trip. It caused *Time* to gush—even before the summit had actually taken place—that "never, perhaps, have two men who so dramatically epitomized the conflicting forces of modern history sat as equals at one negotiating table."[25]

There was substance to accompany the pomp. On February 27 Nixon and Chou released the Shanghai communiqué, a statement of where the new Sino-American relationship stood. The PRC reaffirmed its support of the North Koreans, as the United States did of the South Koreans. Both nations promised that they would not try to "seek hegemony in the Asia Pacific region." The problem of Taiwan was termed an "internal" one that the two Chinas had to work out on their own. However, the United States clearly showed which side it was on in this supposedly internal dispute when it promised to withdraw its troops from Nationalist China by an unspecified date.

Nixon would claim in 1983 that along with the Sino-Soviet split, "the US-China rapprochement in 1972 [was] the most significant geopolitical event of the post–World War II era."[26] This author would not dispute that conclusion. However, Nixon also reaped huge political rewards from the trip. Despite outcries from conservatives, support in Middle America for the move was so overwhelming that it surprised even Louis Harris, pollster and unabashed Nixon supporter. Soon after the China trip, Harris called Chuck Colson to tell him that the big surprise was not that people were reacting favorably to the "substance of the trip, but rather to the way that [Nixon] handled himself personally." Harris went on to explain what the American people had seen:

This could be the beginning of something really tremendous. I think the president has always had this problem of breaking through on the personal dimension. People are fascinated looking at China, looking at Chou En Lai and looking at the president meeting with him and the idea of peace, the possibility of at least no war; it's a very appealing one. But I suspect that over and above and beyond all that is the sense of "My God, here is this man who is our president our leader and look at how well he handles himself." And that's the kind of thing which—odd as it may seem for all the exposure he has received before—that may now be able to stick as an image of the president."[27]

From the vantage point of the White House staff, then, the most important aspect of the China trip was that it had formed the basis of a positive image for their man just in time for the reelection campaign—Nixon the diplomat.

The Moscow summit, which would follow the China trip by only three months, reinforced this image. If the handshake with Chou was the symbol of détente, SALT I, the agreement which was signed by Nixon and Brezhnev in May 1972, represented the substance. The treaty contained two parts: the ABM treaty, an agreement to limit to two the number of ABM sites that each side would construct, one at an ICBM site and one at its capital,* and the ICBM agreement, a five-year interim compact to stop building ICBM launchers and accept limits on submarine-launched ballistic missiles. As had been forecast by the May 20, 1971, "major breakthrough" announcement, SALT I did not call for a reduction of either side's offensive capabilities. As argued above, it was never meant to. The ICBM agreement clearly favored the Soviets. This area of their offensive arsenal was allowed to remain not only intact but larger than that of the United States. However, in areas not covered by the agreement, most notably MIRVs, the United States retained its huge advantage.†

When all was said and done, neither side had conceded anything of importance. Nixon wanted both MIRVs and a summit; Brezhnev wanted both to maintain Soviet superiority in land-based ICBMs and a summit. Both got what they wanted. In effect, SALT I was an agreement to negotiate further. That an agreement had been reached meant that détente had occurred. The agreements reached with the Chinese earlier that year were of much greater world import. SALT had no more stopped the arms race than détente had ended the Cold War. Both problems, however, had been stalled.

Nixon's eight-day visit to Moscow to sign the SALT treaty was accompanied by as great a media blitz as the Peking trip had received. Over one hundred reporters followed Nixon on his second trip into a land heretofore unvisited by an American president. Beginning on May 22 Nixon endured eight days of the handshakes, toasts, ballets, and diplomatic ceremonies that once again enthralled a nation. Yet there was essence to the meeting as well. Along with SALT, the two nations signed agreements for a joint Soviet-American space effort, for pooled research in the medical and environmental fields, and for a joint commission to continue discussions on a future deal to sell American grain to the Soviets. The pace was even more frenetic than it had been in

*In 1974 the treaty was amended to limit the number of sites to one, and in 1975 the United States gave up that one site. This was testimony to what Congress, the Defense Department, and the CIA all knew—the ABM didn't work.

†According to one published source, at the time of the signing of SALT I the Soviets held a lead of 1,618 to 1,054 in land-based ICBMs. In MIRVs the United States led, 5,700 to 2,500.

China. A Mike Peters cartoon showed Nixon and Brezhnev dazedly signing something in front of them as one aide whispered to another, "I think they need a rest . . . they just signed their napkins." On his final night in the Soviet Union, Nixon made a historic television address to the Soviet people; on the same evening a team of burglars under the command of Gordon Liddy and E. Howard Hunt successfully broke into the offices of the Democratic National Committee at Washington's Watergate complex.

When he returned from the Soviet Union, Nixon's image as a diplomat was secure. Nixon champion Hugh Sidey, Washington bureau chief for *Time*, gave the president his stamp of approval:

> Nixon moved through this landscape seemingly a lonely man, clinging to his American habits—dry cereal, cottage cheese, no vodka, only modest sips of champagne—and his singleness of purpose. There was something very admirable about the man in these circumstances, determined to bring something home, to make a supreme effort to get a little more order into the world.[28]

Nixon had indeed brought a new order into U.S. relations with China and the Soviet Union. However, while Cold War America had centered its attention upon its conflict with worldwide communism, other areas of the world had grown in power and influence. The situation in the Middle East festered like an open sore, waiting to infect and destroy détente. That it almost did just that is clear testimony to the limits that the United States now felt upon its role as a world leader.

The United States had been the first nation to formally acknowledge the creation of the state of Israel in 1948. Yet from that moment on, U.S. policy toward Israel revolved less around the needs of the Israelis than it did around three other factors—the desire to check Soviet growth in the Middle East, a growing dependence on Arab oil, and a growing inability of both the Soviet Union and the United States to control their client states in the region. In 1967 the Soviets harassed Egypt, their oldest ally in the area, into demanding the removal of the United Nations peacekeeping force that stood between itself and Israel. Once the United Nations took out its force, the Soviets recanted and urged Egyptian strongman Gamal Abdel Nasser to be more careful. Nasser ignored the advice, closing off Israel's access to the Gulf of Aqaba, its southern entry to the Red Sea.

The United States was as incapable as the Soviets of keeping its client in line. On June 5, 1967, the Israeli Air Force initiated a surprise attack over the Mediterranean, destroying most of the air forces of Egypt, Jordan, Syria, and Iraq on the ground. By agreement between Kosygin and Johnson, neither superpower intervened in what would become known as the Six-Day War. This did not, however, stop Nasser from claiming that the United States had been the force behind the Israeli attack. As a result, several Arab nations, including Egypt, broke off relations with the United States and initiated a brief shutoff of oil exports to it and Great Britain. These measures were largely ineffectual against the Western nations and did little to blunt the overwhelming nature of the Israeli victory. When a cease-fire was finally signed, Israel occupied territory in Egypt (the entirety of the Sinai Peninsula and the Gaza Strip), Syria (the Golan Heights), and Jordan (the city of Jerusalem and the West Bank of the Jordan River). Adding to the tension was the fact that the West Bank and the Gaza Strip were full of refugee settlements, most of them Palestinian, from the 1948 and 1956 Arab-Israeli wars. The refugees were quickly influenced by a growing radical movement, the Fedayeen, led by Yasir Arafat of the Palestine Liberation Organization. Arafat demanded a formal homeland for the refugees, and his organization sponsored terrorist attacks into Israel. By 1970 the PLO was leading a virtually autonomous existence within Jordanian borders.

The Six-Day War initiated a seemingly interminable stalemate in the region. The Egyptians had been humiliated, and through the rest of 1967 and 1968 they slowly backed off their sanctions against the West. The Israelis, however, became more strident with each day that they held onto their conquered territories. Not even a mutual agreement on the part of both Israel and Egypt to a United Nations resolution (Security Council Resolution 242) eased the tension. The resolution called for a Palestinian homeland, Israeli withdrawal from the occupied territories, and Egypt's acceptance of Israel's right to exist. However, each side insisted that its part of the bargain was contingent on first seeing the other side initiate its part of the bargain—which, of course, got both sides nowhere. In early 1969 Nasser once again lit the Middle Eastern fuse. Using Soviet arms, he began a series of commando raids and artillery barrages of Israeli fortifications along the Suez Canal. Nasser called it a "war of attrition"; Golda Meir, who was months away from becoming Israel's prime minister, wryly noted in her memoirs that "for us, the War of Attrition was a real war."[29] By July the Israelis were responding by flying raids of their own across the Sinai and into Egypt.

Despite this new spate of violence, the Middle East was clearly a subsidiary issue for the new Nixon administration; China and Vietnam topped the list. Evidence of this was that Nixon assigned the trouble spot not to Kissinger but to Secretary of State William Rogers. Rogers had been a Nixon confidant since 1947. He had counseled Nixon to pursue the Alger Hiss inquiry, and he had helped write the Checkers defense. When Eisenhower suffered his heart attack, Nixon turned to Rogers, then deputy attorney general, for advice (in fact, Nixon moved into Rogers's home for the duration of the crisis). Rogers served as a policy adviser during the 1960 campaign, returning to his law practice following the election. While he had not been a member of the Nixon team in 1968, Rogers was completely trustworthy and knew Nixon's mind-set as well as anyone. He also had absolutely no background as a diplomat. Yet Nixon felt that his old friend was enough of a politician and bureaucrat to work well in a system where foreign policy would not be initiated at State but at the White House. And, as several observers have pointed out, Rogers knew full well what he was getting into and accepted Nixon's view that the role of a secretary of state in the making of foreign policy was a purely advisory one. Giving Rogers the Middle East portfolio was a clear statement to insiders that Nixon was not planning to give the region his personal attention.

Through the first months of 1969 Rogers and Joseph Sisco, the State Department's expert on the Middle East, struggled to develop an approach that would both defuse the situation and be acceptable to Nixon. They operated on the basic premise that the problem with U.S. policy toward the Middle East was that the United States had been patient with Israel long past the point of reason. The first "Rogers Plan" came close to abandoning Israel altogether in exchange for stability in the region. The plan was essentially a rehash of the demands made in Security Council Resolution 242; Rogers suggested that the United States work with the Soviet Union to ensure that all sides live up to the terms of the resolution: that Israel withdraw to its pre–Six Day War boundaries and that Egypt accept Israel's right to exist.

As Jimmy Carter would later write in his memoirs, "It is easy to understand why [the Rogers Plan] was not named the Nixon Plan, since it was rejected by all the negotiating parties almost as soon as it was revealed."[30] The Soviets would have been foolish to accept it; to limit Egypt's actions would be to limit their own options in the area, and they quickly rejected the plan in the diplomatic back channel. The Israelis, not surprisingly, also opposed the plan. There was bitterness in Israel for what Meir later called "any solution for the Middle East that would be imposed upon us by others." Rejecting what became derisively known as the "big power approach," Meir noted her "strong opposition to Mr. Rogers' idea that the Russians, the Americans, the French, and the British should sit down comfortably somewhere and work out a 'feasible' compromise."[31]

Most important, however, was the fact that Nixon did not support the plan. The proposition of having to deal with the intransigence of the Israelis made him plainly nervous. He was also worried about their taking further military action, much as they had done in July 1967. Hersh reports that Len Garment, a former Nixon law partner and a Jew, was sent to Meir to reassure her that the plan did not have the president's full backing.[32] The president himself made this clear during a speech to the Jewish Leadership Conference on January 25, 1970, when he promised the delegates that "the United States stands by her friends. Israel is one of its friends."[33] Rogers had been publicly undercut.

With U.S. diplomacy in the Middle East in a state of chaos, the Soviets once again began to move into the area. In February and March 1970 Soviet crews and hardware arrived in Egypt to help repulse the Israeli raids across the Sinai. Kissinger privately pleaded with the president for a tough response, but Nixon, only days away from committing ground troops in Cambodia, was not about to risk a second front in Egypt. Nor would he jeopardize his plans for a summit with Brezhnev. Instead he issued a warning to the Soviets about the consequences of their actions during a March 21 press conference, then turned the policy back over to Rogers.

This time Rogers concentrated upon a more limited objective—the end of the war of attrition. Announced on June 25, "Rogers Plan II" called for a ninety-day cease-fire and internationally monitored talks to begin after the cease-fire was in place. All parties had reason to accept this proposal. Having been badly bloodied by the intense public reaction against his Cambodian strategy, Nixon was quick to sign onto a plan that would allow him to claim a diplomatic victory somewhere. The Soviets had also become sick of the situation. On June 30 Brezhnev told Nasser that the Soviets were gravely concerned about the war of attrition and its potential for provoking an Israeli response.[34] This effective withdrawal of support left the Egyptians with no choice but to accept Rogers's plan, which they did on July 23. Their acceptance of the cease-fire led to a split between Egypt and much of the rest of the Arab world, including Arafat's PLO, which strongly opposed the plan.

For their part the Israelis were sharply divided over the new plan. Yitzak Rabin, Israeli ambassador to the United States, led the opposition, which argued that to accept the plan meant to accept less than a full victory over the enemy. Ultimately, however, Nixon bribed Israel into accepting the plan. In late July he wrote Meir to assure her that he would sell her nation the Phantom and Skyhawk jets that she had asked him for during her September 1969 visit to Washington. Nixon also promised that there need be no withdrawal of Israeli troops from the occupied territories until an acceptable peace treaty had been negotiated.[35] On July 31 the Israelis accepted the terms of the cease-fire, which went into effect on August 7.

Almost immediately the Egyptians violated the cease-fire by moving SAM missiles into the neutral zone with the help of the Soviets. The White House also received Central Intelligence Agency reports of movement by Syrian tanks, with their Soviet advisers, toward the Jordanian border. Nixon, however, was unwilling to push Egypt too far.

A combination of forces—the domestic reaction against Cambodia, a fear that the Soviets might retaliate against any U.S. military action, and the upcoming congressional elections—dictated the caution. He decided to increase arms shipments to the Israelis and file mild protests with both the Soviets and the Egyptians. For the moment there would be no attempt to force the Egyptians to keep Rogers's peace treaty. Besides, attention soon shifted away from the Rogers cease-fire and onto the volatile situation in Jordan, where the Nixon administration faced the very real possibility of the outbreak of World War III.

The PLO had never supported the Rogers Plan, and despite the cease-fire it had continued to use its foothold in Jordan as a springboard for terrorist raids into Israel. Jordan's King Hussein, a moderate whose support for U.S. initiatives had led to reports that he was receiving CIA aid for his army, made it known that he did not approve of the PLO's actions. For its part, neighboring Syria was upset that Hussein would not allow Palestinian raids into Israel from Jordan, and by the summer of 1970, under the leadership of General Hafez al-Assad, it began to arm troops near the Jordanian border to take advantage of the situation. As the PLO and Syria grew stronger and more organized, the prospect of civil war in Jordan loomed greater with each passing day.

The crisis peaked on September 6, 1970, when the Popular Front for the Liberation of Palestine, a radical arm of the PLO, hijacked three airliners, one Swiss and two American. A seventy-two-hour deadline for the release of all PLO terrorists in Swiss, German, and British jails was issued. Seeing not only the necessity of aiding the hostages but also the opportunity to strike at the Fedayeen and show his support for Hussein, Nixon acted over Rogers's objections and ordered the immediate bombing of PLO encampments in Jordan. He also ordered the movement of the U.S. Sixth Fleet to the coast of Lebanon and placed several army units in Europe on alert. These actions, along with the intervention of both the Soviets and the Israelis, prompted the terrorists to release their hostages on September 29, but not before destroying all three planes on the ground.

The PLO hijacking was the straw that broke Hussein's back. On September 15, despite the urging of both the Soviet Union and the United States and with the hostages still in terrorist hands, Hussein turned his army loose on the PLO enclaves in Amman. Nixon's response was swift: two aircraft carrier task forces were moved to the Mediterranean and a third was moved to the coast of Lebanon. Three army battalions in Europe, fighter planes in Turkey, and the Army's 82d Airborne Division at Fort Bragg, North Carolina, were placed on full alert. Hussein's army dealt well with the PLO, and in a week the PLO had been temporarily neutralized as a threat to the Hussein regime.

The Syrians used the unrest in Jordan to advance their own agenda.

On September 19 and 20, 250 Syrian tanks crossed the Jordanian border near the Golan Heights. Immediately after news of the invasion was received, Nixon told Sisco to contact Yuri Vorontsov, the minister counselor of the Soviet Embassy, and make it clear that if the Syrians were not called off, Nixon "could not predict what actions the U.S. might take."[36] The next day Nixon himself met with Israeli Ambassador Rabin and promised him that if the Syrians continued their advance or joined forces with the PLO, the United States would support any retaliatory action taken by Israel.[37] It was clear that Nixon viewed the Syrian invasion as a crisis between the United States and the Soviet Union. It is just as clear that he was prepared for war.

That war did not come was less a result of reasoned negotiation among the superpowers than of the unexpected success of Hussein's counterattack. By September 25 the Jordanian Air Force had won a number of victories, and the Syrians were withdrawing to their own borders. Casualty estimates range from 5,000 to 20,000 dead on both sides. Nevertheless, both Nixon and the Israelis had backed up their friendship for Hussein, made clear by the fact that the king was entertained at the White House during the first week of December—the second state visit to the United States for Hussein in the space of eighteen months. The region, however, was left as volatile as before, virtually ignored by the administration as détente and devolution took precedence over all other policies.

Some ten months later Anwar Sadat, who had become president of Egypt after the death of Nasser in late 1971, carried out his own brand of devolution. On July 18, 1972, he demanded the withdrawal of all Soviet military personnel from Egypt, numbering some 20,000, within a week's time. There were many reasons for Sadat's taking such a bold and risky step. Since succeeding Nasser he had become disillusioned by the inability of the Soviets to help Egypt rid the Middle East of Israel. Yet he was also concerned that the Soviets, who had opened new channels to the Americans, would not support an Egyptian military attempt to disengage Israel from the territories it had gained in the 1967 war. It is also likely that Sadat, a proud man and a fiery nationalist, had had enough of having his people treated as second-class citizens in their own country by the Soviets. Kissinger believed that Sadat saw the move as an opportunity to increase Egypt's stature in the world and perhaps to allow him to court the Americans in the process.[38]

The Soviets did not disregard these warning signs. When, a year later, the Egyptians and Syrians came to them with a plan for an attack on the Israelis, the Soviets, masking their bitterness at being expelled from Egypt, agreed to sell them the necessary armaments. Both CIA and Israeli intelligence estimates concurred, however, that the Egyptians could not win a war. Therefore, went the argument, the Egyptians would not be foolish enough to attack. Caught up in the throes of Watergate, Nixon continued to ignore a situation that was ready to escalate into war.

The Egyptians and Syrians struck at approximately 8:00 A.M. on October 6, 1973. It was Yom Kippur, the day of atonement—the most holy of the Jewish holidays. Within one hour of the initial assault, Egyptian forces were crossing the Suez Canal. Beyond that point, however, the extended front took its toll on the invaders. Although they advanced several miles into the Sinai Peninsula, they could not reach the Sinai passes. The Syrians drove the Israelis off the Golan Heights, but they too stalled.

Ignoring the advice of Defense Minister Moshe Dayan, who wanted to fall back, Meir ordered a counterattack on the Egyptian front. Within three days the Israelis had pushed the Egyptians to the 1967 border and were poising for more. An Israeli general, asked by reporters if he would stop at the 1967 borders, answered cryptically, "I have to remind you that the cease-fire lines are not marked in the terrain." On October 8 the *Jerusalem Post* trumpeted that "Israel will not cease fighting until all invading enemy forces have been driven back across the borders." However, despite Israeli advances, Egyptian resistance along the lines of retreat was unexpectedly heavy, and the fighting along the Syrian front was particularly bloody. In three days of combat the Israelis lost about 1,000 men, and their resources to stage a counteroffensive were thin. Also, Palestinian commandos under Yasir Arafat had begun to harass the Israeli flanks, and there were rumblings that pro-American Jordan would soon be forced to enter the conflict on the side of Egypt. Immediately the Israelis began to press their U.S. allies for assistance.

In his memoirs Nixon argues that he ordered Kissinger on October 9 to "let the Israelis know that we would replace all their losses."[39] It took a week for any aid to arrive. Nixon explained away the delay as being the result of bureaucratic foot dragging. An element of inertia was certainly present, as the Americans, convinced of the infallibility of their own intelligence, had been caught by surprise. But in truth, Nixon was simply so preoccupied with Watergate that despite his later excuses, aid to the Israelis was simply not his first priority. There was also the threat of Arab retaliation. The nations which belonged to the Organization of Petroleum Exporting Countries (OPEC) made it clear that if Nixon reinforced the Israelis, they would cut off the flow of oil to the United States. Several of Nixon's advisers, particularly Secretary of Defense James Schlesinger, counseled against doing anything that would upset the moderate Arab leadership. This also concerned Nixon, who later wrote that "I hoped that we could support [the Israelis] in such a way that we would not force an irreparable break with the Egyptians, the Syrians, and other Arab nations."[40] It was not until October 13, one week after the Egyptian attack and three days after the Soviets began to ship material to both Syria and Egypt, that the United States began an airlift to the Israelis. The delay infuriated the Israelis, particularly Meir, and put a severe dent in the relationship between the two nations.

When it finally arrived, U.S. aid quickly created a crisis for détente. The Israeli counterattack, which began on October 15, was a smashing success. Surprising no one, the Israelis bulldozed past the 1967 borders, crossed the Suez Canal at two points, and cut off the Egyptian Third Army, the heart of Sadat's fighting force. On the Syrian front the Israelis also went beyond the cease-fire line, pushing the Syrians back past the Golan Heights. As Meir's troops rolled victoriously onward, Nixon's worst diplomatic fears were realized: the Israelis were now poised to annihilate the Arab forces, an event that would destroy both the balance of power in the Middle East and any opportunity that the United States might have to maintain ties with the Arab world. As if to hammer home the gravity of the situation, on October 17 OPEC made good on its threat and placed an embargo on all oil exported to the United States.

There seemed to be little that the superpowers could do to control the situation. On October 22 (two days after Nixon fired his Watergate special prosecutor, Archibald Cox, in the "Saturday night massacre"), both the Soviets and the Americans forced a cease-fire agreement upon the combatants. However, the Israelis immediately violated the terms of the agreement (claiming Egyptian transgressions), and completed their encirclement of the Third Army. The Soviets rightly blamed Israel for the breakdown of the cease-fire. On the evening of October 23 Brezhnev sent Nixon a letter that came terrifyingly close to blaming the United States for instigating the war. Nixon's reply was conciliatory, telling him that the Americans had prevailed on the Israelis to hold to the cease-fire and that Brezhnev should do the same with the Egyptians and the Syrians. A second cease-fire was proclaimed, but no one held high hopes for its success. In what may well have been a decision made out of a belief that Watergate had crippled Nixon's decision-making power, Brezhnev took a step that brought the world to the precipice of nuclear destruction.

On the morning of October 24, almost eleven years to the day since the Cuban missile crisis, intelligence reports confirmed that seven Soviet airborne divisions in the Ukraine and the Caucasus as well as the Soviet Mediterranean fleet had been put on alert and that the Soviets were flying additional troop and cargo support to Cairo. Later that evening a letter from Brezhnev arrived at the White House carrying a message so shocking that Kissinger reportedly called Ambassador Dobrynin to verify its contents. Brezhnev called for the United States to join with the Soviet Union in a joint peacekeeping force or face the consequences: "I will say it straight, that if you find it impossible to act together with us in this matter, we should be faced with the necessity to urgently consider the question of taking appropriate steps unilaterally. Israel cannot be allowed to get away with violations."[41] Following a brief meeting of the Washington Special Actions Group (WSAG) of the NSC, the decision was made to put all U.S. forces on worldwide alert. A letter was sent to Brezhnev, signed by Nixon, which made it clear that "in these circumstances, we must view your suggestion of unilateral action as a matter of the gravest concern involving incalculable consequences."[42] It was what Kissinger would later call "a deliberate overreaction"; as Kennedy had done with Khrushchev in October 1962, Nixon had called Brezhnev's hand.* The following morning both Brezhnev and Sadat cabled the White House to say that they would accept a U.N. peacekeeping force. The Israelis agreed, angrily, to hold back from annihilating the Third Army. The formal cease-fire was signed on November 11. The Soviets had blinked, and the crisis abated.

It had taken the Yom Kippur War to put into place the first Rogers Plan. Nixon simply refused to endanger U.S. ties with Egypt by allowing the Israelis to completely crush the Third Army. The Americans had in effect abandoned their ally. Nevertheless, Yom Kippur left a sobering pall, if only temporarily, over the Middle East. The stage was now set for the negotiation of a treaty between Israel and Egypt, constructed through Kissinger's frenetic shuttle diplomacy during the last months of 1973 and based on his skill in breaking up the wartime coalition between Egypt and Syria. Signed on January 18, 1974, it called for a mutual pullback and disengagement along the Suez and a U.N. buffer zone to be placed between the two states. A fragile peace had come at last to the Middle East. Yet it was a victory that could be ascribed to nothing more than Nixon's and Kissinger's ability to react quickly to a crisis that their apathy and shortsightedness, dating back to the scuttling of the first Rogers Plan in 1970, had helped cause.

*A question that has been hotly debated is whether Nixon, despondent over Watergate, delegated his authority to Kissinger on the evening of October 24, leaving Kissinger to order U.S. forces on alert. Several journalists later reported that information had been leaked to them stating that Nixon, upon reading the Dobrynin letter, "empowered" Kissinger to deal with the situation. Some say that Nixon was not even consulted that evening; others contend that Kissinger went to the president's bedside at 3 A.M. to consult with Nixon. In his memoirs Kissinger describes Nixon as "overwhelmed by his persecution" and moves quickly from the receipt of the Brezhnev letter to the meeting of the WSAG without even mentioning Nixon. He also relates that it was the WSAG, not Nixon, that ordered the move to alert status and that the reply to Brezhnev was drafted by the WSAG and sent "over Nixon's name." In his memoirs Nixon takes the opposite stand, placing himself in the decision loop every step of the way, constantly referring to decisions that "we" made. There is no question but that Nixon, now in the eye of the Watergate hurricane, was preoccupied. However, as several high government sources have told this author, the person who leaked to the press that Kissinger had been "empowered" to deal with the situation was most likely Kissinger himself. There has been no satisfactory resolution of these significant yet contradictory claims

CHAPTER SIX

"Dirty Tricks":
Nixon and His Enemies, 1969–1972

"WATERGATE," that understated misnomer for the aggregate of abuses of power effected by Nixon and his administration, is one of the most emotional topics in modern United States history. Nixon continues to be castigated by those such as New York's Mayor Edward Koch, who cringed and shuddered when he bumped into Nixon on his way to a funeral in 1980.[1] Despite the desire of the author to be objective when researching this topic, it was impossible to sieve the emotion from the voices of any of the persons interviewed on these episodes. No matter what their ideology or party loyalty, when those who lived through Watergate talk about it today, they still speak with a noticeable agony. Aside from its emotional content, however, Watergate is clearly the single most influential event in the nation's postwar politics. Not only did it lead to the first resignation of a U.S. president; it also affected the shape of legislative and presidential politics to this day.

Thanks to the new availability of archival material, the composite picture of Watergate can now be told with a great amount of clarity. The story must begin with two facts that Nixon, much of the general public, and many scholars still refuse to accept. First, the June 20, 1972, burglary at the Watergate Hotel was far and away the least important part of a systematic attack by the Nixon White House against the enemies of Richard Nixon. Previous administrations had used the power of the incumbency to wreak havoc on their political opponents, but there is no doubt that this administration perceived itself to have more enemies than others before it and took immediate evasive action. Undeniably the White House began circling its wagons the moment that suitcases were unpacked in 1969. Yet the evidence makes it clear that far from being, as many have portrayed it, a White House run amok, members of Nixon's staff had a cold single-mindedness driving their neutralization of his adversaries. There was something appallingly efficient about the way they went about stalking their prey. They did it with the calculating style of junior executives preparing for an important presentation. They used memos instead of stealth, presented their plans on flip charts to approving audiences, and made copies of everything for everyone. The administration's vendettas were so painstakingly organized and so well documented that they stand alone in the annals of political "dirty tricks." Even past masters of the art stood in awe; Tommy "the Cork" Corcoran, chief political operative for Franklin Roosevelt, observed with amusement to Nixon aide Ray Price at a party: "The trouble with your people is that they're always writing memos. When we did that sort of thing, we never put it on paper!"[2]

The evidence makes one other point clear. Nixon himself comes in and out of the story at many diverse points—more often than his defenders will admit and less often than Nixon's haters will acknowledge. Yet the involvement of Nixon in these exploits was no accident. His staff did not work entirely without his approval; nor did they involve the president in the subsequent cover up against his will. His protests in his 1990 memoir, *In the Arena,* that he did not use government agencies illegally, that he did not order the CIA to obstruct the FBI investigation of the Watergate burglary, that no payments were either authorized by him or paid to the Watergate burglars, and that he did not deliberately lie to the press about the matter are simply not true.[3] Any researcher can hear Nixon doing all of the above on the copies of the "Watergate tapes" presently available to the public. There is absolutely no question; of the crimes and misdemeanors with which he was charged by the House Judiciary Committee in its 1974 impeachment investigations, Richard Nixon was guilty.

The abuses themselves began with Henry Kissinger's 1969 wiretapping of both his own aides at the National Security Council and of offending newsmen. The story of the tapping of the telephones of William Beecher, the *New York Times* reporter who published a May 1969 story detailing the secret MENU bombings of Cambodia, and Morton Halperin, the NSC staffer suspected of leaking the story to Beecher, has been discussed in a previous chapter. Three days after tapping Beecher's phone, Kissinger ordered Halperin's phone tapped, along with those of three other NSC aides: Daniel Davidson, Helmut Sonnenfeldt, and Colonel Robert E. Pursley. Within a week two others, Richard L. Sneider and Richard Morse, were also under surveillance. By the fall Kissinger had also ordered wiretaps on the phones of three other journalists: Marvin Kalb of CBS News, Hedrick Smith of the *New York Times,* and Henry Brandon of the London *Sunday Times.* By spring of the following year, Kissinger had approved taps on three more NSC staffers: Anthony Lake, Winston Lord, and Roger Morris. All of these wiretaps were known about by both Nixon and Haldeman, approved by John Mitchell at the Justice Department, and cleared through J. Edgar Hoover at the FBI.* The details were handled on the White House end by Kissinger's adjutant, Colonel Alexander Haig; William Sullivan, who had ingratiated himself to Hoover by expediting wiretaps on Martin Luther King, Jr., handled things at the FBI.[4]

It is relatively easy to conclude that Kissinger's wiretap schemes went far beyond any desire to merely ferret out leaks. Most observers, both in and out of the NSC, have concluded that Kissinger raced into this venture out of a desire to prove his loyalty to Nixon. In any case, the taps gained little or no information of substance, except to provide White House voyeurs with a detailed view of the personal lives of their victims. In fact, as Kissinger would admit in his July 1974 testimony before the Senate Foreign Relations Committee, which was investigating the wiretapping episodes, the taps never found the source of the leak to Beecher.[5]

Kissinger's wiretaps are evidence of one of the most enduring facets of the Nixon image: his war with the press. It is difficult not to agree with the observation of Pierre Salinger, Kennedy's press secretary, that there will always be friction between press and president "because the objectives of the two institutions collide."[6] However, Nixon's press relations took on a hostility that remains unsurpassed in the history of the modern presidency. Those who had contact with the Nixon press office recalled for the author that it presented a bunker mentality—an "us versus them" attitude—and that the feeling was mutual. The reason for this antipathy lay in the fact that Nixon saw—and continues to see—the press as his ideological, not merely his political, enemy. In Nixon's view the press simply did not believe in the values that he espoused and would never report his accomplishments in a fair and unbiased manner.

This opinion was shared by Nixon's two closest advisers on his press relations. Pat Buchanan would write in his 1973 synopsis of the Nixon presidency, *The New Majority*, that "an incumbent elite, with an ideological slant unshared by the nation's majority, has acquired absolute control of the most powerful medium of communication known to man." Ron Ziegler, Nixon's press secretary throughout his presidency, concurred in this opinion quite clearly to the author: "There in fact is in the press, a liberal tack. But it's no secret. It's not an ideological statement to make, that is a fact." While both analyses are open to debate, there is no question that Nixon felt the same way. Nixon also understood that most members of the Middle also resented the power of the media and generally sided with their president in his

---

*Mitchell added a few names of his own to the list, including White House political adviser John Sears, whose access to meetings and comments on political matters threatened the attorney general. Sears eventually resigned from the White House, only to resurface as Ronald Reagan's campaign manager in the 1976 primary battle against Gerald Ford.

battles with the press. As a result, Nixon's administration was clearly, as the National Press Club contended, "the most closed [to the press] in decades."[7]

But limited access was the least of the press's problems. Nixon's tenure is saturated with attempts to denigrate, harass, and otherwise discredit offending members of the press. It was an exceptional meeting between Nixon and any of his top aides that did not contain some kind of slight, followed immediately by some flavor of the presidential command to "take the offensive" (February 1971: "Deal w[ith] columnists *individually.* . . . This is like war—go to the heart"[8]). Space does not permit a complete recounting of every example of Nixonian retribution. A few examples must suffice. The wiretappings—the above-mentioned taps placed by Kissinger as well as a June 1969 tap, ordered by Nixon, of Joseph Kraft, a syndicated columnist who had taken an outspoken stand against the administration's conduct of the Vietnam War—were the most flagrant acts. Others were more narrow, as was the case with Nixon's growling during a June 1971 meeting with Colson: "Get rid of NET [National Educational Television]—cut budget. Public Broadcasting Corp[oration]—budget should be cut."[9] Lists were generated from Haldeman's and Ziegler's offices, noting reporters, columnists, and TV commentators who were to receive special treatment.[10] No detail was too small to escape White House attention. After a newscast during which CBS White House correspondent Dan Rather was particularly critical of an administration action, the Office of Communications, responding to the directive of its upwardly mobile deputy director, Jeb Stuart Magruder, sprang into action:

> We generated approximately 50 telegrams to Dan Rather this morning complaining about his treatment of the president last evening. These telegrams were sent by area residents, as well as some of our people from throughout the country. . . . In addition, we have programmed telephone calls throughout the day to Rather's Washington office.[11]

Perhaps the most brazen example of this treatment, and one that forecast the inept manner in which the White House would handle the Watergate cover-up, was the harassment of CBS Washington correspondent Daniel Schorr. Schorr's tough investigative reporting had given Nixon fits. In an attempt to rid himself of Schorr, Nixon ordered Haldeman in August 1971 to request the reporter's FBI file. In the mind of Nixon aide Bill Safire, "the request was immoral: nothing that could possibly be in the FBI file had any bearing on his right to report what he did."[12] There is still debate about whether Haldeman ordered a full field investigation to accompany his request for Schorr's file. Regardless, agents were soon talking to a host of Schorr's intimates and finally to Schorr himself. The agent who met with Schorr at his office fed the reporter his flimsy cover: that Schorr was being recruited for a "position of confidence and trust" in the administration, and the FBI investigation was the usual prenomination background check. The flabbergasted Schorr ran into Nixon's director of personnel, Frederic Malek, at a cocktail party two months later and asked if he was really being recruited for a position. Protesting that he knew of no such offer pending, Malek said that he would get back to Schorr. Malek never called back; he related to the author the reason why:

> I got a call from, I think, Ziegler. And Ziegler said, "Look, the FBI, this is coming out . . . and it's true that there is a directive that somebody here asked us . . . and there was a consideration as to whether Dan could be used in some capacity. . . . But to add credibility to the thing it would be helpful if you back that up, that you were considering it and such." So I did.

When Schorr went public with the story, Ziegler explained that the reporter had been considered for an administration position "in the environmental area." Malek backed up the story (according to Safire, Haldeman ordered that Malek take the rap[13]). When the author later asked Malek if the story had been "fabricated," Malek responded: "Well, I think it was fabricated, but it wasn't fabricated by me."

Clearly Nixon was incapable of understanding either the motives or the tactics of anyone seen as being "liberal" in any way. He reacted to the demands of those who protested against his decisions not with negotiation but with subversion. As he had supported Kissinger's wiretapping of "liberal" NSC members and reporters, so too did Nixon support the Justice Department in its wiretapping of political dissidents. He continued to give presidential support for the FBI's attempts to flood the media with false stories about protesters and to infiltrate their organizations. Nixon also supported the CIA's Operation CHAOS, which had been created in 1967 to trace foreign links to dissident groups but had evolved into a massive domestic spying program.*

It is clear that Nixon believed then—and continued to believe—that the many taps he ordered put on domestic dissidents were justified by a need for national security (he told a May 25, 1971, meeting, which included Hoover, that "tapping saves police lives"[14]). However, both

---

*Recently declassified materials at the Gerald R. Ford Library clearly show that the original intent of CHAOS was to investigate foreign ties to the antiwar movement. A June 1, 1972, "eyes only" agency memo, "Program Objectives" stated that the purpose of CHAOS was the "clandestine collection abroad of information on foreign . . . efforts to support/encourage/exploit domestic extremism and dissidence in the United States. These efforts include funding, training, propaganda, provision of safe haven, provision of alien documentation, etc. The collection emphasis is on foreign involvement, whether directly or by indirect third national leftist groups or individuals . . ." (in GFL, Richard B. Cheney Files, box 5). That CHAOS eventually strayed beyond its original charge is also unquestionable.

the quality and the quantity of the information that the White House received from these sources was disappointing. Nixon had never had much respect for Richard Helms, his director of central intelligence, and CIA analyses were always held at arm's length (witness the administration's reaction to CIA estimates in the MIRV debate). Nixon had also shed much of the awe with which he had long viewed Hoover. In March 1970 the president bitterly told Moynihan and Ehrlichman that the FBI was "incapable" of mounting an effective intelligence campaign because it was of a "different frame of mind" than was the administration.[15] Later that month Nixon told Haldeman and Ehrlichman to get to Hoover and Mitchell with a "directive" to get "new procedures . . . new people." Next to his note recording this order, Ehrlichman scribbled the name "Huston."[16]

Young, ambitious, and a true believer, White House staffer Tom Charles Huston had first made his mark through his "Cato" response to Bill Safire's memorandum on the New Federalism. Huston was as convinced as Hoover and Nixon that dissident elements in the United States counterculture were being supported by Communists. He had long been arguing for a reorganization of the administration's domestic intelligence capability when the student uprisings that followed the Cambodian incursion presented him the opportunity to press his case. On June 5 a fuming Nixon met with the heads of all of his intelligence agencies. Demanding better intelligence against the student movement, Nixon established an interagency committee headed by Hoover to formulate plans to strengthen domestic intelligence operations. Huston, also at the meeting, was appointed as White House liaison.

The committee went about its work with mixed intentions. Convinced of the infallibility of his organization, Hoover thought that the study was unnecessary. Huston was his polar opposite, working with a frantic zeal while constantly complaining to the White House about Hoover's foot dragging. The committee's report, submitted to the president on June 25, went far beyond Nixon's charge to streamline domestic intelligence (although in a memo written to Haldeman on the same day, Huston did suggest that "all incoming intelligence relating to revolutionary youth affairs come to me"[17]). The bulk of what would be dubbed the "Huston Plan"—increased use of bugging, wiretapping, surreptitious entry, and opening of mail against members of the youth movement—were, as the plan itself admitted, "clearly illegal."[18] That did not immediately concern Nixon, who gave his approval to the plan on July 23.

It clearly concerned Hoover, however. Wary of having his FBI embroiled in an intelligence operation run by amateurs, he complained to Mitchell, who voiced Hoover's reservations to Nixon. Huston counterattacked in a memo written to Haldeman on August 5: "We are not getting the type of hard intelligence we need at the White House. . . .

At some point Hoover has to be told who is president. He has become totally unreasonable and conduct is detrimental to our domestic intelligence operations. . . . What Hoover is doing here is putting himself above the president."[19] Huston lost. Five days after Nixon had approved the plan, he withdrew his approval.

Everyone in the Executive Office, including the president, was expected to protect the administration from outsiders, though only one staff member had this responsibility as a specific part of his job description. Charles Colson joined the White House staff in November 1969 as a special counsel. Contacts made while practicing law in Washington, as well as during his time on the staff of Massachusetts Senator Leverett Saltonstall, made Colson an invaluable liaison to many special interest groups. Colson's burning ambition, however, was to have unlimited access to and recognition by the president. For his part, Nixon liked what he saw of the young go-getter, and he particularly liked his ability to get results. As Nixon later wrote in his memoirs, Colson "was positive, persuasive, smart, and aggr·sively partisan. His instinct for the political jugular and his ability to get things done made him a lightning rod for my own frustrations at the timidity of most Republicans in responding to attacks from the Democrats and the media. When I complained to Colson I felt confident that something would be done, and I was rarely disappointed."[20]

As Colson remembers it, his first real mission for Nixon was to cut through red tape and set up a commission to help study the problems facing Catholic schools. Colson demurred, telling the president that he had no idea where to begin. Nixon exploded: "Break all the ——— China in this building but have an order for me to sign on my desk on Monday morning." Despite the enmity that his haste earned him with Haldeman and Ehrlichman, the order was on Nixon's desk on time.[21] Colson was soon running errands on Capitol Hill for the White House staff, contacting senators on key votes. Colson's office began coordinating Nixon's war against the media, and he was instrumental in working with Nixon on the shifts made in the administration after the congressional elections of 1970. By the end of that year Colson had enough clout to be able to circumvent Haldeman and see the president alone. He inherited the office right next door to the president's at the Executive Office Building, and he began attending Haldeman's early morning briefing for the senior staff. More important, his job description underwent a fundamental change.

No one in the White House could play to the "dark side" of Richard Nixon as could Chuck Colson. He had the foresight to make of himself something that the president at that point lacked: a self-described "flag-waving, kick-'em-in-the-nuts, anti-press, anti-liberal Nixon fanatic."[22] As Ehrlichman described his role, Colson was "called in to

take on the rough chores others wouldn't do";[23] to Theodore White
he was the classic "white-collar hustler as bully."[24] Whenever Colson
went into the Oval Office alone, both Haldeman and Ehrlichman recall, they cringed. They had good reason; Colson and Nixon would
talk for hours on end about what they would do to their enemies.
Whenever Nixon wanted someone "hit," he called upon Colson. The
President's Personal Files are rife with memos of rage sent directly to
Colson and to no one else. For example, Colson's notes taken during
an April 18, 1972, meeting in the Oval Office quote Nixon as fuming,
"Be dirty and hard and tough. Like to see Muskie, HHH, and EMK
pushed hard. . . . Politics be damned—RN do what is right. . . ."[25]
Before the end of 1971 Colson was responsible for the vast majority of
the dirty tricks that typified the Nixon White House.

Colson's influence comes into bizarre focus through his plan to catalog all of Nixon's enemies. Colson recalls in his memoirs a May 1971
evening spent on the presidential yacht *Sequoia* with Nixon, Kissinger,
Haldeman, and Ehrlichman to celebrate the "major breakthrough" on
the SALT treaty. In the course of the after-dinner conversation, Nixon's
thoughts turned, as they so often did in times of triumph, to his enemies. As he fondled his wine glass, the president warned: "One day
we will get them—we'll get them on the ground where we want them.
And we'll stick our heels in, step on them hard and twist—right Chuck?
Right?"[26] As Colson pondered that evening, it may well have led to
the White House enemies project. In May or June 1971 Colson began
to ask his colleagues for names of individuals hostile to the administration. From all corners of the Executive Office, nominations began to
pour onto his desk, often with accompanying résumés and background
information. Nominees included Barbra Streisand, Paul Newman, Joe
Namath, and Arthur M. Schlesinger, Jr.[27] William Rhatican, then an
assistant to Colson, told the author that one office was filled with nothing
but loose-leaf folders of names collected for the project.

The project soon took on a life of its own, and a busy Colson passed
the responsibility for the project to a new member of the staff. Originally a lawyer with John Mitchell's Justice Department, John W. Dean
III had replaced Ehrlichman at the White House counsel's position in
July 1970. A spendthrift and a womanizer with a penchant for the
Georgetown scene as well as an overt desire to achieve upward mobil-
ity, Dean seemed an unlikely prospect to survive long at the Nixon
White House. But Dean had risen to the top by virtue of his razor-
sharp mind and his skill at ingratiating himself to his superiors. Skilled
at organization, Dean bounced his new plan for the project off his
superiors in a confidential memo dated August 16, 1971: "This memorandum addresses the matter of how we can maximize the fact of our
incumbency in dealing with persons known to be in active opposition
to our administration. Stated a bit more bluntly—how we can use the

available federal machinery to screw our political enemies." Dean went on to his plans for the reinvigorated project. He suggested that members of the administration funnel prospective names of enemies through "key members of the staff" and the "project coordinator should then determine what sorts of dealings these individuals have with the federal government and how we can best screw them."*[28] By September Dean had pared down the original group of some 300 nominees to sixteen names. He sent the list directly to Haldeman's personal assistant, Larry Higby. Dean made it clear, however, that this was not the end of the enemies project. He envisioned his assignment to be ongoing and that "we would continue to feed additional names into the process every few months."[29]

When the lists were made public during Dean's 1973 testimony before the Ervin Committee, many persons in official Washington rushed to see if their names were on it. Included on the final list was Dan Schorr, who quipped that "I prize it more than my Emmy award."† Yet the real importance of the enemies project was not who made the list but the meticulous, organized way in which the project was carried out. All correspondence was typed on White House stationery and carefully cross-filed and saved, leaving one of the most bizarre paper trails in the history of executive wrongdoing. One cannot escape the conclusion that Colson, Dean, and the others who worked on the project were convinced that they would never be caught.

For all the tricks and concoctions that Colson came up with, none surpassed the ones stirred by a fear that he shared with Nixon and almost every other member of the senior White House staff—that Nixon's political success would be ambushed once again by a Kennedy. Several of Nixon's psychobiographers have dwelled on his hatred for John Kennedy as the driving force behind all of the dirty tricks of the Nixon administration, from ganging up on Ted Kennedy to breaking into former Kennedy aide Larry O'Brien's office at the Watergate Ho-

---

*Dean's nominee for the project's coordinator, a man whom he described as "most knowledgeable and most interested" and as having some "successes in the field" (and would describe in his memoirs as a man who "specialized in making certain that the press was abreast of bad news about political foes") was Franklin C. "Lyn" Nofziger, a former press secretary and communications director to Governor Reagan then serving as a White House aide.

†The list contained the following names (with notations as written in Dean's memo): Eugene Carson Blake, Leonard Bernstein, Arnold Picker ("On the United Artists Corporation—top Muskie fundraiser"), Ed Dufman ("managing editor, *L.A. Times*"), Maxwell Dane ("Doyle, Dane, and Birnbach"), Charles Dirsen ("associate of Larry O'Brien who bankrolls anti-Nixon radio programs"), Howard Stine ("of the Dreyfus Corporation—Big Democratic Contributor"), Allard Lowenstein, Morton Halperin ("top executive at Common Cause"), Leonard Woodcock ("of UAW"), Dan Schorr, Mary McGrory, Lloyd Cutler ("principal force behind Common Cause lawsuit against RNC-DNC, et al."), Thomas Watson ("a Muskie backer—of IBM"), Tom Wicker ("of the *NYT*"), Clark Clifford (Dean memorandum, Ervin Papers, series 2: Subject File, Watergate Memoranda, box 424, folder 864.)

tel. As will be seen, this, like most assertions made by writers of this genre, is a gross overstatement. Nevertheless, Nixon faced a familiar political problem in 1969: most observers believed that in 1972 Nixon would once again face a Kennedy for the presidency. Even the White House admitted that a race between Nixon and Edward M. "Ted" Kennedy, junior senator from Massachusetts, would be too close to call. The word went out: the president wanted to destroy Ted Kennedy.

In the early days of his tenure at the White House, Colson seemed to have the market cornered on anti-Kennedy material. One incident involved his peddling of a picture of Kennedy and a woman, not his wife, to the *National Enquirer,* which ran the picture.[30] Kennedy's automobile accident on July 19, 1969, at the Chappaquidick Bridge played right into Nixon's hands. From the first it was obvious that the Kennedy family was obfuscating and that the senator's explanation—that he had not run from the scene of the accident but had valiantly tried to save Mary Jo Kopechne, his passenger, who drowned in the car that Kennedy drove off the bridge—was just not believable. Further rumors that Kennedy was sexually involved with Kopechne compounded the senator's troubles, leaving him for the moment at least out of the running in 1972. Not leaving anything to chance, Ehrlichman prevailed on Jack Caulfield to dig deeper into the situation. A former New York policeman whom Ehrlichman had hired to take care of "security," Caulfield had already proved his worth by installing the tap on Joseph Kraft's phone. Busy with other requests from Ehrlichman, Caulfield assigned the Kennedy stakeout to another former New York cop, Tony Ulasewicz. Ulasewicz, who was being paid out of leftover 1968 campaign funds and was not a member of the White House staff, flew immediately to Martha's Vineyard and posed as a reporter, sending information on the story directly to Ehrlichman.[31]

Nixon did not stop with giving aid to Ted Kennedy's self-destruction. He was also obsessed with ridding himself of the ghost of Jack Kennedy. Convinced that there was much in the official record on Kennedy's greatest failure, the botched Bay of Pigs invasion, that could be used to tarnish the myth of the Kennedy presidency, Nixon in his first month as president demanded to see the CIA's file on that mission as well as its file on the Diem assassination. Director Richard Helms balked at the request, but intense pressure from the White House forced him to deliver the files. The dossier clearly showed that the Bay of Pigs had indeed been a CIA operation. More important for Nixon, it suggested that Helms, who had been deputy director for covert operations during the debacle, had played a key role in the postinvasion cover-up. According to some sources, the file showed that it was Helms who had developed the plan of lying to both Eisenhower and Kennedy about the potential success of the invasion.

After seeing the file, Nixon wanted as much additional information on his predecessors as he could get. In the summer of 1971 he told Colson, as Colson's notes state, to get "material for Truman/Eisenhower/Kennedy/Johnson years—get it physically here—Korea, Bay of Pigs, Cuban Missile Crisis, Dominican Republic, Berlin, Suez, Lebanon."[32] Colson complied, spending most of his time that summer on the project. To help him with the Kennedy chase, Colson hired E. Howard Hunt as a special consultant. Hunt seemed made to order for the task. An ex-CIA agent who specialized in Latin American affairs, Hunt had been one of the two senior agency field operators who had made plans for putting in place a provisional government to rule Cuba after Castro was overthrown. When the Bay of Pigs misfired, Hunt was reassigned to a desk job, ostensibly in charge of maintaining CIA relations with Cubans in exile. He and many other members of the Bay of Pigs operation were treated as nonentities after the fiasco, and he would long hold a personal grudge against Kennedy. The appointment of Hunt was far from a careless risk by his fellow Brown University brother Colson. Because of his consistent support of the Cuban freedom fighters, Hunt had earned the genuine respect of much of Miami's Cuban-American community. He had also been in the employ of the Robert Mullen Company, a public relations concern with CIA ties, and his Washington contacts were strong.

A romantic who had spent the years since 1961 writing spy novels, Hunt saw a commitment to Colson as the best way to once again live the life of his literary characters. One of the first jobs that Hunt performed for Colson was the piecing together of two cables from the Pentagon Papers to make one phony communication purporting to show that Kennedy had conspired in the November 1963 assassination of South Vietnamese strongman Ngo Dinh Diem. Although the cables were given to a *Life* reporter, the story was never printed and the doctored telegram was kept in Hunt's office safe at the White House. Its reappearance in 1972 would be one of the first links between the break-in at the Watergate and the dirty tricks that preceded it.

It was the June 1971 publication of the Pentagon Papers that took the White House into the final phase of its fury against outsiders. In so doing it brought in a team of zealous oddballs attached to both Ehrlichman and Colson, who would eventually be put in charge of "security" during the 1972 presidential campaign. That this was done despite their comic failure to get information on the Pentagon Papers leaker, Daniel Ellsberg, is, for the rational mind, inexplicable.

As noted earlier, Nixon flew into a rage when the *New York Times* began publication of the Pentagon Papers on June 13, 1971. It was Henry Kissinger who fueled his rage, for at least two reasons. First, as a result of his earlier consulting work for the Kennedy and Johnson administrations, Kissinger had been mentioned quite prominently in the Pentagon Papers. Several of Nixon's staffers told the author that after members of Congress began to call Defense Secretary Melvin Laird to demand the study, Laird ordered all references to Kissinger excised from copies sent to Capitol Hill.[33] Second, and to Kissinger potentially more damaging, was the fact that Ellsberg not only had been a student of Kissinger's but also a fellow adviser to President Johnson. At that time Kissinger had held Ellsberg in such high regard that despite his leftist reputation, he had been made a member of Kissinger's transition staff after the 1968 election (in an interesting irony, Ellsberg had helped draft the Vietnam option paper that went to Nixon's desk).[34] Ellsberg's initial patience with Nixon's efforts to obtain "peace with honor" soon ran out. He had tried to persuade Kissinger to read the Pentagon Papers as early as 1969 and to follow their lesson by speeding up the withdrawal from Vietnam. During a public debate between the two men sponsored by the Massachusetts Institute of Technology, there was an angry exchange over the pace of the administration's devolution.[35]

Clearly Ellsberg's involvement with the Pentagon Papers would be an embarrassment to Kissinger. On June 17 Kissinger met with Nixon, Haldeman, and Ehrlichman to put his own spin on the crisis. According to Ehrlichman's notes, Kissinger described Ellsberg as a "genius" and the "brightest student [I] ever had." But Kissinger made it clear that he believed that Ellsberg had made a drastic about-face since their time together at Harvard; he had used "drugs," had "shot at peasants" in Vietnam, and had "flipped [from a] hawk to a peacenik in early '69." Kissinger told them about the MIT debate, adding that he had not seen Ellsberg since that time. Kissinger's final conclusion: Ellsberg was "always a little unbalanced."[36] Convinced, Nixon began to compare Ellsberg to Whittaker Chambers and advised his staff, as he was wont to do on virtually any occasion, to reread the section of *Six Crises* on the Hiss case as their primer on treason. By the time Kissinger was done with the president, Nixon saw Ellsberg as the devil incarnate. Colson recalls that at a late June meeting Nixon stormed: "I don't give a damn how it's done, do whatever has to be done to stop those leaks and prevent further unauthorized disclosures; I don't want to be told why it can't be done. . . . I don't want excuses. I want results."

The staff scrambled to find someone to coordinate an all-out war against Ellsberg. The first choice was Nixon's right-wing speech writer, Pat Buchanan, who reportedly declined in writing.[37] On July 17 Ehrlichman finally gave the assignment, with Nixon's approval, to two of his Domestic Council staffers, David Young and Egil "Bud" Krogh, Jr. Of equal importance was Colson's arrangement for a transfer for Howard Hunt from his staff to Krogh and Young's. These three were joined on July 19, on the recommendation of Krogh, by G. Gordon Liddy, an ex-FBI agent who had previously worked at the Treasury Department.

The group's formal name was the Special Investigations Unit. The unit was given an office in the White House basement which Young labeled with a sign describing both its work and its mind-set: "Mr. Young: Plumber."

To suggest that the "Plumbers" were incompetent is to damn with faint praise. Krogh was a Seattle lawyer and a friend of Ehrlichman who had been assigned to the administration's task force on narcotics. He was also the White House liaison to the District of Columbia and as such was responsible for many positive innovations, including the beginnings of the work on the District's subway system. However, Krogh was a far cry from the typical covert personality. He was described by a friend to journalist Theodore White as "the kind of guy who, if you put him in charge of a big wedding back in Seattle, wouldn't have known how to call the police station and get a couple of cops to help with the traffic." [38] Young, a former Wall Street lawyer, was essentially a batman for Kissinger on the NSC (his wife did Kissinger's laundry, and there were rumors that Young even purchased some of his boss's clothes [39]), and he had long been lobbying for another assignment. Neither man knew the first thing about covert operations; more important, neither had sufficient constitution to control either Hunt or Liddy.

Hunt and Liddy were cut from essentially the same cloth, but Liddy's was of coarser quality. Gordon Liddy takes on an almost surreal role in the story of the administration's downfall. If one takes even part of what Liddy has written and said about himself at face value (admittedly a difficult task), the picture that emerges is that of a cartoon spy: as a boy Liddy catches, cooks, and eats a rat to prove his manhood and searches for the perfect Aryan mate; later he becomes a hyperzealous FBI agent, then an assistant district attorney in New York and a far-Right political candidate in Dutchess County; and he likes to show people how to kill a person with one thrust of a pencil. He had enough enthusiasm for ten men and not enough caution for one. In a 1973 article for *Newsweek*, Stewart Alsop typified Liddy as a "crazy-brave," one of the "minority categories of the human race [who] are always doing crazy things that ought to get them killed, or at least maimed." Liddy scared people, particularly those whom he worked for; Alsop characterized others in the Nixon White House, Dean and Magruder particularly, as "phony-toughs" who were consistently challenged by the crazy-brave Liddy to put up or shut up. [40] Best known is the incident at the Committee to Re-Elect the President (CRP) when Liddy threatened to kill Magruder if he didn't immediately remove his hand from Liddy's shoulder. Magruder believed him, and Liddy would have it no other way. Liddy was the perfect man to have if things went wrong; his loyalty could be counted on under any condition. Indeed, he was one of the few participants in the administration's excesses who refused to confess to the authorities after his arrest. Yet the qualities that made Liddy a perfect POW made him a lousy tactician. Things would eventually get fouled up because of his blind zeal.

The Plumbers had been at work for less than a week when yet another leak surfaced. As in June 1969, once again the target of Nixon's wrath was William Beecher of the *New York Times,* who on July 23 published a story detailing the fallback negotiating position of the SALT negotiating team. On July 24 a furious Nixon gave Haldeman, Ehrlichman, and Kissinger their marching orders: polygraphs were to be done on all staffers to find the Beecher leak. Nixon: "In writing—anyone w[ith] access to top secret—if any doc[ument] leaks—take polygraph or lose top secret clearance—Put fear into these people!"[41] These three men were experienced enough to know when to ignore Nixon's ranting, and they did so this time. Krogh, however, was a different story. On the same day Nixon seethed to his head Plumber: "We're not going to allow it. We just aren't going to allow it." Pressure from Colson, Ehrlichman, and now the president was at fever pitch. Krogh had to come up with something, fast.

All ideas, no matter how wild, were considered by the Plumbers. Then it was learned that during the investigation of Ellsberg, the FBI had attempted to interview his psychiatrist, Dr. Lewis Fielding. Fielding had refused, citing the confidentiality of the patient-doctor relationship. Hunt suggested to the group that they circumvent this irritating development by breaking into Fielding's Beverly Hills office and copying Ellsberg's medical file. On August 5 Krogh and Young pitched the idea to Ehrlichman. One month later Fielding's office was raided by Hunt, Liddy, and Hunt's three Cuban compadres, Bernard Barker, who had worked as Hunt's assistant on the Bay of Pigs, Felipe De-Diego, a veteran of combat during the invasion, and Eugenio Martinez, an ex-CIA arms runner to Cuba.

The September 3 break-in, financed through Colson's contacts, was a farce. The burglars were unable to find Ellsberg's file (it had been removed by Fielding) but, rather than leave the scene as quickly as possible, they trashed the office to make it look like a common burglary. They took pictures of virtually everything, including the sign outside Fielding's office which clearly labeled where they had been. Hunt then turned the undeveloped film over to a CIA contact for developing (apparently not thinking that the agency would stop to put two and two together and figure out what Hunt was doing). When they returned, the Plumbers found themselves personae non grata in the White House. The CIA had called Ehrlichman several days after the burglary, complaining about Hunt's demands for equipment (wigs, voice masking machines, and the like), and said that it wanted to cut him off. Ehrlichman recalls that he then called Krogh and told him to stop the covert activity. On December 1 Liddy left the Plumbers and became head counsel of CRP; he would move to CRP's finance department in March 1972. Although the others stayed with their White House assignments—Hunt in Colson's office and Krogh and Young on Ehrlichman's Domestic Council—by the end of the year the Plumbers had folded their tents.

After the burlesque antics of the Fielding break-in, the ineptitude of the Plumbers should have been apparent to all concerned. Instead all were kept in the employ of either the White House or the reelection campaign, and Liddy was even promoted. This carelessness was in large part responsible for the White House's walking blindly down the road toward the final, fatal phase of its campaign of dirty tricks: using the remnants of the Plumbers to gain covert information on Nixon's Democratic rivals for the presidency in 1972.

It was impossible for the men in the White House to think of a world without Richard Nixon. Yet despite their loyalties, the staff had to face the fact that Nixon had yet to prove himself a guaranteed sure thing in presidential politics. Both his defeat in 1960 and his victory in 1968 had been razor thin, and if Johnson had announced the bombing halt but a few weeks earlier, Nixon would probably have lost in 1968. The close calls in the off-year elections of 1970 had convinced many on the staff that Nixon could actually lose his bid for reelection. Early polls confirmed their fears, showing Senator Edmund Muskie of Maine running ahead of the president. The opening of China and the trip to the Soviet Union closed the gap, but Vietnam was still raging. Lost in the hoopla of détente and the size of his eventual victory over George McGovern is the fact that as the 1972 campaign began, the Nixon White House clearly saw itself as the underdog.

It should come as no real surprise, then, that in the early months of 1972 the president's handlers were looking for an edge. One of their major strategies was sophomoric but time-tested and effective. "Dirty tricks"—the unethical, usually illegal games that politicians used to tar and feather each other—were nothing new. Presidents Kennedy and Johnson both had used them. "Deep Throat," the informant who kept reporters Bob Woodward and Carl Bernstein on the right path as they investigated Nixon's transgressions, told them that the inside term for these games was "ratfucking." Appointments Secretary Dwight Chapin, who reported directly to Haldeman, was put in charge of coordinating the campaign's frolics. He recruited a fellow USC alumnus, lawyer Donald Segretti, to "mastermind" the plots. Liddy and Hunt, who felt that they should have drawn this assignment, met with Segretti and pronounced him an amateur. Despite the pot-calling-the-kettle-black flavor to this, they were right. Segretti's tricks were witty and effective but, as it turned out, all too easy to trace. A few examples will suffice: a girl was paid to stand naked outside Muskie headquarters and yell,

"I love Ed Muskie"; smoke bombs were tossed into Muskie headquarters; letters were circulated charging that Scoop Jackson had fathered an illegitimate child and that Hubert Humphrey consorted with prostitutes. Segretti used a credit card to pay for most of his expenses and even signed his vouchers without using an alias. Like Dean and his enemies project, it would be easy for investigators to track Segretti's whereabouts from the paper trail that he so conveniently provided.

Others in the White House joined in the fun. The most notable example of their work was the "Canuck letter," which more than anything else cost Muskie the Democratic nomination. A letter was written on Muskie stationery and sent to the ultraconservative *Manchester Union Leader*. In the letter, an unnamed Muskie aide charged that the senator had referred to French Canadians as "Canucks," a racial slur. The gleeful *Union Leader* published the letter on page one. Furious and exhausted, Muskie made an emotional off-the-cuff rebuttal on the steps of the newspaper's office. Standing in a snowstorm, he looked for all the world as if he were crying. He was immediately branded as soft, and his support quickly evaporated. Who wrote the Canuck letter is still not known. Some say it was Ken Clawson, director of White House communications; others blame Pat Buchanan or Colson.

Liddy had something in mind for "campaign security" that was considerably more complex than Segretti's sophomoric "ratfucking." As chief of the Nixon reelection committee's intelligence system (a job for which, despite his awful performance in the Fielding break-in, had been procured for him through the recommendation of Bud Krogh) Liddy had developed a plan which he promised would give the Republicans all the information on their opponents that they would need. On January 27, 1972, in Mitchell's Justice Department office, Liddy made one of the most extraordinary business presentations in the history of modern politics. The stunned audience consisted of Mitchell, Dean, and Jeb Magruder, now Mitchell's assistant at CRP. Liddy's plan was code-named GEMSTONE, and each of the nine subportions of the plan, presented to his audience with the use of color-coded flip charts, was named after a precious gem. Operation EMERALD, for example, called for the use of a chase plane to eavesdrop on the Democratic candidate's phone conversations while he was flying from city to city; SAPPHIRE called for the use of a luxurious houseboat bugged with video equipment and staffed with top-shelf call girls to "entertain" delegates to the Democratic convention. Operation CRYSTAL called for selected targets for wiretapping. But OPAL was the most ambitious. It called for covert entries into the Washington headquarters of McGovern and Muskie, the Fontainebleau Hotel in Miami, and a fourth place to be named later. The total price tag for the GEMSTONE package was one million dollars. Dean recalls that the presentation was "mind-boggling." Magruder says that he was "appalled." Perhaps. The most important reaction came from the poker-faced Mitchell, who simply puffed on his pipe through the entire proposal. At the end, however, Liddy's plan was not completely rejected. Mitchell merely told him that it was too expensive, that he had to pare down the cost and report back later to the three men.[42]

When the Ervin Committee later asked Mitchell why he didn't send Liddy packing after that first meeting, Mitchell mused, "In hindsight, I not only should have thrown him out of the office, I should have thrown him out of the window."[43] There were several reasons, however, why Mitchell could not afford to leave any stone unturned in Nixon's re-election effort, no matter how slimy that stone was. Mitchell had been in the doghouse for some time. Nixon held him responsible for his setbacks on his Supreme Court appointments and on busing. Mitchell's wife, Martha, had become a media darling through her nocturnal phone calls to reporters, and her conversations were almost always embarrassing in some way to the administration. Before the spring was over, Mitchell would spend hours in a courtroom being grilled on Justice's role in a scheme to elicit the help of International Telephone and Telegraph (ITT) in overthrowing the Marxist government in Chile, in exchange for donations to CRP. As a result, reports began to circulate that he was drinking more heavily than usual. In a November 1971 meeting with Ehrlichman and Haldeman, Nixon mused about his attorney general: "Can a Cabinet Officer take a leave of absence?"[44] Mitchell was indeed replaced in February 1972 by his assistant, Richard Kleindienst, and made head of CRP. But he had long been persona non grata with the staff at the White House, and Nixon was doing his best to keep his distance. If Liddy could give Mitchell information to relay back to the White House, perhaps that information could be used to buy a bit of goodwill.

In his distinguished study of the administration's abuses of power, *Nightmare: the Underside of the Nixon Years,* J. Anthony Lukas reports that some days after Liddy's presentation, Dean called Liddy and told him that the plan was basically good but that "some means would have to be found for deniability for Mr. Mitchell."[45] Apparently Liddy's reworked plan still did not provide enough of a safety net, because his second presentation, made to the same three men on February 4, also ended without an approval. This was in spite of the fact that Liddy had cut GEMSTONE's budget down to $500,000, leaving only the OPAL covert entries intact. According to everyone but Mitchell, at this meeting the men discussed several possible additional targets for OPAL entries. The Watergate Hotel office of the head of the Democratic National Committee, Larry O'Brien, was added to the list.[46] So too, according to Magruder, was the office of Hank Greenspun, publisher of the *Las Vegas Sun.* Dean recalls that he protested the direction of the meeting, saying that "I don't think this kind of conversation should go on in the Attorney General's office."[47] The meeting broke up, but no one had told Liddy to stop his efforts.

Throughout the month of March Liddy honed his plan and fumed at how long it was taking Mitchell to make up his mind. He finally gave up waiting and asked Hunt to talk to his friend Colson to see if he could intercede on behalf of GEMSTONE. According to Liddy, when Colson heard that the plan had been stalled, he immediately picked up his phone, called Magruder, and demanded that he "get on it."[48] Colson's intercession broke the roadblock. When Magruder visited Mitchell and Frederick LaRue, Mitchell's chief aide, in Key Biscayne on March 30, OPAL was one of the topics of discussion. According to Magruder, Mitchell approved the plan over the objections of LaRue. Mitchell denied approving the plan at the meeting, and LaRue later testified that he left with the feeling that nothing had been decided.[49] Nevertheless, on Monday, April 1, Liddy recalled, he received a call from Bob Reisner, Magruder's administrative assistant: "You've got a 'go' on your project."[50]

The mind-set in the Nixon White House was clear. Enemies of Richard Nixon must be neutralized. Be they Black Panthers, the press, or any Democratic contender, their possible threat to the Nixon presidency must be neutered. One cannot help but look at the organization of the White House for "security" matters with a bit of awe. Historians can point to one or two men who in previous administrations did the dirty work for the man in the Oval Office. In the Nixon White House it was an entire subbureaucracy of the Executive Office, whose only purpose was political subversion. While that bureaucracy was staffed with men who were either too intense or too incompetent to make good spooks, the organization itself and its cold, memorandum-pushing approach to the dirty tricks are truly awe-inspiring.

This makes even more puzzling the biggest question asked by the general public about the break-in at the Watergate: why? Why, when Nixon was running so far ahead; what information could they hope to find that they didn't already have? As for the argument that "Nixon had it in the bag," the reader should be reminded of polls in early 1972, taken during the same weeks that the high command was debating and revising GEMSTONE, that showed Nixon running neck-and-neck with Muskie. Nevertheless, there exists the nagging belief that there just didn't seem to be anything of value at the DNC headquarters. McGovern's headquarters made a bit more sense. But why the Watergate?

A few analysts subscribe to Jim Hougan's analysis in *Secret Agenda* that "Hunt and McCord were secretly working for the CIA while using the White House as a cover for domestic intelligence operations" and that "clients of prostitutes in the Columbia Plaza Apartments, hard by the Watergate complex, were the real targets of the bugging operation."[51] The thesis on the CIA connection is one that is as old as the break-in itself; the FBI began to blame it on the CIA within twenty-four hours of the burglars' capture. For the most part the argument came to the public's attention through Lukas's work, but he did not give the same credence to the argument as did Hougan. Despite his prodigious use of memoirs and published testimony, Hougan was not privy to certain unpublished material, now opened, which does not corroborate either the CIA or the call girl theories.

Several scholars quietly hold to an alternative theory: that the White House wanted to know how much the Democrats knew about 1968 campaign contributions to Nixon in exchange for his agreement to prolong the war in Vietnam. But not only do such contributions run counter to every bit of fiber that made up Richard Nixon; there is no evidence to back up the claim.

One theory, however, is corroborated by testimony given both at the time of the incidents and at the time of this writing, by the memoirs of the participants, and by the newly opened manuscript sources. Operation OPAL held the potential for finding out how much information there was in the files of both Greenspun and O'Brien on a topic that could severely embarrass the administration: the financial largess and political clout of Howard Hughes.

In 1956 Nixon's brother Donald had taken out a $205,000 loan from the rich and reclusive Hughes to help finance a fast-food restaurant. The loan was secured by Nixon's mother's lot in Whittier, worth much less than the value of the loan, and it was never repaid. Despite Donald's protests of innocence of any wrongdoing, the Hughes loan was an issue in his brother's 1960 and 1962 political campaigns. This was at best a relatively minor embarrassment, but it concerned the White House enough to monitor court cases that dealt with Hughes's finances and to bring them to John Dean's attention for follow-up.

The fate of Don Nixon was not the White House's only concern in connection with Hughes. In 1970 Richard Nixon himself was the recipient of Hughes's largess. In an attempt to grease the skids for the purchase of the Dunes Hotel in Las Vegas, Hughes arranged for Nixon confidant Bebe Rebozo to receive a $100,000 contribution for the Nixon coffers. The deal was negotiated by Robert Maheu, an ex-FBI agent and Hughes confidant who also worked for the CIA while working for Hughes (it would later be charged that Maheu had been the contact man for the CIA's efforts to have the Mafia assassinate Fidel Castro in the early 1960s[52]). The contribution was never reported, and was illegal. One set of investigative reporters, Larry DuBois and Laurence Gonzales, wrote in 1976 that this was but the tip of the iceberg. Over the next few years at least $150,000 was funneled to Nixon by Hughes, using Robert Bennett, owner of the Robert Mullen Company, a public relations firm and CIA front that also employed Howard Hunt, as an intermediary.[53]

Although there is no solid evidence as to how much money changed hands, events would show that Hughes clearly got his money's worth. Hughes hired Richard Danner, a Nixon friend who claimed to have first introduced Nixon and Rebozo, as his "lobbyist" to the Nixon administration. Danner later told reporters that he passed money along to Rebozo, then went to see Mitchell. The attorney general then put pressure on the Justice Department's Antitrust Division so that Hughes might purchase more hotels in Las Vegas and acquire Air West. As DuBois and Gonzales piercingly observed, "Clearly, Nixon hadn't been president long before he had a great deal to protect."[54]

In the fall of 1970 the Hughes empire experienced several shock waves. Long rumored to be deathly ill, Hughes disappeared from his Las Vegas hotel. His disappearance was followed one month later by Maheu's being tossed out of his office by Intertel agents, who also seized his files. The shakeup threatened to expose the relationship between Hughes and Nixon, as Maheu was a wealth of information on their financial dealings. On January 18, 1972, CBS reported that it had learned "new details" on the loan to Don Nixon, most notably that after Donald received the money, Hughes was given an IRS exemption on a medical foundation he had started. Donald was interviewed, and he continued to protest his innocence.[55] The story, then, was still hot when Liddy made his first GEMSTONE presentation.

On February 3, 1972, the day before Liddy's second presentation, it got hotter. The *New York Times* reported that Greenspun had several memos from Maheu in his Las Vegas safe. The story made sense. Greenspun's newspaper had long been a supporter of Hughes. However, after Maheu was kicked out of the Hughes organization, Greenspun sided with Maheu and began to attack Hughes in his editorial pages. It was safe to assume that Maheu had made available to Greenspun copies of the memos which Hughes had entrusted to him during his employ. One of these memos was rumored to be from Robert Merhige, a CIA agent also in the employ of Hughes, to Haldeman. The memo, which DuBois and Gonzales obtained in their research, was dated September 2, 1968, and labeled "Proposed Fund-Support List as Through Local Outlets." It listed thirty-one U.S. politicians whom the CIA wanted to receive funds from Hughes. Included on the list were the names of Wilbur Mills, Strom Thurmond, Paul Laxalt, John Tower, Robert Byrd, and Gerald Ford.[56] While no evidence exists that Hughes ever actually channeled any money to these politicians, there was clearly a great deal of private nervousness over the matter. It is understandable, then, why Mitchell added Greenspun to the list of OPAL targets.

Maheu had another important contact who had also been a thorn in Nixon's side. After Lawrence O'Brien left his position as postmaster general in the Johnson administration, he opened a consulting firm. One of his first and biggest clients was the Hughes Tool Company, which gave O'Brien a $15,000-per-month contract. The contract was negotiated by Maheu on Hughes's instructions. After Maheu and Hughes severed their relationship, Hughes ended his relationship with O'Brien as well.[57] O'Brien lobbied hard to keep the contract, or at least to get a hefty severance settlement, but to no avail. The initial reaction in the White House to this news was favorable. Now O'Brien would be denied Hughes money, and even more helpful, the Hughes account had been turned over to Bob Bennett's Mullen Company.[58]

The joy quickly turned to dread. Up to the time of Maheu's firing, the relationship between O'Brien and Maheu was close. The White House realized that Maheu would soon advance his cause against Hughes, if he hadn't done so already, by telling O'Brien everything that he knew about the Hughes-Nixon relationship. When O'Brien became head of the Democratic National Committee in 1970, his second tour of duty as chairman, he was clearly in a position to use that information. It therefore made sense for OPAL to include his office as a target; if CRP knew exactly what O'Brien had in his files regarding the Nixon-Hughes relationship, it would be able to plan a counteroffensive.

Whispers about the Hughes connection being the reason for the break-in at the Watergate circulated almost immediately after the story broke in June 1972. It continued as a "rumor" for several years, but it was largely ignored by the public, which seemed to find it too complicated an explanation. Lukas documented much of the Hughes link with success, however, and the point was expanded even further in Michael Drosnin's 1985 book, *Citizen Hughes*. No one from the Nixon White House had written or spoken specifically on this matter until November 1987, when, responding to a question posed by Lukas during Hofstra University's Conference on the Nixon Presidency, Jeb Magruder made this startling statement: "As far as I know, the primary purpose of the break-in was to deal with the information that has been referred to about Howard Hughes and Larry O'Brien and what that meant as far as the cash that had supposedly been given to Bebe Rebozo and spent later by the president possibly." Magruder continued that this information had been made clear to him at the third meeting on GEM-STONE in Key Biscayne.[59] Documents in the Nixon Papers as well as several off-the-record comments to this author from highly placed sources in the Nixon White House, confirm Magruder's story. It is clear, then, that the Nixon people went into the Watergate for two reasons: to document the relationship between O'Brien and Hughes and to see to it that Nixon's relationship with Hughes never saw the light of day.

The question of Nixon's role (or, in the soon to be immortal words of Senate Watergate Committee member Howard Baker, "What did the president know and when did he know it?") would surround the Nixon presidency until its end, chase the president's reputation through his retirement, and become a key debating point for historians of the period. Unlike the question of why the offices of Greenspun and O'Brien were chosen for OPAL, the answer to this question is easy for the historian. What evidence do we have proving that Nixon approved GEMSTONE? None. Not in the testimony or memoirs of any of the participants, not in the tapes, nor, most important, in any of the available manuscript sources, including the Nixon Papers.

The matter cannot end there, however. Grumblings from former administration officials to this author show that old beliefs die hard. Stephen Ambrose speaks for many when he concludes that "the president himself, while he did not know everything, knew more than anyone else."[60] While admitting the dearth of evidence, many continue to believe that Nixon somehow "knew" (interviewees who were asked to speculate on the matter invariably mused that if anyone told Nixon about GEMSTONE in advance, it was Colson). This belief may have its genesis in a portion of John Dean's memoirs, where he writes that immediately after Liddy's February 4 presentation in Mitchell's office, Dean told Haldeman all the details about GEMSTONE. Dean also later testified that "Magruder had a conversation with Mr. [Paul] O'Brien [CRP lawyer], in which he told O'Brien that he had received his final authorization for Liddy's activities from Haldeman's assistant Gordon Strachan, and that Strachan had reported that Haldeman had cleared the matter with the president."[61]

Quite aside from the fact that so far this is the only evidence on this point and that its acceptance necessitates trusting the word of Dean and Magruder, the claim makes little sense. This was precisely the type of thing that Haldeman had a record of keeping *from* the president. It also makes no sense to believe that Mitchell, struggling to regain his status in the White House, would endanger his boss by giving him this knowledge. Everyone else involved was so low on the ladder of power that they had no direct access to the president. The debate seems to want to rage on. Nevertheless, one thing is clear: there is absolutely no evidence to prove that Nixon was briefed on GEMSTONE before the break-in occurred.

That is not to say that Nixon is to be completely absolved from blame for the break-in. The climate in the White House, set by Nixon himself, was certainly open to such a venture. Indeed, in one of his many musings on his enemies, he may well have set the ball rolling. On January 14, 1971, in a memo that he dictated to Haldeman, Nixon stated: "It would seem that the time is approaching when Larry O'Brien is held accountable for his retainer with Hughes. Bebe has some information on this although it is, of course, not solid but there is no question that one of Hughes' people did have O'Brien on a very heavy retainer for services rendered in the past. Perhaps Colson should make a check on this."[62]

Once Mitchell had finally given his approval, plans for GEMSTONE chugged into gear. Liddy quickly recruited Howard Hunt for the operation, and Hunt contacted the Cubans who had helped bungle the Fielding break-in. (It should be noted that, strictly defined, the Watergate break-in was not a "Plumbers" operation; the group had been disbanded after the Fielding break-in, and Krogh and Young had no role in the Watergate caper.). Two men were added who would contribute not only to the break-in but also to the unraveling of the cover-up of the crime. James McCord, an ex-CIA agent who had been hired on January 9 as a security consultant for CRP, was given responsibility for procuring and installing the surveillance equipment. This was a key decision, one made by Liddy and not cleared with anyone at either CRP or the White House. Using Hunt's Cubans was one thing; if they were caught, they could stonewall about their relationship to Hunt and Liddy and the affair would not necessarily be traced back to CRP. With McCord, however, the team ran the risk of getting caught with a registered CRP employee bugging the phones. Liddy, however, believed that McCord was the best of the bunch at electronic surveillance—a fact that, given the complete ineptitude of the lot, was relative. On May 1 McCord contacted Alfred Baldwin, a former FBI agent and bodyguard for Martha Mitchell, and offered him a job as a security guard for CRP. Baldwin would be used as the lookout on the job as well as the man who would monitor the taps once installed. He would also be the first man to talk to the federal prosecutors.

Financing the operation was relatively uncomplicated but completely illegal. Quite aside from the fact that CRP was footing the bill for breaking and entering and wiretapping, it was doing so with laundered campaign contributions. On April 3 Nixon's finance chairman, Maurice Stans, approved the Mexican transfer of four checks totaling $89,000. Four days later, according to the testimony of Hugh Sloan, treasurer of CRP, Liddy told Sloan that he would soon need $83,000, the first installment in a $250,000 budget authorized for him. Sloan checked with Magruder, who confirmed that Sloan should give Liddy the money. Unconvinced, Sloan double-checked with Stans, who a few days later confirmed to Sloan that he should follow Magruder's instructions. McCord later testified that on April 12 Liddy gave him $65,000 in $100 bills from the $83,000 that Sloan had given him. Furthermore, Liddy told McCord that Mitchell had approved the operation and wanted it to be done within thirty days. Not one to ask questions, McCord spent the money on tape recorders, walkie-talkies, and other electronic paraphernalia.[63]

Not surprisingly, it took the burglars three attempts to get it right.

On May 26 they went into the Watergate but were forced to abort the mission, leaving Hunt to spend the night locked in a closet. From that point on, Hunt stayed with Baldwin and Liddy as lookouts from their post at Howard Johnson's Hotel across the street from the Watergate. In their second try on May 27 they failed to gain entrance because Gonzalez had not brought the proper tools. They finally succeeded in breaking into DNC headquarters on Sunday, May 28. They used up two rolls of 36-exposure 35-mm film to photograph material from O'Brien's desk, and McCord planted bugs on two phones, one belonging to O'Brien's secretary, Fay Abel, and a second belonging to R. Spencer Olivor, a DNC operative responsible for links with state chairmen.

The only problem was that the bugs didn't work. The day after the break-in, Baldwin began to monitor the tap on Olivor's phone but was unable to locate Abel's. Olivor's phone yielded nothing of substance except details on his personal life. Nevertheless, Baldwin made daily logs of the conversations (Baldwin would later tell the Ervin Committee that he kept logs on about two hundred conversations[64]) and passed them along to McCord, who gave them to Liddy. Liddy's secretary, Sally Harmony, transcribed the conversations. On June 8 Liddy gave Magruder the transcripts of the taps from DNC phones as well as copies of the photographs. According to Liddy, the next day Magruder called him into his office and reprimanded the team, saying that the content of the logs was not worth either the risk or the expense. Magruder then asked if the bugs could be fixed or moved. Liddy's response was that "that would mean another entry, one that had not been budgeted."

On June 15 Liddy met with Mitchell, Magruder, and a few others. Liddy took more logs with him. It was at this meeting, according to Liddy, that Mitchell approved another break-in, which was attempted on June 17.[65] The final attempt was handled even more carelessly than previous Hunt-Liddy escapades. The burglars advertised their presence by taping back the lock on the door of entry so that they could get out, but anyone on the outside could see the tape. The night watchman, Frank Wills, called the District police, whose job was made easier when the burglars, seeing flashlights, turned off their walkie-talkies and could not be given guidance from Howard Johnson's. At 1:52 A.M. the burglars were arrested.

CHAPTER SEVEN

Beyond the ''Third-Rate Burglary'': Cover-up and Departure

O N NBC's "Meet the Press" on April 10, 1988, Nixon responded to moderator Chris Wallace's question about breach of trust in his administration by arguing that in 1972 there were many "big things"—the Soviet Union, China, and the end of the Vietnam War— and Watergate was "a small thing, and we fouled it up beyond belief." A moment later Tom Brokaw pressed Nixon to explain: "Is it fair, really, to characterize it as only a small thing that was a mistake?" Nixon persisted in his defense, arguing that "it was a small thing that became a very big thing . . . the break-in, and break-ins have oc- curred previously in other campaigns as well."

This narrow view of Watergate is exactly what Nixon always wanted the country to believe. From the moment he learned of the break-in, Nixon and his staff maintained that the burglary was merely an iso- lated incident within the administration, what Ron Ziegler described to the press on June 19, 1972, as a "third-rate burglary." But despite the administration's best attempts to keep the country's attention fo- cused only on the burglary, forces from both within and outside the administration began to piece the whole story together. For almost two years the administration worked night and day to keep earlier covert activities from coming to the surface. It was these activities, not the details surrounding the break-in at the DNC, that were being covered up.

Nixon's first recorded reaction to the news of the botched burglary was made, predictably, to Colson, whose memory of the phone call from Key Biscayne ("[Nixon] was so furious that he [threw] an ash- tray across the room . . . and thought it was the dumbest thing he had ever heard of"[1]) presents a realistic enough scenario. When he returned to Washington on June 20, Nixon held numerous meetings and conversations that dealt directly with Watergate. First he met with Haldeman. It is inconceivable that Watergate was not a topic of discussion; Hunt and Liddy had been arrested, and Hunt's White House safe had been opened, revealing the doctored cables on the Diem assassination as well as psychological profiles of Ellsburg provided by the CIA.* When reviewed the following year by Nixon's counsel, the tape of this conversation was found to have a mysterious gap of eighteen and one-half minutes.

The transcript of this tape has not been released to the public, though others have been. Yet as soon as the White House confirmed its existence, many observers both in and out of the administration concluded that the erased portion of the conversation had contained Haldeman's briefing of Nixon on the history of GEMSTONE. If so, then Nixon learned of the details surrounding the planning of the burglary less than seventy-two hours after it happened—a far sight earlier than he would later admit to the American public. Two days later, on June 22, Nixon publicly referred to the break-in for the first time. What he said was a complete lie, as he stated to the press that the White House was not involved in the Watergate matter.[2]

Nixon knew that if investigations could be contained to just the break-in at DNC headquarters, then the damage would be light. The Justice Department posed little problem. The Watergate investigation had been assigned to Assistant Attorney General Henry Petersen, head of the Criminal Division. Transcripts of the available tapes clearly show that Petersen kept Dean, and eventually Nixon, completely informed of his investigation every step of the way. Justice Department prosecutors, led by Earl Silbert, consistently failed to check leads and in general ran a shoddy investigation (as Petersen said when telling Dean of Silbert's assignment to the case, "Earl knows better than to wander off beyond his authority into other things"[3]). The FBI soon proved to be another matter. By June 22 it had solid evidence linking the break-in to the Nixon campaign; on the same day the FBI informed Silbert that money in Bernard Barker's bank account had been traced to CRP checks.[4] From the White House's point of view, the FBI needed to be slowed down.

On June 23, in the most fateful hour and thirty-five minutes of his entire presidency, Nixon met with Haldeman to discuss a plan to decelerate the FBI's investigation before it went beyond the burglary and uncovered the administration's other scorpions. The early moments of the White House tape recording that became known as the "smoking gun conversation" (named after the slang legal term for a piece of evidence that will convict without any other corroborating evidence)

*This material was turned over to L. Patrick Gray, then acting director of the FBI, who burned all of it with his Christmas trash.

is tinny, and Nixon's voice is muffled. But Haldeman's plan is crystal clear:*

> HALDEMAN: Now, on the investigation, you know, the Democratic break-
> in thing, we're back . . . in the . . . problem area because the FBI is
> not under control . . . their investigation is now leading into some pro-
> ductive areas, because they've been able to trace the money, not through
> the money itself, but through the bank . . . and it goes in some direc-
> tions we don't want it to go . . . the way to handle this now is for us
> to have Walters call Pat Gray and just say, "Stay the hell out of this
> . . . this is ah, business here, we don't want you to go any further on
> it."[5]

Nixon's full agreement with the plan and his marching orders to Haldeman are equally clear:

> HALDEMAN: And they seem to feel the thing to do is to get them to stop?
> NIXON: Right, fine.
> HALDEMAN: They say the only way to do that is from White House instruc-
> tions. And it's got to be Helms and, uh, what's his name . . . [Deputy
> Director of the CIA Vernon] Walters.
> NIXON: Walters.
> HALDEMAN: And the proposal would be that Ehrlichman (cough) and I call
> them in, and say, ah . . .
> NIXON: Alright, fine. . . . You call them in.

Nixon and Haldeman had broken the law. Despite the later protes-
tations of many scholars and politicians, including Nixon, the June 23
conversation clearly shows Haldeman suggesting and Nixon ordering
an end to a legal investigation of a felony—a clear obstruction of justice.

At first glance it seems that Nixon's trust in the CIA, an organization never trusted by the administration and one that not only had
disagreed with the president on several key occasions but also had
given him misinformation on other occasions, was very poorly placed.
Yet he knew that he could count on Helms this time. Both men knew
of a razor that they could hold to Helms's throat—the CIA file that
Nixon had received on the Bay of Pigs, which as noted in the preceding chapter clearly showed Helms's complicity in the disaster. In a second conversation with Haldeman on the afternoon of June 23, Nixon
made it clear that he expected his aides to blackmail Helms into co-
operating:

> NIXON: When you get in these people . . . , say: "Look, the problem is
> that this will open the whole, the whole Bay of Pigs thing, and the

*For a detailed discussion of the "Watergate Tapes" and which of the many sets of
transcripts have been utilized in this chapter, see "An Essay on the Sources."

president feels that" ah, without going into the details . . . don't, don't lie to them to the extent to say there is no involvement, but just say this sort of comedy of errors, bizarre, without getting into it, "the president believes that it is going to open up the whole Bay of Pigs thing again. And, ah, because these people are plugging for, for keeps and that they should call the FBI in and say that we wish for the country, don't go further into this case," period![6]

Helms and Walters arrived at the White House while Haldeman was still talking with Nixon. When the chief of staff emerged to speak with them, he got right to the point. Walters wrote a memo about that meeting and its subsequent effect for the record:

> Haldeman said that the whole affair was getting embarrassing and it was the president's wish that Walters call on Acting FBI Director Patrick Gray and suggest to him that since five suspects had been arrested, that this should be sufficient, and that it was not advantageous to have the enquiry pushed, especially in Mexico, etc. . . .[7]

Helms reacted precisely as Nixon expected. As Haldeman would report back to Nixon later that day, once he told Helms that "the problem is that it tracks back to the Bay of Pigs," the director responded that "we'll be very happy . . . to handle everything you want. . . ."[8] At 2:30 that afternoon, Walters saw Gray and asked him not to push the FBI investigation into Mexico. Gray agreed.[9] The plan, for the moment, worked.

Coinciding with Nixon's maneuvering to stop the FBI was the genesis of another arm of the cover-up: the plot to raise money to keep the imprisoned burglars quiet. At a June 29 meeting in Washington's Lafayette Park, Herbert Kalmbach, Nixon's chief fund raiser since 1968, agreed to Dean's request to raise money for the defendants. Kalmbach began his fund-raising efforts with the CRP finance chairman, Maurice Stans, who gave him $75,000. The next day Tony Ulasewicz agreed to deliver the money; he gave it to Hunt's wife, Dorothy, who began to distribute it to the burglars and their lawyers.[10]

Yet at the very moment that it began, the cover-up was starting to disintegrate. On June 25 Alfred Baldwin agreed to cooperate with the government. A week later CRP treasurer Hugh Sloan told Jeb Magruder that if asked he would not falsify figures on the amount of money that Liddy had been given by CRP. Also, the heads of the FBI and the CIA were belatedly trying to distance their agencies from the mess. On July 6, going against the direct request of the president, Helms told Gray that there was in fact no CIA operation in Mexico to protect. Realizing that he had been duped, a furious Gray called Nixon. Gray reportedly told the president that "people on your staff are trying to mortally wound you by using the CIA and the FBI."[11]

The unraveling was accelerated by the reporting of two *Washington Post* city beat reporters, Bob Woodward and Carl Bernstein. A Yale graduate, Woodward had spent a five-year stint in the navy, service that included his assignment as a command watch officer at the Pentagon. This position had given him access to top-secret communications and, according to several recent reports, the role of briefer to Nixon's Joint Chiefs of Staff. Woodward had joined the *Post's* metro desk in 1970 and had been assigned to cover the arraignment of the Watergate burglars on the evening of June 18. He made good use of his wide range of Washington sources. The most famous, christened "Deep Throat" by one of his editors, was, according to Woodward, "a source in the Executive Branch who had access to information at CRP as well as at the White House."*[12] Woodward was teamed, not entirely by choice, with Bernstein. A quixotic, somewhat bohemian womanizer, Bernstein had risen from copyboy to a 1966 appointment as city reporter on the basis of his street smarts and his writing skills, which clearly outshone Woodward's. Aside from his gifted prose, Bernstein's main contribution to the team was, as one writer would later say, to use "his charm and brains to get in the doors of people who knew they shouldn't talk."[13]

The two men proceeded to dig past the story of the break-in and to come achingly close to tying the White House in with the earlier covert operations. On August 1 the *Post* published their first big story on the scandal—based on information already obtained and suppressed by the FBI—that the Barker check came from CRP. After several subsequent stories that traced the money to CRP safes controlled by Mitchell and used by Magruder and others, the *Post* ran a story on October 10 which read in part: "FBI agents have established that the Watergate bugging incident stemmed from a massive campaign of po-

---

*Who was Deep Throat? In *The Ends of Power*, Haldeman writes that he believes that it was Fred Fielding, Dean's assistant in the White House counsel's office. In *Lost Honor*, the second volume of his memoirs, Dean spends an elaborate final chapter telling of his search for Deep Throat, how one of the Watergate special prosecutors told him that it was Earl Silbert, and how Dean publicly accused Silbert, only to come to the final conclusion that the culprit was Kissinger's assistant Al Haig. There are three other serious contenders whose names came to the author from several Nixon White House insiders. One, long-time Nixon loyalist Peter Flanigan, was clearly being pushed out of the inner circle long before the break-in, a fact made clear by the archival record in both Haldeman's and Ehrlichman's papers. Another, staff secretary Jerry Jones, has been charged with being a Woodward confidant before the burglary as well as having access to the information that Woodward published. A third, David Gergen, worked in the Communications Department in both the Nixon and the Ford administrations and was widely suspected of being a prodigious leaker to the press. This author believes—along with many journalists and members of the administration—that rather than being one person, Deep Throat was an ensemble of sources, all of whom offered Woodward something. As an aside, what was truly remarkable about the *Post's* reporting was not that Deep Throat leaked but that by the time the story began to break, so many of the Nixon insiders— members of the presidential family, Cabinet members, and key staffers—all *chose* to talk to Woodward and Bernstein.

litical spying and sabotage conducted on behalf of President Nixon's reelection and directed by officials of the White House and the Committee for the Re-Election of the President." The story described Segretti's operations and said that the activities were financed by a secret campaign fund, which fluctuated between $350,000 and $700,000. The story implicated Segretti, Chapin, and Kalmbach.

The *Post's* key sources were usually quoted anonymously, and many observers have challenged their very existence. Nevertheless, the *Post* clearly got the jump on the Watergate story (the *Los Angeles Times* was its only competition; television largely missed the boat and was covering the story from wire reports), and the imaginative though somewhat questionable journalistic efforts of Woodward and Bernstein ushered in a new era of investigative reporting. After October 1972, however, the story slowed down. The Watergate trials and congressional investigations were largely a matter of public record, and Woodward and Bernstein began work on their book, *All the President's Men*, to be released the following year. While their reporting won a Pulitzer Prize for the *Post* and angered Nixon beyond belief, Woodward and Bernstein did not establish the final, incontrovertible link between the White House and the dirty tricks. It would take the tapes to do that.

Throughout the late summer and fall of 1972, the White House struggled to keep its finger in the dike. On August 26 the General Accounting Office (GAO) released a report that cited eleven "apparent and possible violations" by CRP of the Federal Election Campaign Act. The GAO referred these matters to Justice and asked for an investigation into a possible secret fund. Nixon tried to blunt the impact of the report two days later in a press conference when he charged that "both sides" apparently made "technical violations" of the campaign finance law, but he refused to specify Democratic violations. Nixon also said that Stans was directing an investigation of the mishandling of campaign funds and Dean was conducting a full investigation "under my direction" of the Watergate mess. Nixon then told his audience what Dean's investigation would ultimately find: "I can state categorically that this investigation indicates that no one in the White House staff, no one in this administration, presently employed was involved in this bizarre incident. . . . What really hurts is if you try to cover it up."[14] Dean later testified that this was the first he had ever heard of such an investigation.[15]

On September 15, thanks largely to the testimony of Baldwin, a grand jury returned an eight-count indictment against Hunt, Liddy, and the five burglars. It did not indict any members of the White House staff, due in large part to the fact that Magruder, after being coached in his testimony by Dean, had perjured himself before the grand jury on August 16.[16] This victory was enhanced for the White House by the decision of Federal District Judge John Sirica, who would be hearing the case, not to begin the trial of the burglars until after the election. That evening a triumphant Nixon waxed vengeful: "We'll have a chance to get back at them some day. . . . This is war. We're getting a few shots and it'll be over, and we'll give them a few shots and it'll be over. Don't worry. I wouldn't want to be on the other side right now. Would you?"[17]

Despite the cover-up's being challenged by Gray, Helms, and the *Washington Post,* it was nevertheless strong enough in the summer of 1972 to achieve the desired result—the scandal had been confined to revelations about the break-in. In August a vast majority of Americans who were asked about Watergate answered that they did not know anything about it, and the minority who did said that they did not care. Watergate was not a factor in that fall's presidential election; George McGovern made sure of that.

As in 1968, Nixon's basic political strategy in 1972 was to appeal to Middle America, now labeled by him the Silent Majority. To them the issues were nearly the same as they had been in 1968 and 1970: law and order, the economy, and the war. Yet it was clear from the start that even though these problems were far from being solved, the Middle wanted Nixon to stay at the helm. There was no serious challenge to Nixon in the primaries. Liberal Republican Representative Paul N. "Pete" McCloskey ran in the New Hampshire primary on an anti-war platform, was swamped, and immediately withdrew. Of more long-range import was the brief conservative challenge of Ohio Representative John Ashbrook, meant to highlight the dissatisfaction of hard-line conservatives with many of Nixon's first-term policies, particularly détente with China. Despite receiving a surprising amount of support from the Republican Right, Ashbrook was also swamped by the CRP machine. Nixon and Agnew were easily renominated on the first ballot in Miami.

Despite the success of the Nixon steamroller, the Democrats began the 1972 election cycle with an air of optimism. Throughout 1970 and 1971 polls showed that Nixon was vulnerable in many areas of traditional Democratic power: civil rights, the war, and the economy. If the Democrats could nominate a candidate who would appeal to Middle America, they would be able to mount a strong challenge to Nixon. This was not to be; in 1972 the Democratic party acted as if it believed that the Middle did not even exist.

In his meeting notes, Chuck Colson consistently referred to George McGovern as "the Preacher." Most scholars have concentrated their analysis of McGovern's 1972 presidential campaign on his unwavering demand that the United States immediately withdraw its troops from South Vietnam. McGovern's sincere pacifist tendencies—conceived in the later Johnson years, hardened by Tet, and cemented in Chicago during the riots at the Democratic convention—led him to try again after a short-lived candidacy in 1968. With the demise of Eugene McCarthy, the antiwar mantle gravitated naturally to the former history professor from South Dakota, who sponsored several bills in the Senate calling for immediate withdrawal from Vietnam. His hold over the issue was strengthened by the respect in which he was held by his colleagues on both sides of the aisle and his distinguished war record (in World War II he flew a B-24 bomber on many sorties and won the Distinguished Flying Cross). Besides, few people entertained a serious thought that he could win the nomination.

Yet it was not the antiwar issue that got McGovern nominated. Rather it was his shrewd promulgation of his own brand of prairie populism within the Democratic party. McGovern had initiated revolutionary reforms that balanced the composition of convention delegations for the first time in the party's history. Recognizing, perhaps before anyone, the importance of the youth vote in 1972 (it would be the first time that eighteen-year-olds would be allowed to vote for president), McGovern had begun a campaign to change the party rules in favor of the young and the traditionally disfranchised. In the midst of the upheaval at the 1968 convention, the Rules Committee had upheld McGovern's minority report, calling for a commission to study reform in the delegate selection process. He was chosen to head the inquiry, and in November 1969 the McGovern Commission proposed that the party set quotas for the number of black, female, and younger delegates. In late 1971 the party agreed, deciding that these quotas had to represent "the proportion of these groups in the total population." The voting power on the floor of the convention thus shifted away from political bosses who had long controlled the makeup of their delegations to a coalition of factions that had long been excluded from the power base of both parties. This new political foundation would be expected to support a candidate who was progressive on economic policy and firmly against the war. In effect McGovern engineered a rules change that complemented his ideals, fit his strategy, and ended up guaranteeing him a convention packed with delegates who supported his candidacy.

At first it seemed that fate was helping McGovern. A challenge from the microscopic Democratic Right over busing fell with George Wallace in Laurel, Maryland, as an assassin's bullet left him paralyzed from the waist down. Chappaquidick neutralized Kennedy, and Muskie's near defeat in New Hampshire, thanks to the Canuck letter, emaciated his campaign and allowed McGovern to completely co-opt the antiwar issue. The departure of Muskie left the Democratic Middle, which was terrified of McGovern's unabashed populism from the start, with no established candidate around whom to coalesce. The mainstream Democratic party began to search frantically for a candidate who could stop McGovern. Hubert Humphrey came out of retirement to try, but his candidacy never really materialized and he lost virtually every primary he entered. Humphrey's last hope was the California primary, and he pulled out all the stops in an attack that was so ferocious that many observers labeled it as decidedly "un-Humphrey." In a series of four highly publicized debates, his painting of McGovern as soft on welfare (centering his wrath on an ill-advised McGovern promise to give $1,000 to every American family) and defense spending made the race close. However, McGovern's organization and the appeal of the antiwar message on the college campuses made the difference, as he beat Humphrey, 44.3 percent to 39.2 percent.

California, however, chose its delegation under the unit rule. Although McGovern had not won a majority, he still was awarded all of the state's 271 convention delegates. In a decision of some irony, the party's Credentials Committee used McGovern's own reform commission to deny him his victory; they decided that the new rules of diversity and equity precluded use of the old unit rule and turned the entire delegation over to Humphrey. However, McGovern's reforms had led to the seating of a convention that was ready to do battle with the machines. It was the convention that George built, 23 percent of whose delegates were under thirty, 15 percent black, and 38 percent women. (Mayor Daley, looking around him at the Miami Convention Center, groused about the New York delegation: "What kind of delegation is this? They've got six open fags and only three AFL-CIO people on that delegation! Representative?"[18]) When the issue was put to a floor vote, the delegates voted to seat McGovern's California delegation, thus ensuring his nomination. In his acceptance address, when he urged America to "come home." McGovern doubtless believed that he had begun the process through his party reforms.

McGovern proved to be as inept in the fall campaign as he had been skillful in the fight for the nomination. His dismissal of Larry O'Brien, who only one month before had been paid a visit by the Watergate burglars, was a slap in the face to party regulars who had been bruised during the convention. His search for a new DNC head was little short of embarrassing. His summary reversal of a previous promise to Pierre Salinger, ex-Kennedy press secretary, not only angered the Kennedy wing of the party but also painted the McGovern campaign as indecisive and deceitful. The eventual choice, former campaign lieutenant Jean Westwood, did little to heal the breach with the Kennedy wing and opened wider the rift with the regulars as they fumed about being led into battle by a woman.

It was, however, the choice of his running mate that finished the McGovern campaign before Nixon had even been formally renominated. McGovern's first choice, Ted Kennedy, never had any intention of accepting, but his silence kept the McGovern forces waiting until the edge of the deadline. His second choice, Mayor Kevin White of Boston, was scuttled by the Massachusetts delegation as being an affront to Kennedy. At the literal last moment, the McGovern staff proposed the name of Thomas Eagleton, senator from Missouri. Despite rumors about Eagleton's drinking problems, there was little serious objection. Within twenty-fours hours of Eagleton's nomination, news reports alleged that his problem was far from minor: he had been hospitalized three times since 1960 for recurring bouts of mental illness. Within a week, stories were flying about Eagleton's imminent demise.

In a scene reminiscent of Eisenhower during the Nixon fund crisis of 1952, McGovern waffled. Struck by an indecision that lasted for almost two weeks, he consistently denied that he was going to dump Eagleton: "I am 1,000 percent behind Tom Eagleton." When Eagleton was finally abandoned, as all observers had known from the start that he would be, McGovern's credibility was destroyed. As Theodore White observed, "lost was McGovern's reputation as a politician somehow different from the ordinary—a politician who would not, like others, do *anything* to get elected." [19] The muddled and comic search for a new running mate, which turned through some ten candidates, finally settled on an embarrassingly transparent olive branch to the Kennedy wing, as the nomination was accepted by Kennedy in-law Sargent Shriver.

Nixon's strategy remained as it had been since the beginning of the year. He would once again aim for the Middle by acting presidential, playing up his foreign policy exploits of the spring, pointing toward an impending cease-fire in Vietnam, cornering the market on old-time patriotic values (in July he ordered Ehrlichman to "coopt the American flag lapel button—have at all rallies" [20]). The flip side of this was, as Ehrlichman told the author, to "move McGovern as far to the left as possible" without alienating the Democratic party regulars. Republican surrogates referred to "McGovernites" and "McGovern Democrats," and Nixon constantly reminded his staff to "never attack Democrats" and "never use word Democrats." This reinforced the image of McGovern as a liberal interloper whose beliefs were not those of the Democratic party. To make certain that the job was done right, the Nixon staff continued, despite the disaster at the Watergate, to use dirty tricks to pressure the opposition. McGovern's phone was tapped, his background was investigated, and RNC Chairman Robert Dole initiated an investigation into McGovern's campaign finances that turned up nothing. [21]

Nixon, however, needed no more help. McGovern's positions alienated just about everyone except the far Left. Statements such as the one he made in South Carolina ("Begging is better than bombing. . . . I would go to Hanoi and beg if I thought that would release the boys one day earlier" [22]) showed a single-mindedness for peace and a complete lack of political prescience. One by one, prominent Democrats left the fold, taking thousands of moderate Democrats with them. George Meany called McGovern "the candidate of amnesty, acid, and appeasement";[23] Dean Rusk characterized McGovern's defense posture as "insane."[24] In the end McGovern was abandoned by all the old constituencies of the Roosevelt coalition except for African Americans, who once again voted against Nixon in solid numbers. Nixon told Ehrlichman in September that McGovern was "the worst candidate of the century."[25]

The election produced the expected slaughter, with Nixon receiving 60.7 percent of the vote to McGovern's 37.5. It was the second largest plurality of any president in history, with McGovern losing every state except Massachusetts (he was the first candidate since Adlai Stevenson in 1956 to lose his home state). The defeat is made all the more telling when it is noted that in 1972 the GOP was at its lowest level of membership since 1964, trailing the Democratic party in registered membership by a whopping 45 to 27 percent. Nixon continued the trend he had begun in 1968, as the South and the Sunbelt went solidly Republican. One McGovern aide summed up the Democrat's frustration: "McGovern couldn't carry the South with Robert E. Lee as his running mate and Bear Bryant as his campaign manager."[26] Nixon had shown once again the strength of his stranglehold on Middle America.

Nixon's coattails were surprisingly short. The landslide did not extend itself to congressional races. Despite impassioned pleas from both members of Congress and the RNC, Nixon completely wrote off local races, telling Ehrlichman that the Republicans had raised the "worst crop of candidates in history."[27] As a result, both houses of Congress stayed in Democratic hands. Nixon's refusal to work for a Republican Congress in a year when it might have been won was unforgivable to many party stalwarts. His callous treatment of Congress would soon come home to roost. It would be only a matter of weeks before Nixon would have to marshal his forces on the Hill for the last battle of his presidency. When that time came, his friends in Congress were few indeed.

Throughout the campaign Nixon had been able to hold Congress at bay on Watergate. His treatment of Congress had left open sores, however; that there would be a postelection investigation was never in doubt. Senator Sam Ervin, a Democrat from North Carolina, agreed to chair a Senate panel that would investigate charges of abuses during the presidential election of 1972. Nixon's description of Ervin—"for all his affected distraction and homely manner, [he] was a sharp, resourceful, and intensely partisan political animal"[28]—was on the mark. On February 7 the Senate Select Committee on Presidential Campaign Activities was presented to the press. Counting Ervin, there would be four Democrats and three Republicans, the minority being led by Howard Baker of Tennessee.* The choice of Baker was a key one. Nixon privately had little respect for Baker,[29] but the evidence is clear that the senator was in constant contact with the White House, filling it in on developments as the investigation went along. The notes of all White House principals are full of references to Baker's funneling of information to the White House through Kleindienst, as are the tape transcripts.[30] It seems clear that Baker served roughly the same role as did Henry Petersen; like Petersen, he is left open to charges of conflict of interest.

Yet the Ervin Committee was not as immediate a problem as was Pat Gray's confirmation hearings before the Senate Judiciary Committee, also chaired by Ervin. Against the advice of most of his aides, Nixon had announced on February 17 that he was nominating Gray to permanently succeed Hoover as director of the FBI. This was one of Nixon's biggest mistakes of the cover-up. The Judiciary Committee immediately subpoenaed White House staff members to testify about the FBI's role in the investigation of the break-in. Nixon believed that Gray was a reliable soldier, but that turned out to be a false hope. By March Gray had testified that Dean had turned the contents of Hunt's safe over to the FBI (but not that he had personally destroyed that material). Not surprisingly, the senators demanded to know both the contents of the safe and what happened to it.

Nixon immediately exerted both executive privilege and presidential immunity—the hotly debated and implied rights of executive officials to refuse to appear before, and to withhold information from, a legislative committee. On March 12 the White House issued a formal statement proclaiming that members and former members of the president's personal staff would refuse to testify to a congressional committee.[31] Two days later, also citing executive privilege as well as lawyer-client confidentiality, Dean declined to testify before the Judiciary Committee.

The cover-up was straining at the seams, but so far everyone's flimsy stories had held. There just wasn't much evidence linking the break-in to the earlier abuses of power. It is distinctly possible that the unraveling would have stopped in March had John Dean not thrown in the towel. During a March 17 meeting Nixon pushed Dean to begin work on the "Dean Report" that Nixon had told the press seven months earlier was already being written.[32] Dean believed that Nixon, Haldeman, and Ehrlichman had come to see a "Dean Report" as a panacea for their problems; it would certainly not satisfy the press, but it just might make Dean the scapegoat for the entire affair. Two days later

---

*The other members: Republicans Edward Gurney (Florida) and Lowell Weicker, Jr. (Connecticut), and Democrats Daniel Inouye (Hawaii), Joseph Montoya (New Mexico), and Herman Talmadge (Georgia).

Dean received an appallingly high demand from Hunt for more money.[33] According to Dean's memoirs, he had finally had enough. He asked for a lengthy appointment with the president. He planned to lay all his cards on the table, tell Nixon everything he knew about the cover-up, and then get out.

At the same time that Dean was planning to end his role in the cover-up, Nixon had decided to strengthen it. The day before their meeting, Nixon met with his chairman of the RNC, George Bush, who promised him that "Watergate [and] executive privilege won't be an issue in '74."[34] Nixon, however, knew better. He had come to the conclusion that he had to do everything possible to make it certain that Hunt would continue his silence. Given his past record of what Dean would himself call "blind ambition," Nixon had every reason to believe that his chief counsel would handle this for him. On March 21 at 10:12 A.M. in the Oval Office, Dean and Nixon were at cross purposes for the first time. Dean was going to tell Nixon that he could not do a report and that the cover-up could not go on; Nixon was going to tell Dean how he wanted the cover-up to be continued.

As one listens to the tape of this critically important conversation,[35] the high quality of Nixon's acting job is apparent. Dean's cathartic recounting of all the details of the burglary and cover-up told Nixon absolutely nothing that he didn't know already, yet for the entire conversation Nixon acted as if it was the first time he had heard these things. Not knowing the full extent of the president's knowledge, Dean wanted to get his immediate attention. He did so with a phrase that for many would forever summarize the excesses of the Nixon White House:

DEAN: I think, I think that, uh, there's no doubt about the seriousness of the problem we're, we've got. We have a cancer—within, close to the presidency, that's growing. It's growing daily . . . it is basically because (1) we're being blackmailed; (2) uh, people are going to start perjuring themselves very quickly that have not had to perjure themselves to protect other people and the like. And that is just—and there is no assurance—
NIXON: That it won't bust.
DEAN: That it won't bust.

Dean went on to tell Nixon that everything had started with Haldeman's 1972 request to set up a "perfectly legitimate campaign intelligence operation." Dean then recounted Liddy's plan ("the most incredible thing I have ever laid my eyes on") and the information that was eventually gained from the bugs; he went on to say that Magruder was "totally knowledgeable" on the entire project and that Haldeman assistant Gordon Strachan knew where the transcript information was coming from. Dean then talked about the payoffs to the burglars. He made it clear that Haldeman, Ehrlichman, Mitchell, and himself were involved, and he talked about the $350,000 in Haldeman's safe, kept for "polling purposes." As if he had had no prior knowledge of the issue, Nixon pounced on the problem of continuing the hush money:

NIXON: How much money do you need?

DEAN: I would say these people are going to cost, uh, a million dollars over the next, uh, two years.

[Pause]

NIXON: We could get that. . . . What I mean is, you could, you could get a million dollars. And you could get it in cash. I . . . know where it could be gotten . . . the question is, who the hell would handle it?

More money for Hunt was not something that Dean wanted to approach, but it was at the heart of Nixon's agenda. As Dean vainly tried to get back to his script, Nixon pressed his point: "Let me put it this way, let us suppose that you get . . . the million bucks. . . . It would seem to me that would be worthwhile."

Haldeman then entered the room, and it was decided that he, Dean, and Ehrlichman should confer on the situation. Nixon made it clear that their first priority should be "the Hunt problem. That ought to be handled." Nixon then adjourned the meeting and, in a moment of no small irony, thanked Dean: "You had the right plan. . . . And you handled it just right. You contained it. . . ." Dean did meet with Ehrlichman later that afternoon. He later testified that they talked about blanket immunity for all the White House staff; Ehrlichman said that the subject never came up.[36] The subject did come up, however, in a taped conversation still later that afternoon between Nixon, Dean, Haldeman, and Ehrlichman, but the idea was rejected by all.[37]

Nothing had been settled on the tension-packed day of March 21. Dean had laid out facts that Nixon already knew; immunity was discussed and rejected; and staff members were feuding among themselves as they saw the inevitability of prosecution for each of them. Not surprisingly, in a phone call that evening Nixon turned to Colson, who had departed the White House in January, for help in putting things into perspective. Instead Colson gave the president more bad news about Dean—that if things fell, Dean would have "an obstruction of justice problem."[38] If Dean had a problem in this area, so did they all.

On March 23 Judge Sirica sentenced the Watergate burglars: a stunning thirty-five years in jail for Hunt and an astonishing forty years for the Cubans and Liddy. He then made the cryptic statement that these sentences were "provisional." The reason for his warning was soon clear. Sirica immediately released a letter written to him on March 19 by McCord which claimed that the Watergate defendants were under "political pressure" to plead guilty and remain silent. McCord also charged what everyone had long suspected: that "higher-ups" were involved in the break-in.[39] It was the bombshell that Ervin and the press had been waiting for. For the White House it was the beginning of the end. Within seven weeks Nixon's entire cover-up team would be gone from the administration.

McCord had been a weak link from the start. In the fall of 1972 he had written seven letters to CIA officials warning that the White House was trying to blame Watergate on the agency.[40] The White House secretly offered McCord clemency if he would maintain his silence, but he had steadfastly refused to take the bait.[41] On the same day that Sirica read his letter, McCord met for the first time with Samuel Dash, the chief investigator for the Ervin Committee, telling him that "I've got one slice of it. I think Mr. Hunt has the other slice you want, the biggest slice."[42]

Within a week the *Los Angeles Times* reported that McCord had named Dean, Magruder, and Mitchell as the planners of both the burglary and the cover-up. On March 24 McCord also asked for a private meeting with Sirica; during that meeting he told the judge that perjury had been committed at the trial. The Watergate grand jury reconvened two days later and began hearing new testimony in an attempt to reconsider whether or not anyone besides Hunt, Liddy, and the burglars should be indicted for Watergate. Between March 28 and April 4 McCord testified once again to the grand jury, telling them that Mitchell had knowledge of the break-in.[43] Hunt, who had now been granted immunity by Sirica, also spent four hours in closed session with the grand jury. Dean, Magruder, and Mitchell now faced certain indictment. On April 3 Dean told his story to a lawyer and made preliminary contacts with the investigators at the Justice Department. Magruder followed suit quickly. He resigned from his position at the Commerce Department on March 26. One week later he testified to the grand jury about the cash payments to the burglars, then confessed his earlier perjury to U.S. attorneys.

Glad to be rid of Dean and Magruder and convinced that nobody would believe their stories anyway, Nixon faced with regret the fact that Mitchell also had to go. On April 14 Haldeman, Ehrlichman, and Nixon met to discuss the situation. They agreed that Mitchell had to come forward to make a statement about his complicity. Nixon mused that "I'm not convinced he's [Mitchell] guilty . . . but I am convinced that he ought to go before a Grand Jury."[44] The discussion then led into a volatile area, one that had not yet seen the light of day, but one that sealed Mitchell's fate.

Nixon had been aware of allegations of financial improprieties made against Vice-President Spiro Agnew while he was governor of Maryland. Nixon was completely unprepared, however, for the startling news that Mitchell was a key part of this flourishing scandal on the periph-ery. The transcript of the conversation bears quoting at length: *

HALDEMAN: . . . There's a . . . area in here which has the vice-president absolutely scared shitless. There's a Grand Jury in Baltimore going on that . . .

NIXON: That isn't about us, I hope . . .

HALDEMAN: Well, he tried to get it into us in order to jar us into being worried about him, but we're avoiding that . . . because he says if that thing runs its course he will be through.

NIXON: Huh.

HALDEMAN: . . . That guy—that finance chairman . . . is involved in this Kline† case and what the vice-president tells me is, in other words, to scare us into being worried about the case, is that Kline . . . in the Grand Jury they've developed that Kline came to Mitchell's office with a bag of cash which he turned over to Mitchell and which . . . and it was allegedly involved in his receiving some very good government contracts. What the vice-president is worried about—that's what he's trying to get us worried about—so that we will worry about what he's worried about which is—

NIXON: How in the name of God could you give government contracts—Kline got government contracts as a result of this?

HALDEMAN: He doesn't have to get them—he just has to be promised them.

NIXON: Oh, I see.

HALDEMAN: He apparently got them.

NIXON: And Mitchell took the money?

EHRLICHMAN: Shapiro told me about this.‡

HALDEMAN: That's what the vice-president . . .

NIXON: I can't believe that—I can't believe that John Mitchell would take money in his office. A candidate never takes money . . .

HALDEMAN: Kline may have done it after Mitchell left us—this may have been when Mitchell was the campaign manager.

NIXON: Well, that's a different matter—he's not guilty then.

Quite aside from Nixon's faulty legal logic and the disaster that the conversation portended for Agnew, Nixon had now been confronted

*This material, excised from the original *White House Transcripts* by Nixon, was found by the author in the Nixon Presidential Papers, President's Personal Files.

†Joel Kline, a stock and land speculator and onetime candidate for Maryland bank-ing commissioner, pled guilty on August 3, 1973, to charges of obstructing a Securities and Exchange Commission investigation into his finances and on October 26, 1973, to charges of perjury, conspiracy, and obstructing justice. A government witness in the Agnew investigation, Kline admitted to being a "conduit" for up to $100,000 in cash to Agnew (*New York Times*, October 27, 1973, p. 9). Nowhere in the public record did Kline discuss his dealings with Mitchell.

‡Probably David Shapiro, law partner of Chuck Colson after the latter's resignation from the White House. The firm of Shapiro and Colson supplied Agnew with legal aid throughout the investigation. As described by journalists Jules Witcover and Richard Cohen, "the political defense was the responsibility of [third partner Judah H.] Best, with Colson and . . . Shapiro in the wings: finding out what the prosecutors were up to, then working with the White House to try to strike a deal" (*A Heartbeat Away*, p. 147).

with new evidence of Mitchell's guilt. Mitchell had to be convinced to go before the grand jury and take the blame for Watergate. Ehrlichman and Haldeman reluctantly delivered the news, but Mitchell made it clear that he was not about to take the fall for the entire team. Nixon was furious with his old friend, and he sputtered to his aides: "You *know* he'll [Mitchell] never go to prison. . . . Does a trial of the former Attorney General of the United States bug you? This god damn case . . ."[45]

With Mitchell refusing to accept any responsibility for his decisions regarding covert activities, neither Haldeman nor Ehrlichman could continue to protect themselves from the charges of Dean and Magruder. On April 30 Nixon announced to the nation that he had accepted the resignations of Haldeman and Ehrlichman, "two of the finest public servants it has been my pleasure to know." The malleable Kleindienst also resigned, forced out so that Nixon could appoint an attorney general of unquestionable principle and thereby quiet critics in Congress and the press. Nixon dryly noted that he was accepting the resignation of Dean, but he did not comment on it. He announced that Elliot Richardson would replace Kleindienst, and his old law partner Len Garment would replace Dean. Yet of greater importance than even these announcements was Nixon's decision to use the same speech to offer what he hoped would be perceived as a full explanation of his role in Watergate. Continuing the strategy that had been decided upon from the start, Nixon limited his admission of involvement to the break-in at the DNC. He took "official responsibility" for the crime, but he made it clear that he was not personally involved with it. He conceded for the first time that there had been "an effort to conceal the facts" and that Richardson would be empowered to appoint a special prosecutor who would take the case away from Justice and find those facts.

Over the next few days Nixon continued the reshuffling of his team. Alexander Haig was transferred from the NSC to replace Haldeman as chief of staff. John Connally rejoined the White House as an unpaid adviser (and soon formally switched his registration to the Republican party). Melvin Laird replaced Ehrlichman as head of the Domestic Council, and J. Fred Buzhardt, late of the Justice Department, was brought in as a special adviser to work with Garment on Nixon's defense. There was now a "new team" in the Nixon White House; its responsibility was to plot Nixon through the most troubled waters of any American presidency.

Members of the team were to deal immediately with the public's fascination with the two public investigations into Watergate. The first was the televised hearings of the Ervin Committee, which began on May 17. Technically speaking, the hearings were supposed to investigate claims of abuses on both sides during the 1972 presidential elections. However, it quickly became clear that the senators were interested only in Nixon. Watching the Ervin Committee that summer became a more popular form of daytime television entertainment than the soap operas that it often preempted. Ervin dug into his job with the tenacity of a bulldog; the next year, one week before Nixon resigned, Ervin wrote a fellow Nixon adversary, George McGovern: "Our job was to expose what was done wrong, not to extol what was done right."[46] The second investigation belonged to Archibald Cox, whom Richardson had appointed Watergate special prosecutor, thus taking the Justice Department investigation away from Silbert and Petersen. There were many at the time who questioned the legality of this action.* Nevertheless, the appointment of the Harvard professor who had been solicitor general in the Kennedy administration and was still close to the Kennedy family would place an aura of fairness and bipartisanship around the investigation. The appointment misfired badly, however; Cox promised that if he found it necessary, he would follow the investigation into the Oval Office.

In the minds of most Americans the essence of Watergate soon boiled down to the question of John Dean's word against that of the president of the United States. It was, at the start, a situation that suited Nixon quite nicely. While Dean certainly made a convincing witness before the Ervin Committee from June 25 to 29, particularly when the television audience found itself entranced by his almost photographic memory for dates and conversations, there was absolutely no proof of his claims. But there was also no proof for Buzhardt's written rebuttal to Dean's testimony, read by Daniel Inouye, which said that Dean was the "mastermind" of the cover-up and Mitchell his "patron."[47] Certainly no light would be shed on the confusion by the White House. On July 6, in a letter to Ervin, Nixon formally notified the committee that "I shall not testify before the Committee or permit access to presidential papers." Nixon argued that "no president could function if the private papers of his office, prepared by his personal staff, were open to public scrutiny."[48] Despite Howard Baker's famous demand, "What did the president know and when did he know it?" no one could be sure what or when either Dean or Nixon really knew about Watergate. The proof would come from an unexpected source.

On July 17 Alexander Butterfield, an aide to Haldeman, dropped a bomb on Ervin Committee investigators in closed session: "There is tape in the Oval Office. The tape is maintained by the Secret Service, and only four Secret Service men know about it."[49] Stunned, the investigators contacted Buzhardt, who publicly confirmed its existence on the same day. The next day Cox wrote to Nixon asking to hear the

---

*In the 1978 Ethics in Government Act, Congress affirmed the legality of the office of special prosecutor, arguing that it insulated high-level investigations from White House interference. In *Morrison v. U.S.* (1988), the Supreme Court upheld the constitutionality of the special prosecutor law.

tapes, and Ervin quickly took out a formal subpoena. One week later Nixon defied Ervin's subpoena, arguing that "the principles stated in my letter to you of July 6th preclude me from complying with that request [for the tapes], and I shall not do so." He also hinted that in any case the tapes "would not finally settle the central issues before your Committee" because to fully understand them would take the help of other executive documents, which Nixon was not about to turn over.[50] Watergate had entered its final phase—the battle for the tapes.

An unidentified Nixon aide told Robert B. Semple of the *New York Times* in January 1971 that Nixon's image problem would be solved if they could just get "somebody to stick a small television camera in the upper corner of the president's office, turn it on in the morning, leave it running all day, and not tell him about it."[51] An interesting thought; at that very moment, a semi-sophisticated taping system was running in the Oval Office. Nixon did not come into the White House with plans for taping his conversations, despite the fact that in one of their meetings during the transition Lyndon Johnson told him that from a historical viewpoint it would be a good idea. In fact, Nixon immediately ordered that Johnson's personal taping system be torn out of the Oval Office. Nevertheless, he soon had a change of heart. After meeting with Johnson a second time during the dedication of the LBJ Library, Nixon came away convinced that the taping system should be reinstalled. In February 1971 the Oval Office and the Cabinet Room were wired; in April, Nixon's hideaway office in the Old Executive Office Building and the telephones in the Oval Office, the EOB, Lincoln Sitting Room; and in May, Nixon's study at Camp David's Aspen Lodge.

Nixon argues in his memoirs that the decision to reinstate the taping system was based on a decision "that my administration would be the best chronicled in history."[52] Such a claim is at least worthy of consideration. Nixon's concern about his eventual place in history is well documented, and there is no evidence of the tapes being used for blackmail or for any other unethical purposes. However, another related theory, shared with this author by several Nixon intimates, is the most convincing: Nixon installed the system so that Kissinger would not be able to take complete credit for Nixon's foreign policy after the administration.[53]

Its installation was one of the most closely guarded of the secrets in Nixon's White House. The system was controlled through the Secret Service's First Family Indicator, an electronic unit that kept track of the whereabouts of the Nixon family at all times. If the president was in the White House, the power to the taping system was automatically turned on. In the Oval Office the trigger to the system was voice activated; a voice or any other noise (the tapes are full of car backfires, rattling coffee cups, and door slams) started the recorder. In the Cabinet Room, the system was controlled by either a switch under the table or a push button on Butterfield's phone. A Secret Service agent had the responsibility to change the tapes once a day, and up until the time that Butterfield revealed the system to the world, there had been no transcription of any of the tapes. Before the system was finally dismantled, Nixon had recorded some 950 tapes of six hours each.

Yet if Nixon wanted an accurate, clean record of his conversations, his staff could not have chosen a worse system to do it. The actual hardware of the system—Sony 800B recorders—were far below the top of the line. They were also badly installed. In the Oval Office, the microphones were embedded in the kneewells of the president's desk, and above the fireplace, hidden in wall sconces that held two lamps. The positioning of the mikes was so accoustically bad that much of the conversations are, as the famous phrase in the transcripts stated, "unintelligible." In most of the tapes Nixon sounds muffled, almost slurring—a result of the fact that the mikes were below his desktop. Perhaps this was the fault of the haste with which the system was installed. The White House staff bypassed the White House Communications Agency, and the system was installed by the Secret Service and fine-tuned by burglar alarm specialists. To make matters worse, the recordings were made on the cheapest recording tape possible, bought at a Drug Fair near the White House; one observer noted that the tape was so thin that it looked like "thick Saran Wrap."[54]

The result: tapes that are muffled, full of extraneous background noise and incomprehensible conversation. It is difficult, and in some cases impossible, to separate intent from musings, orders from speculation. Nevertheless, what is clearly heard is clearly damning. The White House tapes are perhaps the most extraordinary historical documents ever compiled by a public figure. Without them, one thing is clear—whether or not he ever came to trial, there would always be some doubt about whether Nixon willfully obstructed justice. With them, there is no doubt of his guilt.

The war of the tapes, which lasted until the day before Nixon's resignation, unearthed questions of executive power that had, to this point, been muted in the headlines of burglaries and break-ins. Nixon continually invoked his interpretation of executive privilege. Judge Sirica argued that the tapes were necessary evidence in the deliberations of the second grand jury and, if indictments were handed down, would be germane to any subsequent trials. Congress argued that its investigations meant nothing if it was denied any evidence that would shed light on the subject. The bottom line, however, was simple. All arguments were moot if Nixon refused to turn over the tapes. Throughout the fall of 1973 all of Ervin's and Cox's requests and subpoenas were met with brusque refusals from the White House.

The pressure on the administration was becoming tremendous. Agnew's fight for life was public property by the end of the summer; he would resign in October. Ervin, Cox, and Sirica only increased their demands to listen to the tapes. Tension in the Middle East would lead to October's Yom Kippur War. William Rogers had resigned as secretary of state, and Nixon's nomination of Henry Kissinger as his successor was sure to lead to a particularly probing line of congressional questioning. The press was digging into Nixon as it had never done before, and press conferences were becoming a shooting gallery. Few were surprised when, late that August, pictures were taken of an exhausted Nixon shoving Ron Ziegler out of his way while entering a speaking engagement. Most important, Watergate had taken its toll on Nixon's electoral mandate. At the end of the summer of 1973 a Gallup Poll found that only 31 percent of Americans approved of the way Nixon was doing his job. Pressure began to come from every corner of Washington for Nixon to make some kind of concession.

On September 28 Nixon decided to review the tapes that Cox and the Ervin Committee had subpoenaed. He asked Rose Mary Woods, his personal secretary since 1951, and presidential assistant Steven Bull to begin the arduous task of transcribing the conversations. They began their work at Camp David the next day, only to be interrupted by Al Haig, who cryptically reminded them that the June 20 conversation between Nixon and Haldeman was not part of the subpoenaed batch. Despite Haig's warning, Woods continued to transcribe that conversation. According to Woods's later testimony, it was she who first told the president that there was a gap of approximately eighteen and a half minutes on the tape. Nixon said that this was not a problem, as the tape had not yet been subpoenaed. After the review of the transcripts, it was clear that the tapes had to be kept from Congress and Cox; their contents alone could destroy the administration.

In a desperate search for time, Nixon came up with a novel idea. On October 17 the White House proposed that instead of giving the tapes to Cox and Ervin, they be turned over to a third party who would transcribe the tapes, decide which portions of the tapes were relevant to the investigations, and turn those portions of the transcripts over to the grand jury. During an October 19 meeting with Ervin and Baker, Nixon suggested that the third party be John Stennis, Democratic senator from Mississippi. Stennis was, as we have seen, no blind enemy of the White House. He had proved himself to be a cagey adversary on civil rights, but his Armed Services Committee had supported Nixon on the ABM. Nevertheless, at the time that the "Stennis compromise" was proposed, the senator was in a hospital recovering from gunshot wounds suffered during a mugging attempt. Aside from the question of whether his health would allow him to perform his end of this deal was the question of whether any one man could listen to all those tapes.

It certainly seemed that, as Ervin later remembered, the Stennis compromise was a "spurious proposal, which I don't believe [Nixon] ever intended to carry out. I think he was using it as an excuse to fire Cox, trying to show Baker and myself were reasonable people and that Cox was incorrigible."[55] The argument seems plausible, as aside from his intransigence on the matter of the tapes (Cox refused to accede to any plan that was predicated on someone else's version of what was on the tapes, and told Richardson so[56]), Nixon had a much more important reason for wanting to get rid of Cox. On October 18 Haig called Richardson to advise him of Nixon's concern that Cox had begun an investigation into the 1968 Hughes cash contribution.[57]

Hoping to force Cox's hand, the administration took a calculated risk. On October 19 it publicly announced the Stennis compromise idea. After quickly contacting Stennis, both Baker and Ervin announced that they would be satisfied with Stennis's report. The White House had now forced Cox to refuse the compromise in public, which he did at a tense press conference the next day, Saturday, October 20. Cox's tenure as special prosecutor was now over, and all of Washington knew it.

Despite the hand wringing that followed what the press would dub as the "Saturday Night Massacre," Nixon had the authority to fire his special prosecutor. That he asked Richardson to do the deed is entirely consistent with Nixon's aforementioned inability to face the executive's duty of firing a subordinate. It may also have been a calculated move, designed to rid Nixon of the independent Richardson as well; Richardson refused to fire Cox and resigned. In a tragicomic domino effect, the knife passed to Assistant Attorney General William Ruckelshaus, who also resigned rather than fire Cox. Both Ruckelshaus and Richardson prevailed upon Solicitor General Robert Bork to do the deed rather than present Nixon with a total insurrection; this Bork did.*

What followed was the sharpest reaction against the administration since the May 1970 crisis over Cambodia, a response that Haig aptly termed a "firestorm." Some 275,000 telegrams flooded the Western Union office in Washington, the overwhelming majority carrying a demand for the president's resignation. Within two days of the Saturday Night Massacre some forty-four Watergate-related bills and resolutions were introduced in the House of Representatives, twenty-two of them calling either for Nixon's impeachment or for an investigation of impeachment measures. The AFL-CIO voted to demand Nixon's resigna-

---

*Bork, who believed that Nixon had the constitutional right to fire Cox, would be nominated for the Supreme Court by Ronald Reagan in 1987 but rejected by the Senate.

tion. Senator Adlai Stevenson III introduced a bill giving the office of special prosecutor "a firm statutory basis." Nixon did not help his cause during an October 25 press conference when he responded to a question from Dan Rather concerning how he felt about people talking of impeachment with a bitter "I'm glad we don't take the vote in this room" and a defiant "we will not provide any presidential documents to a special prosecutor." It was a threat he could not keep. Caught off guard by the intensity of the reaction, the White House announced that Nixon would yield the subpoenaed tapes and documents to Sirica and that a new special prosecutor would soon be appointed.

Nonetheless, it was much too late for any conciliatory gestures. The most significant reaction to the Saturday Night Massacre was the decision by House Democratic leaders to have the Judiciary Committee begin hearings to see if Nixon had committed an impeachable offense. It began its deliberations on October 30; one of its first actions was to grant subpoena powers to its chairman, Representative Peter Rodino of New Jersey. Now there was a third investigative body demanding the tapes from the White House. Chief counsel for the Judiciary Committee's staff was John Doar, who had worked in the South during the sixties as a member of Robert Kennedy's Justice Department. It was quickly made obvious that Doar was not going to allow his staff to race into the breach with the headlong speed that seemed to mark the work of the Ervin Committee. One clue to this might have been Doar's refusal to use computers to categorize the incredible amount of material that his staff amassed; rather, each fact was handwritten on three-by-five filing cards.[58] As 1974 came, critics of what was now called the Rodino Committee began to carp that the committee was going too slow.

One reason for this was the murky definition of the constitutional requirement that the "president . . . shall be removed from Office on Impeachment for and conviction of Treason, Bribery, and other high crimes and misdemeanors." Did Nixon *personally*—not the White House staff or CRP—commit a high crime or misdemeanor? This was the key issue that had to be faced by the Judiciary Committee. Unlike the Ervin Committee, which had concentrated primarily on the culpability of the staffers, the Rodino Committee concentrated on the guilt or innocence of Nixon himself. If it found evidence of high crimes and misdemeanors, it would vote in favor of specific articles of impeachment, thus setting into motion the chain of events that could lead to the nation's second impeachment trial.

More so than the Ervin Committee, then, the Rodino Committee had to present a sound legal foundation for its case. In a February 20, 1974, memorandum to the committee, Doar admitted the difficulty of doing this. The Ervin Committee had shown that, without a doubt, illegal and immoral acts had occurred on Nixon's watch—what Doar called "vindictive uses of power." But how many of these acts could be traced to Nixon himself? To deal with this problem, Doar chose to take a very broad interpretation of the definition of impeachment. He noted that impeachment was not a criminal but a political "remedial" act; therefore, there was no need to look for one specific criminal act that could be shown to be a high crime. Rather, as Doar put it, "unlike a criminal case, the cause for the removal of a president may be based on his entire course of conduct in office." In their various responses to Doar, Nixon's lawyers argued that his interpretation separated high crimes from misdemeanors and thus perverted the constitutional mandate for impeachment. This, they argued, was the result of the president's being placed at the whim of a politically malicious Congress. The president's lawyers demanded that the scales be righted again: "If there is any doubt as to the gravity of an offense or as to a president's conduct or motives, the doubt should be resolved in his favor. This is the necessary price for having an independent executive."[59]

As Doar prepared his case against Nixon, the fight to gain access to the tapes continued. Cox's successor as special prosecutor, Texan Leon Jaworski, wanted to introduce them as evidence during the deliberations of the second Watergate grand jury, hoping that they would lead to more indictments of the White House staff. Nixon met Jaworski's demands with his usual derision, as he utilized executive privilege to continue to deny access to any further tapes. However, a March 1 announcement from the grand jury rattled Nixon badly. Six Nixon officials—Ehrlichman, Colson, Haldeman, CRP political coordinator Robert Mardian, Mitchell, and CRP lawyer Kenneth Parkinson—were indicted and would now face trial in Sirica's courtroom. More important was the sealed report that the grand jury gave to Sirica and recommended that he turn over to the Judiciary Committee. In it Nixon was named as an unindicted co-conspirator. A new spate of subpoenas for the tapes followed. Looking for an out, Nixon hit upon the strategy of releasing an official version of the transcripts of the subpoenaed tapes, edited by himself.

As the transcripts came out of Rose Mary Woods's typewriter, Nixon excised them with his trademark felt-tip pen. In keeping with the linchpin of the original cover-up strategy, if Nixon saw that the statement on the transcript had nothing to do with the break-in, he cut it out. As a result, material on Hughes, Agnew, and the earlier abuses of power were cut. The puritanical streak in Nixon also led him to cut out most obscenities. Usually, but not always, these obscenities as well as utterances such as "God" and "Jesus Christ" were replaced with the now famous "expletive deleted." Nixon also routinely changed complete phrases to cast his demeanor in a better light. For example, in a transcript of an April 15 meeting with Petersen, Nixon changed the phrase "haul his ass in here" to "haul him in here." What emerges, then, is a brutally edited version of what Woods and Bull thought that they heard on the tapes, a version that reflected Nixon's desire to continue to contain the scandal only to the events relating directly to the actual break-in.

On April 29 in a nationally televised address, Nixon released transcripts of forty-three of the taped conversations, including edited portions of twenty of the discussions that had been demanded by the Rodino Committee (not including the June 23 "smoking gun" conversation, which the Rodino Committee had also subpoenaed). As he spoke the transcripts sat behind him on a table, bound in impressive black leather folders emblazoned with the presidential seal. Keeping from the nation the fact that they were *his* version of the conversations, Nixon promised that "they include all the relevant portions of all the subpoenaed conversations that were recorded; that is, all portions that relate to the question of what I knew about Watergate or the coverup and what I did about it . . . these materials . . . will tell it all."[60]

It was quickly evident, however, that nothing of the sort was going to happen. Nixon's deletions were immediately discovered by the committee, as members saw that their version of many of the transcripts—which had been both leaked to them and provided by Doar's investigation—were completely different from those that Nixon now released to the public, not to mention that Nixon had refused to supply transcripts of *all* the subpoenaed tapes. For its part, the public reacted less to the specifics of the conversations than to the locker-room language that it deemed reprehensible when used by the president of the United States. Hugh Scott, long out of favor with the White House, publicly said that the transcripts show a "deplorable, shabby, disgusting, and immoral performance."[61] Within two weeks of the release of the White House transcripts, a Harris poll found that for the first time a majority of Americans favored Nixon's impeachment.

Most important, the release of the transcripts did nothing to ameliorate the Judiciary Committee. The very day they were released, Judiciary Committee members voted (20-18) to tell Nixon that he was still not in compliance with committee demands. They soon made it clear that unless Nixon gave them the 141 additional conversations that it had subpoenaed on April 19, it would serve the White House with a second subpoena. White House lawyers countered with statements arguing that the story was now complete and there would be no more releases. As both a public relations stunt and a calculated political gamble, the release of the edited transcripts was a complete flop.

On May 10 the Rodino Committee opened its impeachment hearings. True to his earlier memorandum, Doar argued that he would make his case not on any one specific bit of criminal information but on a pattern of illegality and immorality that had permeated every fiber of the Nixon White House: "When you get into the proof, and try to find the proof of the means, you find yourself down in the labyrinth of the White House in that Byzantine Empire where 'yes' meant 'no,' and 'go' was 'stop,' and 'maybe' was 'certainly' . . . but, that is just the very nature of the crime."[62] After all its deliberations and all the evidence—eight volumes, 4,133 pages—that the Judiciary Committee had amassed, it had not located a smoking gun.

Where the Rodino Committee failed, Jaworski succeeded. On May 20 Judge Sirica had finally sided with the special prosecutor and ordered all the tapes to be turned over to the court on or before May 31. Four days later the White House filed an appeal of Sirica's decision with the District of Columbia Court of Appeals. Jaworski immediately countered by filing a petition in the Supreme Court for writ of certiorari before judgment. If the writ was granted, the Court of Appeals, the next step in the appeals process, would be bypassed and the case would be taken directly to the Supreme Court. This was a highly unusual procedure, and as such it was a colossal gamble for the special prosecutor. If his request was refused, the process would drag out for months, perhaps at the same time that an impeachment trial had begun in the Senate. However, the gamble paid off; one week after receiving Jaworski's request, the Supreme Court agreed to hear the case.

Warren Burger's Supreme Court, which had demonstrated a shocking independence in *Alexander, Swann,* and the Pentagon Papers case, now sealed Nixon's doom. On July 24, in *U.S. v. Richard Nixon,* the court voted 8-0 against the president.* The decision is one of the most important court opinions on the subject of presidential power, and it offered absolutely no cracks for Nixon to slip through. It concluded that Nixon could not withhold the tapes subpoenaed by Jaworski on the grounds of executive privilege and must surrender them immediately. While it recognized the need for executive privilege, it found that the defense was not absolute: "We find it difficult to accept the argument that even the very important interest in confidentiality of presidential communications is significantly diminished by production of such material for *in camera* inspection with all the protection that a district court will be obliged to provide." On top of all this, the court also upheld the action of the grand jury in naming Nixon as an unindicted co-conspirator.

It was now over, and everyone but the blindly loyal knew it. Despite some counsel to the contrary, Nixon immediately announced that he would comply with the Supreme Court's demands. Three days later Rodino's committee turned out the first of three articles of impeachment, charging that Nixon had "prevented, obstructed, and impeded the administration of justice" (the other two, voted on within the next

---

*Justice Rehnquist recused himself, arguing that his past employment in Mitchell's Justice Department disqualified him from sitting on the case.

two days, charged Nixon with abuse of power and an unconstitutional defiance of subpoenas). The Senate Rules Committee began to debate how the impending trial would be run, and the full Senate voted to televise any subsequent impeachment hearings.[63] There was now no question but that the tapes would be heard by the entire nation; there was no longer any point in holding anything back.

It took Nixon a week to get to Jaworski the tape of the June 23 conversation with Haldeman. Once the transcript of the tape was released to the public, any hope of Nixon's mounting a defense in the Senate was gone. George Bush wrote Nixon a private letter, imploring him to resign.[64] Hugh Scott, John Rhodes, and Barry Goldwater visited the White House on August 7 and told Nixon point-blank that he had no support on the Hill; he would without a doubt be impeached in the House and most likely convicted in the Senate.

It was the defection of men closest to him, pressure from family members, and, finally, the realization that defeat in the Senate was imminent that led Nixon to resign. His speech to the nation on the evening of August 8 was at once cathartic and pathetic. Nixon looked exhausted. He explained the last year and a half by claiming that "I felt it was my duty to persevere," and he explained his resignation not by admitting guilt but by observing that he had "not a strong enough political base in Congress." Before the talk was moments done, critics began to chastise him for not apologizing for Watergate, a charge that would plague him for years to come.

His farewell to his staff and Cabinet the next day, also televised, eclipsed his resignation in drama. As Nixon entered to the strains of "Hail to the Chief," he received a lengthy and thunderous standing ovation. As he spoke, clearly fighting back his emotions, he put on his eyeglasses, a view of their president that few Americans had ever seen. He said that "this office, great as it is, is only as great as the men and women who run it." In what was perhaps a fitting epitaph for Watergate, Nixon apologized to the assembled staff for not staying in closer touch with them, saying that "I wanted to come by your offices, but I just haven't had the time."[65]

CHAPTER EIGHT

Gerald Ford and the
Thirty-Day First Term

A FTER enduring a grueling eleven-month hospitalization to treat the devastation caused by his third and fourth heart attacks, the seventy-eight-year-old soldier was ready. Telling his son "I want to go; God take me," Dwight D. Eisenhower died in the early morning hours of March 28, 1969. The United States fell into a mourning that had become all too familiar after the assassinations of the previous years. This time, however, it was not a man of the Left who had passed but the patron saint of the Middle; his conservative values had been its values for over two decades. As one observer noted, Eisenhower "embodied in his wide smile, high ideals, and down-to-earth speech all the virtues of a simpler and a more serene America."[1] It had been only nine years since he left office, but it seemed like an eternity for those who still revered Ike's memory. The decade of the sixties had seen a wholesale assault on the values that Dwight Eisenhower held dear; with him seemed to go any hope of regaining that way of life in the decade to follow.

Sex had been at the center of social consciousness in the sixties; so too did it dominate the seventies. The book that led the best-seller list on the week of Eisenhower's death was Philip Roth's *Portnoy's Complaint,* a novel based on a young man's guilt-ridden exposé of his sex life to his psychiatrist. It was edged off its plateau several months later by Jacqueline Susann's *The Love Machine.* The 1969 Broadway show *Che* promised copulation on stage (it didn't happen, but the actors did a realistic enough job of faking it); Andy Warhol's *Blue Movie* went even further, boasting forty-five minutes of simulated sex. An October 1969 *Time* cover story dealt with "The Homosexual in America"; *The Boys in the Band,* a play dealing with a gay life-style, opened to rave reviews in 1970. Americans had long since been used to sex in their movies—the new ratings system had resulted only in a glut of X-rated movies. Even in less graphic fare, Hollywood was taking sex for granted;

the first scene of 1969's *John and Mary* showed Dustin Hoffman and Mia Farrow introducing themselves to each other *after* making love. It was no longer enough to say that sex preoccupied the United States. By the end of the seventies, sex was a cornerstone of society in a way that it had not been since the 1920s. It had become, in the caustic words of one national magazine, the country's favorite "spectator sport."

Along with sex, violence continued its stranglehold on the American psyche. The United States and the world were no saner in the seventies than they had been in the sixties. Not even the cease-fire of 1973 could stop the horror of Vietnam and Cambodia from being what it had been since 1965—the most important issue on the minds of Americans and the usually bloody lead story in virtually every newscast. Competition in terms of gore came from the stories of bloodshed in Belfast, Northern Ireland, and the seemingly endless stories of Middle Eastern terrorism. In September 1971 thirty-two inmates and eleven guards or officials were killed in the bloody retaking of New York's Attica prison. The summer of 1972 saw the massacre of Israeli athletes at the Olympic Games in Munich. The most grisly reminder of society's sickness, however, was the summer 1969 slaying of actress Sharon Tate and six others at the hands of Charles Manson's "family." The grisly California murders had sickened the entire nation; a pregnant Tate was found with one breast slashed off and an "X" carved into her abdomen. During the following year's trial, defendant Sadie Atkins admitted "Yes, I killed her." When the prosecutor asked her, "But how can it be right to kill somebody," she replied with a smile, "How can it not be right when it's done with love?"*

It is not surprising, then, that like sex, violence continued to be an acceptable and widespread venue of entertainment. Quite clearly the constant media bombardment of bloodshed on the news had numbed America to carnage on the screen. In 1970 the movie *M*A*S*H*, based on a satirical book that ridiculed the military during the Korean War, scored at the box office chiefly because of its bloody operating room scenes; before decade's end the television series of the same name— also quite graphic, particularly in its earliest episodes—would be the most popular show in the country. It is not surprising that the three top-grossing films of that same year—*A Clockwork Orange, Dirty Harry,* and *The French Connection*—all based their plots on graphic violence. The following year saw the release of *The Godfather,* one of the most popular movies of all time and the standard by which films revolving around violence would ultimately be judged.

*The guilty verdicts in the Tate trial would not be the end of the Manson family's trip into the American consciousness. In Sacramento on September 4, 1975, family member Lynette "Squeaky" Fromme attempted to assassinate President Gerald Ford. Some three weeks later in San Francisco, a depressed matron, Sara Jane Moore, also tried to take Ford's life. In both attempts, Ford was unhurt; both Fromme and Moore received life sentences.

Yet worse for Middle Americans than having to hold their children back from sneaking into movies such as 1971's sex-filled *Carnal Knowledge* and 1972's gory *Deliverance* was that the general lack of respect for America that the sixties engendered had also refused to go away. The 1969 New York Drama Desk Award went to *Peace,* a play in which the god of war flushed nations down a huge toilet. The occupation at Berkeley in May 1969, the frenzied reaction to the Cambodian incursion, and the success of the moratoria movement showed that observers who had predicted the end of student protests after those at Columbia University were greatly mistaken. In many quarters the "Chicago Seven," Jane Fonda, the Berrigans and others who opposed U.S. violence in Vietnam were held forth as folk heroes. Rock and rollers such as the group Chicago penned songs such as the 1970 "Song for Richard and His Friends," which begged Nixon to "go away, please"; Crosby, Stills, Nash and Young eulogized Kent State with the bitter lyrics "Tin Soldiers and Nixon Coming, we're finally on our own. This summer I hear the drumming, Four Dead in Ohio." Yet the revulsion against government violence at home and abroad went far beyond rock and roll musicians. During a 1971 White House performance by the Ray Conniff Singers, a squeaky-clean choral group that Nixon truly enjoyed, one of the singers held up a sign of protest and openly pleaded with the shocked president to "stop bombing innocent women and children."

In retrospect it is clear that the upheaval of the 1960s and early 1970s had a striking permanence that eclipsed any previous social protest in United States history. Attempts to turn back the clock, like the graphic artists at the *New York Daily News* who sketched in crude bra straps to cover backless models in the paper's movie ads, seem either comic or pitiful. By any definition of the term, there had been a societal revolution. One of the countless examples of its permanence: in June 1969 *Oh, Calcutta* opened on Broadway, prompting a reviewer to note that it was "the nudest show outside a nudist camp"; at this writing, it is *still* running on Broadway, to packed houses. The Middle, however, continued to hope that something could stem the tide—that was one reason it had helped elect Richard Nixon.

Nixon's political reputation has obscured the fact that he held some of the same traditional values as did Eisenhower. While the tapes treat us to a Nixon who is at best coarse and often obscene, in his everyday family and personal life Nixon's mores were severely puritanical. To suggest that Nixon would have countenanced an extramarital affair, as did, by all reliable accounts, his three immediate predecessors, is absurd. He eschewed what he called "modern music" (anything besides his beloved choral music and "instrumentals" such as Mantiovani and Lawrence Welk) as much as he did loud clothing—there would be no pictures of Nixon walking the beach in a Hawaiian shirt. What he called in his memoirs his "unabashed patriotism" was straight out of a John Wayne movie, and completely sincere.

All this led inextricably to Nixon's inability to accept the social change that had taken place in the United States during the sixties. One of the great goals of the Nixon administration was to wash out America's minds and return American culture and mores to the days of Eisenhower. In his memoirs Nixon wrote that as president he was "anxious to defend the 'square' virtues," so dearly held by the Middle. In his eulogy to Eisenhower, delivered as the general lay in state in the Capitol Rotunda, Nixon observed that "he made Americans proud of their president, proud of their country, and proud of themselves." Nixon hoped that, like Eisenhower, he would come to typify the president as the nation's moral guardian. This hope is spelled out in a rather remarkable series of documents—several pages of handwritten notes that he kept nearby in his desk to the very last day of his presidency. In these notes Nixon scrawled his ideas and thoughts on the state of the presidency, and how he hoped to use that office. On one legal-size sheet, dated September 7, 1969, Nixon scribbled that he should constantly remind himself that "each day [is] a chance to do something memorable for someone—need to be good to do good," and he listed one of his long-term goals as being that the "nation is better in spirit at end of term." On another, dated December 6, 1970, Nixon mused: ". . . Purpose—goals for generation—vision—Dignity—respect—prestige—a man the people can be proud of."[2]

His administration's abuses of power kept Nixon from achieving these lofty goals for himself. They shocked the Middle to its core, and by 1974 Americans were sickened by their government as they had never been before. Although television's Archie Bunker continued his uncompromising defense of "*my* president, Richard E. Nixon," the Middle held Nixon personally accountable for the excesses of his administration. There was clearly a national sigh of relief upon his resignation. Bob Woodward recalled it for the author as "a real moment that was quasi-therapeutic," while a former New Hampshire supporter of Nixon paralleled the resignation to getting an inoculation: "You hate to get it because you know it's going to hurt. But when it's over, you're glad you got it." A future Republican senator from Minnesota, Rudy Boschwitz, was blunt in his assessment for *Time:* "Dick Nixon doesn't have us to kick around any more." A poll taken in California only hours after the resignation found that 54 percent felt that it would be wrong to give Nixon immunity from prosecution, and a sign left on a fence outside the White House proclaimed, "Ding, Dong, the Witch is Dead." Americans hoped that their new president would be a dignified antidote to Nixonism. As Margaret Campbell, a librarian in Shaker Heights, Ohio, put it, "I'm looking forward to another and a better day."[3]

Something better seemed to be happening inside the White House in August 1974. The vitality of the new first family reminded many people of the Kennedys. The first daughter refused to give up wearing jeans in the White House; one of the first sons invited Beatle George Harrison for lunch. The First Lady certainly broke the mold; her candor when talking about her children, her bravery when undergoing surgery for breast cancer, and her firm support for the women's movement made Betty Ford a national figure in her own right.

The new occupant of the Oval Office was, in a word, a comfortable man to be around. Before moving into the White House he would fetch his morning *Washington Post* while still in pajamas and bathrobe and wave to curiosity seekers in the street. He was prone to taking laps in the White House pool with an inflatable rubber duck at his side, and urged reporters to take all the pictures that they wanted. One of his first orders was to stop the playing of "Hail to the Chief" when he entered a room; he contended that the school song of his alma mater, the "Michigan Fight Song," would do. His ever-present pipe made him look easygoing even when he was reading a stack of state papers. White House staffers were quietly told that their new boss would like to see office doors left open as much as possible. A true social life returned to the White House after its Watergate-imposed sabbatical; the president loved to dance, and the new first couple were always the last to leave the party. It wasn't long before the American people were giving their president the highest possible compliment one can give to a new acquaintance: he was a regular guy. As he himself had said in his Inaugural Address, he was clearly a Ford, not a Lincoln.

Yet as the wags said at the time, Lincoln had made a fairly good president; Ford only made cars. The country was clearly in a mood to like its president in 1974, but Watergate had destroyed any movement on policy and had left the American people believing that all politicians were incompetent liars. The new guy didn't seem to be a liar. However, a nagging question kept popping up: was Gerald Rudolph Ford up to the job?

Gerald Ford reflected his midwestern small-town upbringing throughout his political career. On the banks of the Grand River in western Michigan, turn-of-the-century Grand Rapids was a magnet for austere, puritanical, and hard-working Dutch immigrants. Their Christian Reformed Church frowned upon drinking, music, and socializing. They also brought with them their trade of furniture making. The town, and families such as that of Gerald R. Ford, Sr., flourished as a result. Ford owned a moderately successful paint business that sold to furniture dealers. Living in a spacious home in the upper-middle-class section of East Grand Rapids, the Fords were, by comparative standards, financially well off. Young Jerry and his three brothers were disciplined not with an iron fist, as were their Dutch Reformed playmates, but with the Golden Rule. Ford would later write that "[Dad] and Mother had three rules: tell the truth, work hard, and come to dinner on time."[4] Ford's youth was a midwestern cliché: church every Sunday, Boy Scouting (he would earn his Eagle badge, scouting's highest award), and sports at South High School, where he excelled in football.

It did not have to be thus. Young Jerry had originally been the product of a violent, unhappy environment. He was born on July 14, 1915, in Omaha, Nebraska, and christened Leslie Lynch King. His parents fought and argued their way to a divorce before their child's second birthday (Ford would later write that "I heard that he hit her frequently"[5]). The baby and his mother, Dorothy Gardner, moved back to her family's home in Grand Rapids, where she met the senior Ford. After their marriage, Ford adopted the baby boy, who was renamed Gerald R. Ford, Jr.

It was football that consumed young Jerry, and he excelled at the sport, taking South High to the Michigan state championship in his senior year. The Depression weakened the family business, so an athletic scholarship was the only way that he would be able to attend college. His high school coach helped him to obtain a prestigious full-tuition scholarship at the University of Michigan, where he enrolled in 1931. Ford developed into one of the Big Ten Conference's all-time leading centers, and the Wolverines won the national championship two of his four years. He was sought after by several professional teams, but he had long since decided that he was going to study law. Money was again a problem, and again a coach intervened. The Michigan skipper, Harry Kipke, recommended Ford to the head football coach at Yale, and Ford went to New Haven in the fall of 1935 as an assistant coach. After two years of part-time coaching he was able to enroll full time in the Law School. Ford graduated in January 1941, returned to Grand Rapids, and founded a firm with a friend from Ann Arbor, Philip Buchen.

World War II interrupted, and Ford was commissioned an ensign in the U.S. Navy in early 1942. His first assignment was as a physical training officer for aviation cadets, but he earnestly wanted to see active duty. He eventually was assigned to the aircraft carrier *Monterey* as an assistant navigator. During the last year of the war, he took part in most of the major naval action in the Pacific theater. Indeed, he almost lost his life—not from enemy fire, but from a violent typhoon that killed several of his mates in December 1944. When Ford was discharged, he held the rank of lieutenant commander and had earned ten battle stars, three medals, and a ribbon.

It was not particularly surprising that when he returned from the war, Ford gravitated to politics. While he returned to Grand Rapids as fiscally conservative as any Taft Republican, Ford's experience in the Pacific would not allow him to accept postwar isolationism. This stance was strengthened by the transformation of Michigan's senior senator, Arthur Vandenberg, into an internationalist. Vandenberg's conversion set up the scenario for political change in Ford's hometown. Michigan's Fifth Congressional District, which included Grand Rapids, had long been represented by Bartel A. Jonkman, a Taft conservative who was one of the scourges of Harry Truman's "do-nothing 80th Congress." For example, Jonkman attacked the Marshall Plan while Vandenberg supported it, profoundly irritating the senior senator. Vandenberg decided to oust Jonkman, and he began to look for a candidate.

He found young Jerry Ford, who had already begun to ally himself with Grand Rapids Republicans who felt that Jonkman was beatable. Ford built his entire primary campaign in 1948 around criticisms of Jonkman's foreign policy and made it clear that he was for Vandenberg, the Marshall Plan, and the United Nations, roughly in that order. He emphasized his veteran's background in a novel way: he converted an army surplus quonset hut into a rather conspicuous red, white, and blue campaign headquarters. The voters of the Fifth District were impressed by the energy of the young lawyer, a vigor that was made all the more conspicuous by the complacent campaign of Jonkman, who seemed never to have considered that he might lose. Ford's victory in the primary and his easy fall election victory (which, for purposes of modern comparisons, cost Ford a grand total of $3,500 for both campaigns), were small elements of the shift in the Republican party away from the Right that would destroy the presidential hopes of Taft and lead to the candidacies of Thomas Dewey and Dwight D. Eisenhower.

Ford was always a man of the House; his was always a legislative temperament. His twelve terms in Congress were a story of steady growth of power, if not of flashy accomplishment. He began as the most junior member of the Public Works Committee, and by his second term he was on the influential Appropriations Committee, the body that concerns itself with budgetary matters. As a member of the defense appropriations subcommittee, Ford became fluent in military spending, and while on the foreign operations subcommittee he dealt with the ticklish task of the CIA budget. The Korean War and the accompanying acceleration of defense spending quickened Ford's education, and he was soon regarded as an expert on defense matters. His growing influence was evidenced by a Ford for vice-president boomlet in 1960.

If it had come to pass, a Nixon-Ford ticket in 1960 would have made a particularly odd union, even odder than the combination that was to come in 1973. Ford had become increasingly impatient with his party during the Eisenhower administration. He found himself becoming more and more of an activist, and he deplored what he saw as an arrogance of power and a dependence upon Eisenhower's name in the party, views that had backfired in 1958 and had led to huge Republican losses at the polls. As Ford watched Nixon go down to defeat in 1960, and as he watched the new president run the Executive Office with a well-publicized "vigor," Ford found himself attracted to John Kennedy. In 1961 he surprised his party by leading a floor revolt against a foreign military aid bill that was substantially less than what Kennedy wanted. Ford was able to put together a coalition of Democrats and Republicans that pushed the bill back up to Kennedy's original price tag.

This streak of independence would take Ford tantalizingly close to the summit of legislative power. In 1963 a group of "Young Turks"—men who, like Ford, were upset with the turtlelike pace of Republican leadership—overthrew sixty-seven-year-old Charles Hoeven of Iowa and elected Ford the leader of the House Republican caucus. In 1965, sickened by the Goldwater debacle, the same group engineered the election of Ford as House minority leader. Ford made it clear from his very first press conference that he was going to be bird-dogging Lyndon Johnson's Great Society. His most publicized method was a weekly television show with Senate Minority Leader Everett Dirksen of Illinois. A half-hour show that always began with a "question of the week" for Johnson ("Mr. President: Why are we *losing* the War on Poverty?"), the "Ev and Jerry Show" tore into Johnson's programs and served as a marvelous public relations vehicle for both men. Despite his leadership of the "loyal opposition," however, Ford liked Johnson. He saw in him many of the same qualities that he had seen in Kennedy—boldness, decisiveness, and humor.

Ford was developing a reputation for being a partisan leader who was nevertheless respected on both sides of the aisle. Perhaps the most visible sign of this trust was Ford's inclusion on the most sensitive and scrutinized committee of the decade—the Warren Commission, which investigated the assassination of President Kennedy. It was Ford who accompanied Chief Justice Earl Warren to the Dallas jail to interview Jack Ruby, the assassin of Lee Harvey Oswald. Ford came away from this experience reassured that Oswald had indeed killed Kennedy. To this day Ford remains convinced of the validity of the Warren Commission's conclusions. In 1978, when called upon to testify before the House Select Committee on Assassinations, he defended the Warren Report and called the new committee "the most inexcusable waste of the taxpayer's money."[6]

By mid-1973 Spiro Agnew was at the end of his rope. A lengthy *Wall Street Journal* investigation made public what had been rumored in Washington for months: Agnew was suspected of tax evasion, bribery, and extortion schemes while he was governor of Maryland. As

noted in the preceding chapter, Nixon was well aware of the seriousness of the allegations and of the tie between those charges and John
Mitchell. However, Nixon was preoccupied with his own problems; in
an April 4 telephone conversation he told Ehrlichman that "under [the]
circumstances Agnew should chart his own course, as will the president."[7] Agnew tried to take his case to the House of Representatives
for review, but no one in the House leadership—including Ford—wanted
to touch the case. After months of wrangling with the Justice Department, Agnew finally surrendered. On October 10 he plea-bargained his
case and pled nolo contendere to a charge of income tax evasion. Later
that day he resigned.

Loyalty to the president was not the primary reason that Ford was
tapped to succeed Agnew. Although he had voted with the administration approximately 90 percent of the time, Ford had also shown that
he could be unpredictable. He certainly was not chosen for the ease
with which he would fit in with the beleaguered White House staff;
both he and Hugh Scott, his partner in the Senate, never got along
with any of Nixon's handlers. The reason that Ford was selected instead of Nixon's first choice, John Connally,[8] was that Ford was something that Connally would never be—confirmable.

Ford was masterfully prepped for his confirmation hearings by his
two closest aides. The lion's share of the work was done by Robert
Hartmann. A wily veteran of Washington's political wars, Hartmann
had covered Washington for the *Los Angeles Times* during the Truman
and Eisenhower years but was farmed out of the *Times* by the ruling
Chandler family in 1962 because he was philosophically out of sync
with the Kennedys. In 1966 Hartmann began to serve Ford as a legislative assistant and quickly became his indispensable right hand. In
preparing Ford for the hearings Hartmann was assisted by Phil Buchen,
who had stayed close to Ford since their days as law partners in Grand
Rapids; his advice had been solicited on a number of occasions. During
the hearings Buchen served as a volunteer researcher and prepared
many of the documents that were included in the voluminous briefing
books that Ford studied prior to his questioning. Thanks not only to
this detailed preparation but also to the reputation for integrity that
Ford had built with his colleagues over twenty-seven years in Congress, there was never any real doubt that he would be confirmed.

What Nixon needed from his new vice-president was a public defender, a lightning rod for the bunkered president. Ford was perfect for
this job. His sense of loyalty to party and office overcame any doubts
he may have had about Nixon, and as minority leader he had evolved
into one of the president's most vocal congressional defenders. Even
when faced with the Saturday Night Massacre just days after his nomination, Ford wrote to a constituent that "I feel it was unfortunate that
Mr. Cox did not go along with the compromise worked out between

the president and Senators Ervin and Baker. The president had no alternative at the time but to dismiss Cox." As he wrote in his memoirs, Ford "still believed that Nixon was innocent" in late 1973; Nixon's only fault was that he had acted "politically dumb."[9] Once confirmed, Ford began an exhaustive whirlwind of speeches in defense of Nixon. By early 1974, however, Ford had seen enough of the Nixon White House to want to soften the tone of his defense. Yet, as he wrote in his memoirs, "by the nature of the office I held, I was in an impossible situation. I couldn't abandon Nixon, because that would make it appear that I was trying to position myself to become president. Nor could I get too close to him, because if I did I'd risk being sucked into the whirlpool myself."[10] Hartmann soon hit upon the idea of criticizing Nixon's staff rather than Nixon, thus getting the best of both worlds. On March 30 at a convention of Midwest Republicans in Chicago, Ford blamed the abuses of power on the machinations of Nixon's "elite guard." The speech was met with a wild ovation, and Ford used it as the basis of his talks for several weeks after.

Ford's position was made more complicated by the continuing Watergate revelations. Despite the adverse media reaction, Ford failed to see the April release of Nixon's version of the transcripts as a crushing blow. He had long been pushing the president to release all relevant evidence, and while the transcripts provided ample examples of oafishness in the White House, there was as yet no smoking gun. Ford responded to a reporter's question on the transcripts with the observation that "there is no question in my mind that the documentation which has now been made available to the American people . . . proves that the president is innocent and exonerates him of any involvement in either the planning of Watergate or any cover-up."[11] Yet events conspired to undercut Nixon's front man. On June 5 Ford spoke at a Republican fund-raiser in Columbus, Ohio, and argued that the evidence showed that Nixon "is innocent of any involvement in the cover-up." That same evening the press released the story that Nixon had been named by the Watergate grand jury as an unindicted co-conspirator. As Ford charitably remembers it, "I damn near blew my stack"—an outburst which was most certainly done in private.[12]

Ford was quickly coming to the conclusion that innocent or not, Nixon could not hang on much longer. He began to waver, not in his public defense of Nixon but in his private belief that Nixon would survive. In a moment of disarming candor aboard Air Force Two, Ford told John Osborne of the *New Republic* that a future Ford cabinet would not include either Defense Secretary James Schlesinger or Press Secretary Ron Ziegler. After Osborne wrote the story, Ford did not deny having made the observations. The furor that the story caused, however, forced him to back off his statement, saying during a Kansas City speech that Schlesinger "would make a good Secretary of Defense in anybody's cabinet."[13]

And yet even when faced with the most damning evidence of all—the smoking gun conversation—Ford still could not cut the umbilical cord that tied him to his president. Nowhere is this more evident than during the most dramatic meetings of the Ford vice-presidency. The story of whether or not Gerald Ford and Nixon's chief of staff, Alexander Haig, constructed a deal that promised a presidential pardon for Richard Nixon after he left office has just enough loose threads in it to titillate the imagination of conspiracy seekers. Ford's version of the meeting—as stated in his memoirs and testified to before the House Judiciary Committee's subcommittee on criminal justice later that year—is, with some exceptions, corroborated by both the memoirs of Hartmann and Woodward and Bernstein's *Final Days*. It is not a story of a deal but rather a story of Ford's indecision, as well as his resistance to making a final break with his president.

At about 8:00 A.M. on the morning of Thursday, August 1, Haig called Ford to ask for a meeting. Hartmann came along. Haig told them that while he had not yet heard the tapes that the Supreme Court had ordered Nixon to relinquish, he had been assured that there was new evidence that would prove that Nixon knew of and approved plans for the cover-up as early as six days after the break-in. Haig said that James St. Clair, Nixon's lawyer, was angry about this new development; predictably, Ford recalls in his memoirs that "I was angry too."[14] The meeting was a short one, and after Haig left, Ford swore Hartmann to secrecy.

Haig went back to his office to read the transcripts of the June 23 tapes. As soon as he read them, he emphatically told the president that those conversations would sooner or later end his presidency. According to Woodward and Bernstein, Nixon then directed Haig to prepare a list of options that were still available to the president. Haig returned to his office and arranged with White House Counsel Fred Buzhardt to begin work on the list. Haig then called Ford and requested a second meeting, this time without Hartmann present.

At 3:30 P.M. Haig summarized the June 23 transcripts for Ford. In a flourish of melodrama, Haig asked: "Are you ready, Mr. Vice-President, to assume the presidency in a short period of time?" Ford, who had expected this moment for several months, answered in the affirmative. Then Haig turned to the subject of the list that he and Buzhardt had prepared earlier that day. The options were that Nixon (1) step aside briefly under the 25th Amendment, then reassume power if he was cleared in a Senate trial; (2) delay his resignation in the hope that a miracle would happen; (3) maneuver for a censure vote rather than an impeachment trial from Congress (à la Joseph McCarthy); (4)

pardon himself and everyone else related to the crimes of his administration, then resign; (5) resign, then be pardoned by his successor. Haig made it clear to Ford that these were not *his* suggestions. What Haig wanted to know was whether or not Ford agreed with him that these were the only viable options, and whether or not the vice-president had any other recommendations to make to the president.

Several reports suggest that at this point Ford became confused. Ford recalls in his memoirs that he told Haig point-blank that he was not going to make any recommendations, but "because of his references to pardon authority, I did ask Haig about the extent of a president's pardon power." This seems a bit odd—a lawyer asking a general for a legal interpretation. Nevertheless, there is little question that Ford did want more information on the possibility of a Nixon pardon. Haig responded that it was his understanding "from a White House lawyer" that a president did indeed have the right to pardon someone even before criminal action was taken. The meeting was now over.[15]

Ford's and Hartmann's memoirs generally agree on what followed. When Ford told his chief of staff that Haig had mentioned a pardon, Hartmann demanded to know, "What did you tell him?" According to Hartmann, Ford said, "I told him I needed time to think about it." Hartmann was flabbergasted that his boss would even consider such a heinous thing as a pardon. Ford reminds his readers that Hartmann's reaction "was typical of Bob . . . [he] was suspicious of everyone."[16] Nevertheless, the vice-president agreed to Hartmann's request that he consult Jack Marsh, an ex-Virginia congressman serving as an assistant to Ford, who had a better rapport with Haig than did Hartmann.

Ford's schedule for the rest of the day kept getting in the way, and by evening he had not yet spoken to Marsh. Finally Hartmann could stand it no more. He cornered Ford, who was dressing for a formal dinner engagement, and told him, "You ought not even be thinking about pardons." According to Hartmann, Ford replied, "Well, I'm going to sleep on it. I want to talk to Betty."[17] Ford recalls that he went home and talked to his wife, who agreed with his instinct that he shouldn't make any recommendations from Haig's options list. Haig phoned him later that evening to check in, and Ford reiterated to his caller that "we can't get involved in the White House decision making process."[18] When Hartmann was told of the phone call the following morning, he was more convinced than ever that Haig was conniving to extract a promise of a pardon from his unwitting boss.

If that was ever the case, the events of that day—agreed upon by all observers—ended the matter. Marsh and Hartmann finally got their chance to jointly make their feelings known to Ford (Hartmann: "We both lit into him like Dutch Uncles"[19]). But sensing that Ford was still wavering, they suggested that Bryce Harlow be consulted, to which

Ford agreed. It was midafternoon before Ford talked with the three men. Agreeing with Marsh and Hartmann that Haig was soliciting a pardon, Harlow confirmed the worst fears of the two aides when he remarked that "I cannot for a moment believe that all this was Al Haig's own idea."[20] Wanting to end the matter, Ford picked up the phone (he recalls that he first wrote out what he wanted to say) and with all three advisers present told Haig that he had no intention of recommending whether or not the president should or shouldn't resign. He also emphasized that nothing from the previous day's conversation should be given any consideration in whatever decision Nixon would ultimately make. According to Ford, Haig responded, "You're right."[21]

The question of whether Haig was canvassing for a deal on the pardon with Ford is still an open one. Hartmann told the author that he remains convinced that Haig was fishing for a deal, and he recalls that Marsh and Harlow agreed with him at the time. Ford, however, does not agree. He writes that he told Hartmann that far from a deal, Haig's suggestion was "just one of the ideas kicking around at the White House."[22] Haig has not yet discussed or written on the matter. On one point, however, the record is clear. If Haig was offering a deal, Ford never accepted it.

On August 5, 1974, the public release of the "smoking gun conversation" liberated Ford from his dilemma of defense and allowed him to disengage himself from Nixon. In a statement to the press that evening, Ford announced that "I have come to the conclusion that the public interest is no longer served by repetition of my previously expressed belief that . . . the president is not guilty of an impeachable offense." The next day in the Oval Office Nixon told Ford of his decision to resign. On August 9, in an Inaugural Address written by Hartmann and delivered in the East Room of the White House, Ford asked the audience to "confirm me with your prayers" and began his administration by proclaiming that "our long national nightmare is over."

The suddenness of the transition did not find Ford without a plan of attack for the opening days of his administration. For several weeks, without Ford's knowledge, a secret "transition team" had been planning for the first decisions of a Ford presidency. Clay Whitehead, who had served in various positions in the Nixon White House and was then head of the Office of Telecommunications Policy, had linked up with Phil Buchen by virtue of the fact that their Washington offices were in the same building. Together they agreed that Ford would need to have specific recommendations in hand on his very first day in office. With the help of three other young alumni of the Nixon White House—Brian Lamb, Lawrence Lynn, and Jonathan Moore—they dis-

cussed problems that Ford would face when he took office and con-
signed their ideas to a binder that would be presented to Ford after his
inauguration. Their motives were clear; as Lamb told the author,

> I remember saying to [Whitehead]: "You better get Phil and that black
> book into that limousine on the morning of the ninth [Nixon's resigna-
> tion] when he leaves . . . because if he is not there to meet and greet
> him, the game's over. [Ford] will be in the hands of others, including Al
> Haig and Henry Kissinger, and he'll never have a chance to be his own
> man.

Their meetings were held in secret to shield them not only from the
press but also from Ford's vice-presidential staff. They needed to distance themselves from Ford lest the vice-president be accused of helping to plan a "palace coup." Ford says in his memoirs that had he
known about the deliberations of these men, he would have stopped
them.[23] Buchen agrees, musing to the author that if he had found out,
Ford would have "blown his top".

On August 7, when it was evident that Ford would become president within hours, Buchen went to Ford's home in Virginia and told
him about the transition team's efforts. As Buchen recalled that meeting for the author, he told Ford bluntly that "you're not quite ready to
go . . . you better get some work done, even though I've done some
work." Both men agreed that the transition team would now have to
ask people who were close to Ford to join its ranks; with the exception
of Buchen, no one on the team was a Ford intimate. It is not surprising
that several of Ford's suggested additions were either present or former
congressional colleagues: Robert Griffin of Michigan, John Byrnes of
Wisconsin, and Rogers Morton of Maryland, along with Bryce Harlow,
William Wythe, a vice-president of operations for U.S. Steel, and former Pennsylvania Governor William Scranton. Over the next two days
this new team expanded upon Whitehead's report and formulated a
series of specific recommendations for Ford. One recommendation was
that a general housecleaning was in order. While Ziegler should be
asked to resign immediately, Haig should be given more time and handled more gently, yet eventually be asked to "move on." Thanks to
the efforts of his two transition teams, Ford was starting out with well-
prepared options. Nevertheless, it was soon obvious that options would
not be enough as Ford's administration stumbled to its start.

The transition period from one presidential administration to another is normally about sixty days. Counting Whitehead's secret efforts, Ford's transition planning had gone on for two weeks; after Ford
was made aware of that group's efforts, the formal passage from the
Nixon administration took place in less than forty-eight hours.
Throughout August 1974 the Ford presidency looked more like a tran-

sition team that was planning its takeover than an administration in its first days of power. Forced into a peculiar on-the-job training, the team had a wild, disorganized thirty days, during which the administration tried to come to grips with how it wanted to run itself. It did so with an unavoidable mixture of Nixon holdovers and elements of Ford's congressional and vice-presidential staffs that instantly became entangled in dissension and indecision. When Ford brought his thirty-day "first term" to an abrupt end with his decision to pardon Richard Nixon, he had yet to find his way out of a Ford transition and into a Ford administration.

When he had inherited the office of vice-president, Ford had taken along his congressional staff of about a dozen people, some of whom had been with him since 1946. By February 1974 the staff had grown to about sixty people, ostensibly run by Hartmann, who had been promoted to chief of staff. The new size and responsibilities of the vice-presidential staff created immediate difficulties. A man of congressional, collegial mind-set, Ford was innately uncomfortable with the idea of heavy-handed management of his staff. He preferred a more open office and a staff that constantly bombarded him with ideas. Hartmann's job description was never intended to resemble either Haldeman's or Haig's. A man of somewhat shoddy scheduling habits, prone to working all night on speeches and then being somewhat lax about attending the next day's meetings, Hartmann ran the loose ship that Ford liked. It was soon obvious, however, that running the office of the vice-president like a congressman's office was not working. Hartmann was quickly overwhelmed by the complexities of running such a large office; in his memoirs, Ford would characterize Hartmann's promotion to chief of staff as a "dreadful mistake."[24] Hartmann received little help from Ford, who was constantly on the road. The vice-president's office was soon in a state of chaos.

Buchen, who at this point was making frequent trips to Washington to serve on several commissions for the vice-president, was appalled by what he saw. As he recalled in an interview with the author, "There weren't any staff meetings; people were just not knowing what to do, and [you were] never certain if the correspondence was getting answered promptly. . . . It just seemed to be a terrible operation." He began to press Ford to make changes. Acting on Buchen's advice, in May 1974 Ford asked William Seidman, highly successful in the world of financial accounting, to come in and do a study of how the vice-presidential staff could be streamlined. Seidman's study made it clear that Ford needed a strong chief of staff and a more focused organization below. The study designated Hartmann as that chief, with direct responsibility for three heads of the operational staff: Richard Buress as congressional liaison, Jack Marsh at defense and international affairs, and Seidman, now aboard as head of administration and services.

Ford moved into the Oval Office before Seidman's changes really had an opportunity to take hold; besides, an operation like Seidman's wasn't Ford's style. Instead of bringing a strong staff system into his White House, Ford kept the loose structure of the vice-presidential office. All of his top advisers would ideally have equal access to the president, be on an equal plane with each other in terms of level of influence, and not be managed or controlled by any one staffer. Hartmann explained this system to the press: "Ford is number one, we are *all* number twos."[25] This was soon dubbed the "spokes in a wheel" concept. All staff members were equidistant on the rim of this administrative "wheel," with each having direct access to the "hub" of the Oval Office. Hartmann was named counselor to the president with Cabinet rank and was also put in charge of the Editorial Office, which included responsibility for the White House speechwriters. Jack Marsh received the same rank and continued his role as ad hoc adviser to Ford, with particular emphasis on congressional and Defense Department relations. Buchen replaced Fred Buzhardt as White House counsel and was immediately put in charge of researching the thorny question of a pardon for Nixon. Seidman was given charge of a revamped Economic Policy Board, but he also offered advice on a wide-ranging array of domestic issues. Rounding out the top-level staff were Kissinger, who kept both the State and NSC portfolios, and Al Haig.

It was the decision to keep Haig on that caused the most immediate trouble. For several reasons Ford had agreed with the recommendation of both his transition teams that Haig be temporarily kept on as assistant to the president. As Ford recalled for the author, he "didn't think it was in the nation's best interest to make a clean sweep overnight. I needed some continuity on a short-term basis." There was also the issue, as Ford wrote in his memoirs, that "I was determined to be my own chief of staff, and Al Haig was agreeable to this change."[26] Hartmann, who had been passed over for Haig's position, was furious. He argued that Haig, Kissinger, and the other Nixon holdovers would smother any attempts to ignite a true Ford administration. Hartmann's disgust with the Nixon alumni was expanded in his memoirs, *Palace Politics.* He derisively labeled them the "Praetorian Guard," named after the elite military force that was chosen to protect the lives of the Roman emperors.

In an interview with the author, Hartmann made it clear that he continues to believe that Ford's refusal to immediately clean house, "combined with the pardon, really doomed Ford's brief romance with the American people and probably doomed his reelection, although you can put a lot of other reasons on that." The author, however, found few who served in the Ford administration who agree with Hartmann. Buchen, for example, told the author that he crossed swords with Hartmann at the time, telling him that in the first place, Haig was the only man who knew how to take care of the nuts-and-bolts "routing stuff," and that in the second place, Haig wasn't enough of a Nixon ideologue to try to convert Ford to anything. Yet it is unquestionable that the decision to keep Haig on and, to a lesser extent, the decision to keep Kissinger sowed the seeds of dissension in a Ford staff that was already coming into office quite disheveled.

It was quickly clear that the spokes in this particular wheel needed a much clearer line of organization than Ford had furnished them. Within days of the inauguration Haig had once again assumed the de facto duties of chief of staff and was shuffling the paperwork in what he felt to be the right direction. This infuriated Hartmann, who made his feelings on his diminishing influence well known. Staff meetings continued to be poorly attended; key personnel were not getting information needed for proper decision making. By the end of his first month, a disappointed Ford had given up on the "spokes in a wheel" and was searching the market for his own Haldeman. On September 15 Ford asked Donald Rumsfeld, back in the United States from his post as ambassador to NATO to attend his father's funeral, to rein herd over his brawling staff. Anxious to avoid any comparison in the press with Haldeman, Ford gave Rumsfeld the title of "staff coordinator." Rumsfeld's appointment gave at least the impression that someone was at the top. It also generated one added advantage by opening a position for the exhausted Haig at NATO.

Rumsfeld added to the large number in the Ford White House who had served in the House with Ford; indeed, Rumsfeld had supported Ford's successful 1965 candidacy for minority leader. His stint at Nixon's Office of Economic Opportunity as head of the Cost of Living Council had provided testimony to his managerial skills. Rumsfeld's appointment was an admission that Ford's experiment in giving his staff a wide berth of autonomy had run aground only one month into the administration. However, the appointment served to exacerbate the problem, fueling the long-standing speculation that Rumsfeld's ambitions reached far beyond a mere manager's role. One Ford staffer, speaking for many, acerbically told the author that Rumsfeld "was only for himself—I don't think he served the president well. He wanted to be vice-president so badly."[27] Rumsfeld was also quite heavy-handed in his managerial style, and as established staff members saw him co-opting areas once reserved for them, the predictable sparks flew. Hartmann, with whom tension with any new chief of staff was natural, did battle with Rumsfeld for the rest of the administration. But the final arbiter of the situation was satisfied; Ford would later tell this author what he told several national publications at the time: "Don Rumsfeld was an excellent chief of staff."

This feuding staff was one of Ford's biggest problems as president. There are those, including this author, who would argue that it helped

cost him the 1976 election. In any case, in September 1974 many observers had written off any chance for Ford's election to the job he had
inherited. Indeed, the new president fueled such observations by making a fateful decision that threatened to ruin his presidency before it
had hardly begun.

The question of whether Ford would offer a pardon to Nixon was
on the front burner of the administration from the moment Ford took
the oath of office. Ford was lobbied from all sides. Buchen recalled for
the author that before the new administration was hours old, Len Garment gave him a memorandum to pass on to Ford making the case for
a pardon and also arguing that it should be done quickly. Buchen gave
the memo to Ford but disagreed with Garment's conclusions, saying
that it was too early for such a risky move. Ford agreed with his counsel, and Buchen returned the memo to Garment. Ford was also besieged with reports from San Clemente informing him that Nixon's
phlebitis was acting up to the extent that his life might be threatened.[28]
Press Secretary Jerald terHorst was constantly harassed with questions
on the issue, as were members of Congress. In fielding the inevitable
question, an exasperated Hugh Scott answered, "For God's sake, enough
is enough. He's been hung, and it doesn't seem to me that in addition
he should be drawn and quartered."[29]

When Ford gave his first televised press conference as president on
August 28, the problem of a pardon was not a new thought in his
mind (as his August 5 conversation with Haig clearly shows). Yet he
professed surprise at the first question, asked by Helen Thomas of United
Press International: did he think Nixon should have immunity from
prosecution? Ford made it clear that he was "the final authority" on
any question of a pardon but that "there have been no charges made,
there has been no action by any jury, and until any legal process has
been undertaken, I think it is unwise and untimely for me to make
any commitment." Yet Ford refused to rule out the pardon option, and
he further muddied the issue by asserting that the special prosecutor
had "an obligation to take whatever action he sees fit, and that should
include any or all individuals." The contradictions were obvious, and
most of the remaining questions in the press conference dealt with the
possibility of a quick pardon. Ford recalls walking back to the Oval
Office afterward and asking himself, "Was I going to be asked about
Nixon's fate every time I met with the press?"[30]

For Ford's staff the press conference confirmed their worst fear:
Ford was still having trouble making up his mind on the pardon. Buchen
told the author that he was concerned that Ford's "answers weren't
consistent," a result of Ford's being genuinely confused about what to
do. Hartmann wrote that he felt that Ford was "groping his way toward
a firm decision, fighting for a little more time."[31] They were not the

only ones who sensed Ford's indecision; seeing an opening, both Haig and Kissinger began to openly lobby him for a pardon.[32]

Just when Ford made his final decision to offer a pardon to Nixon is still open to debate. Ford's version of the events depicts him as grappling with the decision until the last possible moment. In his memoirs he says that immediately after the press conference he contacted Buchen and asked him to research both the possible criminal charges that Jaworski might bring against Nixon and the full scope of the presidential pardoning power. Over the next two days, as Ford recalls in his memoirs, he "agonized over the idea of a pardon." His gut feeling after these days of introspection was that "it was the state of the *country's* health at home and around the world that worried me. . . . America needed recovery, not revenge. The hate had to be drained and the healing begun." Ford further recalls that on August 30 he summoned his top five aides—Buchen, Haig, Kissinger, Hartmann, and Marsh— and "urged them to give me their most candid feelings." Ford's recollection is that he already knew Buchen to be in favor of the idea, as were Haig and Kissinger; Marsh and Hartmann expressed reservations on the timing. Hartmann expressed the view that the president's popularity was sure to suffer; Ford shot back: "I'm aware of that. It could easily cost me the next election if I run again. But damn it, I don't need the polls to tell me whether I'm right or wrong." Ford, then, would have us believe that on August 30 he was still making up his mind about the pardon; indeed, he recalls that his mind was not made up until about a week later.[33]

Both Hartmann and Buchen differ with this view of events. Buchen told the author that at the August 30 meeting "there wasn't much discussion." Hartmann agrees. He recalls that Ford sat back, "elaborately filled his pipe," and, rather "matter-of-factly, . . . said that he was very much inclined to grant Nixon immunity from further prosecution as soon as he was sure he had the legal authority to do so." Both of Ford's key aides believe that on August 30 they were being informed, not consulted. It is important to note that none of them violently objected to Ford's decision, despite Hartmann's earthy public relations analysis that "the fit is going to hit the shan."[34]

Given that Buchen believed Ford's mind was already made up, the president's directive to research the pardon took on a critical urgency. Ford had decided to pardon Nixon, but he knew little about his power to do so. To compound the problem, the issue was essentially one of criminal law, not Buchen's area of specialty. Also, once Ford had confided his decision to his closest aides, it would be only a matter of days before it leaked. Ford suggested that Buchen enlist Benton Becker, an ex–Justice Department investigator, to handle the research. Becker had met Ford during Justice's 1964–1966 probe of the finances of New York Representative Adam Clayton Powell. Becker was impressed with

Ford's evenhanded treatment of Powell, and he struck up a friendship with the minority leader.[35] Becker had also provided investigatory backup for Ford's probe of Justice William O. Douglas and had lent his services to Hartmann on Ford's confirmation hearings.

Buchen and Becker conducted their research quickly, spending most of that Labor Day weekend at their task. On September 3 Buchen reported their findings to the president. Their results essentially boiled down to two points. There was never any question that the president could pardon before *conviction,* but Buchen and Becker were just as convinced that the president had the power to pardon before *indictment.* More important for this particular case, the two men also concluded that the offering of a pardon carried with it the assumption of guilt, and they cited two Supreme Court cases to back up their conclusion that the acceptance of a pardon constituted a *confession* of guilt.[36] Ford now felt that he had the legal authority to proceed with his plan.

Buchen and Becker's work was not limited to legal research. Ford had also asked them to assess the extent of the crimes with which Nixon might be charged by the special prosecutor. For this, Buchen dealt directly with Jaworski. Both men were staying at Washington's Jefferson Hotel, and they met there informally several times. As a result of these meetings as well as a more formal meeting on the morning of September 4, Jaworski sent Buchen a letter. Dated that day, it estimated that to seat an impartial jury and to try Nixon would take approximately "nine months to a year and perhaps longer." Jaworski also made available to Buchen a memorandum written by a member of his staff, Henry Ruth, which outlined ten areas in which Nixon would probably be under investigation.[37]

It was also important for Buchen to ascertain from Jaworski whether his office would challenge the pardon in court after it was announced. Richard Ben-Veniste, a member of the special prosecutor's team, suggests in his memoirs that a deal was cooked up between the two men, that in their September 4 meeting, "by words or by silence, [Jaworski] intimated that as long as the pardon was based on the premise that prejudiced publicity made it impossible for Nixon to get a fair trial, Jaworski would not oppose it."[38] In a later interview with the author, Buchen did not question the need to sound Jaworski out on this point, offering only that "I knew he wouldn't challenge it."

The final step involved the Nixon camp, and it was twofold. An arrangement regarding the massive aggregate of Nixon's tapes and papers had to be negotiated, and Ford had to be certain that Nixon would not publicly reject a pardon after it was extended to him.

Despite attempts by leftover Nixon staff members to sneak tapes and papers out of the White House during the days after Ford's inauguration, the vast majority of the material was still being stored in the White House basement. There was a case to be made for keeping the material at the disposal of the special prosecutor's office; it might be needed as evidence in the trial of the Watergate defendants due to begin on September 30, or in subsequent prosecution of Nixon. However, Nixon's lawyers insisted that the presidential materials were his personal property and as such should immediately be shipped to San Clemente. Attorney General William Saxbe agreed, arguing in a memorandum to Ford that "to conclude that such materials are not the property of [Nixon] would be to reverse what has apparently been the almost unvaried understanding of all three branches of the government since the beginning of the Republic."[39]

Confusing the issue was the method by which Nixon had donated his presidential material to the government. Since Herbert Hoover, past administrations had established the custom of simply turning over all presidential papers to the government to be processed and stored in a library maintained by the General Services Administration and made available to qualified researchers. In 1973 Nixon made arrangements for the usual bestowal of his material (in a twist, he backdated this donation so that he might claim a $432,000 income tax deduction). With the prospect of a possible impeachment trial or resignation near at hand, Nixon reneged on this decision. On the day before he resigned, Nixon wrote a letter to Arthur Sampson, head of the General Services Administration. In it he changed his deed of gift to read that "the undersigned [Nixon] shall have the right of access to any and all of the materials and the right to have copied any and all of the materials by any means of his selection, and to take and retain possession of any and all of such copies for any purpose whatsoever." After his resignation Nixon's argument was that this new deed of gift gave him the right to claim any of the records left behind at the White House that he wanted—and he wanted them all.

Although no one at the time knew for sure, the tapes were estimated to number between 850 and 900 reels, and there were about fifty million pages of written records. Lack of proper archival care jeopardized the safety of these invaluable records (the tapes were kept in a safe under a stairwell, where heat threatened to destroy them). While Buchen told the author that Ford made it clear to him that the pardon was not contingent on such an agreement, a deal which both got the material out of the White House and maintained the widest possible access for their future use was the key to fulfilling Ford's dream of putting Nixon behind him. The deal that Becker and Buchen worked up with Nixon attorney Jack Miller called for Nixon to once again amend his deed of gift so that he and the government would share ownership for a period of three to five years and the material would be available for subpoena by the courts. During this period of joint ownership the material would be stored at a federal facility near San Clemente, and two keys—one held by Nixon, one by the General Services Administration—would be needed to gain access. After that time the material would belong solely to Nixon, to dispose of as he pleased. This agreement satisfied neither Nixon's demand for free access nor the special prosecutor's demand for a full and open disclosure of all possible evidence. Nor did it adequately protect the availability of the papers for future historical research. It was at best a feeble stopgap measure.

As for the question of Nixon's reaction, several members of the White House staff confided to the author that they lived in private fear that a recalcitrant Nixon would announce to the world that he would rather rot in jail than accept a pardon and admit his guilt. A major miscalculation by Buchen almost caused this to happen. In a September 4 meeting with Miller to hammer out the final details, Buchen suggested that Nixon should offer a statement of contrition when he publicly accepted Ford's pardon. When Becker arrived in California the next day with the charge of personally presenting the package to Nixon, he was met by an indignant Ziegler, who barked that "President Nixon is not issuing any statements whatsoever regarding Watergate, whether Jerry Ford pardons him or not." Becker countered by suggesting that there was no longer a reason for him to stay; Ziegler offered to call the pilot. Miller calmed the two men down. The next day Ziegler made it clear that Nixon was not happy with the proposal concerning the materials. Becker soon realized that if he didn't allow Nixon substantially more access to his papers, any hopes of working out an acceptable scenario for the pardon would be lost. Miller's alternative proposal was startling. Nixon would give the material to the government, and the GSA would act as a trustee. Scholars who wanted access to the materials would have to subpoena the materials, and both the GSA and Nixon had the right to object. After five years Nixon could order the destruction of any document or tape. Feeling that it was the best he could do, Becker proposed it over the phone to Ford, who immediately accepted. Becker then had to sidestep the issue of contrition, eventually accepting from Ziegler a six-paragraph statement that did not acknowledge guilt, only that Nixon was "wrong in not acting more decisively and forthrightly in dealing with Watergate."[40] The final stumbling block on the way to a pardon had been cleared.

Sunday, September 8, marked the end of the first month of the Ford presidency. It also marked the end of whatever honeymoon Ford had enjoyed with the American people. Early that morning he attended services at St. John's Episcopal Church across the park from the White House. He then returned to the Oval Office, where he made final corrections in the draft announcement that had been written by Hartmann. The word then went out privately. Ford personally called senators and representatives (Tip O'Neill's response to the president summed up the reaction of many on Capitol Hill: "You're crazy."[41])

Buchen notified Jaworski. The secret had held; even Ford's Press Secretary, Jerry terHorst, was not notified until thirty-six hours before the speech.[42]

At 11:00 A.M. Ford made his announcement from the Oval Office. In a steady, almost defiant voice, he read without deviating from his script.

> Theirs [the Nixons'] is an American tragedy in which we have all played a part. It could go on and on and on, or someone must write the end to it. I have concluded that only I can do that, and if I can, I must. . . . I deeply believe in equal justice for all Americans. . . . I do believe that right makes might and that if I am wrong, ten angels swearing I was right would make no difference.

Ford then read from the pardon proclamation, which granted a "full, free, and absolute pardon" to Nixon for all crimes he "committed or may have committed or taken part in" while in office. He then signed the proclamation, and the broadcast was over.[43]

As Hartmann predicted, "the fit hit the shan" with lightning speed. The timing of the broadcast was in large part responsible. Since Ford spoke on a Sunday morning without much prior warning (necessary, according to Buchen, because it was thought that the story would leak by the next day), many people did not even see the broadcast. They then jumped to an inaccurate conclusion—that Ford's decision meant pardons for all those involved in Watergate crimes. Although thousands of letters were sent out from the White House to try to correct this impression, the damage had been done.[44] The response was venomous and often violent. Letters criticizing Ford began to pour into the White House; Buchen told the author that Ford was particularly upset by the large number of letters from ministers who fiercely disagreed with his decision. The outpouring of sentiment from Congress was so negative that the White House congressional liaison Bill Timmons sent the comments on to Haig with specific instructions not to show them to the president. Becker told the author that he was physically attacked by protestors. One reaction would lead to its own peculiar problem. Feeling both upset with the decision and angered because he had not been consulted, terHorst resigned as press secretary on the same day that the pardon was announced. Within a month, approval among Americans of how Ford was doing his job dropped from 71 percent to 50 percent in the polls.

The investigatory wheels of Congress also churned into motion. Immediately after the announcement the Subcommittee on Criminal Justice of the House Judiciary Committee, chaired by William Hungate of Missouri, began an inquiry into the events surrounding Ford's decision. Committee members Bella Abzug and John Conyers introduced privileged resolutions of inquiry and sent to Ford a series of questions to which they requested a written response. One question specifically inquired about whether a deal had been struck and consummated between Ford and Nixon.

Against the advice of Buchen, Ford decided to go to Capitol Hill and testify in person before the Hungate subcommittee. On October 17, 1974, Ford faced the subcommittee on national television.[45] During his appearance, it seemed like prepardon times; Hungate and Judiciary Committee chairman Peter Rodino were deferential, almost reverent, in their public praise of Ford's appearance. But when Ford got to the point that everyone wanted to hear, he was emphatic: "In summary, Mr. Chairman, I assure you that there was never at any time any agreement whatsoever concerning a pardon for Mr. Nixon should he resign and I become president."

Despite the congeniality of the situation to that point, it was clear that Ford had not convinced Elizabeth Holtzman, a represenative from Brooklyn. When her turn came to cross-examine Ford, she went on a lengthy harangue, charging that there were still "very dark suspicions" about his role in the pardon, an act whose very "secrecy . . . made people question whether or not there was a deal." Ford finally interrupted Holtzman's filibuster with a voice clearly shaking from anger: "I assure you that there was no deal, period, under no circumstances." It was clear that no single appearance by Ford was going to charm away the problem of the pardon. It stayed through the elections of 1974 and 1976; it is the major question that hounds Ford about his presidency today.

For Gerald Ford, his pardon of Richard Nixon was not an act of mercy or compassion. As he told the author, "I did it because it was the right thing from the point of view of the country." Ford was much more concerned about the suffering of both his nation and his administration than he was about Nixon, and he felt that until the Nixon issue was put to rest he would be incapable of concentrating on more important issues. A criminal trial for Nixon would divert the attention of the administration well into the 1976 election. With the pardon, however, Nixon would be neither indicted nor tried, and it was hoped that, like President Truman's firing of General Douglas MacArthur (a parallel which pops up in the memos of many of Ford's aides at the time), the storm would soon blow over, and Ford would be seen to have been right in the long run.

But the very nature of the Ford pardon made it unlikely that the ghost of Nixon past would go away in the near future. As previously noted, the available evidence makes it clear that there was no deal between Ford and anyone else on an early Nixon pardon (if anything, there was a "deal" between Buchen and Jaworski that made sure that Jaworski would not challenge the pardon). However, the timing of

Ford's decision, coming so quickly on the heels of Nixon's resignation, and the fact that Nixon came out so well in the process—he did not have to admit any wrongdoing, and he got access to his tapes—left the unmistakable stench of a deal in the air. Nothing that Ford said or did could erase it, and it was clear that whispers about the pardon would last well into 1976.

For all of Ford's good intentions and political calculations, he had made a critical mistake. The mistake was not in pardoning Nixon but in issuing a pardon on Nixon's terms. As a result, Ford had left himself open to a plethora of charges of favoritism, bad judgment, bad timing, and "dealing." From Nixon's point of view, the pardon was a welcome end to his personal anguish and uncertainty; from Ford's point of view, the pardon was a dismal failure that would color the rest of his presidency. Ford's thirty-day "first term" was over.

CHAPTER NINE

A Search for Direction:
The Ford Presidency, 1975–1976

FORD'S "second term" began the moment he signed the pardon. It was instantly clear that he had lost a great deal of the goodwill that his affable personality had gained for him. More important, the pardon had so consumed Ford and his staff that they had not had time to stop and see where the administration was headed. In an interview with the author, Phil Buchen said it best:

> I think it's true that it was very difficult to settle in, because the first hectic days were . . . we weren't doing any forward planning to speak if. Then . . . as '75 went on, then you finally got to '76, and there was the Bicentennial and the election year. . . . And so it seemed much too short a time to really sit back and say, "Now look, this is where we should be a year from now, or two years from now." I mean, you never got the sense that we gave it much direction.

Ford's administration never found that direction. Ford fought to get it, but he was continually plagued by the same three forces that had plagued Nixon. As noted in the preceding chapter, Ford's staff setup was a barrier in the way of his success. There were two other factors that also hurt the Ford ship of state. One was a political revolution, and the other was the opening gun in what many would later call another political revolution.

To historian Arthur M. Schlesinger, Jr., the events of Watergate made perfect sense. Indeed, Nixon's abuses of power were the natural culmination of an evolution of the presidency begun in earnest during the Civil War. In his landmark 1973 work, *The Imperial Presidency*, Schlesinger defined this pattern: "It deals essentially with the shift in the *constitutional* balance—with, that is, the appropriation by the Presidency, and particularly by the contemporary Presidency, of powers reserved by the Constitution and by long historical practice to Congress."[1] The title of Schlesinger's book was used by critics to label everything that had gone wrong in the United States government— most notably, that the presidency had run amok and that Congress had been left gasping for air in its wake. The revelation of the abuses of power in the Nixon administration sparked Congress to try to regain this lost power. The resignation of Nixon was but the most dramatic act of a major revolution in U.S. politics which Hedrick Smith, in *The Power Game,* aptly termed the "power earthquake" of 1974.

The first step of this revolution was Congress's attempt to reassert its constitutional mandate to declare war. Article I, Section Eight of the Constitution expressly delegates this right to Congress. However, Korea and Vietnam had chipped away at that power, until the power to make war had become a virtual executive prerogative. For the most part the president did not have to seize this power. A Congress whipped into submission by a series of strong presidents gave up its war-making power with a minimum of fuss—thus the relatively easy presidential moves in Korea, the Cuban missile crisis, and Tonkin Gulf. But the Vietnam debacle spurred Congress into action. On October 12, 1973, the House gave final approval to a joint War Powers Act. In it Congress stipulated that "the president in every possible instance shall consult with Congress before introducing United States Armed Forces into hostilities or into situations where imminent involvement in hostilities is clearly indicated by the circumstances." The bill also designated that in the absence of a declaration of war by Congress, this consultation must take place a full forty-eight hours before the deployment of troops, and unless Congress gave its approval to the action, the troops must be withdrawn within sixty days. At the end of the resolution, Congress protested that "nothing in this joint resolution is intended to alter the constitutional authority of the Congress or the president." The bill's supporters argued that it merely restored a balance to the war-making power that had disappeared over the years.

That is clearly not how Nixon saw the bill. In one bitter sentence in his memoirs, Nixon coupled the War Powers Act with Congress's refusal to aid South Vietnam after the peace treaty and argued that the two actions "set off a string of events that led to the Communist takeover in Cambodia and . . . the North Vietnamese conquest of South Vietnam."[2] On October 24, four days after the Saturday Night Massacre, Nixon vetoed the measure, arguing that the restrictions were "both unconstitutional and dangerous" and that they "seriously undermine this nation's ability to act decisively and convincingly in times of international crisis." In a November 7 vote, trumpeted by many as a test of Nixon's congressional support should he be impeached, Congress overrode his veto. In the House, the vote was 284–135—just five votes short of sustaining it; Nixon also lost in the Senate, 75 to 18.

Having won an unexpectedly lopsided victory on war powers, Congress next moved to establish itself as the sentry standing guard over the Executive Office. It began with an assault on the almost unilateral power that the president had over the federal budget process. Throughout his tenure, Nixon had used a technique for controlling federal spending that had been exercised by virtually every one of his predecessors. He refused to spend monies—impounding them—that had been allocated for programs which he did not support. Where Nixon differed from his predecessors was the obvious relish with which he used impoundment to weaken many of Johnson's Great Society programs. Congress was so infuriated that the House Judiciary Committee briefly considered listing it as an impeachable offense.[3] One month before Nixon's resignation, Congress struck out at this practice with the Budget and Impoundment Control Act. It called for congressional intervention in case of presidential impoundment of funds that either cut total spending or canceled a program. More important, however, was the bill's creation of the Congressional Budget Office (CBO) to oversee the budget process, produce its own information on the economy, and submit a draft budget of its own. Now the president's budget would not be the only draft upon which Congress held its annual debate.

"Congressional oversight" of the executive branch now became the hottest debate in Washington. The previously discussed Hungate subcommittee which investigated the pardon would have been unthinkable only three years before. In 1975 Senator Frank Church of Idaho initiated an investigation into the antics of the CIA (particularly OPERATION CHAOS) as well as the agency's plots to assassinate unfriendly heads of state. When the work of the Church Committee was done, it had established congressional oversight of intelligence operations once and for all. Quite clearly there had been a shift in the balance of power toward Capitol Hill.

The American public was far from an innocent bystander during this political revolution. It had been sickened by its government as it had never been in the past; during an October radio talk show in Maine, a caller asked, "Why do we need a governor at all? What can any of these men do for us?" The piercing downturn in the economy worsened the public mood; an early November poll for *Time* reported that the proportion of Americans living in "economic distress" was 33 percent, a 10 percent increase from the previous May.[4] In its frustration the country lashed out at Ford and his party, holding the Republicans responsible for all of the events of the past several years. The result was Democratic victories. The Republicans lost forty-three House seats and four Senate seats, giving the Democrats a majority of four in the Senate and a stunning 147 in the House; House Democrats now had one vote more in their majority than the two-thirds necessary to override a presidential veto. The Democrats also took nine governorships that had previously been Republican and gained control of an additional eight statehouses, increasing their total to thirty-six.

Thus appeared the "Class of '74," quickly dubbed the "Watergate Babies" in the press. They were the youthful Democratic leaders who rode the issues of Watergate, the pardon, and the "mess in Washington" to victory. In the Senate, men such as John Glenn of Ohio, David Boren of Oklahoma, Gary Hart of Colorado, and Patrick Leahy of Vermont—the first Democrat that Vermont had ever sent to the Senate—were the beneficiaries of public indignation over the Nixon-Ford policies. In the statehouses, men such as Hugh Carey of New York, Edmund Brown, Jr., of California, and Michael Dukakis of Massachusetts profited from the nation's bitterness. The landslide was not so much a victory for the Democrats as a lashing out at the Republicans. As columnist Hugh Sidey put it, "The old political style is dead. It should be buried, particularly by presidents. Everybody except the politicians seems to sense that."[5]

Some politicians did, however, sense the change. As we will see, Jimmy Carter and Ronald Reagan sensed it. So did the "Watergate Babies." Congressional etiquette had long dictated that a freshman should be seen and not heard; the "Class of 1974" made itself known before it was even sworn in. Three fixtures as House committee chairmen, including Wright Patman of the Banking Committee, were ousted in a coup led by the seventy-five Democratic freshmen. The seniority system was tottering; it was brought to its knees with the adoption by House Democrats of the "subcommittee bill of rights," which dispersed power from the relatively few standing committees to a greatly increased number of subcommittees (172). A joke soon circulated that all a member had to do if he didn't recognize another member was greet him with a jovial "Good morning, Mr. Chairman"; with so many subcommittees, almost every member was in charge of something.

Thanks to the shocking independence of the "Watergate Babies," the chasm that had developed between Congress and the White House was stretched to the point where Ford could expect only opposition to his policies. Knowing that getting a legislative package of his own passed would be next to impossible, Ford undertook a deliberate veto strategy, sending legislation back to Congress at an unprecedented rate. This was a high-risk, high-yield plan. If most of Ford's vetoes were sustained, then he might be able to present to the public an image of a man in control that would carry into 1976. If he lost, however, it would be an easy task for Democrats to charge him with legislative ineptitude.

The strategy was a mixed success. All in all, Ford vetoed sixty-six bills during his tenure; that placed him third on the list of presidents in terms of using that power. Twelve of his vetoes were overridden.

Ford put the best face on the results. He told the author that "when they in the Congress knew I meant business, and they certainly did after awhile, they respected me, and they soon learned that they couldn't get away with these various things that they were trying to ram through." However, liberal and moderate Republicans, emboldened by the "power earthquake," often broke with the administration. Although Ford's relationship with Congress was friendlier than Nixon's, the results were essentially the same.

The third and unquestionably the most important force working havoc on the Ford presidency was one that was taking place within his own party. By the end of 1972 Nixon had proved to be a major disappointment to the Republican Right. His social policy was seen as too liberal, his economic policy had shattered the stability of Bretton Woods, and his foreign policy, most notably the opening of China, was anathema to them. Few if any believed that Ford, despite his conservative voting record in Congress, would turn the clock back. It took only a matter of weeks for conservatives to abandon Ford and hitch their wagon to a new star.

Ronald Reagan had been a thorn in Nixon's side since his election to the California statehouse in 1966. His entry into the presidential race in 1968 confirmed his higher ambitions, and his reelection as governor in 1970 by a majority of over 500,000 votes affirmed his power within the party. Despite his distaste for both Nixon and his policies, Reagan kept his own counsel through 1972, recognizing that despite their concerns, conservatives would flock to the Nixon banner rather than chance there being a President McGovern. The elevation of Ford, however, ended this uneasy truce. Reagan's chief biographer, *Los Angeles Times* reporter Lou Cannon, argues that Reagan saw Ford as a "caretaker" president who, if he fell out of sync with the conservative movement as badly as had Nixon, could be challenged and beaten.[6] After the pardon, Reagan began to speak out in favor of "broadening the GOP base"[7]; this meant the replacement in power of the Nixon-Ford Republican moderates with the new leaders of the Republican Right.

Unlike Nixon, Ford consistently underestimated Reagan. Ford, whose dislike for Reagan continues to the present day, admits as much in his memoirs: "Some of my closest advisors—Marsh and Hartmann in particular—had been warning me for months to prepare for a difficult challenge from Ronald Reagan. I hadn't taken those warnings seriously because I didn't take Reagan seriously."[8] Even when Ford finally admitted that Reagan was a threat, his attempts to neutralize the governor were incredibly clumsy. The best example of this was the way that Reagan was offered a clearly token position in the Cabinet. In the fall of 1974 Ford offered him several jobs, including secretary of transportation and ambassador to Great Britain; Reagan declined. Later in

1975 Ford had Rumsfeld offer Reagan the post at Commerce; this time he was insulted. A Reagan adviser sniffed that "they're working their way down the scale."[9]

Reagan contributed to this White House apathy, and infuriated his advisers in the process, by not making a public declaration of his opposition to Ford's policies as soon as the president was inaugurated. As Cannon puts it, "Reagan was as reluctant as ever to make a personal decision before it was absolutely necessary."[10] However, he could not stay quiet long. Within three months conservatives were stunned as Ford pardoned Nixon, offered a limited amnesty program for Vietnam-era draft evaders, showed himself incapable of dealing with the fiscal crisis, seemed to be unwilling to either dismantle or to limit détente, and—the most damning thing of all for conservatives—nominated a Republican liberal to be his vice-president. By the end of 1974 Reagan had become the most outspoken critic of the Ford administration and was clearly readying himself to challenge Ford in the primaries. Ford's policy stumbles gave Reagan hope for an upset victory.

Ford's domestic agenda was dominated by the problems of the economy. Nixon's economic policies had resulted in both skyrocketing prices and more people out of work than there had been in a decade. In July 1974 inflation was at its highest level since 1919. Less than a year later, in May 1975, unemployment was up to 9.2 percent, two percentage points higher than the previous postwar high.[11] Simply put, the economy was in chaos.

Unlike Nixon, Ford actually enjoyed the arena of domestic policy, preferring the give and take of budget negotiations to the realm of summit diplomacy. Ford was also much more of a classical economic conservative than was Nixon. For Ford, solutions such as wage and price controls were both ineffective and dangerous. He immediately pledged that he would not use an incomes policy of any kind. He was supported in this belief by his equally conservative chairman of the Council of Economic Advisers, Alan Greenspan, who had been appointed in July 1974. Greenspan quickly emerged as Ford's leading economic adviser. He counseled a cautious program that would raise revenues and cut government spending, a "pump-priming" program that would, in the long run, lessen unemployment.[12]

In October 1974 Ford submitted such a program to Congress. The package followed strict conservative economic policy, as Ford supported cuts in social programs and other domestic spending that far eclipsed anything that Nixon had ever supported, as well as a tax increase. However, this proposal is best known for its call for a renewed volunteerism that urged all Americans to spend less and save more. The slogan for the plan, "Whip Inflation Now," was shortened to "WIN" by an approving Ford, who took to wearing a WIN button during his

public appearances. As a public relations gimmick, WIN left much to
be desired; it certainly did nothing to lower inflation. By the end of
1974 it had become a laughingstock, with many Democratic candidates lambasting it during the congressional campaigns.

To make matters worse, Greenspan had greatly underestimated the
severity of the recession. By December 1974 unemployment had risen
to 7.2 percent, and the "Watergate Babies" were demanding increases
in government spending to help the unemployed. As he entered 1975,
Ford was forced with an unenviable choice. If he stuck with Greenspan's slow approach, unemployment was certain to continue its rise.
If he abandoned his program and adopted the spending plans that the
Congress demanded, not only would the deficit sharply increase but
Ford also would open himself to charges of flip-flopping on policy.[13]

In his State of the Union Address on January 13, 1975, Ford submitted a new program that he hoped would offer the best of both
worlds. He made clear his belief that this new policy was imperative,
as he opened his address by stating the obvious: "The State of the
Union is not good." Ford proposed a one-shot $16-billion tax cut across
the board. Individuals could look forward to a rebate on their 1974
taxes of approximately $1,000 each, and business stood to benefit from
a reduction in the corporate rate of approximately 42 percent. However, to compensate for the increase in the deficit that these cuts would
cause, Ford put a moratorium on the creation of any new federal
spending programs and a 5 percent ceiling on both Social Security raises
and federal pay raises in 1975.[14]

The reaction was expected. The press scored the president for what
the *Washington Post* called a "self-reversal."[15] George Meany spoke for
many when he called the new Ford program "weird."[16] Congressional
Democrats painted Ford into a corner, as they ignored the president's
program and passed a series of appropriations bills that were substantially more expensive than what Ford had called for. Ford attempted
to keep the lid on spending by vetoing most of these bills, but by the
end of the year the government was spending about $17 billion more
than Congress had appropriated.[17] Nevertheless, Congress proposed a
tax cut of $22.8 billion, some $7 billion more than the president had
asked for. Clearly Ford's 1975 plan had backfired, and he was now
faced with the politically devastating decision of vetoing a tax cut that
was popular with the public but that he knew would only increase the
already staggering federal deficit.

Reacting to the crisis, Ford's economic staff proposed a third plan,
one that included the rather novel method of linking a promise of
lower taxes to reduced government spending. In October Ford proposed a permanent tax reduction of $28 billion, but only if Congress
agreed to a ceiling on federal spending of $395 billion for fiscal year
1977. Not falling for the trap, Congress passed a tax cut but ignored

the spending ceiling. Ford finally vetoed the bill, and in a substantial victory for the administration, had his veto closely sustained by Congress. Early in 1976 both parties finally agreed to a loosely worded bill that provided for the tax cut and promises of spending austerity by Congress.

In the end, figures show that Ford had actually cut inflation in half (the Consumer Price Index had dropped from 11 percent in 1974 to 5.8 percent in 1976). Yet the political damage done by his fight with Congress over the economy was incalculable. Without a friendly Congress and with Reagan sniping at his heels, Ford was forced to change his mind on his legislative packages at an embarrassingly frequent rate. This served to feed the fires set by those who questioned his executive competence. His energy policy met the same fate.

Until about 1970 the United States had little concern that its energy resources might someday be limited. Thanks in large part to quotas on oil imports that had been set during the Eisenhower administration, the U.S. oil industry was booming. The 30 percent or so of oil that was imported still sold for well below domestic price levels, and despite a barely perceptible rise in gasoline and heating oil prices, Americans believed their domestic energy sources to be limitless. Few paid any attention to the banding together of five oil-producing nations in 1960 to form the Organization of Petroleum Exporting Countries (OPEC).* As Nixon took office, then, the possibly of an international energy crisis seemed remote.

The effect of the August 1971 wage and price controls on the oil industry and on U.S. energy consumption was, however, little less than momentous. The controls were initiated in the summer, when the price of gasoline was higher than the price of heating oil and when people traveled in their cars more often than they heated their homes. Since prices would stay the same throughout the life of the controls, it was therefore more profitable for the oil companies to refine gasoline than it was to refine heating oil. Among the consequences of Phase I and Phase II, then, were the devastating fuel shortages of the winter of 1972–1973 and the resulting national preoccupation with the issue of energy. Already under seige from Watergate, the White House had no energy policy (as Herb Stein mockingly though accurately put it, "an energy official at the White House was someone who knew that Abu Dhabi was a place and Qaddafi a person"[18]). It met the crisis of the 1973 Arab oil embargo with a series of half measures, such as Nixon's call for a national daylight savings time and a reduction in the highway speed limit. These measures did nothing to alleviate the hardships caused by the five-month embargo, which resulted in a total price rise

*During Nixon's and Ford's tenures the members of OPEC were Saudi Arabia, Iraq, Kuwait, Iran, Algeria, Venezuela, Libya, Qatar, the United Arab Emirates, Nigeria, Gabon, Indonesia, and Ecuador.

of 367 percent. They also did nothing to alleviate the frustration, felt most keenly by the Middle, over having the nation's energy supply held hostage to the whims of OPEC.

Unlike Nixon, who reacted to the energy crisis only when it was too late, Ford bored in on the issue as soon as he had dealt with the pardon. His logic, supported by his new head of the Federal Energy Administration, Frank Zarb, was that the immediate decontrol of domestic oil prices would offer the best long-term solution to the problem. Additionally, already present tariffs on Middle Eastern oil should be raised, thus helping the price of domestic crude return to a competitive rate. While both Ford and Zarb understood that both of these measures would mean substantially higher gasoline and heating oil prices, they concluded that the wound would heal more quickly if Ford raised taxes on the oil producers. In his 1975 State of the Union Address Ford unveiled his energy package, proposing that Congress lift all leftover Phase II controls on the price of domestic oil as of April 1 of that year and pass a windfall profits tax on oil producers. Ford also announced that he was issuing an executive order raising the tariff on foreign oil, and he promised to order greater hikes in the tariff if Congress refused to deal with the energy situation.[19]

Still stung from the pardon, Congress exploded in opposition. Many legislators called Ford's executive order raising the tariff an abuse of presidential power. Senators Henry Jackson and Ted Kennedy announced that they would spearhead an effort to block the tariff "at least temporarily."[20] House Ways and Means Committee Chairman Al Ullman requested a delay in the imposition of the tax. Initially Ford refused any attempt at compromise, and on January 24 the committee voted for legislation that would nullify Ford's executive order and put a ninety-day freeze on the tariff hike, a measure that was quickly passed by the full House; Ford just as quickly promised to veto it.[21] On March 4 he vetoed the nullification of the tariff increases but agreed to hold up any further tariff increases for sixty days.

The focus of the crisis had now shifted away from the energy issue and onto the battle between Ford and Congress. Ullman had proposed a forty-cent-per-gallon tax increase on gasoline, phased in over a five-year period. The general idea appealed to Zarb, who wrote in a February 13 memo to the president that "the notion of *phasing in* your program over a *one year period* may not be a bad compromise."[22] By midsummer, with the presidential election looming closer, Ford was forced to agree. Abandoning Ford's original call for unilateral decontrol, in July the administration submitted a plan calling for a phased decontrol of oil prices over a thirty-nine-month period (a period which, by no coincidence, would have extended the matter past the election and into Ford's second term). Smelling out his strategy, on July 30 Congress rejected the plan and passed instead a bill extending the life

of oil controls. Ford vetoed the bill but agreed to a forty-five-day waiting period, demanding that Congress produce a plan of its own by
November 15, a deadline which Ford extended for one month.

By early December Congress had produced its own "compromise"
energy bill, which called for the rolling back of domestic oil prices to
$7.66 per barrel but also gave the president the authority to gradually
decontrol prices over a forty-month period. It was a much longer phase-
out period than Ford wanted, but Zarb was convinced that a veto would
not be sustained and that the override vote would come perilously
close to the upcoming New Hampshire primary. On December 22 Ford
signed the Energy Policy and Conservation Act of 1975 and at the
same time formally withdrew his plans for increases in the tariffs on
imported oil.

Ford got an energy bill, but at a heavy price. His actions in dealing
with the energy crisis had further infuriated the Republican Right, which,
like Ford, had long wanted decontrol. Ford's own secretary of the treasury, William Simon, had argued against Zarb's counsel to abandon
decontrol, later writing that the bill was "disastrous," and "[that] Republicans who claim to be dedicated to free enterprise and to the welfare of this nation should have cooperated in the framing of this bill
and that a Republican president should have signed it are tragic."[23]
Ford clearly needed to show the Republican Right that he could be
trusted; for this, New York City's fiscal crisis seemed made to order.

For decades New York had spent and borrowed more than it had
taken in in taxes. Since 1965 its operating budget had more than tri-
pled. Economist Milton Friedman estimated that the city was spending
more than $1,000 per person per year, one-third more than Oakland
and twice as much as Chicago.[24] Clearly thanks to the spending patterns of Governor Nelson Rockefeller and the fiscal mismanagement of
Mayor John Lindsay—both Republicans—New York City was, in
Friedman's words, "the most welfare-state-oriented electorate in the
United States."[25] In the fall elections of 1974, New Yorkers followed
the national trend and elected Democrats Hugh Carey to the governor-
ship and Abraham Beame to City Hall. The two men immediately faced
the fallout of the mismanagement of their predecessors and offered
President Ford a fiscal crisis of significant proportions.

To meet its bills, New York had borrowed millions of dollars in the
tax-free municipal bond market. It did not, however, have the income
flow to meet its obligations. In April 1975 its credit rating was so bad
that several banks told the city that it could no longer borrow in the
market. The city was threatened with default as well as with the prospect of having to shut down many of its necessary services for lack of
funds. Carey and Beame made it clear that they expected help not just
from the state legislature but also from the federal government. On
May 13 Carey and Beame went to the White House. They asked Ford

for a $1-billion ninety-day loan for the city. Ford needed little time to think about it; he recalled later that the request was "ridiculous."[26] The next day Ford told his aides that he would reject any pleas for federal aid from the city. Even Vice-President Rockefeller, during a Columbus Day speech in New York, admitted that the situation had gotten "crucial."

Indeed it had. The state had advanced New York City some $300 million in aid over the summer and had created the Municipal Assistance Corporation to change the city's long-term debts into short-term ones. In September the aid increased, with the state approving a $2.3-billion aid package. Nevertheless, even this amount of money did not solve the crisis, and by October the city was facing default. Despite pleas and threats (in an October 23 meeting with the administration's congressional liaison, Max Friedersdorf, New York Senator James Buckley offered Ford his support in the following year's New York State primary for some federal aid to the city),[27] in an October 29 speech to the National Press Club, Ford declared that "the people of this country will not be stampeded" and that he would veto any bill that "has as its purpose a federal bailout of New York City to prevent a default."[28] The next day's headline in the *New York Daily News* brought shudders to Ford's political advisers: "Ford to City: Drop Dead."

Ford summed up his role in the crisis for the author: "If we, or I, had not taken a hard line, New York City would have gone bankrupt. The only way they could straighten out their fiscal mess was to have somebody tell them, 'If you want help, you have to correct these problems.' " However, when the hoopla had died down, Ford agreed to a modified form of bailout. On November 11 he announced his support of a plan by which the federal government would loan money to New York City with the stipulation that at the end of every fiscal year the city would repay the entirety of the principal, plus an amount of interest which was one percent greater than the prevailing market rate. Ford would later argue that this was a victory for conservative economics. It was not, but the Right had been momentarily appeased by his decisive action in the crisis. It would not be so easily mollified when it examined his foreign policy.

Bob Hartmann told the author that Nixon's last request of Ford was that he continue on the same course in foreign policy, particularly regarding China. With some modifications, Ford would have liked to have done this. He would have preferred to preside over a moderate postdétente foreign policy in which Kissinger was given much more latitude to plan policy than he had been given under Nixon. Ford would then have more time to devote to the debilitating economy, and the country would settle into what he later called a "quiet diplomacy" with the Soviet Union.[29]

This was not to be. Détente had begun to unravel with the Yom Kippur War, and Ford was soon faced with a series of crises in the Third World that once again threatened to pit the Soviet Union against the United States. Faced with such challenges, Ford proved unable to chart a coherent course for his administration. Like his domestic policy, his foreign policy was battered from all sides by his feuding staff, a recalcitrant Congress, and the Republican Right. The Ford administration searched for a common voice for its foreign policy. The search was in vain—there was not to be a "Ford Doctrine." The Ford diplomacy can be more appropriately seen as an emergency-room approach to world affairs that left the patient in a worse condition than when the doctor began to operate.

Despite rough sailing, Henry Kissinger had survived Watergate intact. His incessant courtship of the press paid marvelous dividends, helping him through the worst of the 1973–1974 revelations as the press missed no opportunity to contrast the languishing Nixon with the ever-rising "Super-K." Congress, for all its bluster, was as smitten with Kissinger as was the press. While the line of questioning was often tough, there had never been any doubt that he would be confirmed as secretary of state in the fall of 1973. His subsequent holding of the State and NSC portfolios at the same time only added to his image. Congress had even backed down when presented with evidence of Kissinger's wiretaps in early 1974. Again the questioning was strong; again nothing was done. Kissinger also began the Ford years with a stronger personal relationship with Ford than he ever had with Nixon. If anything, his reputation was enhanced by Ford's inability to deal with the ravaged economy. More than ever, Kissinger was portrayed in the press as the indispensable man.

But with the speed of light, Kissinger's star plummeted. The events of Yom Kippur and the closeness by which the two superpowers came to war led to an attack on détente by conservatives of both parties. They argued that calmer relations with the Soviet Union had not, as Nixon and Kissinger had promised, brought economic benefits. They also observed that despite U.S. concessions, the Soviets had done nothing to moderate their dictatorial regime. Indeed, reports of human rights abuses, most notably Soviet intransigence on the emigration of Soviet Jews, had increased. Nor had the Soviets decreased their desire to expand their sphere of influence. After being ejected by the Egyptians from the Middle East, they had turned their sights on Africa, beginning covert aid to a rebel faction in the Portuguese colony of Angola. These developments were monitored closely by Kissinger's opponents, and before the end of 1974 he was beginning to feel the heat. Many leading Republicans in Congress, long having fawned over the secretary of state, were now beginning to wonder if he should resign. The attacks increased with the fall of South Vietnam.

As historian George Herring has correctly observed, "the 'peace' agreements of January, 1973 merely established a framework for continuing the war without direct American participation."[30] Nixon's "peace with honor" held no lasting peace for the Vietnamese people. North Vietnam quickly exploited Nixon's Watergate-related preoccupations; by the time of Nixon's resignation, they had built a 3,000-mile oil pipeline, expanded their radio communication ability, and tested their forces in a series of short, limited engagements. In Cambodia the situation was much the same, with the Communist Khmer Rouge, under the command of Pol Pot, positioning itself for a final assault on Lon Nol's regime.

There was no way that Ford would recommit U.S. forces to stop this last surge from the North. Neither Congress nor the American people would have countenanced it, and there is no evidence that Ford even wanted to do so. Ford thus returned to where the U.S. commitment in Vietnam had begun; he attempted to buttress the Thieu regime with money. In his budget request for FY 1975, Ford proposed $1.4 billion in total aid for South Vietnam and Cambodia. Congress, citing inflation as its key argument, eventually pared that figure down to $1 billion, but in September appropriated only $700 million, half of which would comprise shipping costs.[31]

The South Vietnamese were now desperate. Recently declassified documents show that one week after the congressional defeat of Ford's request, Thieu wrote to Ford bemoaning the "utterly inadequate amount of military and economic aid to the Republic of Vietnam" and begging for "all necessary military equipments and economic assistance . . . to maintain [our] capabilities of self-defense and to develop [our] national economy." In his reply, sent more than one month later, Ford lamely assured Thieu that "American policy toward Vietnam remains unchanged under this administration" and that "I give you my firm assurance that this administration will continue to make every effort to provide the assistance you need."[32] Ford could not keep his word; Thieu knew it, and the North Vietnamese knew it. In December the North once again invaded the South. Ford immediately asked Congress for $522 million in emergency aid; congressional reaction was skeptical, and Ford's request was soon pared down to $300 million. On March 12 the House Democratic caucus voted in favor of denying any further aid for either South Vietnam or Cambodia.[33]

The speed and devastation of the North Vietnamese advance took everyone by surprise. Ford dispatched the army's chief of staff, General Fred C. Weyland, and White House photographer David Hume Kennerly, a former photographer for *Time* who had won a Pulitzer Prize for his photographs of Vietnam, to view the situation for themselves. On his return Weyland wrote to Ford that the current military situation in the South was "critical" and that the "GVN is on the brink of total military defeat." Weyland's recommendation: "We must make a maximum effort to support the South Vietnamese now."[34] Kennerly was even more blunt in his oral report to Ford: "Cambodia is gone, and I don't care what the generals tell you; they're bullshitting you if they say that Vietnam has got more than three or four weeks left. There's no question about it. It's just not gonna last."[35]

Weyland's and Kennerly's reports led Ford to increase rather than abandon his demand for aid. On April 10 Ford went before Congress to ask for $722 million for the South Vietnamese and Cambodian governments. Again Congress refused. In a meeting with the Senate Foreign Relations Committee, New York's liberal Republican, Jacob Javits, told Ford that "I will give you large sums for evacuation, but not one nickel for military aid."[36] Even this was too late. On October 16, after Ford had ordered U.S. forces to help evacuate the embassy in Phnom Penh (a decision for which several congressmen argued that the War Powers Act should have been invoked), the Cambodian government surrendered to the Khmer Rouge. Three days later Thieu resigned as president of South Vietnam. In a major speech on April 23 at Tulane University, Ford put the best face on the debacle, bringing the predominantly student crowd to its feet with his declaration that "today, [the] war is finished as far as America is concerned."[37]

In reality, the U.S. commitment to Vietnam had ended with the Nixon administration's ignoring of the North Vietnamese buildup during the first half of 1974. Despite subsequent carping by the Republican Right that Ford abandoned an ally, that partner had long been left twisting in the wind by Nixon and Kissinger. Indeed, Ford tried to stall the inevitable, but his inability to get congressional funding sealed Thieu's fate. Ford's Tulane speech was South Vietnam's eulogy, delivered by a man who had had little to do with that nation's fate. On April 30 the South Vietnamese government surrendered, and the next day the North Vietnamese proclaimed Saigon as Ho Chi Minh City. Devolution was complete.

Ford was soon presented with an opportunity to regain a bit of the ground that the U.S. image had lost over the fall of Vietnam. At 3:10 A.M. on the morning of May 12—only thirteen days after the fall of Saigon—the Cambodian navy fired on the U.S. merchant ship *Mayaguez*, a freighter on its way from Hong Kong to Singapore, as it steamed through the Gulf of Siam. Khmer Rouge sailors boarded the ship and captured the thirty-nine-man crew.

Having much to lose and having learned a harsh lesson in the results of passivity from the *Pueblo* crisis, no one in the Situation Room counseled negotiation with the Khmer Rouge (according to Press Secretary Ron Nessen, on the night of the rescue operation Kissinger snarled, "Let's look ferocious"[38]). By noon of May 12 the USS *Coral Sea* had been dispatched to the area and an amphibious task force was being assembled. As Jack Marsh cautioned the president, however, Congress would probably support military action but the president could nevertheless expect keen scrutiny of his decisions. As a result, Ford was careful to term the capture of the *Mayaguez* not an act of war but rather an act of "piracy." That would allow him to treat the crisis as one that required his immediate action through the latitude given the president under his emergency powers, but not as one that was likely to lead to war with Cambodia.

Throughout the evening of May 12 and the morning of May 13, conflicting reports exacerbated the problem. At 9:43 P.M. it was reported that the *Mayaguez* had weighed anchor and was heading toward the port city of Kompong Som (formerly Sihanoukville); five hours later the ship was reported anchored off Koh Tang, a jungle island some thirty-four miles from mainland Cambodia. It was not until 7:15 A.M. that the crew of the *Mayaguez* was confirmed to be on Koh Tang. A half-hour later Ford and General Brent Scowcroft of the NSC met and concluded that it was still possible to prevent the crew from reaching the mainland. Ford ordered a marine unit to be airlifted from Okinawa to Thailand. The events of the next few hours made the situation more acute. During the move, at 6:30 P.M. a U.S. helicopter crashed, killing eighteen air police and five crewmen. Two hours later, three Cambodian patrol boats were spotted trying to leave Koh Tang. Two of them were immediately sunk. Upon learning of the exchange of fire, Ford ordered the third boat destroyed, and it was. Immediately following the altercation an A-7 pilot spotted a boat with "Caucasian" men in the bow leaving the island and heading toward Kompong Som. Despite warning fire, the boat reached its destination.

With the crew of the *Mayaguez* now most likely imprisoned on the Cambodian mainland, Ford ordered the rescue operation to move in the next day. The attack would include a landing on Koh Tang, the securing of the island, and the retaking of the *Mayaguez*. The hope seems to have been that this action would force the Khmer Rouge to release the crew without any need to invade the mainland—an invasion that could well mean war. At 7:09 P.M. on May 14, Marines landed on Koh Tang, where they were met by unexpectedly heavy ground fire. In the first hour, fourteen Americans died and eight helicopters were shot down. An hour later the USS *Holt* pulled alongside the *Mayaguez*, boarded it, and found—to no one's surprise—no crew. Before the inevitable final step was deemed necessary, the Cambodians backed down. At 10:35 P.M. a P-3 pilot spotted a small fishing boat with about forty men aboard waving white flags. Within ten minutes the crew of the *Mayaguez*, which had been transported from the mainland by a Thai fishing boat, was safe aboard the USS *Wilson*.

The crisis provided a temporary respite for the embattled Ford. Hartmann later wrote that "crisis calmed Jerry Ford," and he noted that moments after receiving news of the crew's release, Ford turned to an aide to find out whether the Baltimore Orioles had won that evening's baseball game.[39] Even though the mission had cost almost as many lives as there were crew members of the *Mayaguez* (eighteen marines dead during the assault, plus the thirteen fatalities from the helicopter accident) Ford was generally applauded in the press for his decisive action. Flattering comparisons to Kennedy's handling of the Cuban missile crisis were as prevalent as unflattering comparisons with Johnson's handling of the *Pueblo* crisis, and Ford's approval rating climbed from 39 to 51 percent. Congress was also generally approving; on the morning of May 14 it adopted a resolution of support for Ford, and a bipartisan delegation that had been called to the White House for a briefing some twenty minutes before the rescue operation commenced rose and greeted the president with applause.[40] It is not surprising that one of Ford's most treasured relics of his administration is the steering wheel of the *Mayaguez,* presented to the president by the grateful crew.

Despite this undisputed success, the Republican Right continued to hound Ford with accusations of his perpetuating a policy of détente that had allowed the United States to go "soft on communism." Sharing this view was Ford's own secretary of defense. As Nixon's director of central intelligence and later his secretary of defense, James Schlesinger had developed a belief that both Kissinger and Nixon had vastly underestimated both the power and the resiliency of the Soviet Union. As he testified before Congress in 1975, Schlesinger believed that "the need for steadfastness is no less great than it was a decade or more ago . . . the world remains a turbulent place."[41] For Schlesinger the only thing that had changed about the Soviets during the period of détente was the tone of their rhetoric.

Schlesinger was not alone in his open opposition to détente. Donald Rumsfeld—both as staff coordinator and later at Defense—and Richard Cheney, Rumsfeld's successor at the White House, were both unreconstructed cold warriors who argued that the president should return to a hard line toward the Soviets.[42] They pointed out that since Yom Kippur there had been a notable shift of public opinion away from détente and reminded Ford that this was an issue that the Republican Right was sure to hit hard in 1976.[43] They certainly had a receptive audience in the president, who as a member of Congress had been privately opposed to Nixon's cuts in defense spending and a consistent hawk on Vietnam, and now was much less prone than Nixon had been to pursue a policy designed to placate the Soviets and the Chinese.

Further pressure came from Congress, led by Senator Henry "Scoop" Jackson of Washington. A conservative Democrat who had supported Nixon's Vietnam policies, Jackson had nevertheless been a consistent opponent of détente, which he felt had taken too grave a human toll. In Jackson's view, as the United States became overly cautious in its relations toward the Soviets, their record on human rights had gone unchallenged. He stood ready to move congressional Democrats against the White House in a battle for control over the nation's foreign policy agenda.

In October 1973, immediately following the Yom Kippur War, Jackson and Ohio Representative Charles Vanik had cosponsored an amendment to the East-West trade relations bill that would deny the Soviets "most favored nation" trade status as long as they barred emigration or imposed "more than a nominal tax . . . on any citizen as a consequence of emigration." Nixon and Kissinger feared that the Jackson-Vanik amendment would demolish détente. In June 1974, during Nixon's final summit visit to the Soviet Union, Kissinger was able to extract a pledge from Brezhnev to allow 45,000 Jews to emigrate yearly. Jackson found the number to be too low, and during the first months of the Ford administration Kissinger tried to get Brezhnev to increase the number. Unimpressed, Jackson refused to excise the amendment from the trade bill. Not surprisingly, the Soviets refused to sign the treaty. Furious, Ford blamed Jackson not only for meddling in the foreign policy prerogatives of the president but also for scuttling a trade bill that could help the recession-ravaged economy.

Jackson also opposed the grain deal between the Soviets and the United States, which, as noted earlier, played a large role in moving Brezhnev to sign SALT I. In August 1974 Jackson charged that there had been a "great grain robbery" and that U.S. exporters had made a fortune by selling grain to the Soviets at discount prices while cheating American farmers in the process. Jackson's criticism forced Ford to place an embargo on all overseas shipments of wheat and corn in October 1974. Despite his later argument that he was acting to save the economy because of forecasts that production of grain would be down, Ford's action was a response to direct pressure from a Democratic senator, a response that did little to help the price of grain. It did, however, anger Brezhnev.

The tension was heightened by Ford's awkward reactions to the events of the summer of 1975. In June, Soviet dissident novelist Aleksandr Solzhenitsyn visited the United States. Ford initially accepted the advice of Kissinger and his assistant on the NSC, General Scowcroft, who argued against any action that might antagonize the Soviets. Ford declined an invitation to attend an AFL-CIO dinner honoring Solzhenitsyn and rejected a request by conservative senators Strom Thurmond and Jesse Helms to bring Solzhenitsyn to the White House. The Right quickly denounced what it saw as the president's cowardice. On the floor of the Senate, Helms bellowed that "I must suggest that this is a sad day for our country, if the United States of America must

tremble in cowering timidity for fear of offending Communists." Ford
then changed his mind and invited Solzhenitsyn, only to change it a
third time when the novelist demanded a "public" meeting with the
president.[44]

If the Solzhenitsyn visit opened Ford to criticism, the Helsinki Accords sent the Right into convulsions. The thirty-five-nation Conference on Security and Cooperation in Europe, held in Helsinki during
the last week of July 1975, was the largest meeting of European nations since the Congress of Vienna in 1814-1815. The centerpiece of
the conference was negotiations between the United States and the
Soviet Union. The Soviets had hinted that they would be open to an
accommodation on Berlin, a dialogue on the issue of mutual troop
reductions in Europe, and discussions on the cruise missile, a weapon
whose existence in the U.S. arsenal stood in the way of a SALT II
agreement. Ford's refusal to accept Brezhnev's figures on the capabilities of the missile created an impasse that scuttled any immediate hopes
for a SALT agreement, but the Right could hardly fault him for being
strong on defense. The Soviets had also agreed in advance to sign a
document in which they agreed to follow a more liberal human rights
policy. It seemed that Ford would come back from Helsinki a sure
winner.

However, the final terms of the Helsinki agreement seemed to be
an endorsement of the Soviet position on Eastern Europe. The Soviets
had long hoped to gain U.S. approval of the boundaries set in Eastern
Europe after World War II, particularly the boundary between Poland
and East Germany. At Helsinki the Western nations agreed to accept
these boundaries as "permanent" as well as to open diplomatic relations with East Germany. Even though the boundary clause was followed by one that provided a mechanism for future changes in these
boundaries and Ford did not accept a Soviet proposal to do away with
the European alliance system altogether, the Right was white-hot with
anger. Ford tried to allay its wrath in his closing speech to the conference. Recalling in his memoirs that he "looked directly at Brezhnev"
as he spoke, Ford referred to the human rights clause of the agreement
and proclaimed that "peace is not a piece of paper. . . . To my country, these principles are not cliches or empty phrases. We take this
work and these words very seriously.[45]

It was nowhere near enough to mollify conservatives on the home
front. Hundred of letters were sent to the White House that read like
the one sent by the Veterans of Foreign Wars, expressing its "sharp
disappointment . . . [in your] gratuitous write-off of Eastern Europe
implicit in the Helsinki accords."[46] Reagan attacked the agreement in
his syndicated newspaper column and on the speech circuit. Ford tried
to limit the damage by telling reporters that the agreement was "not
legally binding,"[47] but the attacks continued. Despite his best efforts,

détente would clearly be an issue in the upcoming presidential elections.

In the spring of 1976 it seemed that there was no way that the Democratic party could lose. *Newsweek* had trumpeted the beginning of a "post-Imperial politics" that would certainly whisk Ford from office.[48] Ford was hurt, and the Reagan challenge was making him weaker, but either man would be leading a bitterly divided party into fall battle. No matter who won the nomination, the Republican party was sure to be castigated as the party that had led the country down the road to economic ruin, diplomatic chaos, and ethical impasse—in short, it would be portrayed as the party of Watergate.

It was to be the year of the outsider. A new type of candidate caught the imagination of the voter. These candidates were inexperienced in national politics and quick to see that in 1976 this was a virtue rather than a handicap. They played up their distance from the federal government and attempted to corner the market on virtue. The most unconventional version of this new Democrat was Jerry Brown, Governor of California, whose ascetic life-style and political ideals led to his being dubbed "Governor Moonbeam." Brown ran his campaign on a very basic premise: *"all* government bothers my conscience."[49] This professed revulsion against Washington was the common thread that ran through the campaigns of all of the new Democrats; yet their very inexperience hurt them in the primaries, and they eventually beat hasty exits.

James Earl Carter, however, survived. He combined the political savvy of the Old Guard with the antigovernment emphasis of the new Democrats to forge his victory. His southern roots, machine-politician experience, Christian fervor, boundless ambition, and workaholic tendencies all combined in equal portions to make up a man of incredible complexity. Yet the key to Jimmy Carter, both as candidate and as president, was discipline. It was a trait ingrained into him by a domineering father who bequeathed to his son not just the family peanut business but also the personal skills necessary to run that business successfully. Training at the U.S. Naval Academy automatically increased the young man's discipline, and so did the study of engineering, a rigorous academic endeavor. His class standing when he graduated in 1946—59th out of 820 cadets—was evidence of his diligence as well as his above-average intelligence. Lieutenant Carter's service under Admiral Hyman Rickover, father of the nuclear-powered navy, stiffened his resolve; Rickover was as stern and demanding a taskmaster as Carter's father.

After his return in 1953 to Plains, Georgia, to manage the family business, Carter was successful but bored. In 1962 he ran for a seat in the Georgia Senate, lost by a few votes in an election riddled with fraud, and successfully won a legal challenge that gave him the seat. He was not as successful in 1966, failing to qualify for the runoff election for the Democratic nomination for governor eventually won by Lester Maddox. Carter's inner resolve and discipline refused to let him retreat back into the business world. He spent the next four years planning his next run for governor (Maddox could not succeed himself) and won the office in 1970.

It is not overstating the case to contend that Carter's entire service as governor of Georgia was a stepping stone to the White House. All accounts agree that by 1971 he had decided to make a run for the presidency. In 1972 two of Carter's closest political advisers, Gerald Rafshoon and Hamilton Jordan, tried to convince George McGovern to consider Carter for the second spot on the ticket; their entreaties were spurned. This did not deter either Carter or his ambitious young aides. On November 4, 1972, the day before McGovern went down in flames, Jordan wrote Carter a lengthy memorandum. It was to be the blueprint for the 1976 Carter presidential campaign. Along with such advice as to read the *New York Times* and the *Washington Post* daily and "Visit Sen. Kennedy and Get to Know Him," Jordan argued that Carter must enter every primary, beginning with a contest virtually ignored to that point, the Iowa precinct caucuses.[50] As Carter would later tell reporter Martin Schram of *Newsday*, author of the standard work on Carter's 1976 campaign, "We saw that Iowa was a good chance. There are only about 35,000 Democrats there who participated in the 1972 caucuses. We just saw a good chance to build that up with a major media event.[51] Carter's early start, followed by his upset victory in Iowa, not only sparked his candidacy but also rewrote the rules of U.S. politics by requiring that each subsequent candidate must campaign longer—virtually for four years—to have even a chance at winning the nomination.

According to Jordan's strategy, one big victory in the North would erase any thoughts of Carter as merely a sectional candidate and destroy his nearest competition. That victory came in Pennsylvania, where Carter forced both Scoop Jackson and an ailing Hubert Humphrey out of the race. To emphasize his espousal of a "new system," Carter made a great show of inviting prospective vice-presidential candidates to Plains for "interviews," so that he might make a more careful choice of a running mate than had McGovern four years before.* However, Minnesota Senator Walter "Fritz" Mondale had long been his choice. Mondale's integrity could not be questioned, he would serve to appease the party's liberals, and he would provide Carter with the link

---

*On Carter's "short list" were Governors Hugh Carey of New York and Michael Dukakis of Massachusetts, Representative Peter Rodino of New Jersey, and Senators John Glenn of Ohio, Edmund Muskie of Maine, Alan Cranston of California, Frank Church of Idaho, and Walter Mondale of Minnesota.

to the legislative establishment that he sorely needed. When Carter, with shrewd self-deprecating humor, began his acceptance speech at Madison Square Garden with the opening line of his door-to-door campaign, "I'm Jimmy Carter and I'm running for president," he was underscoring the strategy of the new Democrats: distance yourself from the "mess in Washington" and speak as an outsider.

For many, the Ford administration had become synonymous with that mess. And Ronald Reagan, like the new Democrats, was running as much against Washington as he was against Ford. As the campaign approached, the White House staff was, not surprisingly, divided on how to approach the problem. A very few in the White House, led by Hartmann, argued that Ford should hit the campaign trail as soon as possible. This would allow the public to see the president as he was—a likable, honest leader.[52] Others, most notably Stuart Spencer, Michael Raoul-Duval, and pollster Robert Teeter, argued that since Reagan and Carter both were running as outsiders, Ford should stay in Washington and position himself as the competent insider, an expert at being president who was being challenged by amateurs. This would be dubbed by Raoul-Duval as the "no-campaign campaign"; most students of politics know it as the "Rose Garden strategy." Hartmann was again outgunned. Ford cast his lot with the "no-campaign campaign,"[53] and Hartmann, who uses the episode in his memoirs to bolster his thesis concerning the negative influence of the "Praetorian Guard," was effectively excluded from any further consultation on campaign strategy. It has been suggested by many observers that the first step of the "no-campaign campaign" took the form of actions designed to demonstrate that Ford was a tough executive, capable of making the difficult managerial decision. Journalist Jules Witcover postulates in his book on the 1976 election that the "Sunday Morning Massacre" was the first step in this campaign.[54]

As noted earlier, Ford had never wanted James Schlesinger in his Cabinet. Schlesinger's demeaning of Congress had made him a liability. Recognizing this, Kissinger had long been screaming for Schlesinger's head, but Ford knew that the dismissal of his hawkish secretary of defense would give the Right a martyr. However, reports from White House staffers, who argued that Schlesinger's private statements were sympathetic to the Reagan cause, sealed his fate. Yet these same staffers believed Ford's problems would not be solved simply by dismissing Schlesinger. They also argued that Kissinger had become as big a foreign policy liability with the Right as Schlesinger had become with the Middle.

Ford's solution was a staff shakeup of sizable proportions. It was designed, as was Ford's way, to attempt to give each side something. To appease the Middle, Schlesinger was dismissed. To appease the Right, Kissinger was relieved of his duties as national security adviser and

Nelson Rockefeller removed himself from consideration as Ford's running mate in 1976. Two Nixon appointees would be called in to fill the NSC posts: Donald Rumsfeld took over at Defense, to be succeeded as chief of staff by his protégé Richard Cheney, and Kissinger was succeeded at the NSC by Brent Scowcroft. To complete the overhaul, Ford replaced CIA Director William Colby with George Bush, then Ambassador to China, and Commerce Secretary Rogers Morton, ill with cancer, was replaced by Elliot Richardson.

When the press was informed on Sunday, November 2, of the sweeping changes, it was quickly dubbed the "Sunday Morning Massacre." It turned out to be a series of fateful miscalculations. Cheney was no more capable of stopping the sniping between members of Ford's staff than Rumsfeld had been. In terms of foreign policy, Reagan and Jackson both decried the firing of Schlesinger (ignoring the demotion of Kissinger) and charged the administration with caving in like Nixon to the Soviets.

The withdrawal of Rockefeller proved disastrous for the campaign. In nominating Rockefeller as his vice-president, Ford had chosen one of the most savvy political operators in the Republican party. He had also chosen a man whose progressive views on most domestic issues allowed Democrat Hugh Carey to observe that he "operated one party and occupied the other."[55] Of all Rockefeller's strengths, however, Ford made it clear in an interview with the author that he had been chosen for his political status:

> I picked Nelson Rockefeller in the first place, one, because of his stature as a public official. And secondly, because I wanted to show, not only to the American people but the world that we had a strong administration. He added stature to the Ford administration.

However, while Rockefeller might indeed legitimize the administration to the world, he was also the man who more than any other living politician—except Ted Kennedy—embodied everything that the Republican Right hated. If there was ever an opportunity for Ford to win back the Right, it was smashed by his choice of Rockefeller. Reagan immediately charged that Ford had abandoned "the conservative philosophy." While it is perhaps true, as Lou Cannon suggests, that Reagan was "disappointed that he had been passed over himself," it is also probably true that the appointment convinced Reagan to run against Ford in the primaries.[56]

The reason for Rockefeller's departure is simple. Ford became convinced that with Rockefeller and his liberal reputation on the ticket with him, he would lose the nomination to Reagan. Several of Rockefeller's White House adversaries lobbied hard for his departure. Ford was most impressed with the argument voiced by his first campaign manager, Howard H. "Bo" Callaway. Secretary of the army under Nixon and an ex-Republican representative from Georgia who had served in the House with both Ford and Rumsfeld, Callaway put the dilemma into its most basic political terms: if Rockefeller stayed on the ticket, conservative Republican friends of Callaway's would support Reagan. Callaway told the author that his advice to Ford was to throw the choice of vice-president open to the convention and let the delegates pick their own candidate. However, some evidence suggests that Callaway was not alone and that Rumsfeld was also lobbying for Rockefeller's early departure.*

When asked by the author if Rockefeller withdrew from the ticket of his own volition, Ford replied slowly and deliberately: "I think he withdrew understanding the reasons why his continued service would potentially undercut my capability to get the nomination." Ford is virtually alone in this belief. With very few exceptions, those in the Ford administration who have either written on the subject or have spoken to the author contend that it was a deliberate firing. As so devastatingly stated by Hugh Scott, Rockefeller's ouster from the ticket was "a deliberate hatchet job."[57] There is no doubt, however, that if the Rockefeller move was part of a grand strategy to make Ford seem more presidential, it didn't work. The exit of Nelson Rockefeller did as little to quiet the Right as the exit of Schlesinger did to quiet the Middle. Ford was treated in many quarters as duplicitous, and stories of the staff feud over Rockefeller also embarrassed the administration.

The wobbly start of Ford's campaign was one of the many factors that led to the closest race for the Republican presidential nomination since 1952. In New Hampshire Ford's early lead was cut by a last-minute announcement that Nixon was visiting China and accompanying reports of his being treated like a visiting head of state. The news of the trip on the front page gave fresh life to memories of the pardon, and Ford won by only 1,317 votes. For all intents and purposes, it was a tie, and Reagan's campaign donations immediately increased. The next few weeks found Reagan hitting hard at détente, but the issue that worked the best, particularly in the South, was that of the Panama Canal. Reagan's violent criticism of the administration's decision to continue treaty negotiations with the regime of Omar Torrijos, with an eye toward turning the canal over to the control of the Panamanians, hit home to a public whose pride had been badly wounded by the loss of Vietnam.

*In a December 1976 interview with journalist John Osborne, cited by Hartmann in his memoirs, Rockefeller contended that Rumsfeld, who wanted to be vice-president, pushed for Rockefeller's dismissal and that Ford "allowed it to happen." When Osborne later asked Ford if Rockefeller's version was accurate, Ford replied, "There may be some credence to that" (Hartmann, *Palace Politics*, pp. 366–367). When asked about this allegation in a 1989 interview with this author, Rumsfeld was crystal clear: "Absolutely false. It's just absolutely false."

The boost that the Reagan campaign received from Panama showed itself in North Carolina, a state that had been organized for Reagan by Jesse Helms. There Reagan's campaign was reborn, thanks to a 52-46 percent trouncing of Ford. Reagan then threw his hopes into Texas, where the canal issue helped, as did the ability of conservative Democrats to cross tickets and vote for a Republican candidate. Reagan swept all twenty-four of Texas's congressional districts, and the press immediately dubbed the race a tossup. On May 25, six states—including California—would be up for grabs. The nomination could be decided after that one day of voting.

Terror set in at the Ford campaign headquarters. Several of Ford's staffers argued for the death of the "no-campaign campaign" and a renewed emphasis on the nice guy image. These advisers were led by White House photographer David Kennerly, who told the author that he did not feel that "the personality of the man was getting out at all or the positive things that he had done," and by humor writer Don Penny. Two young, somewhat irreverent advisers who were particular favorites of Ford, Kennerly and Penny persuaded Ford to modify the Raoul-Duval strategy. During the California primary campaign, "slice-of-life" commercials—such as those showing Ford supporters talking to their friends about high prices—were run. According to Kathleen Jamieson, a knowledgeable critic of presidential advertising, the actors used in the commercials "reeked of fakery," thus "undercut[ting] Ford's cultivated persona as an open and candid individual and president." The ads were soon dropped, and Penny and Kennerly incurred the wrath of the staff.[38] The confusion in Ford's public relations machinery was largely responsible for his 66-34 percent defeat at the hands of Reagan in California. However, on the same day Ford blunted the Reagan landslide with sizable wins in both New Jersey and Ohio, thus keeping the race very much alive.

As the primary season ended, Reagan held the lead with 178 committed delegates, followed by Ford's 114 and 64 uncommitted. Some 270 delegates were yet to be chosen by nonprimary methods (state nominating convention, caucus, and the like), and some 100 would be elected as members of uncommitted delegations. It was in the race for these delegates that Ford surged ahead, using the power of the incumbency to make sure that the composition of nonprimary delegations favored him. Ford also made maximum use of several high-profile appearances at Bicentennial celebrations to buttonhole potential delegates. By the time the convention opened in Kansas City, Ford had a slim lead which, if his ranks held, would give him a first-ballot victory.

John Sears, Reagan's campaign manager, suggested a daring strategy. Reagan would become the first candidate in modern memory to announce his vice-presidential choice to the delegates before the balloting commenced. Reagan chose Pennsylvania Senator Richard Schweicker, who had been rated by the AFL-CIO's Committee on Public Education as voting liberal 100 percent of the time in 1975—the only senator to be so designated. The move immediately backfired. The Ford forces had a field day; Rockefeller went to every television network—no doubt with some amount of inner glee—deriding Reagan's flip-flop. More important, several Reagan delegates withdrew their support, furious at what they saw to be their leader's capitulation to politics at the expense of the conservative cause. This assured Ford's first-ballot victory, by the razor-thin margin of 1,187 to 1,070 votes.

Ford had, however, been grievously wounded by his clash with the Reagan Right. This was hammered home by the way that Ford had his vice-presidential choice thrust upon him. According to Rockefeller, Mississippi Republican boss Clark Reed contacted Cheney to tell him that the southern candidates would nominate Reagan from the floor for vice-president if Reagan's choice, Senator Robert Dole of Kansas, was not chosen.[59] Dole, former head of the Republican National Committee with impeccable conservative credentials but with a reputation for sarcasm and a short-fused temper on the campaign trail, certainly balanced the ticket. However, the circumstances surrounding his choice left little doubt as to how badly weakened the Reagan challenge had left the president.

It had been too close a call. Ford's staff was convinced that the upcoming campaign would be just as close. Now led by James Baker III, a Texan whose initial work for Reagan had impressed the Ford team, the campaign moved to regain the initiative. Baker would try a new tack, one that combined elements of both the nice guy strategy and the no-campaign campaign. In a nutshell, the plan suggested that Dole would attack, Ford's advertising would emphasize the nice guy image, and Ford would stay in Washington and attend to the responsibilities of the presidency. Using a relatively new concept of which Baker would soon become the undisputed expert—that of the quick twenty-second "news bite"—Ford would be pictured on the evening news doing his job, thus countering the image of him as inept, while his advertising could concentrate on showing what a regular guy he really was.

Yet events quickly conspired to tarnish Ford's character, producing news clips that reflected not his presidential judgment but rather outside criticisms of his competency and credibility. It began with a short-lived furor over U.S. Steel President William Whyte's financing of several pleasure trips for Ford. It was brought to a head by accusations in John Dean's new autobiography, *Blind Ambition,* that as minority leader Ford had put pressure on Wright Patman, chairman of the House Banking Committee, to slow the initial phases of the Watergate investigation. Even more damaging was another Dean scoop. While sitting on an airplane returning from the Republican convention, Dean and singer Pat Boone had overheard Secretary of Agriculture Earl Butz telling a lewd and racist joke. Without identifying Butz by name, Dean reported the story in an article for *Rolling Stone*. After the story broke, Ford took an agonizingly long time to resolve the situation, finally asking Butz to resign.[60] Added to these embarrassing episodes were stories revolving around the discovery of a 1973 tax audit done on Ford which, although it showed no illegalities, raised a few eyebrows when the amount of his deductions was reported.

Yet for most voters the most lasting image of Ford was that of a president who did not know the map of Europe. During his acceptance speech at the convention, Ford had challenged Carter to engage in debates. Debates could be the perfect vehicle for both candidates to prove themselves to be both presidential and competent. However, the second debate, held in San Francisco, contained one of the most famous gaffes in presidential campaigning history. The Helsinki Accords had brought to the fore the issue of the legitimacy of governments in the European satellites of the Soviet Union. Ford's staff knew that the debate, centering on foreign policy, would bring interrogation on this issue, and Ford had practiced his answer.[61] When Max Frankel of the *New York Times* asked the question, however, Ford responded that "there is no Soviet domination of Eastern Europe, and there will never be under a Ford administration." Astonished, Frankel asked for a clarification. Completely oblivious to the danger, Ford drove his own knife deeper.

> I don't believe, Mr. Frankel, that the Yugoslavians consider themselves dominated by the Soviet Union. I don't believe the Rumanians consider themselves dominated by the Soviet Union. Each of these countries is independent, automomous. It has its own territorial integrity and the United States does not concede that those countries are under the domination of the Soviet Union.[62]

Carter's response was sluggish ("I would like to see Mr. Ford convince the Polish-Americans and the Czech-Americans and the Hungarian-Americans in this country that those countries don't live under . . . the Soviet Union behind the Iron Curtain"), but it was swift compared to the snail's pace that Ford and his staff responded to the gaffe. Scowcroft stumbled through a postdebate press conference in which he not only refused to admit that Ford had made an error but also failed to remember how many Soviet troops actually were in Poland. Ford stuck it out for two days, telling audiences that he had meant that he did not "concede" that the Soviets had eternal control of Eastern Europe. But the press was having a field day. Two full days after the debate, Ford finally admitted his mistake. But by that time the Poland gaffe had heightened doubts about Ford's competence.

It was heart-stoppingly close. Carter's victory was razor thin—297 electoral votes to Ford's 241, and a bare 50.1 percent popular vote plurality to Ford's 48 percent. Ford kept the Republican West, Southwest, and Midwest intact; Carter won several states of the Northeast, but 90 percent of his plurality came in the South, based largely on his winning 90 percent of the southern black vote. The truly deciding factor, however, was the votes of the Middle, as it had been for most of the century. The two men literally split the vote of the Middle in half, with Carter taking the small edge necessary for victory. Carter now had the opportunity to heal the nation.

CHAPTER TEN

The Limits of Power

UNTIL the late 1960's Americans generally perceived the United States to be the most powerful and most glorious nation in the world. This author has called this public attitude the "God Bless America Myth"—the belief, held by most Americans, that their nation was both all good and all powerful, and that God Himself had blessed this nation and no other with power and glory. Mixed with this belief was the image that the public held of the chief executive. Americans long assumed that the president had the power to do just about anything that he wanted and, given his assumed moral fortitude, would exercise this power in a "good" way. Even when faced with outright lying or bumbling (of which there are many examples in the twentieth-century presidency), the presidents involved were forgiven, as the idea of their being "crooks" was unthinkable. Theodore White viewed this too as a national myth, one that "binds America together" in the belief that "somewhere in American life there is at least one man who stands for law, the president."[1] The present author has called this belief the "Myth of the Omnipotent President."

Vietnam rocked the foundations of both these myths. A newly multipolar world challenged America's power hegemony, and domestic and world disgust with the U.S. military commitment knocked the nation off it moral pedestal. By the end of Lyndon Johnson's presidency, U.S. power was limited throughout the world, and its glory, while still trumpeted by patriots, had been sorely tarnished. Johnson's conduct of the war had also presented a challenge to presidential power. As he became more and more ensnared in Vietnam, he found himself incapable of offering the public either an acceptable or ultimately a believable explanation of his actions. The press refused to trust him, antiwar protests made him a prisoner in the White House, and his standing in the polls plummeted. This "credibility gap" ultimately weakened Johnson's ability to influence the course of public opinion and led to his being chased from office. Richard Nixon then inherited both a nation and a presidency that had been restricted as never before. The ultimate tragedy of the Nixon administration was in Nixon's inability to fully grasp these new, post-Vietnam limits on his power.

In the realm of foreign policy Nixon was at his most sophisticated. He had accepted the limits of U.S. power in the new multipolar world earlier and more completely than most of his contemporaries. With a notable exception to be mentioned in a moment, Nixon grew beyond the bellicose Cold War rhetoric that had typified conservatives—like himself—of both parties during the postwar period. This growth allowed Nixon to evolve into a true internationalist, believing that the United States was indeed one of many coexistent nations. This belief spurred Nixon to disengage both from Vietnam and from Cold War hostilities with the Communist powers.

This is not to say, however, that Nixon's foreign policy was a complete success. Just as clear as the success of détente and devolution is that these two achievements were realized at tremendous political and social costs. Détente was established only as a result of sacrificing Taiwan as an ally and agreeing to a SALT treaty that left much to be desired. Nixon extricated the nation from Vietnam, but the human and diplomatic costs of both the war on the periphery and the renewal of the bombing of the North stained Nixon's "peace with honor," further tarnished the nation's glory, and led directly to many of his administration's abuses of power. Just as important was that while his administration concentrated its efforts on achieving détente and devolution, Nixon deliberately put the Middle East on the back burner. His refusal to treat the Middle East as a unique regional issue—one of the many new "poles" of world power—led to the continuation of brinksmanship rhetoric with the Soviets on Middle Eastern issues and an inability to either predict or effectively react to conflict in the region. As a result, the situation in the Middle East, most notably during the Syrian invasion of 1970 and the Yom Kippur War, soured both the Soviets and the Americans on détente even before Nixon had left office. It was the single largest policy failure of the Nixon presidency.

On the domestic front Nixon's policies revolved around the conservative canon that the federal government should limit its role in people's lives (that, after all, was the basis of the "New Federalism"). His belief that Washington was limited in how fast it could make school districts enforce *Brown v. Board of Education* made him a more acceptable partner to southern politicians than any president since 1954; as a result, the integration rate was faster under Nixon than any previous or subsequent administration. Revenue sharing funneled new tax dollars back to the badly needed localities and gave hope to those who longed for the pre-FDR days of limited governmental intervention in local affairs. However, both of these true achievements must be tempered by the realization that they were not the sole accomplishment of the administration. *Alexander v. Holmes County* pushed Nixon into having to face up to the problem of de jure segregation, and Nelson Rockefeller's coterie of governors rammed revenue sharing down the throat of a recalcitrant Congress. Executive reorganization, however, was an unchallengeable success, as Nixon streamlined the presidency and provided for a more rational line of command for the creation of domestic policy.

Yet despite Nixon's strongly felt desire that he would, as he stated in his memoirs, "get rid of the costly failures of the Great Society,"[2] his administration did not do so. The basic structure of Johnson's revamping of the New Deal and the New Frontier existed after Nixon left office. The most notable example was the failure of the Family Assistance Plan, which suffered from staff infighting and brutal mismanagement on Capitol Hill. Also, Nixon's belief that the federal government should not make itself the instrument of integration led him to denounce busing at every opportunity and effectively turn his back on de facto segregation. In so doing Nixon left racial tensions in the cities essentially as he had inherited them from Johnson—a powder-keg, waiting for the next opportunity to detonate.

There were other failures. While Nixon recognized that the nation could no longer play the international economic role that it had written for itself at Bretton Woods, Phase II destroyed whatever good might have come out of the initial decision to freeze wages and prices and close the gold window, and his inability to cut domestic spending left his predecessors with a staggering federal deficit. He also failed to reinject the country with a dose of Eisenhower morality, leaving the social revolution of the sixties intact.

Nixon's was far less than the domestic "revolution" that his admirers profess and much more than the utter failure in domestic policy that the vast majority of observers believe. It was instead the beginning of a transitional period in domestic affairs, a tempered traditionalism residing between the Great Society liberalism of the 1960s and the Reagan conservatism of the 1980s. Taken alone, this mixed legacy of accomplishment and missed opportunity might well have placed Nixon higher in the presidential rankings than he now stands.* Yet it is not for his domestic policy—the "ends" of power—that Nixon has been remembered. Rather it is for the "means" by which he pursued his policy goals.

In a more recent volume of memoirs, *In the Arena* (1990), Nixon professes to believe that "the President's power is far more circumscribed

---

*In 1989 Nixon ranked thirty-fourth among presidents in effectiveness—only Grant and Harding ranked below him (see Jack E. Holmes and Robert E. Elder, "Our Best and Worst Presidents: Some Possible Reasons for Perceived Performance," *Presidential Studies Quarterly,* Summer 1989, pp. 529 558).

than that of most other world leaders."[3] This may well represent the
former president's present beliefs. It is a far cry, however, from what
he believed, and how he acted, as president. Nixon never accepted that
Johnson's "credibility gap" had created any irreversible limitations on
his power to advance his own agenda. He firmly believed, and continues to state, that a strong use of executive power was not only within
his consititutional prerogative but would eventually restore the presidential "glory" that had been squandered as Lyndon Johnson muddled his way through Vietnam. This was an integral part of Nixon's
desire to reform Johnsonism—he would personally stop the erosion of
presidential power. Nixon failed to do so. In fact, he left the presidency
an infinitely more limited office than the one he had inherited from
Johnson. The key to this irony lies in Nixon's dreadful relationship
with Capitol Hill.

As Richard Neustadt points out in *Presidential Power*, "most Wash-
ingtonians reacted to [Johnson], lies and all, with cool professional-
ism."[4] Despite his elevation to the presidency, Johnson—like Ford—
remained a legislator at heart. He liked and courted Congress throughout his presidency; it strains the imagination to think of his successor
beginning a speech to Congress, as Johnson did in his very first such
address, with the phrase "I need your help." Although his actions in
Vietnam lost him the support of what was then a very small percentage of legislative doves, Johnson left Washington with the majority of
those in Congress on his side. While he was universally seen as a crude
power broker, few of his peers argued that Johnson had gone beyond
the scope of his constitutional limits, and those who tried were reminded of the lopsided congressional approval of his 1964 actions in
Tonkin Gulf. Under Johnson there was no attempt to statutorily limit
the power of the presidency as there would be in 1973, no serious calls
for Johnson's impeachment, no congressional committees formed to
investigate his administration's transgressions. Politically expendable in
1968, Lyndon Johnson was nevertheless still respected by his congressional friends. He would always be one of them.

Nixon's disdain for Congress is clear; he recently wrote that "the
alternative to strong Presidential government is government by Congress, which is no government at all."[5] Nixon never made any attempt
to court Congress—indeed, quite the opposite was true. He browbeat
its members, Republican and Democrat alike, with the expectation that
they would either do his bidding or suffer the consequences. By the
end of 1970 there were effectively no relations between the White House
and Capitol Hill. They had been destroyed by Haynsworth-Carswell,
the heavy-handedness of the ABM debate, the deception of Cambodia,
and the attempted purge during that fall's congressional elections. The
political reality, of course, is that the definition of "high crimes and
misdemeanors" is, as John Doar realized, whatever Congress wants it

to be. It can ignore transgressions in someone it respects and penalize those it does not respect. It can do so more easily when public opinion is on its side, as was clearly the case in 1973 and 1974. Richard Nixon was held in lower regard by Congress than any of his predecessors or successors, except perhaps the man with whom he will be forever linked—Andrew Johnson, the first president to be impeached.

By spring 1974 Congress had little doubt about its ability to remove Nixon from the presidency; its victories on the War Powers Act, the Budget and Impoundment Act, and support of the Thieu regime after the cease-fire had made this fact clear. It also had few pangs of conscience about initiating the impeachment procedure. While Nixon spared himself the ultimate indignity of an impeachment trial, there is no doubt that he would have been convicted. In his attempt to turn the clock back to the days of a presidency that Arthur M. Schlesinger, Jr., had called imperial, Nixon had brought about his own destruction and the emasculation of the office's powers, and in the process he had tarnished its glory before the nation and the world.

Schlesinger's "imperial" presidency had degenerated under Johnson and Nixon into a "constricted" presidency. The congressional "power earthquake" that followed Nixon's resignation continued to limit the powers of the office. Gerald Ford's power and influence, then, were more limited than any other president. There was never any way that he could be the type of president whom political scientist Clinton Rossiter had described as a "magnificent lion, who can roam freely and do great deeds" with "virtually no limit to what [he] can do."[6] The presidency, as well as its occupant, was indeed a Ford, not a Lincoln anymore. Add to this the fact that Ford was hampered by a weak staff and chased by Reagan counterrevolutionaries, and the scene for disappointment was set. Congress forced an end to a détente that was already unraveling, and it completed devolution in Vietnam. Congressional opposition also prolonged the agony of inflation, and staff infighting weakened the energy proposals. The Reagan challenge forced the administration to abandon its set policy at several junctures, only to adopt proposals that were blatantly political in nature and thus difficult to defend.

From an image point of view, Ford did not help his own case. His ability to persuade the American people was never on a par with any of his immediate predecessors. Philip Buchen summed up this problem for the author: "A president should be able to make people awe-struck"; Ford could not. His inability to line the public up behind his program of economic volunteerism ("WIN") is a case in point, as was his inability to keep the Republican Right in line as Nixon had. However, Ford's pardoning of Nixon offers the best example. Despite what can now be seen as a valid need to rid himself of his predecessor's shadow, Ford was never able to communicate to either Congress or the American people his true motives for pardoning Nixon. Unable to mount an offensive against the talk of a backroom deal, the pardon became, as A. James Reichley observes, the event that "linked" his administration to Nixon's in the public mind.[7] As a result, Ford was unable to restore the "glory" of the presidency; he would forever be, in the words of journalist Clark Mollenhoff, "the man who pardoned Nixon."[8] It was, as we have seen, a large factor in his defeat in 1976.

What Ford did bring back into the presidential equation was respect. Johnson and Nixon had misplaced the presidency's ethical compass. Ford proved that a truly nice guy could still be president. Two *Newsweek* reporters called it the "DHB Factor—the Decent Human Being Factor."[9] Even the pardon could not displace American's gut feeling that Gerald Ford was a truly nice man. This is the most endearing part of his presidency; it is the most positive component of his legacy.

In January 1977, as he began his Inaugural Address, Jimmy Carter turned to Gerald Ford and said, "For myself and for our nation I want to thank my predecessor for all he has done to heal our land." Yet despite Ford's proclamation in the title of his memoirs that his administration had been a time to heal, the task had been only partially completed. Ford's depth of character had healed the nation's most gaping wounds. Yet as Carter observed in his memoirs, "in spite of Ford's healing service, the ghosts of Watergate still haunted the White House."[10] The experience of the limits of power would be the most lasting legacy of the Nixon and Ford years.

Notes

Unless otherwise noted, quotations from personal interviews with the author are identified in the text.

PREFACE

1. Richard M. Nixon, *The Memoirs of Richard Nixon* (New York: Grosset and Dunlap, 1978), p. 1084.

1. TO REFORM THE SIXTIES

1. John Hersey "1968: Year of the Triphammer," *Syracuse Herald-American* (special insert), November 26, 1978.

2. William Manchester, *The Glory and the Dream: A Narrative History of America, 1932-1972* (Boston: Little, Brown, 1973), p. 1379.

3. George C. Herring, *America's Longest War: The United States and Vietnam, 1950-1975* (New York: Knopf, 1986), p. 191.

4. Nixon, *Memoirs,* p. 14.

5. Nixon, *Memoirs,* p. 16.

6. Stephen E. Ambrose, *Nixon: The Education of a Politician, 1913–1962* (New York: Simon & Schuster, 1987), p. 58.

7. Ambrose, *Nixon*, p. 110.

8. Ambrose, *Nixon*, p. 139.

9. Garry Wills, *Nixon Agonistes: The Crisis of the Self-Made Man* (New York: New American Library, 1969), chap. 4.

10. Quoted in Nixon, *Memoirs*, p. 56.

11. Nixon, *Memoirs*, p. 56.

12. John Robert Greene, *The Crusade: The Presidential Election of 1952* (Lanham, Md.: University Press of America, 1985), pp. 90, 116.

13. Nixon to George Creel, October 30, 1951, Richard M. Nixon Pre-Presidential Papers, Laguna Niguel Branch, National Archives, series 320, Name File, box 189.

14. Greene, *Crusade*, pp. 190–192.

15. Stewart Alsop, *Nixon and Rockefeller: A Double Portrait* (Garden City, N.Y.: Doubleday, 1960), p. 69.

16. Nixon, *Memoirs*, p. 108.

17. James Hagerty interview, Columbia Oral History Collection, vol. 2, pp. 292–293.

18. Ambrose, *Nixon*, p. 452.

19. Eleanor Roosevelt to John F. Kennedy, September 27, 1960, Eleanor Roosevelt Papers, Franklin D. Roosevelt Library, General Correspondence: 1960, box 4415.

20. Ambrose, *Nixon*, p. 645.

21. Nixon, *Memoirs*, p. 244.

22. Theodore H. White, *Breach of Faith: The Fall of Richard Nixon* (New York: Atheneum, 1975), pp. 72–73.

23. Quoted in William Rusher, *The Rise of the Right* (New York: Morrow, 1984), p. 194.

24. William Safire, *Before the Fall: An Inside View of the Pre-Watergate White House* (Garden City, N.Y.: Doubleday, 1975), p. 263.

25. Lewis Chester, Godfrey Hodgson, and Bruce Page, *An American Melodrama: The Presidential Campaign of 1968* (New York: Viking, 1969), p. 615.

26. Quoted in Theodore H. White, *The Making of the President, 1968* (New York: Atheneum, 1969), p. 65.

27. White, *Making of the President, 1968*, p. 404.

28. Strom Thurmond interview, Southern Oral History Project (Series A), University of North Carolina, Chapel Hill (1974), p. 16.

29. "45–85," ABC News Special (1985).

30. White, *Making of the President, 1968*, p. 386.

31. Safire, *Before the Fall*, p. 78.

32. Chester et al., *An American Melodrama*, p. 682.

33. See Joe McGinniss, *The Selling of the President, 1968* (New York: Pocket Books, 1969).

34. Alexander P. Lamis, *The Two-Party South* (New York: Oxford University Press, 1984), p. 30.

35. Wills, *Nixon Agonistes*, p. 248.

36. Nixon, *Memoirs*, p. 366.

2. THE ROCKY ROAD TO A "NEW FEDERALISM"

1. Quoted in Nicholas Lehmann, "The Unfinished War, Part II," *Atlantic Monthly*, January 1989, p. 64.

2. Quoted in George H. Nash, *The Conservative Intellectual Movement in America since 1945* (New York: Basic Books, 1976), pp. 320–321.

3. Samuel Kernell and Samuel L. Popkin (eds.), *Chief of Staff* (Berkeley: University of California Press, 1986), p. 185.

4. Kenneth W. Thompson (ed.), *The Nixon Presidency* (Lanham, Md.: University Press of America, 1987), pp. 86–87.

5. Seymour Hersh, *The Price of Power: Kissinger in the Nixon White House* (New York: Summit Books, 1983), p. 372.

6. John Ehrlichman, *Witness to Power: The Nixon Years* (New York: Pocket Books, 1982), p. 4.

7. Nixon PP, 1969, pp. 694–702.

8. Safire, *Before the Fall*, p. 220.

9. Safire, *Before the Fall*, p. 226.

10. Safire, *Before the Fall*, pp. 227–228.

11. Thurmond interview, Southern Oral History Project.

12. Nixon PP, 1969, pp. 208–216.

13. Hersh, *The Price of Power*, chap. 13.

14. Haldeman Notes, March 19, 1969, NP, WHSF-Haldeman, box 40.

15. Nixon, *Memoirs*, p. 418.

16. Nixon *Memoirs*, p. 418.

17. John H. Choper, *Judicial Review and the National Political Process: A Functional Reconsideration of the Role of the Supreme Court* (Chicago: University of Chicago Press, 1980), p. 145.

18. Nixon, *Memoirs*, p. 419.

19. Haldeman Notes, May 7, 1969, NP, WHSF-Haldeman, box 40.

20. Herbert Brownell, interview with author, October 10, 1990: confidential sources.

21. Several examples in NP, WHCF: Subject, folder EX FG 51 (Fortas Conflict).

22. Sobelhoff to Kennedy, February 18, 1964, and Kennedy to Sobelhoff, February 28, 1964, Samuel J. Ervin, Jr., Papers, Southern Historical Collection, University of North Carolina, series 2, box 414, folder 567.

23. Press release, October 8, 1969, NP, WHSF-PPF (President's Desk), box 186, Haynsworth folder.

24. Ehrlichman Notes, October 1, 1969, NP, WHSF-Ehrlichman, box 9.

25. Ehrlichman Notes, October 2, 1969, NP, WHSF-Ehrlichman, box 9.

26. Ehrlichman Notes, October 21, 1969, NP, WHSF-Ehrlichman, box 9; Haldeman Notes, October 21, 1969, NP, WHSF-Haldeman, box 40.

27. Nixon PP, 1969, pp. 814–820.

28. Ehrlichman Notes, October 21, 1969, NP, WHSF-Ehrlichman, box 9.

29. Hugh D. Scott, Jr., United States Capitol Historical Society Oral History Program (1976, 1978), p. 62.

30. Bayh remarks at panel discussion, "Appointments to the Supreme Court," November 21, 1987, Hofstra University Conference on the Nixon Presidency.

31. Quoted in Leonard Levy, *Against the Law: The Nixon Court and Criminal Justice* (New York: Random House, 1974), pp. 118–119.

32. Ehrlichman Notes, March 26, 1970, NP, WHSF-Ehrlichman, box 9.

33. Ehrlichman Notes, March 31, 1970, NP, WHSF-Ehrlichman, box 9.

34. Ehrlichman Notes, February 12, 1970, NP, WHSF-Ehrlichman, box 9.

35. Ehrlichman Notes, March 10, 1970, NP, WHSF-Ehrlichman, box 9.

36. A. James Reichley, *Conservatives in an Era of Change: The Nixon and Ford Administrations* (Washington, D.C.: Brookings Institution, 1981), p. 184.

37. Alfred H. Kelly and Winifred A. Harbison, *The American Constitution: Its Origins and Development* (New York: Norton, 1970), pp. 937–938.

38. Nixon PP, 1969, p. 892.

39. Nixon PP, 1969, pp. 1003–1013 (during a December 8, 1969, televised press conference).

40. Ehrlichman Notes, March 10, 1970, NP, WHSF-Ehrlichman, box 9.

41. Nixon PP, 1970, pp. 304–320.

42. Quoted in Rowland Evans, Jr., and Robert D. Novak, *Nixon in the White House: The Frustration of Power* (New York: Vintage Books, 1972), p. 174.

43. Reichley, *Conservatives,* p. 189.

44. Nixon, *Memoirs,* p. 424.

45. Haldeman Notes, February 12, 1969, NP, WHSF-Haldeman, box 40.

46. Quoted in Reichley, *Conservatives,* p. 145.

47. Ehrlichman Notes, November 7, 1970, NP, WHSF-Ehrlichman, box 9.

48. Quoted in *U.S. News and World Report,* April 15, 1983, p. 43.

49. Thomas J. Peters and Robert H. Waterman, Jr., *In Search of Excellence: Lessons from America's Best-Run Companies* (New York: Harper and Row, 1982), pp. 45–46.

50. Confidential source.

51. Evans and Novak, *Nixon,* p. 237; Larry Berman, *The Office of Management and Budget and the Presidency, 1921–1979* (Princeton, N.J.: Princeton University Press, 1979), pp. 105–106.

52. Staff Paper—The Independent Agencies, July 7, 1969; Study Plan—Organization: The Executive Office of the President, July 9, 1969; Notes of Ash Council Member, July 1969, NP, WHCF: Subject, EX FG-250 (PACEO).

53. Quoted in Stephen Hess, *Organizing the Presidency* (Washington, D.C.: Brookings Institution, 1976), footnote, p. 131.

54. Quoted in Berman, *Office of Management and Budget,* p. 111.

3. RADICLIBS, RECESSION, AND REVENUE SHARING

1. Nixon, *Memoirs,* p. 491.

2. Ehrlichman Notes, September 5, 1969, NP, WHSF-Ehrlichman, box 9; Haldeman Notes, September 24, 1969, NP, WHSF-Haldeman, box 40.

3. Unless otherwise noted, the excerpts from Agnew's speeches can be found in *Collected Speeches of Spiro Agnew* (New York: Audubon Books, 1971).

4. Quoted in Jules Witcover, *White Knight: The Rise of Spiro Agnew* (New York: Random House, 1972), p. 314.

5. Quoted in John R. Coyne, *The Impudent Snobs: Agnew vs. the Intellectual Establishment* (New Rochelle, N.Y.: Arlington House, 1972), p. 7.

6. Ehrlichman Notes, February 12, 1970, NP, WHSF-Ehrlichman, box 9.

7. Quoted in Witcover, *White Knight,* p. 365.

8. Ehrlichman Notes, November 1, 1970, NP, WHSF-Ehrlichman, box 10.

9. Safire, *Before the Fall,* p. 328.

10. Nixon PP, 1970, pp. 1033–1038.

11. Nixon, *Memoirs,* p. 494.

12. Safire, *Before the Fall,* p. 336.

13. Walter J. Hickel, *Who Owns America?* (Englewood Cliffs, N.J.: Prentice-Hall, 1971), p. 251.

14. Nixon, *Memoirs,* p. 495.

15. Nixon PP, 1969, pp. 665–668.

16. Ehrlichman Notes, September 16, 1969, NP, WHSF-Ehrlichman, box 9.

17. Nixon PP, 1970, pp. 85–87.

18. Quoted in Robert H. Connery and Gerald Benjamin, *Rockefeller of New York: Executive Power in the Statehouse* (Ithaca, N.Y.: Cornell University Press, 1979), p. 403.

19. Nixon PP, 1971, pp. 158–169.

20. Ehrlichman Notes, September 28, 1971, NP, WHSF-Ehrlichman, box 10.

21. Ehrlichman Notes, February 4, 1970, NP, WHSF-Ehrlichman, box 9.

22. Morgan to Nixon, July 6, 1971, NP, WHSF-POF, President's Handwriting File, box 12.

23. Ehrlichman Notes, April 21, 1971, NP, WHSF-Ehrlichman, box 11.

24. Nixon PP, 1972, pp. 429–443.

25. Memorandum, Buchanan to Nixon, NP, WHCF: Subject, folder EX FG-51 (Supreme Court).

26. Nixon, *Memoirs,* p. 423.

27. Ehrlichman Notes, August 11, 1970, NP, WHSF-Ehrlichman, box 10.

28. Nixon comments in margins of Buchanan to Nixon, October 1, 1971, NP, WHSF:POF, President's Handwriting File, box 14.

29. John Dean, *Blind Ambition: The White House Years* (New York: Simon & Schuster, 1976), p. 50.

30. Ehrlichman Notes, October 14, 1971, NP, WHSF-Ehrlichman, box 11.

31. Ehrlichman Notes, September 11, 1969, NP, WHSF-Ehrlichman, box 9.

32. Memorandum, Nixon to Haldeman, March 2, 1970, NP, WHSF: PPF, box 2.

33. Safire, *Before the Fall,* pp. 497–508.

34. Nixon PP, 1970, pp. 600–602.

35. Quoted in Reichley, *Conservatives,* p. 217.

36. Quoted in Ehrlichman, *Witness to Power,* p. 224.

37. *New York Times,* June 18, 1970, p. A1.

38. Evans and Novak, *Nixon,* p. 206.

39. Nixon PP, 1970, pp. 674–676.

40. Safire, *Before the Fall,* p. 585.

41. Ehrlichman Notes, October 23, 1970, NP, WHSF-Ehrlichman, box 10.

42. Herbert Stein, *Presidential Economics: The Making of Economic Policy from Roosevelt to Reagan and Beyond* (New York: Simon & Schuster, 1984), p. 180.

43. Memorandum, Stein to Nixon, October 12, 1973, NP, WHSF: WHCF, Confidential Files [CF], BE-5 (National Economy).

44. Reichley, *Conservatives,* p. 226.

45. Stein, *Presidential Politics,* p. 183.

46. *Time,* December 28, 1987, p. 58.

4. "PEACE WITH HONOR"

1. Speech quoted in Nixon, *Memoirs,* p. 284.

2. Quoted in C. L. Sulzberger, *The World and Richard Nixon* (New York: Prentice-Hall, 1987), p. 21.

3. Speech quoted in Nixon, *Memoirs,* p. 200.

4. Quoted in Ralph Blumenfeld et al., *Henry Kissinger: The Private and Public Story* (New York: New American Library, 1974), p. 59.

5. Blumenfeld, *Henry Kissinger,* p. 80.

6. See Rockefeller Brothers Fund Special Studies Collection, 1956–1964, Rockefeller Archive Center, Tarrytown, N.Y.

7. Blumenfeld, *Henry Kissinger,* p. 158.

8. Blumenfeld, *Henry Kissinger*, p. 160.

9. Quoted in Stanley Karnow, *Vietnam: A History* (New York: Penguin, 1983), p. 585.

10. Blumenfeld, *Henry Kissinger*, p. 167.

11. Nixon PP, 1969, pp. 544–556.

12. Quoted in H. R. Haldeman, *The Ends of Power* (New York: Times Books, 1978), p. 81.

13. Hersh, *The Price of Power*, p. 63.

14. Hersh, *The Price of Power*, p. 54.

15. Nixon, *Memoirs*, p. 382.

16. Nixon PP, 1969, pp. 585–587.

17. Nixon, *Memoirs*, p. 396.

18. Interview, Frank Church, Lyndon B. Johnson Oral History Project (1969), p. 18.

19. Nixon, *Memoirs*, p. 399.

20. Quoted in Karnow, *Vietnam*, p. 599.

21. Nixon, *Memoirs*, p. 405.

22. Nixon PP, 1969, pp. 901–909.

23. Ehrlichman Notes, November 5, 1969, NP, WHSF-Ehrlichman, box 9.

24. Nixon, *Memoirs*, p. 413.

25. The story of My Lai was broken by Seymour Hersh, a free-lance reporter who had served as press secretary and speech-writer to Eugene McCarthy in 1968. The story was not entirely new—the Associated Press had run a brief story on it the previous September, but it was largely ignored. It was not until Hersh confirmed the story through a Pentagon source, sold it to Dispatch News, and had it picked up by the *New York Times* that the story received national attention. The story was fleshed out through a Mike Wallace interview with Paul Meadlo on "60 Minutes," which cost CBS a $10,000 fee with Dispatch News. Many of the grisly details came to light in this interview. See Seymour Hersh, *My Lai 4* (New York: Random House, 1970), and Mike Wallace, *Close Encounters* (New York: Morrow, 1984).

26. Haldeman Notes, November 25, 1969, NP, WHSF-Haldeman, box 40.

27. Quoted in Nixon, *Memoirs*, p. 450.

28. Safire, *Before the Fall*, p. 187.

29. Richard M. Nixon, *In the Arena: A Memoir of Victory, Defeat and Renewal* (New York: Simon & Schuster, 1990), p. 47.

30. Karnow, *Vietnam*, p. 610.

31. *New York Times*, May 1, 1970.

32. Safire, *Before the Fall*, p. 187.

33. Quoted in Evans and Novak, *Nixon*, p. 276.

34. James Michener, *Kent State: What Happened and Why* (New York: Random House, 1971), pp. 340–341.

35. Quoted in Evans and Novak, *Nixon*, p. 277.

36. Confidential sources.

37. Hickel, *Who Owns America?*, p. 247.

38. Hickel, *Who Owns America?*, pp. 230–238.

39. Ehrlichman, *Witness to Power*, p. 98.

40. Nixon PP, 1971, pp. 75–78.

41. Quoted in Neil Sheehan and the *New York Times*, *The Pentagon Papers* (New York: Bantam, 1971), p. xviii.

42. "The War Exposes: Battle Over the Right to Know," *Time*, July 5, 1971, p. 8.

43. Sanford J. Ungar, *The Papers and the Papers: An Account of the Legal and Political Battle over the Pentagon Papers* (New York: Dutton, 1972), chap. 12.

44. Address reprinted in *Facts on File: 1972,* pp. 31–32.
45. Richard M. Nixon, *No More Vietnams* (New York: Avon, 1985), p. 143; Nixon PP, 1972, pp. 100–106.
46. Nixon, *Memoirs,* p. 594.
47. Herring, *America's Longest War,* p. 249.
48. Herring, *America's Longest War,* p. 250.
49. Karnow, *Vietnam,* p. 649.
50. Karnow, *Vietnam,* p. 650.
51. Quoted in Karnow, *Vietnam,* p. 651.
52. Nixon, *No More Vietnams,* p. 155.
53. Nixon, *No More Vietnams,* p. 156.
54. Herring, *America's Longest War,* pp. 253–254.
55. "45–85" (ABC News Special).
56. Notes in Hugh D. Scott Papers (#10200), Manuscripts Division, Special Collections Department, University of Virginia Library, series 3: Congressional, Foreign Relations Committee, box 67, folder 1.

5. "HARD-HEADED DÉTENTE"

1. Nixon, *Memoirs,* pp. 284–285.
2. Quoted in Robert D. Schulzinger, *Henry Kissinger: Doctor of Diplomacy* (New York: Columbia University Press, 1989), p. 210.
3. Richard Nixon, *The Real War* (New York: Warner Books, 1980), p. 15.
4. C. L. Sulzberger, remarks at panel discussion, "The Opening to China," November 19, 1987, Hofstra University Conference on the Nixon Presidency.
5. Jerome A. Cohen, remarks at panel discussion, "The Opening to China," November 19, 1987, Hofstra University Conference on the Nixon Presidency.
6. Nixon, *Memoirs,* p. 281.
7. Nixon PP, 1969, pp. 179–194.
8. Nixon, *No More Vietnams,* p. 111.
9. Henry Kissinger, speech, November 19, 1987, Hofstra University Conference on the Nixon Presidency.
10. Hersh, *The Price of Power,* p. 365.
11. Memorandum, Nixon to Kissinger, November 22, 1970, NP, WHSF: PPF, box 2.
12. Hersh, *The Price of Power,* p. 366.
13. Evans and Novak, *Nixon,* p. 403.
14. Nixon, *Memoirs,* p. 551.
15. Memorandum, Colson to Nixon, March 2, 1972, NP, WHSF: POF (President's Handwriting File), box 16.
16. Roger Morris, *Uncertain Greatness: Henry Kissinger and American Foreign Policy* (New York: Harper and Row, 1977), p. 208.
17. Hersh, *The Price of Power,* p. 149.
18. *New York Times,* January 20, 1969.
19. Hersh, *The Price of Power,* pp. 66–67.
20. Robert S. Litwak. *Detente and the Nixon Doctrine: American Foreign Policy and the Pursuit of Stability, 1969–1976* (Cambridge: Cambridge University Press, 1984), p. 111.
21. Confidential sources; Hersh, *The Price of Power,* chap. 20.
22. Hersh, *The Price of Power,* p. 343.
23. Quoted in "A Guide to Nixon's Journey," *Time,* February 21, 1972, p. 27.
24. Hersh, *The Price of Power,* p. 489.
25. *Time,* "Guide to Nixon's China Journey," p. 27.

26. Richard M. Nixon, *Real Peace; A Strategy for the West* (Boston: Little, Brown, 1983), p. 72.

27. Memorandum, Colson to Nixon, March 2, 1972, NP, WHSF: POF (President's Handwriting File), box 16.

28. Hugh Sidey, "Eating Cereal in the House of the Czars," *Time*, June 2, 1972, p. 14.

29. Golda Meir, *My Life* (New York: Putnam, 1975), p. 382.

30. Jimmy Carter, *Keeping Faith: Memoirs of a President* (New York: Bantam, 1980), p. 275.

31. Meir, *My Life*, pp. 382–383.

32. Hersh, *The Price of Power*, p. 220.

33. Department of State, reprint, January 25, 1970, David Henry Dietz Papers, Arents Research Library, Syracuse University, box 16.

34. Litwak, *Detente and Devolution*, p. 99.

35. Hersh, *The Price of Power*, p. 229; Meir, *My Life*, pp. 386–394.

36. Evans and Novak, *Nixon*, pp. 263–264.

37. Evans and Novak, *Nixon*, p. 264.

38. Henry Kissinger, *Years of Upheaval* (Boston: Little, Brown, 1982), p. 205.

39. Nixon, *Memoirs*, p. 922.

40. Nixon, *Memoirs*, p. 922.

41. Quoted in Morris, *Uncertain Greatness*, p. 246.

42. Nixon, *Memoirs*, p. 939.

6. "DIRTY TRICKS": NIXON AND HIS ENEMIES, 1969–1972

1. Photo in Robert Sam Anson, *Exile: The Unquiet Oblivion of Richard M. Nixon.* New York: Simon & Schuster, 1984.

2. Quoted in William E. Leuchtenburg, *In the Shadow of FDR* (Ithaca, N.Y.: Cornell University Press, 1983), p. 171.

3. Nixon, *In the Arena*, pp. 33–43.

4. Richard Gid Powers, *Secrecy and Power: The Life of J. Edgar Hoover* (New York: Free Press, 1987), p. 447.

5. Schulzinger, *Henry Kissinger*, p. 42.

6. Pierre Salinger, *With Kennedy* (New York: Avon, 1966), p. 151.

7. National Press Club report quoted in Arthur M. Schlesinger, Jr., *The Imperial Presidency* (Boston: Houghton Mifflin, 1973), p. 230.

8. Ehrlichman Notes, February 6, 1971, NP, WHSF-Ehrlichman, box 10.

9. Colson Notes, June 8, 1971, NP, WHSF-Colson, box 14.

10. See memorandum, Buchanan to Ziegler, NP, WHSF-Buchanan, box 8.

11. Memorandum, Magruder to Colson, January 3, 1972, NP, WHSF-Colson, box 17.

12. Safire, *Before the Fall*, p. 354.

13. Safire, *Before the Fall*, p. 355.

14. Ehrlichman Notes, May 25, 1971, NP, WHSF-Ehrlichman, box 11.

15. Ehrlichman Notes, March 12, 1970, NP, WHSF-Ehrlichman, box 9.

16. Ehrlichman Notes, March 13, 1970, NP, WHSF-Ehrlichman, box 9.

17. Memorandum, Huston to Haldeman, June 25, 1970, NP, WHSF-Haldeman, box 70.

18. WH, pp. 748–751.

19. Memorandum, Huston to Haldeman, August 5, 1970, Ervin Papers, box 424, series 2: Subject File, Watergate Memoranda, folder 862.

20. Nixon, *Memoirs*, p. 496.

21. Charles W. Colson, *Born Again* (New York: Bantam, 1976), pp. 31–32.

22. Quoted in J. Anthony Lukas, *Nightmare: The Underside of the Nixon Years* (New York: Bantam, 1976), p. 15.

23. Ehrlichman, *Witness to Power*, p. 60.

24. White, *Breach of Faith*, p. 142.

25. Colson Notes, NP, WHSF-Colson, box 17.

26. Colson, *Born Again*, pp. 42–43.

27. Memorandum, John Dean to Larry Higby, September 14, 1971, Ervin Papers, series 2, Subject File: Watergate Memoranda, folder 864.

28. Confidential memorandum from Dean, August 16, 1971, Ervin Papers, series 2: Subject Files, Watergate Memoranda, box 464, folder 863.

29. Dean memorandum, Ervin Papers, series 2: Subject File, Watergate Memoranda, box 424, folder 864.

30. Lukas, *Nightmare*, p. 23.

31. For copies of material sent back from the White House plant, see NP, WHSF-Haldeman, box 40.

32. Colson Notes, NP, WHSF-Colson, box 14.

33. Confidential sources.

34. Hersh, *The Price of Power*, p. 325.

35. Lukas, *Nightmare*, p. 95; Hersh, *The Price of Power*, pp. 330–331.

36. Ehrlichman Notes, June 17, 1971, NP, WHSF-Ehrlichman, box 11.

37. Lukas, *Nightmare*, p. 99.

38. White, *Breach of Faith*, p. 149.

39. Hersh, *The Price of Power*, p. 390.

40. Stewart Alsop, "The Crazy-Brave and the Phony-Tough," *Newsweek*, September 10, 1973.

41. Ehrlichman Notes, July 24, 1971, NP, WHSF-Ehrlichman, box 11.

42. See Jim Hougan, *Secret Agenda* (New York: Ballantine, 1984), pp 115–121; Lukas, *Nightmare*, pp. 232–234; WH, p. 70; White, *Breach of Faith*, pp. 156–157.

43. Quoted in Hougan, *Secret Agenda*, p. 120.

44. Ehrlichman Notes, November 1, 1971, NP, WHSF-Ehrlichman, box 12.

45. Lukas, *Nightmare*, p. 234.

46. Lukas, *Nightmare*, pp. 235–236.

47. Dean, *Blind Ambition*, p. 86.

48. G. Gordon Liddy, *Will* (New York: St. Martin's Press, 1980), p. 212.

49. Lukas, *Nightmare*, p. 256.

50. Liddy, *Will*, p. 215.

51. Hougan, *Secret Agenda*, p. xvi.

52. Dean, *Blind Ambition*, p. 70.

53. Larry DuBois and Laurence Gonzales, "The Puppet and the Puppet-masters: Uncovering the Secret World of Nixon, Hughes, and the CIA," *Playboy*, October 1976, p. 112.

54. DuBois and Gonzales, "Puppet," p. 112.

55. Kerhli to Haldeman, January 18, 1972 (Report on News Summary), in Bruce Oudes (ed.), *From: The President—Richard Nixon's Secret Files* (New York: Harper and Row, 1989), p. 357.

56. DuBois and Gonzales, "Puppet," pp. 182–183.

57. Lukas, *Nightmare*, p. 244.

58. See Memorandum, Colson to Chapin, December 12, 1970, NP, WHSF:WHCF, Confidential Files, box 12 [CF], FG 1.

59. J. Anthony Lukas, "Why the Watergate Break-in?" *New York Times*, November 30, 1987, p. 14.

60. Stephen E. Ambrose, *Nixon: The Triumph of a Politician, 1962–1972* (New York: Simon & Schuster, 1989), p. 559.

61. Quoted in Hougan, *Secret Agenda*, pp. 127–128.

62. Nixon to Haldeman, January 14, 1971, WHSF:PPF, box 3.

63. WH, pp. 71–72.

64. In Ervin Papers, box 422, series 2: Subject File, folder 801 (Biographical Information).

65. Liddy, *Will*, pp. 236–240.

7. BEYOND THE "THIRD-RATE BURGLARY": COVER-UP AND DEPARTURE

1. Quoted in White, *Breach of Faith*, p. 161.

2. Nixon PP, 1972, pp. 690–701.

3. Dean, *Blind Ambition*, p. 112.

4. WH, p. 78.

5. Transcript of conversation in Mitchell Trial Transcripts, NP. Not found in *White House Transcripts* or PPF.

6. Portion of conversation from Mitchell Trial Transcripts, NP. Not found in *White House Transcripts* or PPF.

7. Walters memo for the record, June 28, 1972, Ervin Papers, series 2: Subject File, Watergate Memoranda, box 424, folder 862.

8. Portion of conversation in Mitchell Trial Transcripts, NP. Not found in *White House Transcripts* or PPF.

9. WH, p. 79.

10. WH, p. 82.

11. WH, p. 82.

12. Carl Bernstein and Bob Woodward, *All the President's Men* (New York: Warner, 1974), p. 71.

13. Walt Harrington, "Still Carl Bernstein after All These Years," *Washington Post Magazine*, March 19, 1989, p. 46.

14. Nixon PP, 1972, pp. 827–838.

15. Dean, *Blind Ambition*, pp. 128–129.

16. WH, p. 81.

17. *White House Transcripts*, pp. 57–68.

18. Quoted in Theodore H. White, *The Making of the President, 1972* (New York: Bantam, 1973), p. 237.

19. White, *Making of the President, 1972*, p. 275.

20. Ehrlichman Notes, July 5, 1972, NP, WHSF-Ehrlichman, box 12.

21. See material in NP, WHSF: J. Fred Buzhardt, Correspondence—McGovern Campaign, box 5.

22. "Twenty Quotations of Mr. McGovern," in NP, WHSF-Buchanan, box 8.

23. *Washington Post*, July 8, 1972.

24. *New York Times*, September 19, 1972.

25. Ehrlichman Notes, September 8, 1972, NP, WHSF-Ehrlichman, box 13.

26. Quoted in Charles Press and Kenneth Verburg. *American Politicians and Journalists* (Glenview, Ill.: Scott, Foresman, 1988), p. 168.

27. Ehrlichman Notes, no date, NP, WHSF-Ehrlichman, box 13.

28. Nixon, *Memoirs*, p. 773.

29. In a part of a March 17 taped conversation that was excised from public release by Nixon, the president was musing with Dean about whether

to invite Ervin and Baker together to the White House for a meeting. Nixon's conclusion: "I think I would see [Ervin] alone. . . . Baker's a little whipper-snapper and he'll try to make his mind up—I've seen Baker" (in NP, PPF; not in Mitchell Trial Transcripts or *White House Transcripts*).

30. See, for example, Ehrlichman Notes, January 23, 1973, NP, WHSF-Ehrlichman, box 7.

31. WH, p. 99.

32. Portions of conversation found in Mitchell Trial Transcripts, NP; *White House Transcripts;* and PPF.

33. WH, p. 101; Dean, *Blind Ambition,* p. 193.

34. Ehrlichman Notes, March 20, 1973, NP, WHSF-Ehrlichman, box 7.

35. Portions of conversation in Mitchell Trial Transcripts, NP, and *White House Transcripts.* Not found in PPF.

36. WH, p. 102.

37. Portions of conversation in Mitchell Trial Transcripts, NP, and *White House Transcripts.* Not found in PPF.

38. Complete transcript of conversation in PPF; incomplete transcript in Mitchell Trial Transcripts. Not in *White House Transcripts.*

39. WH, p. 101.

40. Lukas, *Nightmare,* pp. 359–360.

41. WH, pp. 93–95.

42. Samuel Dash, *Chief Counsel* (New York: Random House, 1976), p. 36.

43. WH, p. 104.

44. In Mitchell Trial Transcripts, NP; *White House Transcripts;* and PPF.

45. Portions of conversation in Mitchell Trial Transcripts, NP; *White House Transcripts;* and PPF.

46. Ervin to McGovern, July 26, 1974, Ervin Papers, series 2: Subject Files, Watergate Correspondence, box 422, folder 809.

47. WH, p. 119.

48. Nixon PP, 1973, pp. 636–639.

49. Copy of Butterfield's testimony in Alexander Butterfield Papers, GFL, box 1.

50. Nixon PP, pp. 657–668.

51. *New York Times,* January 10, 1971.

52. Nixon, *Memoirs,* p. 500.

53. Confidential sources.

54. Confidential source.

55. Interview, Sam Ervin, Mississippi State University: John Stennis Oral History Program (1976), p. 21.

56. Memorandum, Cox to Richardson, October 18, 1973, Ervin Papers, series 2: Subject Files, Watergate Correspondence, box 422, folder 809.

57. Richardson testimony, November 8, 1973, before the Senate Judiciary Committee. Found in undated memorandum to Nixon from Ervin [unsent], Ervin Papers, series 2: Subject Files, Watergate Correspondence, box 422, folder 809.

58. White, *Breach of Faith,* p. 284.

59. Quoted in White, *Breach of Faith,* pp. 286–291.

60. Nixon PP, 1974, pp. 389–397.

61. WH, p. 251.

62. Quoted in White, *Breach of Faith,* p. 310.

63. S. Res. 371 (July 30, 1974).

64. David Broder, "What George Bush Has Not Said," *Washington Post,* December 22, 1986.

65. Videotape of speech at NP.

8. GERALD FORD AND THE THIRTY-DAY FIRST TERM

1. "Eisenhower: Soldier of Peace," *Time,* April 4, 1969, p. 19.
2. Handwritten Notes, NP, WHSF: PPF (President's Desk), box 185.
3. "The People Take It in Stride," *Time,* August 19, 1974, pp. 59–64.
4. Gerald R. Ford, *A Time to Heal* (New York: Harper and Row, 1979), p. 45.
5. Ford, *Time to Heal,* p. 42.
6. Henry Hurt, *Reasonable Doubt* (New York: Holt, Rinehart, and Winston, 1985), pp. 28–33; Ford, *Time to Heal,* pp. 74–76.
7. Ehrlichman Notes, April 4, 1973, NP, WHSF-Ehrlichman, box 7.
8. Nixon, *Memoirs,* p. 925.
9. Ford, *Time to Heal,* p. 111.
10. Ford, *Time to Heal,* p. 122.
11. Quoted in Robert Hartmann, *Palace Politics: An Insider's Account of the Ford Years* (New York: McGraw: McGraw-Hill, 1980), p. 119.
12. Ford, *Time to Heal,* p. 122.
13. Hartmann, *Palace Politics,* pp. 115–117; *Kansas City Star,* April 14, 1974, p. 3A.
14. Ford, *Time to Heal,* p. 3.
15. Ford, *Time to Heal,* pp. 3–4; Bob Woodward and Carl Bernstein, *The Final Days* (New York: Simon & Schuster, 1976), p. 326.
16. Ford, *Time to Heal,* p. 6.
17. Hartmann, *Palace Politics,* p. 133.
18. Ford, *Time to Heal,* pp. 9–10.
19. Hartmann, *Palace Politics,* p. 135.
20. Hartmann, *Palace Politics,* pp. 136–137.
21. Hartmann, *Palace Politics,* p. 137; Ford, *Time to Heal,* p. 13; Woodward and Bernstein, *Final Days,* p. 337.
22. Ford, *Time to Heal,* p. 6.
23. Ford, *Time to Heal,* p. 24.
24. Ford, *Time to Heal,* p. 118.
25. Lee Byrd, "The President's Right Hand Men," *Ann Arbor News,* October 20, 1974, pp. 50.
26. Ford, *Time to Heal,* p. 147.
27. Confidential source.
28. Milton Friedman, interview with author, July 22, 1988.
29. Quoted in Anson, *Exile,* p. 42.
30. Ford PP, 1974, pp. 56–66; Ford, *Time to Heal,* p. 158.
31. Hartmann, *Palace Politics,* p. 253.
32. Anson, *Exile,* p. 46.
33. Ford, *Time to Heal,* p. 160–172.
34. Hartmann, *Palace Politics,* p. 259.
35. Benton Becker, interview with author, April 7, 1989.
36. Philip Buchen, interview with author, July 15, 1988.
37. James Doyle, *Not above the Law: The Battles of Prosecutors Cox and Jaworski* (New York: Morrow, 1977), p. 368.
38. Richard Ben-Veniste and George Frampton, Jr., *Stonewall: The Real Story of the Watergate Prosecution* (New York: Simon & Schuster, 1977), p. 308.
39. Ford, *Time to Heal,* p. 164.
40. Anson, *Exile,* pp. 52–54.
41. Tip O'Neill, *Man of the House* (New York: Random House, 1987), p. 268.

42. Hartmann, *Palace Politics,* p. 262.

43. Ford, *Time to Heal,* pp. 176–178.

44. See GFL, WHCF, JL-1-Nixon, boxes 4 and 5.

45. Copy of the Hungate subcommittee hearings at Rockefeller Archive Center, Tarrytown, New York.

9. A SEARCH FOR DIRECTION: THE FORD PRESIDENCY, 1975–1976

1. Schlesinger, *Imperial Presidency,* p. viii.

2. Nixon, *Memoirs,* p. 889.

3. Stanley I. Kutler, *The Wars of Watergate: The Last Crisis of Richard Nixon* (New York: Knopf, 1990), p. 136.

4. "The Electorate: Feeling Helpless and Depressed," *Time,* November 11, 1974, p. 17.

5. Hugh Sidey, "The Long Party Is Over," *Time,* November 18, 1974, p. 15.

6. Lou Cannon, *Reagan* (New York: Putnam, 1982), p. 198.

7. Gerald C. Lubenow, "Broadening the GOP Base," *Newsweek,* March 24, 1975, p. 22.

8. Ford, *Time to Heal,* p. 294.

9. Cannon, *Reagan,* pp. 195, 199.

10. Cannon, *Reagan,* p. 198.

11. Stein, *Presidential Economics,* p. 204.

12. Reichley, *Conservatives,* p. 384.

13. John W. Sloan, "Economic Policymaking in the Johnson and Ford Administrations," *Presidential Studies Quarterly,* Winter 1990, pp. 111–125.

14. Ford PP, 1975, pp. 36–46.

15. *Washington Post,* January 14, 1975.

16. *Washington Star-News,* January 24, 1975.

17. Reichley, *Conservatives,* p. 397.

18. Stein, *Presidential Economics,* pp. 191–192.

19. Cheney memorandum to the file, January 22, 1975, GFL, SMF: Richard Cheney, Subject Files, box 4; Ford, *Time to Heal,* p. 242; Reichley, *Conservatives,* p. 366.

20. *Washington Star-News,* January 20, 1975.

21. *Washington Post,* January 25, 1975.

22. Memorandum, Zarb to Ford, February 13, 1975, Frank G. Zarb Papers, GFL, Memoranda to President File, box 1.

23. William E. Simon, *A Time for Truth* (New York: Berkley, 1978), p. 87–88.

24. Milton Friedman, *Bright Promises, Dismal Performance: An Economist's Protest* (New York: Harcourt Brace Jovanovich, 1983), p. 178.

25. Friedman, *Bright Promises,* p. 179.

26. Ford, *Time to Heal,* p. 316.

27. Memorandum, Rourke to Fridersdorf, October 23, 1975, GFL, SMF: John Marsh, Subject Files, box 22.

28. Ford PP, 1975, p. 1729.

29. Ford, *Time to Heal,* p. 138.

30. Herring, *America's Longest War,* p. 257.

31. Herring, *America's Longest War,* p. 263.

32. Thieu to Ford, September 19, 1974; Ford to Thieu, October 24, 1974, GFL, WHCF, CO 165-2.

33. Herring, *America's Longest War,* pp. 264–265.

34. Weyland to Ford, April 4, 1975, GFL, WHCF, CO-165-2.

35. Quoted in Ford, *Time to Heal,* p. 253.

36. Ford, *Time to Heal,* p. 255.

37. Hartmann, *Palace Politics,* pp. 321–322.

38. Ron Nessen, *It Sure Looks Different from the Inside* (Chicago: Playboy Press, 1978), p. 129.

39. Hartmann, *Palace Politics,* p. 324.

40. Nessen, *It Sure Looks Different,* p. 123.

41. Quoted in Schulzinger, *Henry Kissinger,* p. 216.

42. Confidential sources.

43. Litwak, *Detente and Devolution,* p. 171.

44. Richard Steele, "What Price Detente?" *Newsweek,* July 28, 1975, pp. 14–15; Hartmann, *Palace Politics,* pp. 338–339.

45. Ford, *Time to Heal,* p. 305.

46. Quoted in Shulzinger, *Henry Kissinger,* pp. 213–214.

47. Quoted in Shulzinger, *Henry Kissinger,* p. 213.

48. Larry Martz, "Say Nay Politics," *Newsweek,* June 9, 1975, p. 23.

49. Peter Goldman, "Mr. Small-Is-Beautiful," *Newsweek,* December 15, 1975, p. 47.

50. The Jordan memorandum is reprinted in its entirety in Martin Schram, *Running for President, 1976: The Carter Campaign* (New York: Stein and Day, 1977), pp. 55–61.

51. Quoted in Schram, *Running for President,* p. 6.

52. Hartmann, *Palace Politics,* p. 376.

53. Jules Witcover, *Marathon: The Pursuit of the Presidency, 1972–1976* (New York: Viking, 1977), p. 537.

54. Witcover, *Marathon,* p. 82.

55. Quoted in Michael Kramer and Sam Roberts, *"I Never Wanted to Be Vice-President of Anything!" An Investigative Biography of Nelson Rockefeller* (New York: Basic Books, 1976), p. 365.

56. Cannon, *Reagan,* p. 194.

57. Scott interview, United States Capitol Historical Society Oral History Program, p. 104.

58. David Hume Kennerly, interview with author, September 14, 1988; Don Penny, interview with author, August 9, 1990; Kathleeen Hall Jamieson, *Packaging the Presidency: A History and Criticism of Presidential Campaign Advertising* (New York: Oxford University Press, 1984), pp. 337–338.

59. Transcript, Nelson Rockefeller interview with Trevor Armbrister, James M. Cannon Papers, GFL, p. 38.

60. See John Dean, *Lost Honor* (Los Angeles: Stratford Press, 1982), chap. 8.

61. See material in Ronald Nessen Papers, GFL, Campaign: Subject Files, Debates Folders, box 35.

62. Quoted in Schram, *Running for President,* p. 317.

10. THE LIMITS OF POWER

1. White, *Breach of Faith,* p. 322.

2. Nixon, *Memoirs,* p. 424.

3. Nixon, *In the Arena,* p. 205

4. Richard E. Neustadt, *Presidential Power: The Politics of Leadership, with Reflections on Johnson and Nixon* (New York: Wiley, 1976), p. 188.

5. Nixon, *In the Arena,* p. 207.

6. Clinton Rossiter, *The American Presidency,* 2d ed. (Baltimore: Johns Hopkins University Press, 1987), p. 59.

7. Reichley, *Conservatives,* p. 284.

8. Clark R. Mollenhoff, *The Man Who Pardoned Nixon* (New York: St. Martin's Press, 1976).

9. Peter Goldman and Thomas M. DeFrank, "Ford as Mr. Right," *Newsweek,* August 11, 1975, p. 22.

10. Carter, *Keeping Faith,* p. 27.

An Essay on the Sources

The literature on Richard Nixon is vast, but in general it is thoughtlessly disparaging of its subject. The literature on Gerald Ford is in its formative stage, and therefore it is quite limited and incomplete. The primary and archival record of both administrations, however, is growing day by day. While what follows is by no means an exhaustive treatment of the available material nor an inclusive list of the works used in the preparation of this book, it is hoped that this essay will help steer readers in a profitable direction for their own study of the period.

Two excellent reference tools are available. Eleanora W. Schoenebaum (ed.), *Profiles of an Era: The Nixon-Ford Years* (New York: Harcourt Brace Jovanovich, 1979), is a collection of biographies of principals from the period. Howard F. Bremer (ed.), *Richard M. Nixon: Chronology, Documents, Bibliographical Aids* (Dobbs Ferry, N.Y.: Oceana, 1975) is a good bibliographical starting point.

MANUSCRIPT AND OTHER SOURCE COLLECTIONS

Necessary for an understanding of Nixon's early career are the Richard M. Nixon Pre-Presidential Papers (National Archives, Laguna Niguel Branch). At this writing the Richard M. Nixon Presidential Library (Yorba Linda, California) is in the process of acquiring archival collections and will eventually house Nixon's postpresidential papers. However, the overwhelming majority of the relevant archival material from the Nixon White House is at neither repository. It is housed in a small warehouse in Alexandria, Virginia, at an extraordinary archive: the Richard M. Nixon Presidential Materials Project.

The story of the August 1974 agreement between Nixon and the General Services Administration (GSA) on joint ownership of his presidential materials has been told earlier in this work. In December 1974, with many lawsuits pending against the arrangement, Congress passed the Presidential Recordings and Materials Preservation Act. This statute gave sole custody of the Nixon papers to the administrator of the GSA, who was required to keep the material in the Washington metropolitan area, catalog it, and "within ninety days after the date of the enactment of this title . . . propos[e] and explai[n] regulations that would provide public access to the tape recordings and other materials." Nixon immediately sued to have the law declared unconstitutional, arguing that it was an invasion of executive privilege. The case was litigated for three years until the Supreme Court ruled in June 1977 that the the law was constitutional.

This decision did not lead to the immediate opening of the papers. Nixon and members of his administration initiated further legal challenges. These delays were only compounded by the fact that the newly named Nixon Project had been assigned far too few archivists to catalog the material within the agreed-upon time frame. It was not until 1980 that the project was able to open a center for the public to listen to the twelve and one-half hours of the Watergate tapes.* The next opening did not come until 1986 with the release of the project's vast audiovisual holdings. The singular nature of this archive was confirmed the next year by the wealth of material discovered when the project opened the White House Special File (WHSF).†

The Nixon White House established a new system for the filing of its documents, a system which the Nixon Project has retained. Before Nixon, the normal routing procedure for an Executive Office document was to send it to the White House Central File (WHCF), a permanent unit in the White House complex, for duplication and elaborate cross-filing. In the Nixon White House, however, Bob Haldeman saw a need to provide, as a later affidavit described it, a "central storage location for sensitive material." The WHSF, a unit independent of the WHCF, was thus created in September 1972. It was maintained by Gertrude Brown Fry, then staff assistant for security. Fry was asked to undertake the task by Bud Krogh; he told her that she would have a free hand to decide which documents went from the desk of a staffer directly into the WHSF. Fry and her one assistant proceeded to build the WHSF by pulling documents of a particularly sensitive nature that had already been filed in the WHCF; they added to the WHSF by intercepting sensitive documents that had been sent by their writer to the WHCF. Far from being a secret file (as claimed by several contemporary writers), the WHSF was known to everyone in the White House as well as to the staff at the Office of Presidential Papers Archives—indeed, the OPPA helped Fry set up the WHSF.

It is the WHSF that is the backbone of the Nixon Project. Much of the material is filed using the same method used in the WHCF. In addition, the Staff Member and Office Files (SMF) of several White House principals are included. Especially valuable for this study were the files of John D. Ehrlichman and H. R. Haldeman, which were seized by the FBI following their April 1973 resignations and given to Fry to store in the WHSF for security reasons. John Dean's files, confiscated at the same time, are also available for research but are less helpful. Other valuable collections included in the SMF series are the files of Patrick J. Buchanan, J. Fred Buzhardt, Dwight L. Chapin, Charles W. Colson, and Frederick V. Malek. The Colson, Ehrlichman, and Haldeman files include their handwritten notes takes during meetings with the president—for this author, the single most valuable source at the project. The sig-

---

*These thirty-one taped conversations, used as evidence in the U.S. District Court's 1974 cases *U.S. v. John B. Connally* and *U.S. v. John D. Ehrlichman, Harry R. Haldeman, Robert Mardian, John N. Mitchell,* and *Kenneth W. Parkinson* include the "smoking gun" and the "cancer on the presidency" conversations. The general public may listen to them at the Nixon Project. Also available are the transcripts made of these tapes by the FBI in 1974.

†See "The Strange and Convoluted History of the Nixon Materials: A Retrospective," *Society of American Archivists Newsletter,* part I, January 1987, pp. 11–14; part II, May 1987, pp. 16–21. To avoid a recurrence of the battle over the Nixon papers, Congress passed the Presidential Records Act in October 1978. This statute directs that presidential records become the property of the federal government as soon as they are written. Beginning with Ronald Reagan, all presidents must surrender their materials to the archivist of the United States upon leaving office. Although not covered by the act, Ford and Carter voluntarily gave their materials to the National Archives. An interesting viewpoint from a not entirely dispassionate observer is John Ehrlichman, "Should Richard Nixon's Papers Be Public?" *Parade,* November 30, 1986, pp. 4–9.

nificance of the WHSF is enhanced by the President's Handwriting File, an invaluable collection of memoranda and letters on which Nixon wrote responses in the margins. Also of great value in the WHSF are the Transcripts of Recorded Presidential Conversations, which include Rose Mary Woods's and Steven Bull's typed transcripts of the tapes, with Nixon's excisions and deletions penned in.

The Audiovisual Collection at the Nixon Project is also singular. Aside from having the strongest video collection of any of the presidential libraries, it holds the entirety of the approximately 4,000 hours of material taped between 1969 and 1973, with approximately eighty hours of tapes now available for public listening. However, a word of warning is necessary at this point. There are three sets of transcripts of the White House tapes—the above-mentioned transcripts found in the WHSF, the FBI transcripts of the original thirty-one conversations, and Nixon's version of some of those same conversations, which he released to the public on April 30, 1974 (their formal title is "Submission of Recorded Presidential Conversations to the Committee on the Judiciary of the House of Representatives"; better known as the *White House or Presidential Transcripts*, they are available in two paperback versions). None of these three sources exactly agrees with the available tapes, or with the other two sources. As noted earlier, the *White House Transcripts* are appallingly (and perhaps criminally) incomplete. For this work I have drawn most heavily upon the two most credible sets of transcripts: those found in the WHSF and the FBI transcripts.

The Gerald R. Ford Library (Ann Arbor, Michigan) holds the wealth of the Ford presidency records in one building, and without the restrictions that often plague the Nixon researcher. Ford's Vice-Presidential Papers include the files of many of his chief aides, including Jack Marsh and Bob Hartmann (Hartmann's handwritten notes on the confirmation hearing are particularly helpful). The WHCF from Ford's administration is more valuable than that of Nixon, as the staff of the National Security Council used it for their nonclassified material (the bulk of the classified material is under restriction in Brent Scowcroft's Papers).* Valuable staff member files include those of John G. Carlson, Richard B. Cheney, James E. Connor, Alexander M. Haig, Robert T. Hartmann, John O. Marsh, and William E. Timmons. Several donated sets of papers are also quite helpful, including those of Alexander Butterfield, James Cannon, Ronald Nessen, William Syers, Robert Teeter, and Frank Zarb. It should be added that like all the libraries of the more recent presidents, the Ford Library is at this writing actively soliciting manuscript collections, and available material on the Ford presidency has already grown exponentially since the writing of this book.

The speeches, press conferences, and publicly released documents of both Nixon and Ford are found in *The Public Papers of the Presidents* (Washington, D.C.: Government Printing Office, 1971–1978). University Microfilms of America is in the process of releasing several sections of the Nixon Project's material, and one edited work of the archival material has been published: Bruce Oudes, *From: The President—Richard Nixon's Secret Files* (New York: Harper and Row,

---

*It should be noted that there is precious little in the area of foreign policy in either the Nixon Project or the Ford Library; the most valuable material is still classified. Henry Kissinger's papers, housed at the Library of Congress, are presently closed to researchers.

1989), a weakly edited and uneven collection of snippets from the WHSF. Other more helpful published source collections are *The Nixon Presidential Press Conferences* (New York: Earl Coleman Enterprises, 1978), and *The Collected Speeches of Spiro Agnew* (New York: Audubon Books, 1971).

Other manuscript sources of value include Hugh L. Carcy Gubernatorial Papers (New York State Archives), Samuel J. Ervin, Jr., Papers (Southern Historical Collection, University of North Carolina), Hubert H. Humphrey Papers (Minnesota Historical Society), Kenneth Keating Papers (University of Rochester, Rush Rhees Library), Charles S. Murphy Papers (Harry S. Truman Library), Rockefeller Brothers Fund Special Studies Project Collection (Rockefeller Archive Center), Rockefeller Family Audio-Visual Collection (Rockefeller Archive Center), Winthrop Rockefeller Papers (University of Arkansas), Hugh D. Scott Papers (University of Virginia, Alderman Library), Maurice H. Stans Papers (Minnesota Historical Society), and the Harry S. Truman Papers, Post-Presidential Files (Harry S. Truman Library).

The *New York Times* is the indispensable starting point for a chronology of events, not only because it is the established newspaper of record for the contemporary period but also because key battles in the war between Nixon and the press were fought in its pages. Before June 1972 the *Times* consistently scooped the *Washington Post* on major stories (the Pentagon Papers being a case in point). Then, with its seminal coverage of Watergate, the *Post* also became a newspaper of record. From that point on, to obtain the breadth of reporting available on both political and cultural developments, the *Times* and the *Post* must both be read.

INTERVIEW SOURCES

The following individuals consented to interviews with the author:

Anderson, Gwen (July 30, 1988, Washington, D.C.)
Ash, Roy L. (August 23, 1988, telephone)
Becker, Benton (April 7, 1989, Hofstra University)
Brownell, Herbert (October 10, 1990, Gettysburg, Pa.)
Buchen, Philip W. (July 15, 1988, Washington, D.C.)
Callaway, Howard (March 7, 1991, Washington, D.C.)
Cannon, James M. (April 8, 1989, Hofstra University)
Carlson, John G. (December 7, 1988, telephone)
Colby, William E. (April 6, 1989, Hofstra University)
Duncan, John (September 9, 1988, Syracuse, N.Y.)
Dunlop, John T. (August 25, 1988, telephone)
Ehrlichman, John (April 26, 1987, Erie, Pa.)
Eisenhower, David (November 12, 1988, Boston)
Finch, Robert (November 20, 1987, Hofstra University)
Ford, Gerald R. (September 1, 1988, Vail, Colo.)
Friedenberg, Dr. Robert (April 20, 1990, Hofstra University)
Friedman, Milton (July 22, 1988, Washington, D.C.)
Fuller, Jon W. (January 3, 1989, telephone)
Glod, Stanley (March 26, 1991, Cazenovia, N.Y.)
Goodpaster, Gen. Andrew (April 25, 1987, Erie, Pa.)

Halperin, Morton (March 23, 1990, Washington, D.C.)
Hartmann, Robert T. (July 27, 1988, March 22, 1990, Washington, D.C.)
Hathaway, Stanley (August 22, 1988, telephone)
Hess, Stephen (October 12, 1990, Gettysburg, Pa.)
Hoxie, Dr. R. Gordon (April 24, 1987, Erie, Pa.)
Kennerly, David Hume (September 14, 1988, telephone)
Kupferman, Theodore R. (April 21, 1990, Hofstra University)
Lamb, Brian (August 7, 1990, Washington, D.C.)
Lance, Bert (April 8, 1989, Hofstra University)
Malek, Frederic (July 16, 1988, McLean, Va.)
Morgan, Ray (November 21, 1987, Hofstra University)
Penny, Don (August 9, 1990, Washington, D.C.)
Raoul-Duval, Michael (April 8, 1989, Hofstra University)
Rhatican, William (August 8, 1990, Washington, D.C.)
Rumsfeld, Donald (April 7, 1989, Hofstra University)
Saxbe, William B. (September 19, 1988, telephone)
Scammon, Richard M. (April 26, 1987, Erie, Pa.)
Sears, John P. (July 29, 1988, telephone)
Sorg, Leslie (June 19, 1988, Syracuse, N.Y.)
Speakes, Larry (April 8, 1989, Hofstra University)
Stans, Maurice H. (November 19, 1987, Hofstra University; October 13,
    1990, Gettysburg, Pa.)
Stein, Herbert (November 19, 1987, Hofstra University)
Stevenson, Adlai E. III (March 30, 1987, Chicago)
terHorst, Jerald F. (August 26, 1988, telephone)
Watson, Jack H., Jr. (April 25, 1987, Erie, Pa.)
Whitaker, John (November 19, 1987, Hofstra University)
White, Lee C. (April 25, 1987, Erie, Pa.)
White, F. Clifton (April 8, 1989, Hofstra University)
Wilderotter, James A. (April 7, 1989, Hofstra University)
Woodward, Bob (April 6, 1989, Hofstra University)
Zarb, Frank (April 7, 1989, Hofstra University)
Ziegler, Ronald (July 22, 1988, Alexandria, Va.)

Also helpful were various oral history depositories, particularly the Columbia University Oral History Project, the Harry S. Truman Oral History Project (Harry S. Truman Library), the Lyndon B. Johnson Oral History Project (Lyndon B. Johnson Library), and the Southern Oral History Project (University of North Carolina). The author is also grateful to James Rafferty for making available his unpublished 1988 interview with General William Westmoreland.

The published record of the University of Virginia's Miller Center Forums, where forty-four intimates of the Nixon and Ford years made presentations and answered audience questions, is of inestimable value. The transcripts are available in Kenneth W. Thompson (ed.), *The Nixon Presidency* (Lanham, Md.: University Press of America, 1987), and *The Ford Presidency* (Lanham, Md.: University Press of America, 1988).

BOOKS BY NIXON AND FORD

Richard Nixon has evolved into a prolific author. His controversial books must be approached with the same care that any historian would give to an autobiography. Nevertheless, these books document both his presidency and his ideology in more detail than is available for any other American president; this author would also be prepared to argue that in terms of writing ability, Nixon puts all the other postwar presidents to shame.

In a sense, each of Nixon's books is a component part of a nine-volume set of memoirs. His first, *Six Crises* (New York: Pocket Books, 1962) was on the bestseller lists for half a year. Remarkably well written, it allows more than the usual amount of insight into the author's character. Four years following his resignation came Nixon's second and most controversial book, *The Memoirs of Richard Nixon* (New York: Grosset and Dunlap, 1978). Overly long but again written gracefully, the book is peppered with memoranda, letters, and diary entries that make it come alive (the research work was done largely by Nixon aide Diane Sawyer, presently of ABC News). The discussion of Watergate is self-serving, but the attention to detail given to every area of policymaking, particularly that of foreign policy, is superb.

Nixon followed *Memoirs* with a thoughtful series of books that explored his viewpoints on foreign policy. One set can easily be seen as a trilogy on détente (although Nixon never claimed it to be such). *The Real War* (New York: Warner, 1980) warns the reader of growing Soviet power and the expense of American softness; *Real Peace: A Strategy for the West* (Boston: Little, Brown, 1983) offers several solutions that closely resemble Reagan's initial bellicose foreign policy; and *1999: Victory without War* (New York: Simon & Schuster, 1988) argues that the nation should now embrace the opportunity for rekindling the stalled negotiations on arms control. Nixon's views on devolution are set out in *No More Vietnams* (New York: Avon, 1985). This work is an often infuriating but well-reasoned interpretation of his Vietnam policy. It argues that the United States had won a military victory in 1974, only to have Congress throw it away within a year's time. His other books are of lesser value. The lightest of his volumes, *Leaders* (New York: Warner, 1982), is a series of anecdotes on world leaders whom Nixon knew, concluded by some rather loose thoughts on the concept of leadership. *In the Arena: A Memoir of Victory, Defeat and Renewal* (New York: Simon & Schuster, 1990) is a loosely organized and anecdotal treatment of many themes, but the book is best known for its analysis of Watergate. In it, Nixon both misrepresents and ignores key parts of the available evidence. His astounding conclusion, that "no obstruction of justice occurred," is simply untrue (p. 35). His most recent book, *Seize the Moment: America's Challenge in a One-Superpower World* (New York: Simon and Schuster, 1992), is a rousing call to arms, arguing that America must utilize its singular global and economic power to shape the post–Cold War world.

President Ford's literary endeavors are nowhere near as compelling. His memoirs, *A Time to Heal: The Autobiography of Gerald Ford* (New York: Harper and Row, 1979), are the complete opposite of Nixon's. While often entertaining and easy to read, the book is not as well written, and it reveals little of substance about its author. Preparatory to a conference on the subject held by the Gerald R. Ford Institute, Ford also wrote *Humor and the Presidency* (New

York: Arbor House, 1987), an anecdotal book that makes for entertaining reading but has no depth of analysis.

OTHER MEMOIRS

A greater wealth of memoir material is available for the Nixon and Ford years than for any other American presidency. The vast majority of it is predictably shallow and self-serving. Nevertheless, the dearth of general secondary studies makes these memoirs necessary reading. William Safire, *Before the Fall: An Inside View of the Pre-Watergate White House* (Garden City, N.Y.: Doubleday, 1975), is clearly the best of this genre. While incomplete (Safire went to the *New York Times* in 1972), it is an admirable study of policymaking and personalities in the White House; it is *the* memoir source for the first-term fate of Safire's creation, the "New Federalism." John Ehrlichman, *Witness to Power: The Nixon Years* (New York: Pocket Books, 1982), also deserves attention. It is by far the most entertaining of all the alumni memoirs, strong on both the abuses of power and domestic policy. Most important, its reconstruction of the facts can, for the most part, be corroborated from Erhlichman's papers at the Nixon Project. For the Ford tenure, Robert Hartmann, *Palace Politics: An Insider's Account of the Ford Years* (New York: McGraw-Hill, 1980), is critical and often acerbic, but it is nevertheless the best book available which deals exclusively with the Ford years.

A complete list of other relevant general memoirs would be too voluminous to be of use. Nevertheless, the reader should consult Ollie Atkins, *The White House Years: Triumph and Tragedy* (Chicago: Playboy Press, 1977); Patrick J. Buchanan, *Right from the Beginning* (Boston: Little, Brown, 1988); John J. Casserly, *The Ford White House: The Diary of a Speechwriter* (Boulder: Colorado Associated University Press, 1977); Betty Ford, *The Times of My Life* (New York: Harper and Row, 1978); Barry M. Goldwater, *Goldwater* (New York: Doubleday, 1988); Alexander M. Haig, Jr., *Caveat: Realism, Reagan, and Foreign Policy* (New York: Macmillan, 1984); Walter J. Hickel, *Who Owns America?* (Englewood Cliffs, N.J.: Prentice-Hall, 1971); David Hume Kennerly, *Shooter* (New York: Newsweek Books, 1979); Frederic V. Malek, *Washington's Hidden Tragedy: The Failure to Make Government Work* (New York: Free Press, 1978); Clark R. Mollenhoff, *Game Plan for Disaster: An Ombudsman's Report on the Nixon Years* (New York: Norton, 1976); Lawrence O'Brien, *No Final Victories: A Life in Politics from John F. Kennedy to Watergate* (New York: Ballantine, 1974); Tip O'Neill, *Man of the House* (New York: Random House, 1987); and Ray Price, *With Nixon* (New York: Viking, 1977).

Other memoirs pertinent to specific subjects are listed below.

BIOGRAPHIES OF NIXON AND FORD

The work of Nixon biographer Stephen Ambrose stands alone. His three-volume work (*Nixon: The Education of a Politician, 1913–1962, Nixon: The Triumph of a Politician, 1962–1972,* and *Nixon: Ruin and Recovery, 1973–1990,* New York: Simon & Schuster, 1987, 1989, 1991) is a superb example of the craft, based on an exhaustive use of archival material and written with a judiciously balanced tone. This author has drawn heavily from Ambrose's work, particularly his portrayal of Nixon's prepolitical years. Roger Morris, *Richard Milhous Nixon: The Rise of an American Politician* (New York: Holt, 1990), and Tom Wicker, *One of Us: Richard Nixon and the American Dream* (New York: Random House, 1991), are written by longtime Nixon critics. Neither is as objective as Ambrose; neither do they approach his depth of research. An engagingly written study of the first years of Nixon's forced retirement is Robert Sam Anson, *Exile: The Unquiet Oblivion of Richard M. Nixon* (New York: Simon & Schuster, 1984).

Two excellent essays that place Nixon in the context of his America are available. The classic is Garry Wills, *Nixon Agonistes: The Crisis of the Self-Made Man* (New York: New American Library, 1969). Wills's treatment of Nixon as a classical liberal is an insightful undertaking in intellectual history. Herbert S. Parmet, *Richard Nixon and His America* (Boston: Little, Brown, 1990), is an equally thoughtful assessment of why Nixon has been such a "commanding figure" in contemporary history.

The other biographies of Nixon have all been supplanted by the above-mentioned works of scholarship. Those biographies that are pro-Nixon in tone are little more than campaign advertisements, based on no real depth of research—save for interviews with Nixon intimates. This school is led by Ralph deToledano's two works, *Nixon* (New York: Henry Holt, 1960) and *One Man Alone: Richard Nixon* (New York: Funk and Wagnalls, 1969). See also Earl Mazo, *Richard Nixon: A Political and Personal Portrait* (New York: Harper, 1959), and Bela Kornitzer, *The Real Nixon: An Intimate Biography* (Chicago: Rand McNally, 1960).

The vast majority of Nixon biographers have been shrilly critical of their subject. The best written of this angry lot is Frank Mankiewicz, *Perfectly Clear: Nixon from Whittier to Watergate* (New York: Popular Library, 1973). The rest seem to fall into the school of "psychobiographers," all of whom purport, as claimed in the title of Arthur Woodstone's book, to get *Inside Nixon's Head* (New York: Popular Library, 1976). The best known of this group is Fawn Brodie, *Richard Nixon: The Shaping of His Character* (New York: Norton, 1981), but it is the epitome of the genre—accusatory and speculative with little substantive underpinning. For further examples, consult David Abrahamsen, M.D., *Nixon vs. Nixon: An Emotional Tragedy* (New York: New American Library, 1976); Gary Allen, *Richard Nixon: The Man behind the Mask* (Boston: Western Islands, 1971); and Bruce Mazlish, *In Search of Nixon: A Psychohistorical Inquiry* (Baltimore: Penguin, 1973).

There is at present no scholarly biographer of Gerald Ford. The closest thing is Jerald terHorst, *Gerald Ford and the Future of the Presidency* (New York: Third Press, 1974). A reporter for the *Detroit News*, terHorst had begun work on a biography of Ford before he became press secretary. He completed it as a study of the fledgling presidency after resigning in protest of the decision to pardon Nixon. The pardon sparked several bitterly anti-Ford books, including Clark R. Mollenhoff, *The Man Who Pardoned Nixon* (New York: St. Martin's Press, 1976), and Richard Reeves, *A Ford, Not a Lincoln* (New York: Harcourt Brace Jovanovich, 1975).

While not biographies in the strict sense of the word, two extraordinary studies emerged from Ford's desire to reopen the White House to the press.

Time correspondent Hugh Sidey and photographer Fred Ward collaborated to do a photographic essay, based on pictures taken by Ward, who was given unprecedented access to the working day of a president. Their result, *Portrait of a President* (New York: Harper and Row, 1975), is a unique work, with Ward's extraordinary photographs and Sidey's graceful prose combining to become the best "biography" presently available of Ford. The second work resulted from author John Hersey's being given virtually unlimited access to the president for every minute of the working day for a full week. Hersey's *The President* (New York: Knopf, 1975) is an intimate view of the president and his staff (particularly good on Rockefeller) that is made even more interesting by Hersey's constant comparisons of Ford and Truman, whom Hersey also saw work in the Oval Office.

Those seeking a full biographical background of these two leaders will also want to consult biographies of the First Ladies: Bruce Cassidy, *Betty Ford: Woman of Courage* (New York: Dale Brooks, 1978); Lester David, *The Lonely Lady of San Clemente: The Story of Pat Nixon* (New York: Crowell, 1978); and Julie Nixon Eisenhower, *Pat Nixon: The Untold Story* (New York: Simon & Schuster, 1986).

GENERAL STUDIES

A. James Reichley, *Conservatives in an Age of Change: The Nixon and Ford Administrations* (Washington, D.C.: Brookings Institution, 1981), is presently the only general study that treats the Nixon and Ford years as one "era." An important theoretical work, it is a lengthy essay that explores the fit between Nixon, Ford, and the conservative tradition. It concludes that "American conservatism, as it was practiced under Nixon and Ford, and as it continues to be practiced today, surely qualifies as an expression of a distinct social ideology" (p. 418). Reichley's demographic and voting data are strong, as is his use of interviews (Reichley served as a staff member in the Ford administration). His discussion of foreign policy is less convincing, and his conclusion on the conservative nature of Nixon's and Ford's policies is highly arguable. Nevertheless, I have drawn heavily from this solid volume.

The other general works available are either incomplete or suffer from a lack of historical distance from the subject. Rowland Evans, Jr., and Robert D. Novak, *Nixon in the White House: The Frustration of Power* (New York: Vintage Books, 1972), is more than the "instant history" that is often written by journalists. This detailed work is a good primer for the first term, although the authors' anti-Nixon bias seeps through. Jonathan Schell's lengthy essay *The Time of Illusion: A Historical and Reflective Account of the Nixon Era* (New York: Vintage Books, 1975) touches upon details from the entire administration, but its true focus is to critique the abuses of power; its shallow research lessens its credibility. Allen Drury, *Courage and Hesitation: Notes and Photographs of the Nixon Administration* (Garden City, N.Y.: Doubleday, 1971), is full of typos ("John Deane") and other mistakes but nevertheless serves as a valuable introduction to the Nixon White House. Drury interviewed practically every staff member, and the photos of them juxtaposed with their job description is particularly helpful. No general study of the Ford years yet exists.

Of the many valuable works on the U.S. presidency, two are necessary for a full understanding of the Nixon and Ford tenures. In 1977 Richard E. Neustadt released a second edition of his enormously influential *Presidential Power: The Politics of Leadership* (New York: Wiley, 1976). In 1960 Neustadt's controversial stand on the subject of presidential power was that the president was simply not as powerful as earlier students of the institution had thought and that it was up to the individual to use or misuse powers greater than those enumerated in the Constitution: his own "presidential influence." His view remained unchanged, even after reflecting upon the events of 1963–1976 for his update, and his conclusion was that neither Nixon nor Ford was able to effectively utilize that influence. James David Barber's seminal *The Presidential Character: Predicting Performance in the White House* (Englewood Cliffs, N.J.: Prentice-Hall, 1972) argued that a candidate's past can lead to an accurate prediction of his effectiveness as president. Many of Barber's conclusions are based on overextended psychoanalytic speculation. He is also violently anti-Nixon, who is characterized as an "active-negative" president. However, many of Barber's observations of Nixon hit home with tremendous predictive accuracy. Ford, on the other hand, is effectively ignored. He is relegated to thirteen pages in the 1977 update (Ford is characterized as an "active-positive" leader), as opposed to ninety-five pages for Nixon and forty-three for a Carter presidency that was less than a year old. For the most recent treatment of the issue of presidential power, see Robert Shogan's anecdotal and probing *The Riddle of Power: Presidential Leadership from Truman to Bush* (New York: Dutton, 1991).

CULTURE AND SOCIETY

Of the several histories of the United States of the 1960s, William L. O'Neill, *Coming Apart: An Informal History of America in the 1960s* (New York: Quadrangle, 1971), offers an acerbic but thoughtful evaluation of the decade. William Manchester, *The Glory and the Dream: A Narrative History of America, 1932–1972*, 2 vols. (Boston: Little, Brown, 1973), is more anecdotal and no less valuable. The crisis of liberalism as it affected the Middle is best described in Allen J. Matusow's admirable study for the New American Nation Series, *The Unraveling of America: A History of Liberalism in the 1960s* (New York: Harper and Row, 1984). The reader should also consult Jim F. Heath, *Decade of Disillusionment: The Kennedy-Johnson Years* (Bloomington: Indiana University Press, 1975).

For two anniversary recollections of the year that brought Nixon to power, see John Hersey, "1968: Year of the Triphammer," (syndicated article, *Syracuse Herald-American*, November 26, 1978), and Lance Morrow, "1968" (*Time*, January 11, 1988, pp. 16–27). For a fascinating analysis of Nixon's America, see E. J. Kahn, Jr., *The American People: The Findings of the 1970 Census* (New York: Weybright and Talley, 1973).

The greatest issue affecting the development of American society during this period, even after its conclusion, was unquestionably the Vietnam War. Two excellent studies of the war's effect on American culture are available: Loren Baritz, *Backfire: American Culture and the Vietnam War* (New York: Ballantine, 1985), and Myra MacPherson, *Long Time Passing: Vietnam and the Haunted Generation* (New York: New American Library, 1984).

Melvin Small, *Johnson, Nixon, and the Doves* (New Brunswick, N.J.: Rutgers

University Press, 1988), is a detailed study of how student protests were treated by the administrations. James Michener, *Kent State: What Happened and Why* (New York: Random House, 1971), is an empathetic and thorough analysis of the tragedy, but it should be accompanied by *The Kent State Tragedy: Special Report,* the President's Commission on Campus Unrest, October, 1970 (Salem, N.H.: Ayer, 1988). For interesting updates on the student movement, see Morris Dickstein, "Columbia Recovered" (*New York Times Magazine,* May 15, 1988, pp. 32ff.), and the 1990 PBS special "Berkeley in the Sixties" (PBS Video).

The author's memory of the period was refreshed by a walk down memory lane taken through the pages of *Time* and *Newsweek,* then the arbiters of both popular and political culture. The fledgling *People* magazine, which began publication in 1974, was also useful for the culture surrounding the Ford years.

DOMESTIC POLICY

A study of Nixon's domestic policy should begin with William Safire, *Before the Fall* (above). Safire spends the majority of his book discussing the fate of the programs that made up the "New Federalism." Richard Nathan's influential study *The Plot That Failed: Nixon and the Administrative Presidency* (New York: Wiley, 1975) is the most often cited study of Nixon's management of domestic affairs. One of the many analysts who served in the Nixon White House (at OMB and HEW), Nathan argues that as Kissinger won over the machinery of foreign policy, Nixon, Haldeman, and Ehrlichman decided to take the management of domestic affairs away from the departments. This "plot" began with the streamlining recommended by the Ash Council and ultimately "failed" because of Watergate. This excellent analysis would have been strengthened with the addition of an exploration of how Watergate might have been caused by such bureaucratic streamlining, but Nathan's thesis is nevertheless an important one.

Staff management played a major role in the successes and failures of both these administrations. All four men who served as chief of staff during this period, along with four other former chiefs, participated in a televised symposium in 1985. A transcript of the panel's discussion was published as Samuel Kernell and Samuel L. Popkin (eds.), *Chief of Staff* (Berkeley: University of California Press, 1986). The insights from this volume are innumerable. Less valuable is Michael Medved, *The Shadow Presidents: The Secret History of the Chief Executives and Their Top Aides* (New York: Times Books, 1979). Medved's view of Haldeman and Rumsfeld is overwhelmingly negative; Cheney is treated more positively; Haig is not even mentioned. Evans and Novak's *Nixon in the White House* (above) is particularly good on Nixon's Cabinet choices; see also Kathryn Christian Conner, "The Nixon Cabinet: 1968–1972" (M.A. thesis, University of Virginia, 1974).

Nathan's *The Plot That Failed* (above) is the established starting point for a study of executive reorganization under Nixon. Stephen Hess's chapter on Nixon in his *Organizing the Presidency* (Washington: Brookings Institution, 1976) is a thoughtful survey of the aims of the Ash Council. Larry Berman, *The Office of Management and Budget and the Presidency, 1921–1979* (Princeton, N.J.: Princeton University Press, 1979), has an excellent chapter on how Nixon changed the Bureau of the Budget into the OMB. However, despite the dates of his study, Berman includes nothing on Ford. See also Henry C. Mansfield, "Reorganizing the Federal Executive Branch: The Limits of Institutionalization" (*Law and Contemporary Problems* 35, Summer 1970, pp. 461–495).

David M. O'Brien, *Storm Center: The Supreme Court in American Politics* (New York: Norton, 1986) is a worthy survey of its subject. Bob Woodward and Scott Armstrong, *The Brethren: Inside the Supreme Court* (New York: Simon & Schuster, 1979) met with instant criticism because of its wide use of usually anonymous law clerks as sources. This only adds to their gripping story of the politicization of the court under Nixon and Ford. Shedding light on the controversy that led to Nixon's first two vacancies on the court are Bruce Allen Murphy, *Fortas: The Rise and Ruin of a Supreme Court Justice* (New York: Morrow, 1988), and Jack Harrison Pollack, *Earl Warren: The Judge Who Changed America* (Englewood Cilffs, N.J.: Prentice-Hall, 1979). Arthur Galub, *The Burger Court, 1968–1984,* vol. 9 of the Supreme Court in American Life Series; (Millwood, N.Y.: Associated Faculty Press, 1986), is the standard source. It includes lengthy excerpts from the major opinions, detailed biographical sketches, and a solid chronology. For an interesting contemporary viewpoint, see Edwin M. Yoder, Jr., "Haynsworth and History" (*Washington Post National Weekly Edition,* December 4–10, 1989, p. 28). See also Donna Gates Thomas, "Richard M. Nixon: Remaking the Judiciary" (paper delivered to Bicentennial Symposium, Center for the Study of the Presidency, April 1987).

On Nixon's war with Congress, George Gregory Raab, "Presidential-Congressional Relations in the Johnson-Nixon Administrations" (M.A. thesis, University of Virginia, 1972), is an excellent beginning. Margaret Chase Smith, *Declaration of Conscience* (Garden City, N.Y.: Doubleday, 1972), is helpful on the ABM fight. Leon E. Panetta and Peter Gall, *Bring Us Together: The Nixon Team and the Civil Rights Retreat* (Philadelphia: Lippincott, 1971), is a critical view of the administration's handling of that issue. Nicholas Lehmann, "The Unfinished War, Part II," (*Atlantic Monthly,* January 1989, pp. 53–68), is a critical study of Nixon and the war on poverty.

A study of welfare reform should begin with Daniel Patrick Moynihan, *The Politics of a Guaranteed Income: The Nixon Administration and the Family Assistance Plan* (New York: Vintage Books, 1973). No fawning memoir, Moynihan's work has excellent detail, and his corroborating research is well balanced. Vincent J. Burke and Vee Burke, *Nixon's Good Deed: Welfare Reform* (New York: Columbia University Press, 1974), is equally valuable as a condensed analysis that also provides its readers with an outstanding chronology of events. Douglas Schoen, *Pat: A Biography of Daniel Patrick Moynihan* (New York: Harper and Row, 1979), is favorable toward its subject, but the one-chapter review of the Nixon years is the standard treatment of Moynihan's wide-ranging influence over domestic policy. A dissenting view on Moynihan during the Nixon years is Nicholas Lehmann, "Slumlord" (*Washington Monthly,* May 1991, pp. 39–49).

An excellent summary of the world economic situation after Bretton Woods can be found in Randall Rothenberg, *The Neo-Liberals: Creating the New American Politics* (New York: Simon & Schuster, 1984). Herbert Stein, a member of the Council of Economic Advisers under Nixon, has written an astute commentary on modern economic history, *Presidential Economics: The Making of Economic Policy from Roosevelt to Reagan and Beyond* (New York: Simon & Schuster, 1984). The most thorough and persuasive study of revenue sharing is David Caputo, "Richard M. Nixon, General Revenue Sharing, and American Federalism" (paper presented at Hofstra Conference on the Nixon Presidency, November 1987). Robert H. Connery and Gerald Benjamin, *Rockefeller of New York: Executive Power in the Statehouse* (Ithaca, N.Y.: Cornell University Press, 1979), has a strong section on the New Yorker governor's role in obtaining final passage of the revenue-sharing bill. Helpful for statistical information is Andrew C. Kimmens (ed.), *The Federal Deficit* (New York: H. W. Wilson, 1985).

R. Gordon Hoxie, "Staffing the Ford and Carter Presidencies" (in Bradley D. Nash, ed., *Organizing and Staffing the Presidency*, New York: Center for the Study of the Presidency, 1980) is the best survey treatment of the subject. The Miller Center of the University of Virginia also held a conference in which seven members of the Ford staff, including Cheney, Rumsfeld, and Scowcroft, participated; *The Ford White House* (Lanham Md.: University Press of America, 1986) contains transcripts of those sessions. See also interviews with top Ford staffers in "How Ford Runs the White House" (*U.S. News and World Report*, September 23, 1974, pp. 28–33). Helpful glimpses of key members of the Ford team are David Gelman, "Nessen's Report Card" (*Newsweek*, January 12, 1976, pp. 52–53); "The President's Eyes and Ears" (on Robert Hartmann, *Time*, September 2, 1974, p. 13); Barbara Rudolph, "A Conservative Who Can Compromise," (on Alan Greenspan, *Time*, June 15, 1987, pp. 50–51); and Lloyd Shearer, "Don Rumsfeld: He's President Ford's Number One" (*Parade*, February 2, 1975, pp. 4ff.).

Lacking a general study of Ford's domestic policies, the best "survey" available is found in Michael Turner, *The Vice-President as Policy Maker: Rockefeller in the Ford White House* (Westport, Conn.: Greenwood Press, 1982). William E. Simon's memoir, *A Time for Truth* (New York: Berkeley, 1978), is particularly good for understanding the Ford economic policies; Robert W. Bailey, *The Crisis Regime: The New York City Financial Crisis* (Albany: State University of New York Press, 1984), is a solid examination of the best-known incident of that policy. See also the helpful comparative essay, John W. Sloan, "Economic Policymaking in the Johnson and Ford Administrations" (*Presidential Studies Quarterly*, Winter 1990, pp. 111–125). Important to an understanding of the battle over environmental policy is John Whitaker, *Striking a Balance: Environmental and Natural Resources Policy in the Nixon-Ford Years* (Washington, D.C.: American Enterprise Institute for Public Policy Research, 1976).

FOREIGN AND MILITARY POLICIES

Any understanding of the Nixon foreign policies should begin with a review of the diplomacy that Nixon's replaced. With the warning that this listing is far from an exhaustive treatment of the Cold War literature,* students should

*The reader would be well served by consulting bibliographical essays in the other books in the America since World War II series: Charles C. Alexander, *Holding the Line: The Eisenhower Era, 1952–1961,* and Jim F. Heath, *Decade of Disillusionment: The Kennedy-Johnson Years* (Bloomington: Indiana University Press). Also useful are Warren Kimball,

begin with the definitive text on modern U.S. diplomatic history, Stephen E. Ambrose, *Rise to Globalism: American Foreign Policy since 1938*, 5th ed. (New York: Penguin, 1988). Follow Ambrose with the declaration of the Cold War, George Kennan ("X"), "The Sources of Soviet Conduct" (*Foreign Affairs*, July 1947, 566–582). John L. Gaddis, *The United States and the Origins of the Cold War* (New York: Columbia University Press, 1972), and Thomas G. Patterson, *On Every Front: The Making of the Cold War* (1979), document the genesis of the conflict. Walter LaFeber, *America, Russia, and the Cold War, 1945–1980* (New York: Wiley, 1980) is a valuable text that not only sets the stage but also carries the story through to more contemporary concerns. To understand the Cold War mentality as it related to Vietnam, nothing comes close to David Halberstam, *The Best and the Brightest* (Greenwich, Conn.: Fawcett, 1969). Also helpful is Gregory T. D'Auria, "Present at the Rejuvenation: The Association of Dean Acheson and Richard Nixon" (*Presidential Studies Quarterly* 28, Spring 1988, pp. 393–412).

By far the best general treatment of Nixon-Ford foreign policy is Robert D. Schulzinger, *Henry Kissinger: Doctor of Diplomacy* (New York: Columbia University Press, 1989). The author skillfully uses all of the available archival material and has written a judiciously balanced review of the entire scope of foreign policy during the period. He sees Kissinger as a player rather than an architect, one who "changed the way the United States conducted foreign policy" but was incapable of "build[ing] a structure that would endure beyond his term" (pp. 237, 241). This book should be accompanied, although carefully, by C. L. Sulzberger, *The World and Richard Nixon* (New York: Prentice-Hall, 1987), an unabashed defense of Nixon's foreign policy based on a host of interviews with Nixon as well as Sulzberger's own diary entries. Robert S. Litwak, *Detente and the Nixon Doctrine: American Foreign Policy and the Pursuit of Stability, 1969–1976* (Cambridge: Cambridge University Press, 1984), is difficult but necessary; the present author's interpretation is drawn largely from Litwak's thesis surrounding détente and devolution. A third book of consequence is Seymour Hersh, *The Price of Power: Kissinger in the Nixon White House* (New York: Summit Books, 1983). As seen several times in the course of this work, Hersh's reporting often *became* the story. His highly interpretive book makes for compelling reading, and recently opened records have substantiated many of his reports. Also of value are Seyom Brown, *The Crises of Power: Foreign Policy in the Kissinger Years* (New York: Columbia University Press, 1979); Roger Morris, *Uncertain Greatness: Henry Kissinger and American Foreign Policy* (New York: Harper and Row, 1977); and Tad Szulc, *The Illusion of Peace: Foreign Policy in the Nixon Years* (New York: Viking, 1978).

The two-volume memoirs of Henry Kissinger, *White House Years* and *Years of Upheaval* (Boston: Little, Brown, 1979, 1982), are encyclopedic in length and the epitome of sycophantic self-service. While necessary for tracing the detail of foreign policy decision making, they read like a press release for Kissinger as the progenitor of Nixon's foreign policy (the volumes do not cover the Ford years). More important than his memoirs is Kissinger's doctoral dis-

"The Cold War Warmed Over" (*American Historical Review* 79, 1974, pp. 1119–1136), and Robert Maddox, "The Rise and Fall of Cold War Revisionism" (*Historian*, May 1984, pp. 416–428).

sertation, published as *A World Restored: Metternich, Castlereagh, and the Restoration of Europe* (Boston: Houghton Mifflin, 1957), as it contains the germ of what would become linkage diplomacy. Biographies of Kissinger include Charles R. Ashman, *Kissinger: The Adventures of Super-Kraut* (Seacaucus, N.J.: Lyle Stuart, 1972); Ralph Blumenfeld et al., *Henry Kissinger: The Private and Public Story* (New York: New American Library, 1974); Marvin and Bernard Kalb, *Kissinger* (Boston: Little, Brown, 1973); and Bruce Mazlish, *Kissinger: The European Mind in American Policy* (New York: Basic Books, 1976). For a view of Kissinger's influence on recent events, see Garry Wills, "The Unsinkable Kissinger Bobs Back" (*New York Times,* January 17, 1989, p. A25).

In one of the more surprising gaps in modern diplomatic historiography, a scholarly study of the China opening has yet to be written. A beginning can be made with Michael Schaller's short text, *The United States and China in the Twentieth Century* (New York: Oxford University Press, 1990). Nixon, "Asia after Vietnam" (*Foreign Affairs* 46, no. 1 [October 1967], pp. 111–125), is the definitive statement of Nixon's philosophy toward China. Détente with the Soviet Union is better chronicled. Begin with Raymond Garthoff, *Detente and Confrontation: American-Soviet Relations from Nixon to Reagan* (Washington, D.C.: Brookings Institution, 1985). For a superb study of the move toward SALT I under Nixon and the failure of SALT II under Ford, see Charles R. Morris, *Iron Destinies, Lost Opportunities: The Arms Race between the U.S. and the U.S.S.R., 1945–1987* (New York: Harper and Row, 1988). See also the memoirs of chief negotiator Gerard Smith, *Doubletalk: The Story of SALT I* (Garden City, N.Y.: Doubleday, 1980). For the view from the Kremlin, see Harry Gelman, *The Brezhnev Politburo and the Decline of Detente* (Ithaca, N.Y.: Cornell University Press, 1984).

Two excellent books should be taken in tandem for a study of covert operations under Nixon and Ford: John Prados, *Presidents' Secret Wars: CIA and Pentagon Covert Operations since World War II* (New York: Morrow, 1986), and John Ranelagh, *The Agency: The Rise and Decline of the CIA* (New York: Simon & Schuster, 1986). Thomas Powers, *The Man Who Kept the Secrets: Richard Helms and the CIA* (New York: Pocket Books, 1979), and the memoirs of William Colby, *Honorable Men: My Life in the CIA* (New York: Simon & Schuster, 1978), are also useful.

Two survey treatments of the war in Vietnam are essential. George C. Herring, *America's Longest War: The United States and Vietnam, 1950–1975* (New York: Knopf, 1986), and Stanley Karnow, *Vietnam: A History* (New York: Penguin, 1983) serve as outstanding texts; both are well written and balanced. Students will also want to consult the Public Broadcasting System's magnificent series based on Karnow's work, "Vietnam: A History" (PBS Video). William Appleman Williams et al. (eds.), *America in Vietnam: A Documentary History* (Garden City, N.Y.: Doubleday, 1985), is a helpful collection of documents, including Nixon's December 1972 secret correspondence with Thieu. Serious students should read all of the documents in *The Pentagon Papers.* The most helpful version was edited by the staff of the *New York Times* (New York: Bantam, 1971); it includes the documents as well as the stories that accompanied them in the *Times.* Nixon's *No More Vietnams* (above) is necessary for an understanding of his policy of devolution. A valuable specialty study is Martin F.

Herz, *The Prestige Press and the Christmas Bombing, 1972* (Washington, D.C.: Ethics and Public Policy Center, 1980).

The established starting point for a study of the history of Cambodia's relations with the United States, North Vietnam, and China, as well as the conflict to follow, is William Shawcross's bitterly anti-Nixon work, *Sideshow: Kissinger, Nixon, and the Destruction of Cambodia* (New York: Pocket Books, 1979). For a more balanced approach, one should also consult Richard Arden Hennig, "Foreign Policy Crisis Decisions in the White House: The Cambodia Case" (M.A. thesis, University of Virginia, 1971), and Donald Peter Cushman, "A Comparative Study of President Truman's and President Nixon's Justifications for Committing Troops to Combat in Korea and Cambodia" (Ph.D. dissertation, University of Wisconsin, 1974). For Ford and the fall of Vietnam, see Alan Dawson, *55 Days: The Fall of South Vietnam* (Englewood Cliffs, N.J.: Prentice-Hall, 1977), and P. Edward Haley, *Congress and the Fall of South Vietnam and Cambodia* (Brunswick, N.J.: Associated University Presses, 1983). For a view of the omnipresence of the war, even to the present day, see Steven Erlanger, "Missing In Action: From a Lost War, a Haunting Echo That Won't Be Stilled" (*New York Times*, August 31, 1988, p. A6).

Seymour Hersh, *The Price of Power* (above) offers the strongest beginning for a study of Nixon's Middle East policy. Also of value: Galia Golan, *Yom Kippur and After: The Soviet Union and the Middle East Crisis* (Cambridge: Cambridge University Press, 1977); Matti Golan, *The Secret Conversations of Henry Kissinger: Step-by-Step Diplomacy in the Middle East* (New York: Quadrangle, 1976); Golda Meir, *My Life* (New York: Putnam, 1975); and Edward R. F. Sheehan, *The Arabs, Israelis, and Kissinger: A Secret History of American Diplomacy in the Middle East* (New York: Reader's Digest Press, 1976).

The history of Ford's foreign policy has yet to be written. See Richard G. Head, F. W. Short, and R. C. McFarlane, *Crisis Resolution: Presidential Decision Making in the Mayaguez and Korean Confrontations* (Boulder, Colo., Westview, 1978), and Christopher Jon Lamb, *Belief Systems and Decision Making in the Mayaguez Crisis* (Tallahassee: University of Florida Press, 1988), for astute analyses of the most famous moment in that policy. An interesting update to the Helsinki Accords, in light of Reagan's second-term advances to the Soviet Union, is Warren Zimmerman, "Making Moscow Pay for Rights Abuses" (*New York Times*, August 1, 1986, p. A-21). See also Daniel Patrick Moynihan, *A Dangerous Place: Defending America at the U.N.* (Boston: Atlantic–Little, Brown, 1978).

POLITICS

A witty and thoughtful analysis of presidential elections from 1960 to 1980 can be found in Robert Shogan, *None of the Above: Why Presidents Fail—and What Can Be Done about It* (New York: New American Library, 1982). Theodore H. White's last book, *America in Search of Itself: The Making of the President, 1956–1980* (New York: Harper and Row, 1982), is a vivid survey of modern presidential politics. On Nixon's maiden voyage into national politics, see John Robert Greene, *The Crusade: The Presidential Election of 1952* (Lanham, Md.: University Press of America, 1985). To trace Nixon's political nadir, consult White's Pulitzer Prize winning *The Making of the President, 1960* (New York:

New American Library, 1961) as well as *The Making of the President, 1964* (New York: Atheneum, 1964).

On the politics of 1968, the established starting point is White, *The Making of the President, 1968* (New York: Atheneum, 1969). White's journalistic style is engaging, but an anti-Nixon bias pervades the work. While overly long, Lewis Chester, Godfrey Hodgson, and Bruce Page, *An American Melodrama: The Presidential Campaign of 1968* (New York: Viking, 1969), shows the point of view of three British journalists and offers a wealth of fascinating anecdotes not found in White. Also helpful is Norman Mailer, *Miami and the Siege of Chicago* (New York: Signet, 1968).

On the candidates in 1968, a helpful source is David Frost, *Frost on Nixon, Humphrey, Kennedy, Rockefeller, Wallace, Reagan, Stassen, Lindsay, and McCarthy* (New York: Stein and Day, 1978), a collection of Frost's interviews with the candidates. Marshall Frady, *Wallace* (New York: New American Library, 1976), a virulently critical look at its subject, is best for the pre-1968 period; see also Jerald Rudolph Burke, *What Wallace Thinks* (Tuscaloosa, Ala.: Portals Press, 1976). For the candidacies of other prominent Democrats, see Lyndon B. Johnson, *The Vantage Point: Perspectives of the Presidency, 1963–1969* (New York: Holt, Rinehart, and Winston, 1971); Eugene McCarthy, *Up 'til Now* (New York: Harcourt Brace Jovanovich, 1987); Arthur Schlesinger, Jr., *Robert Kennedy and His Times* (Boston: Houghton Mifflin, 1978); and Carl Solberg, *Hubert Humphrey: A Biography* (New York: Norton, 1984).

An understanding of southern politics during the Nixon period begins with Jack Bass and Walter de Vries, *The Transformation of Southern Politics: Social Change and Political Consequence since 1945* (New York: New American Library, 1976). It must be quickly followed by Alexander P. Lamis, *The Two-Party South* (New York: Oxford University Press, 1984), which updates Bass and De Vries in a very readable style. Kevin P. Phillips, *The Emerging Republican Majority* (New York: Arlington, 1969), argues that there was a fundamental shift in voting patterns in 1968 based on new southern and western loyalties to the Republican party, what Phillips terms a "new Nixon Majority." Also helpful is Monroe Billington's brief *Southern Politics since the Civil War* (Malabar, Fla.: Robert E. Krieger, 1984).

Kathleen Hall Jamieson, *Packaging the Presidency: A History and Criticism of Presidential Campaign Advertising* (New York: Oxford University Press, 1984), is the definitive treatment of political media campaigns. Joe McGinniss, *The Selling of the President, 1968* (New York: Pocket Books, 1969), is a probing study of Nixon's advertising campaign; it angered the Nixon White House because of its thesis that Nixon was "remade" by media advisers. David Chagall offers one penetrating chapter of his *The New Kingmakers* (New York: Harcourt Brace Jovanovich, 1981) to Humphrey's media campaign. Herbert Alexander, *Financing the 1968 Election* (Lexington, Mass.: Heath, 1971), is authoritative on its subject.

The regrouping and reforming of the Democratic party between 1969 and 1972 is well chronicled. Begin with Herbert S. Parmet, *The Democrats: The Years after FDR* (New York: Macmillan, 1976), which is particularly strong for this period. Richard M. Scammon and Ben Wattenberg's lecture to the Democrats on the "social issue" in *The Real Majority* (New York: Coward, McCann, and

Geoghegan, 1971) became the party's rallying cry in 1970 ("The major thesis of this book is that the center is the only position of political power," p. 200). The McGovern-led reforms of the Democratic party that spanned the elections are detailed in Byron E. Shafer's solid *Quiet Revolution: The Struggle for the Democratic Party and the Shaping of Post-Reform Politics* (New York: Russell Sage Foundation, 1983).

Theodore White, *The Making of the President, 1972* (New York: Bantam, 1973), is not the equal of his first three volumes. It is more laborious in style, and it badly underplays the impact of Watergate. Charles A. Moser, *Promise and Hope: The Ashbrook Presidential Campaign of 1972* (Washington, D.C.: Free Congress Research and Education Foundation, 1985), is the essential book on Nixon's conservative challenger. Gordon L. Weil, *The Long Shot: George Mc-Govern Runs for President* (New York: Norton, 1973), is an excellent survey; Robert Sam Anson, *McGovern: A Biography* (New York: Holt, 1972), and Gary W. Hart, *Right from the Start: A Chronicle of the McGovern Campaign* (New York: Quadrangle, 1973), offer insights into the Democratic challenger's tactics. Norman Mailer, *St. George and the Godfather* (New York: Arbor House, 1972), is an irreverent but prescient look at the fall race. McGovern's personal recollections can be found in abbreviated form in his " 'This McGovern Democrat Business' " (*Washington Post National Weekly Edition*, July 4–10, 1988, p. 29).

The two best known books dealing with the role of the media in 1972 were both written by correspondents for *Rolling Stone*. Hunter S. Thompson is, as always, eminently entertaining. However, his sarcastic, condescending approach to his subjects renders *Fear and Loathing on the Campaign Trail '72* (New York. Warner, 1973) a satire rather than a history. Much more useful is the chronicle written by Thompson's colleague Timothy Crouse, *The Boys on the Bus* (New York: Ballantine, 1973). See also C. Richard Hofstetter, *Bias in the News: Network Television Coverage of the 1972 Election Campaign* (Columbus: Ohio State University Press, 1976), and James M. Perry, *Us and Them: How the Press Covered the 1972 Election* (New York: Clarkson N. Potter, 1973).

Jules Witcover, *Marathon: The Pursuit of the Presidency, 1972–1976* (New York: Viking, 1977), is encyclopedic in length but downplays several important themes. The story of the Reagan challenge is splendidly told in Lou Cannon, *Reagan* (New York: Putnam, 1982). Jimmy Carter, *Keeping Faith: Memoirs of a President* (New York: Bantam, 1980), yields little of substance on the 1976 election; see instead the authoritative book on the subject, Martin Schram, *Running for President, 1976: The Carter Campaign* (New York: Stein and Day, 1977). James Wooten, *Dasher: The Roots and Rising of Jimmy Carter* (New York: Warner, 1979), is also helpful. David Chagall, *The New Kingmakers* (above), has an excellent chapter on Carter's media campaign.

No scholarly study is presently available of Ford's 1976 campaign; the memoirs of advertising adviser Malcolm MacDougall, *We Almost Made It* (New York: Crown, 1977), are of very limited value. For insight on both the hiring and firing of Nelson Rockefeller, consult Peter Collier and David Horowitz, *The Rockefellers: An American Dynasty* (New York: New American Library, 1976). See also Michael Kramer and Sam Roberts, *"I Never Wanted to Be Vice President of Anything!" An Investigative Biography of Nelson Rockefeller* (New York: Basic Books, 1976), and Joseph A. Persico, *The Imperial Rockefeller: A Biography of*

Nelson A. Rockefeller (New York: Simon & Schuster, 1982). For a view of the vice-presidential campaign, Bob and Elizabeth Dole, *The Doles: Unlimited Partners* (New York: Simon & Schuster, 1988), should be taken in tandem with Larry Speakes, *Speaking Out: The Reagan Presidency from Inside the White House* (New York: Avon, 1988)—Speakes served as Robert Dole's assistant press secretary in 1976. Sidney Krause, *The Great Debates: Carter vs. Ford, 1976* (Bloomington: Indiana University Press, 1979), is a helpful analysis. For the point of view of the press during the campaign, see Elizabeth Drew, *American Journal: The Events of 1976* (New York: Random House, 1976).

THE PRESS

An excellent analysis of the press relations of Nixon and his successors is Joseph C. Spear, *Presidents and the Press: The Nixon Legacy* (Cambridge, Mass.: MIT Press, 1984). Its conclusion—that Nixon perfected the art of manipulating the press and his successors co-opted it—is both debatable and important. It should be followed by David Halberstam's fascinating study of the *New York Times, Washington Post, Los Angeles Times,* and *Time* magazine, *The Powers That Be* (New York: Knopf, 1979). This is a vivid survey of the relationship between both administrations and the national press, with splendid behind-the-scenes details on Watergate and the Pentagon Papers. Two other surveys are less helpful. Charles Press and Kenneth Verburg, *American Politicians and Journalists* (Glenview, Ill.: Scott, Foresman, 1988), offers some nuggets but is a much weaker work than Spear's and offers little of value on Ford. John Tebbel and Sarah Miles Watts, *The Press and the Presidency* (New York: Oxford University Press, 1985), is so blindly anti-Nixon, Ford, and Carter that it must be used with a great deal of discretion.

Two valuable memoirs of Nixon's press assistants are James Keogh, *President Nixon and the Press* (New York: Funk and Wagnalls, 1971), and Herbert G. Klein, *Making It Perfectly Clear* (New York: Doubleday, 1980). The works of Ford's two press secretaries are of uneven value. Jerald terHorst, *Gerald R. Ford and the Future of the Presidency* (above), spends too little time on Ford's relationship with the press. Ron Nessen, *It Sure Looks Different from the Inside* (Chicago: Playboy Press, 1978), is a more valuable work for this subject. It mixes a recounting of Ford's press relations with the tales of an administrative "insider." A more disparaging view of Nessen's tenure can be found in Lou Cannon, "Nessen's Briefings: Missing Questions and Answers" (*Columbia Journalism Review,* May–June 1975, pp. 12–16). Other valuable reflections by journalists include Hedley Donovan, *Roosevelt to Reagan: A Reporter's Encounters with Nine Presidents* (New York: Harper and Row, 1985); John Osborne, *The Nixon Watch* (New York: Liveright, 1970–1975); Dan Rather, *The Camera Never Blinks* (New York: Ballantine, 1977); and Mike Wallace, *Close Encounters* (New York: Morrow, 1984).

The story of the *New York Times's* publication of the Pentagon Papers should begin with Halberstam's *The Powers That Be* (above), followed by Daniel Ellsberg's introduction to his *Papers on the War* (New York: Simon & Schuster, 1972) and Sanford J. Ungar's definitive *The Papers and the Papers: An Account of the Legal and Political Battle over the Pentagon Papers* (New York: Dutton, 1972). Halberstam should also be consulted first for a study of the *Washington Post's* coverage of the Watergate story. The works of Carl Bernstein and Bob Woodward of the *Washington Post* have been discussed at some length in this work. *All the President's Men* (New York: Simon & Schuster, 1974) makes for a good detective story and serves as a good chronological treatment of the *Post's* tracing of the abuses of power beyond the break-in. Nevertheless, like their reporting itself, the book yields little fruit on the coverage of the story after 1973. Elizabeth Drew, *Washington Journal: The Events of 1973–1974* (New York: Random House, 1975), finishes out the story from the point of view of the Washington press corps. *Washington Post* editor Barry Sussman's *The Great Cover-Up: Nixon and the Scandal of Watergate* (New York: New American Library, 1974) is less helpful.

THE ABUSES OF POWER AND THEIR AFTERMATH

This subject has produced some of the best as well as much of the worst writing on the Nixon period. Scholars are fortunate to have two balanced, comprehensive, and readable treatments of the abuses of power. J. Anthony Lukas, *Nightmare: The Underside of the Nixon Years* (New York: Bantam, 1976), is the result of investigative reporting at its finest. While often laborious because of its length and attention to detail, this book provides all relevant background to the abuses of power (including quotations from transcripts of White House tapes that are still unavailable to the public). Stanley I. Kutler, *The Wars of Watergate: The Last Crisis of Richard Nixon* (New York: Knopf, 1990), is a welcome addition to Lukas's study. Kutler skillfully weaves a host of scholarly interviews with the newly opened material from the Nixon Project (unavailable to Lukas) to flesh out the tale. Both are lengthy works, but both are necessary for anyone who wishes to understand Watergate. An interesting essay, but based on shakier sources, is Theodore H. White, *Breach of Faith: The Fall of Richard Nixon* (New York: Atheneum, 1975).

Other recent studies of the scandals are less significant, offering theses that are easily challenged using the available evidence, archival and otherwise. Jim Hougan, *Secret Agenda* (New York: Ballantine, 1984), postulates that the break-in was a lesser part of a much bigger operation, a "sex scandal, the unpredictable outcome of a CIA operation that, in the simplest of terms, tripped on its own shoelaces" (p. xvi). Len Colodny and Robert Gatlin, *Silent Coup: The Removal of a President* (New York: St. Martin's Press, 1991), argues that the real cover-up was engineered by Al Haig and Fred Buzhardt to hide a military spy ring that passed White House documents to the Joint Chiefs of Staff. Both books are based on thin secondary research as well as the prodigious use of unattributed interview sources.

Depending on one's point of view, the two Watergate-related books by Carl Bernstein and Bob Woodward can fit several genres. As noted earlier, *All the President's Men* can be treated as a journalistic memoir; the two men started writing the book even before the story had run its course, and it ends several months before Nixon's resignation. It is a riveting story, made all the more compelling by the journalistic conundrum of "Deep Throat." While both Kutler and Lukas offer fuller versions of the story, Woodward and Bernstein provide a strong chronology of the early part of the crisis that cannot be ignored. Woodward and Bernstein's second book poses more problems for the historian. *The Final Days,* covering the end of the Nixon administration (New York: Simon & Schuster, 1976), has been attacked from all quarters. This author could get through nary an interview with either a Nixon or a Ford principal without hearing an attack on this book. The charges ranged from its being exaggerative to its being no more than a compilation of lies elicited from disillusioned Nixon staff and family members. Both books make for compelling reading (much better than either of the two movies based on the books, both of which misrepresent much of the intent of the writing). Many of the details in *All the President's Men* can be corroborated from the archival record; *The Final Days* rests on a largely unsubstantiated body of material and must be read warily.

With the notable exception of Lukas's work, and noting the caution levied above on the writings of Woodward and Bernstein, the vast majority of the studies of Watergate written *before* the opening of the Nixon material can be dismissed. As a whole, their facts are so errant, and they are so quick to take the opportunity to dismiss the entire administration as being corrupt from top to bottom, that they do little except show the frustration of many writers with the abuses of power. This is in itself an important observation, but it is not enough to make a body of literature worthwhile. One exception is Jimmy Breslin, *How the Good Guys Finally Won: Notes from an Impeachment Summer* (New York: Ballantine, 1975). While never trying to hide his acidity toward the administration, Breslin offers an insider's view of how Peter Rodino and Tip O'Neill successfully maneuvered Congress toward impeachment.

Should students wish to ignore the above works and trace for themselves the voluminous minutiae of contradictory details on both the abuses of power and the investigations that followed, begin with the *New York Times's Watergate Hearings* (New York: Viking, 1973) and *End of a Presidency* (New York: Bantam, 1974). Each book contains samples of the *Times's* stories on the unfolding crisis, but it is the blow-by-blow chronology, prepared by Linda Amster, that is one of the most valuable sources available on the crisis. The *Washington Post's Fall of a President* (New York: Delacorte, 1974) equates roughly with the *Times's End of a Presidency,* but it has fewer stories and a much thinner chronology.

Memoirs written by participants in and bystanders of the Watergate disaster form a cottage industry in themselves. While several of the memoirs already mentioned include material on Watergate, many members of the administration wrote books whose sole purpose was to explain away their roles in the mess. The most famous of this genre, John Dean, *Blind Ambition: The White House Years* (New York: Simon & Schuster, 1976), necessitates an enormous act of historical faith: the belief that Dean's memory is perfect, and that he is telling the truth. If such is the case, the book is an incredible diary of the Watergate cover-up, complete with dates and often times of events. If it is not, as a score of principals have said under oath, then this work, used by many scholars as the best study of Watergate, becomes valueless. Others in this genre include Charles W. Colson, *Born Again* (New York: Bantam, 1976); John Dean, *Lost Honor* (Los Angeles: Stratford Press, 1982); H. R. Haldeman, *The Ends of Power* (New York: Times Books, 1978); G. Gordon Liddy, *Will* (New York: St. Martin's Press, 1980); Jeb Stuart Magruder, *An American Life: One Man's Road* to *Watergate* (New York: Pocket Books, 1974); Maurice H. Stans, *The Terrors of Justice* (New York: Everest House, 1978); and Vernon Walters, *Silent Missions* (New York: Doubleday, 1978). For a humorous but prescient view of "all the president's men," see Stewart Alsop, "The Crazy-Brave and the Phony-Tough" (*Newsweek*, September 10, 1973).

While openly hostile to Nixon, William V. Shannon, *They Could Not Trust the King: Nixon, Watergate, and the American People* (New York: Collier, 1974), is the starting point for an understanding of the congressional investigations. It offers a good chronology, is particularly strong on the Ervin Committee, and gives complete introductions of the witnesses and their transgressions. The work of Harvard's Raoul Berger, *Executive Privilege: A Constitutional Myth* (Cambridge, Mass.: Harvard University Press, 1974), is definitive on its subject, as is Howard Ball, *No Pledge of Privacy: The Watergate Tapes Litigation* (Port Washington, N.Y.· Kennikat Press, 1977).

One must then turn to the weakest set of memoirs coming from this period, those written by the principals in the various investigations. They portend to tell the "real story" of Watergate. Not one of them does so, and not one of them is a truly balanced study: Richard Ben-Veniste and George Frampton, Jr., *Stonewall: The Real Story of the Watergate Prosecution* (New York: Simon & Schuster, 1977); Samuel Dash, *Chief Counsel* (New York: Random House, 1976); James Doyle, *Not above the Law: The Battles of Watergate Prosecutors Cox and Jaworski* (New York: Morrow, 1977); Sam J. Ervin, *The Whole Truth: The Watergate Conspiracy* (New York: Random House, 1980); Leon Jaworski, *The Right and the Power* (New York: Pocket Books, 1977); and John Sirica, *To Set the Record Straight* (New York: Norton, 1979). An exception is Archibald Cox, *The Court and the Constitution* (Boston: Houghton Mifflin, 1987), which includes a useful prologue detailing the setup of the special prosecutor's office, Cox's arguments against Nixon, and the legal precedents used by both sides.

A scholarly study of the investigation and resignation of Spiro Agnew has yet to be written. The investigatory works of Jules Witcover are at present our only source; see his *White Knight: The Rise of Spiro Agnew* (New York: Random House, 1972) and, with Richard Cohen, *A Heartbeat Away: The Investigation and Resignation of Vice President Spiro T. Agnew* (New York: Viking, 1977). Agnew's own *Go Quietly . . . or Else* (New York: Morrow, 1980) is less a memoir of his vice-presidency than an attempt to blame the White House, the press, and Elliot Richardson's Justice Department for his troubles.

A sensationalistic approach to an event that drew much attention from the Nixon White House is Leo Danmore, *Senatorial Privilege: the Chappaquidick Cover-up* (Washington, D.C.: Regnery Gateway, 1988). The FBI's role in the abuses of power is well chronicled in Richard Gid Powers, *Secrecy and Power: The Life of J. Edgar Hoover* (New York: Free Press, 1987). For views on the CIA's role, consult the works on the agency mentioned above under "Foreign Policy." Jeb Magruder told a stunned Hofstra University audience in 1987 that the reason for the Watergate break-in was to see what Larry O'Brien had in his files on the Nixon-Hughes connection. J. Anthony Lukas, a member of Magruder's panel, writes of that experience in "Why the Watergate Break-in?" (*New York Times*, November 30, 1987, p. 14). The Hughes connection is well outlined in Larry DuBois and Laurence Gonzales, "The Puppet and the Puppet-masters: Uncovering the Secret World of Nixon, Hughes, and the CIA" (*Playboy*, October, 1976, p. 74), and Michael Drosnin, *Citizen Hughes* (New York: Bantam, 1985). Background to the Bay of Pigs' role in the cover-up can be found in Peter Wyden, *The Bay of Pigs: The Untold Story* (New York: Simon & Schuster, 1979).

Other useful studies include J. Justin Gustainis, "Nixon and Reagan: A Watergate/Iranscam Analog" (paper presented at a meeting of the Speech Communication Association, November 6, 1987), and "Remembering the Discovery of the Watergate Tapes" (several contributors, *Journal of American History*, March 1989, pp. 1222–1262; also in David Thelen, ed., *Memory and American History*, Bloomington: Indiana University Press, 1990). On the longevity of Watergate in the national consciousness, see George McGovern, "On Nixon and Watergate, Reagan and Iran" (*New York Times*, January 6, 1987, p. A21).

THE CONGRESSIONAL REVOLUTION OF 1973–1975

Arthur M. Schlesinger, Jr., *The Imperial Presidency* (Boston: Houghton Mifflin, 1973) is the classic statement on the growth of the modern presidency, beginning with misuses of the war-making power under Roosevelt and Truman and culminating with Nixon's abuses of power. It was the harbinger of the congressional counterrevolution that followed on the heels of Watergate. R. Gordon Hoxie, *Command Decision and the Presidency* (New York: Reader's Digest Press, 1977) is a strong survey of that new relationship in the area of national security. Robert F. Turner, *The War Powers Resolution: Its Implementation in Theory and Practice* (Philadelphia: Foreign Policy Research Institute, 1983), is a theoretical introduction to congressional oversight of foreign policy; P. Edward Haley, *Congress and the Fall of South Vietnam and Cambodia* (above), is a good view of the practical application of the issue.

The War Powers Act has been under fire since its passage; in 1988 the Senate held hearings on the continued efficacy of the law. Virtually all witnesses testified that the law was either unconstitutional or useless; see United States Senate, 100th Congress, Committee on Foreign Relations, *Hearings before the Special Subcommittee on War Powers* (July–September 1988). Also see Tom Wicker's criticism, written at the time of that congressional hearing, "A Law That's Failed" (*New York Times*, January 7, 1988).

On congressional oversight of intelligence matters, see the report of the Rockefeller Commission, available as *Report to the President by the Commission on CIA Activities within the United States* (Washington, D.C.: Government Printing Office, 1975).

Index

Abel, Fay, 151
ABM. *See* Antiballistic Missile
Abrams, Creighton, 85, 86, 89, 92
Abuses of power, Nixon administration: anti-Kennedy campaign, 136–138; backdating of donation of Nixon presidential papers, 199; break-in at Fielding's office by Plumbers, 141–142, 143, 150; break-in at Watergate Hotel, 128, 145–151; CIA ordered by Nixon to obstruct FBI investigation of Watergate break-in ("Smoking Gun Conversation"), 129, 153–155; Colson's role, 134–135; "dirty tricks" in election of 1972, 142–143, 161; and election of 1972, 158–159; and election of 1976, 222; emotional appeal of issue in 1992, 128; and FBI, 129, 153–155, 166; Howard Hughes and illegal campaign contributions to Nixon, 146–147; hush money raised for Watergate burglars, 155, 164–166; "Huston Plan," 133–134; investigation of by Justice Department, 153–155; Kissinger's wiretaps, 129–130, 132; McCord describes for Sirica, 165–166; Nixon on his guilt in, 129; Operation CHAOS, 132–133, 132*fn.*; payoffs to Mitchell while Attorney General, 166–168; perjury of Magruder and Dean, 157–158, 166; planning of Operation GEMSTONE, 143–151; "Plumbers," organization of, 140; press and, 130–132, 156–157; reaction of the Middle, 182; Arthur M. Schlesinger Jr. on, 204–205; and Dan Schorr, 131–132; White House Enemies Project, 135–136, 143
Abzug, Bella, 201
Acheson, Dean, 10
Agnew, Spiro: and academe, 56; and congressional elections of 1970, 58–61; considered for the Supreme Court, 68; and Ford, 187; and investigation by Justice Department, 187; and investigation by *Wall Street Journal,* 186–187; and payoffs while Maryland governor, 166–167, 175, 186–187; on Presidential Commission on Campus Unrest, 95*fn.*; on shootings at Kent State University, 95; resignation of, 186–187; as Vice-President, 56–58; as vice-presidential candidate (1968), 21, 24; as vice-presidential candidate (1972), 57–58, 158; and welfare reform, 48
Aid to Families with Dependent Children (AFDC), 47–48
Aiken, George D., 2
Airline hijackings of PLO, 123
Alexander v. Holmes County Board of Education (1969), 44–46, 64, 65, 66, 177, 233
All the President's Men (Woodward and Bernstein, 1973), 157
Allen, Richard, 82
Alsop, Stewart, 11, 140
Ambrose, Stephen, 5, 7, 14, 149
American Bar Association (ABA), 39, 41, 69
American Federation of Labor—Congress of Industrial Organizations (AFL-CIO), 160, 173–174, 228
American Independent Party (1968), 18
American Legion, 40
Americans for Democratic Action (ADA), 20, 27
Amnesty: Ford program for Vietnam War draft evaders, 209
Andrews, Bert, 8
Angola: Ford policy toward, 215
Antiballistic Missile (ABM): debate over, 34–36, 38, 39, 50, 55, 109, 172, 234; and Johnson-Kosygin Summit (1967), 113; and SALT I, 115–116, 115*fn.*, 118
Apollo XI, 83

John Robert Greene is
Associate Professor of History and Communication
at Cazenovia College.